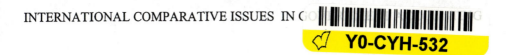

International Comparative Issues in Government Accounting

The Similarities and Differences between Central Government Accounting and Local Government Accounting within or between Countries

Proceedings of the 7th CIGAR Conference

Edited by

Aad Bac

Tilburg University, The Netherlands

KLUWER ACADEMIC PUBLISHERS
BOSTON / DORDRECHT / LONDON

A C.I.P. Catalogue record for this book is available from the Library of Congress.

ISBN 978-1-4419-4881-6

Published by Kluwer Academic Publishers,
P.O. Box 17, 3300 AA Dordrecht, The Netherlands.

Sold and distributed in North, Central and South America
by Kluwer Academic Publishers,
101 Philip Drive, Norwell, MA 02061, U.S.A.

In all other countries, sold and distributed
by Kluwer Academic Publishers,
P.O. Box 322, 3300 AH Dordrecht, The Netherlands.

Printed on acid-free paper

Printed in the Netherlands.

CONTENTS

Part III   National Comparative Research

Part IV   National Non-Comparative Research

CONTRIBUTORS

Aad D. Bac	Tilburg University THE NETHERLANDS
Barbara Bakalarska	Ministry of Finance POLAND
Bernardino Benito	University of Murcia SPAIN
Anatoli Bourmistrov	Bodø Graduate School of Business NORWAY
Krzystof Cichocki	Local Government Partnership Project POLAND
Mark Christensen	Southern Cross University, Lismore AUSTRALIA
James L. Chan	Univesity of Illinois, Chicago U.S.A.
Johan Christiaens	University of Gent BELGIUM
Josèp L. Cortès	University of Balearic Islands SPAIN
Patrick Devlin	Glasgow Caledonian University UNITED KINGDOM
Sheila Ellwood	Aston University, Birmingham UNITED KINGDOM
Jean-Baptiste Gillet	Ministry of Economics, Finance and Industry FRANCE
Alan D. Godfrey	Glasgow Caledonian University UNITED KINGDOM
Ad J.E. Havermans	Court of Audit THE NETHERLANDS

Claude Heiles Ministry of Economics, Finance and Industry
FRANCE

G. Jan van Helden University of Groningen
THE NETHERLANDS

Zhao Jianyong Shanghai University of Finance and Economics
CHINA

Jeanine Kleimo Local Government Partnership Project
POLAND

Harman W.O.L.M. Korte Ministry of Finance
THE NETHERLANDS

James Ley Local Government Partnership Project
POLAND

Helge Mauland Stavanger College
NORWAY

Frode Mellemvik Bodø Graduate School of Business
NORWAY

M. Cherif Merrouche Glasgow Caledonian University
UNITED KINGDOM

Nico P. Mol University of Twente
THE NETHERLANDS

Norvald Monsen Norwegian School of Economics and Business
Administation, Bergen
NORWAY

Vicente Montesinos University of Valencia
SPAIN

Salme Näsi University of Jyväskylä
FINLAND

Wojciech Nowak University of Lodz
POLAND

Hassan A.G. Ouda Tilburg University
THE NETHERLANDS

June Pallot	University of Canterbury, Christchurch NEW ZEALAND
Pieter G. van der Poel	Municipality of Tilburg THE NETHERLANDS
Cees Schouten	Ministry of the Interior and Kingdom Affairs THE NETHERLANDS
Cong Shuhai	Shanghai University of Finance and Economics CHINA
José Manuel Vela	University Jaume I, Castellon SPAIN
Kiyoshi Yamamoto	Okayama University JAPAN
Hiroshi Yoshimi	Hokkaido University JAPAN

FOREWORD

Aad D. Bac

Government is continuously developing all over the world and over time. Especially in the last decades the role of government has changed. In several countries the tasks government has taken up grew out in number and size. The idea that nevertheless the specific characteristics of government from an economic point of view as well as from an organizational point of view, government activities should be able to be performed on an efficient basis and managed in a more business-like way won adhesion. The adherence to this way of looking at government proved even to be exaggerated insofar that blind application of private sector management instruments was seen.

In the same period, which for the majority of countries was characterized by fiscal stress, the interest in accrual accounting increased. The instrumental importance of confronting real cost with fares or usefulness was increasingly recognized. Furthermore it was assumed that control of government activities cost would improve by means of accrual accounting. Nevertheless the consequences of an accounting reform should not be underestimated. Logically a number of countries and especially those who had to cope with important macro-economic challenges still saw advantages in cash-based accounting or at least hesitated whether the advantages of accrual accounting would exceed the disadvantages. ICT-developments increased the possibilities of offering more than one type of accounting figures from the same accounting system. That is why we still see a wide range of different accounting systems all over the world. The variety goes from pure cash accounting to full accrual accounting, with a series of modified variances inbetween, depending the dominant aspects either called modified cash or modified accrual.

The demands on types of information differs when looking at either central government or local and regional government. For instance macro-economic information needs are less to be expected on another level than the central government level.

As far as a judgement on the adequacy of government accounting systems is concerned a financial accounting as well as a management accounting point of view is possible.

Starting from a financial accounting point of view it should be recognized that the financial accounts play a role in the political discharging process of the magerial execution of by means of the budget assigned tasks to the Executive of a government entity. On the other hand they play a role in the accountability of Parliament or Council to the electorate. If regularity, efficiency and effectiveness are the key aspects of accountability, in the first role regularity and efficiency are dominant and in the second role regularity and effectiveness are. In the first role accountability concentrates on budget-execution or policy-execution and in the second role especially policy-choice is.

Of course in the second role the aspects of the first role play a secondary role and are not completely irrelevant.

This being the case it can be stated that dependent on these circumstances the general characteristics of financial reporting can be defined. This stipulates a number of differences between private sector financial reports on the one hand and public sector financial reports on the other hand. Taking the functions of a budget and a financial report as a point of departure they are as follows:

- The allocative function brings about that budgets and financial reports are to be made up on a functional basis and not like in the private sector on a categorical basis. Because of the underlying societal goals of policy information is needed with respect to the intended and realized outcome in order to be able to judge effectiveness.
- The authorization function implies that the budget amounts are esteemed to be limiting and presenting fixed amounts to designated policy areas (functions) and has for a consequence that financial reports have to render insight in the degree of budgetcompliance realized.
- The macro-economic function implies for central government the importance of (additional) cash-based figures irrespective of the current or the capital character of income and expenditure. For local and regional governments this function implies the need of the possibility of aggregation, which brings with it the importance of uniformly defined policy-areas(functions).
- The management function implies the availability of performance indicators in order to have an opportunity to judge efficiency. Especially at the local government level but also for certain central government activities the awareness of the relevance of more business-like management makes a plea for the application of accrual accounting methods. This has also for an advantage the better matching possibilities now matching in government is less matching cost with revenue and more matching cost with usefulness created.
- The control function of the budget demands reference information with respect to regularity, efficiency and effectiveness in order to be able to confront it with realization figures in the financial report.

It is esteemed important, that financial reporting is as understandable as possible in order to involve the electorate more intensively with the democratic process. Who would not agree with such an aim. In that case as less as possible differences between private sector financial reporting and public sector financial reporting is favorable.

From a management-accounting point of view it is obvious that a lot can be learned from the business sector. This implies an increased relevance of the accrual accounting basis. Looking at these circumstances and developments it is logical that a development has come visible to harmonize private sector financial reporting and public sector financial reporting.

But it should not be forgotten that undeniable differences between the private sector and the public sector remain to be of importance. Therefore the motto should be: Harmonize where it could but differentiate where it should.
It could be concluded that the recent initiative of the IFAC Public Sector Committee to produce a set of International Public Sector Accounting Standards (IPSAS) with the

International Accounting Standards (IAS) as a point of departure is completely in line with this view.

This background was the reason to choose the theme for the 7th CIGAR-conference, which in June 1999 was organized by Tilburg University, as:
The similarities and differences between central government accounting and local government accounting within or between countries.

The proceedings of this conference are brought together in this book. The different contributions have been brought in order by creating 4 parts.

The first part contains contributions from plenary speakers dealing with the state of the art with regard to *Dutch Government Accounting*.

In his opening address Ad J.E. Havermans, member of the Dutch Court of Audit, the supreme auditing institution of the Netherlands has set out the view of the Court of Audit on the Dutch government accounting system and the way in which they contribute to accountability and discharging.

In the next contribution Harman W.O.L.M. Korte, Director Budget Affairs at the Ministry of Finance, responsible for accounting and financial reporting at the central government-level sketches the developments within the central government accounting system in the Netherlands.

In the third chapter Cees Schouten, Deputy Director-General Public Administration of the Ministry of the Interior and Kingdom Relations, responsible standardsetter for accounting and financial reporting of provinces and municipalities, elaborates the government accounting systems in use at the provincial and municipal government level and the evolution they are undergoing.

The last contribution of this part is from Pieter G. van der Poel, controller of the City of Tilburg. The city of Tilburg has gained worldwide recognition for its Financial Management System. This chapter contains information on this system and about the continuous developments thereof.

In part II, papers are combined which could be categorized as *International Comparative Research*.

The paper from Mark Christensen and Hiroshi Yoshimi concludes, from a comparison between developments in Australia's New South Wales and Japan's Hokkaido that New Public Management cannot fully explain why differences in development originated. They mention some additional possible explanations, which need further research before they have proven to be relevant. Attention is given to the differences between government in a western type culture and a specific Asian type of culture.

Hassan A.G. Ouda compares in his paper the central government accounting systems of Egypt and the Netherlands. He concludes to a number of influences, which are likely to have been reasons for differences in the existing accounting systems of countries and gives attention to differences between developed countries at one hand and developing countries at the other hand.

Anatoli Bourmistrov and Frode Mellemvik present in their paper an interesting comparison between democratic governance and accounting in Leningrad county (Russia) and Nordland county (Norway) and they interrelate these aspects as explaining factors. Special attention is given to differences between a country with a stable old democracy at one hand (Norway) and a young democracy in evolution at the other hand (Russia)

In part III, papers belonging to the category *National Comparative Research* have been brought together.

Johan Christiaens' paper enters into the comparison of a number of different government levels in Belgium where accounting system changes have been implemented or are in the process of change-preparation. He concludes that the lack of a conceptual framework leads to unexplained and not explicitly considered differences. He predicts a number of conflicts in accounting, because of the use of characteristics of different accounting systems in the new accounting regulations.

The paper of Norvald Monsen and Salme Näsi enters into the question whether departing from a case in a Finnish municipality can be concluded to favorable effects from the accounting reform from cash-based accounting and accrual accounting. In their opinion the favorability of these effects is at least questionable.

Jan van Helden and Nico P. Mol compare the inherent and evolutional aspects of two initiatives in the Netherlands aiming at improvements of management in government. At the lower government level they analyze the so-called Policy and Management Instruments project and at the central government level they analyze the Result Oriented Management Control. They conclude that a number of differences exist and that numbers of practical problems still have to be solved.

June Pallot takes as a point of departure for her study the two ways of viewing at the role of local authorities, either functionalistic or autonomistic, being the international development into the direction of the autonomistic view. She concludes that New Zealand is at a crossroads where both views are recognizable in nowadays local-authorities position. She poses the question whether recent reforms in the local authorities area and with respect to accounting direct into the opposite direction. So the question remains whether these reforms serve central government or local government aims.

Vicente Montesinos, José Manuel Vela and Bernardino Benito present a view on the differences between regional government accounting at one hand and central government and local government accounting on the other hand. The latter being traditionally consistent with each other. The paper enters into this remarkable difference, because of existing autonomy at the regional level as well as into the mutual differences between the several regions.

Sheila Ellwood researched the development of three different parts of the UK public sector during the last two decades and especially focuses on the diversity which nevertheless a lot of convergence remained to exist. She also draws a comparison with the contemporary developments in the private sector.

A similar point of departure, has been chosen by Josep L. Cortès, in his paper on different approaches chosen by different standardsetters in the USA. He enters into the different ways of accounting for capital assets this implies.

Kiyoshi Yamamoto, whilst paying attention to some special aspects of the Japanese legal structure of government, describes and explains the background of similarities and dissimilarities between central and local government accounting systems.

Part 4 contains a number of contributions which are related to the motto of the conference but not comparative and is called *Non-Comparative Research*.

Wojciech A. Nowak and Barbara Bakalarska have presented a country study on the structure of the Polish public sector after very recent State reforms and give a clear insight of the specific solutions, which a country in transition has to choose.

Alan D. Godfrey, Patrick J. Devlin and M. Cherif Merrouche have tried to integrate Lüder's contingency model with theories of diffusion of innovations in an as they call it "new hybrid diffusion-contingency model and tested it through analyzing its application to government accounting innovations in Albania.

James L. Chan, Cong Shuhai and Zhao Jianyong present a study in which the way of economic and social reform from an orthodox socialist economy to a socialist market economy is compared to the way of accounting reform. The unique way of an economy in transition, which can be seen in the People's Republic of China is the object of their research and delivers an interesting view on reform in the largest country of the world. They conclude to some suggestions for further reform.

Jean-Baptiste Gillet and Claude Heiles describe the transitional phase in which the French municipal accounting system has to grow from several different (types) of accounting systems to a more accrual accounting system. They enter into the legal- and public finance constraints which are encountered and have to be solved.

Helge Mauland and Frode Mellemvik deliver a critical analysis of the rather peculiar Norwegian local government accounting system. They doubt the value of information rendered by the system. They confront figures coming from local government financial reports with reports according to private sector accounting regulation and comment them.

The last contribution to this book comes from K. Cichocki, J. Kleimo and J. Ley. They comment on the consequences of the lack of segregation between capital and operating budgets as to the controllability of issuing debts by local governments in Poland. They also make recommendations for adaptations of the accounting system for local governments in Poland.

ACKNOWLEDGEMENTS

I explicitly want to thank the other members of the Scientific Committee of the 7th CIGAR Conference: Ernst Busschor, Eugenio Caperchione, Jim Chan, Jan van Helden, Rowan Jones, Klaus Lüder, Norvald Monsen, Vicente Montesinos, Jean-Claude Scheid and José Manuel Vela for their contribution in the paper-admission process.

The Rector Magnificus of Tilburg University, Professor Len de Klerk, deserves gratefulness for his support to organize the 7th CIGAR Conference at Tilburg University.

The organization of such an event would not have been possible without the important support of the secretariat of the Department of Accounting & Accountancy and especially Loes Lavrijsen and Sharon van Kuijk must be mentioned. Special recognition has to be paid to Sharon van Kuijk for her role in assembling the book in a camera-ready format. She has done so with great accuracy and dedication and was of great help.

Last but not least the authors of the published papers have to be thanked for their contribution.

It should be clear that the final responsibility of this book is mine. It was a pleasure and an honour to work on it.

Tilburg, October 2000

Aad Bac

For further information please contact:

Professor Aad D. Bac
Tilburg University
Faculty of Economics
Department Accounting & Accountancy
Warandelaan 2
PO box 90153
5000 LE Tilburg
the Netherlands
Telephone: +31 13 466 8305
Telefax: +31 13 466 2611
E-mail: a.d.bac@kub.nl

CHAPTER 1

DUTCH GOVERNMENT ACCOUNTING FROM THE PERSPECTIVE OF THE SUPREME AUDITING INSTITUTION

Ad J.E. Havermans

1.1.   Introduction

It was with great pleasure that I accepted the invitation to present the opening address at this conference. My credentials as a mayor of various municipalities between 1963 and 1996 - the last being The Hague, our seat of government - and my membership of the Netherlands Court of Audit since 1996 have placed me in a position which allows me to offer a few introductory observations from the Dutch perspective on the theme of this conference: 'The similarities and differences between central government accounting and local government accounting within or between countries'. My change of appointment also brought about a change in my position with regard to reporting: as a mayor I was responsible every year for drawing up and presenting the municipal accounts on time to the municipal council. My role as a member of the Board of the Netherlands Court of Audit is to independently audit the accounts of central government ministries.

My address will follow a course which reverses the order of my official appointments: first I shall discuss the remit and methods of the institution to which I am currently attached, the Netherlands Court of Audit (to be referred to as 'The Court' in the rest of my address). I shall trace the developments in the reporting practices of central government and then explain how the Court is involved in this. I then intend to briefly explore the potential implications of these developments for local and regional governments.

1.2.   The Position and the Role of the Court of Audit

First, the remit and methods of the Court within the body politic. The Netherlands is a constitutional monarchy. The Constitution allows for a clear separation of powers. Central government comprises the monarch and ministers, but the Constitution specifies that it is the ministers who are accountable to the States General for all the actions of central government. There are 13 ministries. Some of these have central responsibilities, for example, the Ministry of Finance coordinates and supervises the financial management of all ministries. At lower levels of government, both the provinces and the municipalities in the Netherlands are responsible for different aspects of administering and managing local and regional services and programs.

Before 1848 the Court served the King by keeping a check on the ministers. In this year a radical change to the Constitution transferred the power of the monarch to parliament. The Court performed the same function but, this time, in the service of the Lower House.

1

A. Bac (ed.), International Comparative Issues in Government Accounting, 1-7.
© 2001 *Kluwer Academic Publishers. Printed in the Netherlands.*

Ministers are responsible for the proper and effective use of the public money that they administer. This responsibility stretches beyond the walls of their ministries; for it also involves certain important supervisory obligations. First, there is the responsibility that they bear towards local and regional governments. The Netherlands has a highly centralized tax collection system. Local and regional governments may levy taxes only within certain limits. There is no local or regional income tax. Hence, the funding of local projects involves a substantial flow of cash between central and local government. Part of this cash flow takes the form of a general grant and part of it takes the form of specific payments which may be spent by the municipalities only under certain conditions. The ministers must supervise that these specific payments are spent well.

The ministers are also required to monitor the disbursement of public funds that are distributed to organizations in the form of subsidies, loans or guarantees, and the collection and expenditure of public resources by legal entities engaged in carrying out a statutory duty. In recent years, as more and more public sector duties have been hived off, many such legal entities have appeared on the fringes of the ministries. Finally, ministers are also expected to supervise the way local and regional governments and other organizations spend European money.

The Constitution provides for a series of High Councils of State, including the Court. The Court is independent of both the ministers and the States General, and has a high degree of freedom in determining the audit program. The Constitution specifies that the Court is responsible for auditing state revenue and expenditure. The work of the Court is governed by the Government Accounts Act, which provides for the following types of audit to be performed by the Court:
- regularity audits (financial audits) at the ministries: audits of the regularity, orderliness and auditability of departmental financial management and of the reliability of departmental and central government financial statements;
- performance audits at the ministries: audits of the effectiveness and efficiency of departmental policy, management and organization;
- regularity and performance audits at organizations that are financially linked to central government or that perform a statutory duty.

The Court is statutorily authorized to audit these organizations and is hence in a position to monitor the way they use the money. The Court has no authority at the level of local and regional government. Given the ministerial accountability for the expenditure of certain public resources by local and regional authorities, the Court believes that it should be officially empowered to directly demand information on this expenditure. Accordingly, the Court has submitted a request to the central government and the States General that its powers be widened. The Court does not want its authority to extend to local and regional government. It wants additional authorization for the sole purpose of keeping abreast of ministerial accountability. The auditing of local and regional accounts can easily take place on the spot, whenever possible through independent audit offices. The example of the Rotterdam Audit Office is well worth following! The Court has offered to advise local and regional authorities on setting up similar audit offices.

The reports of the Court are submitted to the States General and, being official parliamentary documents, are in the public domain. They are usually considered by the parliamentary State Expenditure Committee, which has the authority to call ministers to account and to seek further evidence from the Court. The Lower House frequently uses the reports of the Court to question ministers. The Court recognizes that it needs parliamentary support if its work is to be successful.

The mission statement of the Court is: 'to audit and improve the operation of central government and the connected bodies'. To achieve this, the Court provides the government, the States General and those who are responsible for the management of the audited bodies with audit-based information, which consists of audit findings and judgements as well as recommendations on organization, management and policy. The Court considers the distinguishing features of its products to be objectivity, reliability and usefulness and believes that independence and efficiency should be reflected in its production process.

In the next few years the Court plans to intensify its performance audits; primarily through assessing the policy information that is obtainable from the ministries. The Court aim in the case of legal entities with statutory duties is to ensure that ministers can be reasonably certain by 2005 that everything is proceeding lawfully in the sectors for which they are accountable, and that regularity and financial management will mirror the situation within central government. I shall return to this presently.

The Court has played a role in two large-scale operations which were of great importance to financial reporting and the underlying financial management at central government. These were the Government Accounting Reform Operation and a recent project on financial reporting quality improvement. I shall now explain these two operations briefly. Mr. Korte of our Ministry of Finance will address the latter of the projects into more detail later on in the program.

1.3.   The Government Accounting Reform Operation

In the late 1980s the Dutch government carried out a large-scale operation to improve financial management at the ministries: the Government Accounting Reform Operation. The primary objective was to improve financial information (budget information and accounting information) and financial management. This operation was given the go-ahead by a motion passed by the Lower House in 1985 and stemming from a report by the Court which indicated that there was an unacceptable delay in the delivery of financial statements from the central government. In those days it was not uncommon for financial statements to be submitted to the States General many years after the budget year. In response to the motion the Minister of Finance announced a plan of action to improve the situation. In the years that followed the Court closely monitored the realization of this long-term plan of action through its reports to the States General. In broad terms, a reasonable degree of order was introduced into the financial management of the ministries, regularity of public expenditure and income was to a large extent assured and, last but not least, financial information became available in an acceptable form at an acceptable moment. Let me give you an illustration: in the initial phase of the Government Accounting Reform Operation the percentage of expenditure over which there was no assurance on regularity stood at around 25% and the percentage of receipts at around 60%. These percentages now stand at over 99% in both cases. The success of the operation was dependent on an interaction of players each of whom accepted that he/she was accountable: the critical audit report by the Court, the parliamentary motion, the plan of the Minister of Finance, actual implementation at the departments and the progress report by the Court were all indispensable factors in the success of the operation.

1.4.   The Follow-up of the Reform

Despite the progress, there was still some dissatisfaction with the budgeting and accounting process. This dissatisfaction was expressed mainly by the Lower House of the States General. In the first instance, it found that accounts were often published too late in the year. Moreover, it was of the opinion that the accounts were not accessible enough, too large, too technical and too narrow in their scope. Although the Government Accounts Act has stated since 1995 that annual ministerial accounts must include information on the realized policy and activities, and on the performance and effects, they were still primarily financial documents. It is partly for this reason, that the parliamentary control function was inadequately exercised.

To enhance its control function, the Lower House itself (in the form of the Public Expenditure Committee) took the initiative to bring forward the publication of the accounts of the previous year from September 1 to May 15 as well as to improve the quality of the financial statements. In consultation with representatives of the Ministry of Finance, the other ministries and the Court, proposals were put forward to achieve these goals.

To bring about the desired qualitative improvement, the departmental financial statements had to provide more insight into the realization of policy objectives and the performance delivered by means of the available budget. Such policy-oriented statements do not come about of their own accord. Policy objectives need to be specified in the budgets in more concrete and quantifiable terms. To this end, indicators must be used more explicitly in the budgets and the statements, particularly with regard to efficiency (cost-related information linked to products and/or performance) and policy effectiveness. The financial statements relating to longer-term policies should provide insight into the progress made towards the policy objectives by means of annual expenditure targets. This must be further refined by the appointment of 'policy priorities' in the budget. The Lower House has already selected the priorities to be addressed in the departmental reports for this year. A working party led by Lower-House member Van Zijl has formulated proposals for this purpose. At its request, the Court recently issued recommendations on the feasibility of justifying policy priorities on the basis of performance data suggested by the working party. Other starting points for qualitative improvements are to organize the financial statements into more general sections and to disclose the relationship between policy, operations and financial resources. The statements will be organized into more general sections by reducing the current number of budget items. Increasingly, each item should represent a distinct and recognizable area of policy. The section on 'operations' should also be organized along general lines. An important aspect of this is a management statement issued by the minister in which the operations are reviewed against certain fixed benchmarks. The initiative to report special events and variances will then rest with the minister. To reflect the increase in the scope of accountability, the term 'annual report' will be used rather than 'financial statements'.

Government-wide accounts, known as the State Annual Report, will be prepared, enabling the government as a whole to report at national level on policy, operations and financial resources. This report will form the basis for an annual plenary debate in the Lower House on or immediately after the third Wednesday in May.

The new version of the annual report will be presented to the States General by 2003 and will serve, together with the relevant audit report by the Court, as a basis for endorsing the ministers' conduct.

The new style annual report of every ministry will have to be audited internally by the ministerial auditing department. The current, mainly financially-oriented audit measures will have to be supplemented with performance-oriented procedures. The focus of the audit will therefore shift. Once all of this has been realized the Court, as external auditor, can base its examination of the annual statements largely upon a review of the departmental audit.

All of this indicates that, in the coming years, the annual statement will gradually cease to be a document in which financial data takes central place and will become an annual report which provides coherent information on policy (activities, performance and effects), business management and finance. The Court has actively helped to pave the way for this key change by participating in the working parties that developed the proposals and by issuing the recommendations on responsibility for policy priorities. Yet again interaction between the parties responsible, initiated by the supervisory body - the Lower House - has lain at the heart of a major change of course.

1.5.   The Central Government Accounting Basis

Another relevant theme in relation to central government reporting is the accounting basis. Mr. Korte will also address this issue into more detail, I will draw some headlines. The central government has traditionally used a cash basis. Many people have argued in the past for a switch to an accruals system - the first time as long ago as 1916! However, up to 1995, accruals accounting was used only in state-owned enterprises.

The accruals system became obligatory for agencies (independent ministerial service units) on January 1, 1995. The arguments in favor of this system are presented from the perspective of internal management: a service can be made more effective by introducing transparency into the expenditure (result-oriented management). Meanwhile, the Minister of Finance, approaching the matter from the same perspective, has suggested that other services be allowed to use an accruals system under certain conditions. The rise in the number of agencies and the prospect of other services using the system have created a situation in which accrual-based accounting is steadily gaining credibility and will soon be applied by many government bodies. Inevitably, this means the parallel existence of two systems for budgeting, administration and accountability in the coming years: an obligatory or optional accruals system for some services and a cash system for the parent departments and the remaining services. Hence, information on cash and commitments in the budgetary and financial documents presented to the States General will have to be accompanied by ever-increasing information on accruals. I fail to see how this can contribute to greater transparency in the information submitted to the States General. Moreover the co-existence of two systems will not make the business operations or the auditing more effective. If this situation continues two types of administrative systems will have to be regulated and maintained; staff will have to be trained to understand both systems and audits will have to be performed from two perspectives.

Accordingly, I believe that it would be legitimate to ask what the ultimate aim of this exercise is. Is accrual-based accounting eventually to be accepted as the main system (supplemented by cash information) or is cash-based accounting to be retained as the main system (supplemented by accruals information from certain departments)?

Over the years discussions have revealed that it is impossible to give an objective answer to this question. What really matters is the importance that is attached to the strengths and weaknesses of each system. It is however clear that the benefits and drawbacks should be weighed up from other relevant perspectives in addition to internal management. Perspectives which are especially important if the States General is to properly fulfill its authorizing and supervisory role. Allow me to mention a few.

- What are the pros and cons of each system regarding:
  - better allocation of financial resources over investment expenditure and consumption expenditure?
  - monitoring and reporting on the size and composition of the public capital?
  - monitoring and reporting on the fulfillment of EMU norms?
- How far are the basic principles of 'result-oriented management' applicable to the relationship between the States General and the ministries as a whole? Which system is better equipped in this context to express the financial resources needed by the ministries for their activities, performance and effects?
- Is it logical or desirable that principles inherent in the accruals system (such as the recognition of provisions) are used only for executive services?
- How do the two systems compare in relation to the complexity and objectivity of information?
- What are the extra costs of introducing and applying the accruals system across the board?

It is important to develop a well-founded vision on the budget system we eventually want to see; a vision which integrates all of these perspectives.

1.6.   Lower Government Accounting Aspects

I shall now concentrate briefly on the local and regional governments. In the last ten years many municipalities and provinces have been strengthening their planning and control instruments. It is for this purpose that the Ministry of Internal Affairs initiated the 'Policy and Policy Instrument' project in the 1980s. Major themes of this project were multi-year planning, product budgeting and interim progress reports. Many local and regional governments have partly or fully adopted the instruments developed by this project. But what about the 'finishing touch': the official annual statement submitted by the executive board to the democratic control body (namely the municipal council and the provincial council)? The legislation states that the annual report of the executive board to the control body consists of an annual statement and a report. The annual statement is purely a financial document drawn up according to an accruals system. There are no general regulations governing the content of the report in relation to the accountability on financial management. How much scope is there for improvement here?

The central government has recently made considerable progress in defining general principles for more policy-related accountability. Particular attention was paid to the primacy of policy: having taken the initiative to improve quality and set policy priorities the Second Chamber will have to accept the proposals that are formulated. One could conceivably ask how these developments will reverberate upon the reporting practices of local and regional governments, where business management has had a powerful boost in the past decade and budgeting and accountability has evolved along modern financial lines. But how far have the local and regional governments progressed in establishing a relationship between accountability for financial data on the one hand and performance on the other? And how far does the democratic control body set requirements for the content of the statements which form the basis for discharging the executive board? These questions are bound to arise later in the program. As has already been mentioned, the Court has declared itself willing to advise the municipalities and provinces on setting up an audit office. This service could also provide useful impulses to enrich accountability.

1.7.   Conclusion

In conclusion: the Court is in a changing political context. The role of government is changing at central, local and regional level. Major trends such as the separation of policy from implementation and the internationalization of policy framing in, among others, a European context are creating complex administrative relationships. Within the complex framework of 'good governance' it is crucial to guarantee transparency of government dealings and electoral accountability. The Court is endeavouring from its specific position to promote these fundamental values at national level and by participating in international alliances such as INTOSAI, EUROSAI. Initiatives are also being developed within these contexts to advise and assist developing nations in setting up their own auditing facilities. Hence, the Court is directing his efforts at English speaking countries in southern Africa. Independent, expert and authoritative audit offices are essential if the government is to enjoy the trust of the people. I sincerely hope that your conference will produce inspiring visions which will help to consolidate this trust.

DUTCH CENTRAL GOVERNMENT BUDGETING AND ACCOUNTING SYSTEM

Harman W.O.L.M. Korte

2.1. Introduction

The subject of this contribution will be approached by means of answering two major questions. These are the following: what is the role for accrual accounting and budgeting in the Dutch central government system and what is the content of recent government proposals to renew the budget and report structure? The answering will be done by means of entering into a number of sub-questions.

As 'the Dutch central government budgeting and accounting system is a rather long and tiresome expression', it will simply be mention 'the Dutch system'. One should keep in mind two things when using that abbreviation. Firstly it is concentrated on central government and secondly it deals with both budgeting and accounting. In the ministry of Finance we are convinced that it is necessary to use the same system for both.

Let us firstly describe the general characteristics of the present system. As holds for most other central governments, the Dutch system is cash based. But in the mid-eighties it was concluded that for better control of public spending, a complete system for control of commitments was needed. The then existing system was not able to produce clear insight into the payments that would result from commitments already entered into in previous years. In the early eighties this shortcoming had resulted in unexpected payments in years that were already characterized by serious fiscal stress due to the almost absence of economic growth. In 1992 the so-called integrated cash/commitments system was implemented. This means that at present all new commitments have to be presented in the budget and have to be authorized by Parliament. Moreover the budgetary information systems must be able to produce the information in which year, what part of a commitment will result in actual payments. To keep such an information system up to date, it is necessary to relate each payment to the commitment it stems from, and to adjust the estimates of future payments resulting from a commitment, as soon as new information on the cash pattern comes available. This system works relatively satisfactorily.

Traditionally the finances of the so-called state enterprises where incorporated in the budget system. These enterprises, like the State Mines, the State Mint and the State Post and Telecom enterprise, used the accrual system. Their budget and report figures were translated into cash terms to consolidate them in the overall totals for the central government budgets and accounts. In the wave of privatization of the nineteen eighties all state enterprises were transformed into private enterprises, so accrual accounting and budgeting was on the verge of disappearance from the Dutch system.

9

A. Bac (ed.), International Comparative Issues in Government Accounting, 9-18.
© 2001 *Kluwer Academic Publishers. Printed in the Netherlands.*

2.2. The Reintroduction of Accrual Accounting and Budgeting in at least Part of the Dutch System

By the time the state enterprises were almost extinct, the Dutch government, influenced by the example set by the United Kingdom, decided to introduce agencies. The status of an agency is assigned to government bodies, which need accrual accounting and budgeting, and some other specific rules, to accomplish greater efficiency than otherwise possible. Another driving force to introduce agencies was that in the late eighties a tendency was discovered to transform government bodies into what in the UK are called *quango's*, quasi autonomous government organizations, for what were felt as the wrong arguments. The first wrong argument was that it would not be possible to work in a result-oriented way under the hierarchy of a minister.

The other wrong argument - never expressed openly - was that as a quango it would be possible to evade budget and staff cuts. Government decided that the only valid argument to transform a government body into a quango should be that there are specific reasons to reduce the ministerial responsibility for its operations. If no reasons for a reduction of ministerial responsibility exist, the government body should remain part of a ministry and could - if necessary to work more result-oriented - become an agency. The first agencies started in 1994. By now there are 21 of them and their number will gradually grow in the next years. Examples are the Government Housing Agency, the Custodial Institutions Service (the jails) and the Plant Protection Service. All agencies have to use the accrual system. So at present the overall system is an integrated cash/commitments system while 21 agencies use the accrual system.

A next question could be how this dual system can work in practice. An important clue to the answer is that each agency has a budget of its own and that money transfers from ministries to agencies are recorded as cash payments in the budgets of the ministries, and as income in the budgets of the agencies, and vice versa. The accrual-based budgets of the agencies have to balance over time. A negative operating-result in any year has to be offset by a positive one later on. Furthermore agencies may use a deposit and loan facility that is provided by the ministry of Finance on quasi-commercial conditions. So the ministry of Finance operates more or less as a commercial bank for the agencies. To prevent unpleasant surprises for the total of the budget outcome in cash terms, agencies have to bid for a maximum use of the loan facility in the process of budget preparation. These provisions ensure that agencies can focus on cost per output, while on the aggregate level, cash totals are kept within limits.

Indeed, the Netherlands has a long tradition of discussing whether some sort of accrual system should be applied by central government as a whole. Between 1927 and 1958 the state budget knew a formal distinction between a current account and a capital account, and was subjected to the golden rule of finance. This implied that in principle current expenditure and the depreciation on capital expenditure should be equal to current income (a balanced current account). It also implied that net borrowing was allowed only for the financing of net capital expenditure.

In 1958 the golden rule of finance was abandoned. Gradually the Keynesian thinking on the macro economic function of the budget led to a total norm for the budget deficit without a role for the difference between current and capital expenditure.

In 1976 the formal distinction between current and capital account was abolished. In the late eighties interest in the issue reappeared. It was argued that the absence of a distinction between treatment of current and capital expenditure had made capital expenditure relatively vulnerable to cuts in periods of fiscal stress. Investment expenditure would be crowded out of the budget by non-investment expenditure. This crowding-out would be caused by the fact that while the investment expenditure has to compete for the full amount with other types of expenditure in any year, the benefits of the investment expenditure are spread over many years ahead.

In 1991 mister Kok, presently Prime-Minister and then Minister of Finance sent a policy document on the capital account to Parliament. It treated both the issues of full accrual accounting and budgeting, and of replacing the norm of the total budget deficit by the golden rule of finance.

On the issue of the accrual system the conclusion was as follows. There are two principal arguments in favour of introducing the accrual accounting system - firstly, that it would enable the cost and utility of government action to be compared and secondly, that it would provide the clearest possible picture of changes in the net asset position of central government. However, these two arguments would not hold for central government, or at least not entirely. On the other hand it was argued that the introduction of the accrual system could be worthwhile for parts of the budget, and that this need not damage the unity of the budget.

On the issue of the golden rule of finance the conclusion was that it was not to be recommended that the golden rule of finance be adopted as one or the main guiding principle for all, or part of the central government budget. Three reasons against were given. Firstly, it was argued that there would be a very real danger that one aspect of the golden rule - financing capital expenditure by means of borrowing - might be embraced, while the other - balancing the current account - was insufficiently respected. This would cause erosion of control of expenditure and would endanger efforts to curb the growth of national debt. Secondly, it would be difficult to arrive at a worthwhile and practical definition of capital expenditure and to tackle the problem of accounting for depreciation. Thirdly, it would lead to 'a new administrative imbalance in connection with budgetary decisions' because when major investment project are carried out, the political/psychological and macro-economic benefits are reaped in the short term, but the full impact of the burden on the budget is not immediately felt.

On the basis of the 1991 policy document Parliament accepted that: firstly, the capital account would not be re-introduced in central government; secondly, full accrual accounting and budgeting would be limited to government agencies; thirdly, the golden rule of finance should serve as an additional point of reference in the budgetary process, but not as the sole, overriding norm.

2.3.   Continuing Discussions

These conclusions have not made an end to discussions in the Netherlands. Already in 1994 circumstances had changed in such a way that a new discussion took place. Let me mention the most important changes. Firstly, the 1994 coalition agreement on which the first cabinet Kok was based, mentioned a perspective of the introduction in time of a capital account. Secondly a trend-based fiscal policy was introduced. Real expenditure ceilings were defined in such a way that under cautious economic assumptions specific ceilings for the budget deficit would be respected automatically. More importantly it was agreed that fluctuations in tax revenues would not automatically affect the expenditure ceilings as long as the budget deficit would remain below its ceiling. This implied that the direct role of the budget deficit as the sole compass for fiscal policy ended. Thirdly, the conviction grew that government should apply a result-oriented management system wherever feasible. This implies working with agreements on output and associated cost. It was recognized that the accrual system is more suited to this model than the commitment/cash system. Fourthly, developments in other countries like New Zealand and the United Kingdom fuelled a renewed discussion. Fifthly, a new Economic System of Accounts was established. Thus came available an international standard for the demarcation between current expenditure and capital expenditure.

Analysis of the ministry of Finance led to the conclusion that given the new circumstances and under certain conditions a total conversion from the commitment/cash system to the accrual system for central government as a whole would be possible without endangering the control of expenditure.

A number of implications of this conclusion are the following: Firstly, indeed central government would make a complete transition to accrual accounting and budgeting. Secondly, the already existing expenditure ceilings would be converted into net cost ceilings. Thirdly, the costs of capital expenditure would comprise depreciation and a capital charge. Fourthly, the demarcation between current expenditure and capital expenditure would be based on the new Economic System of Accounts without exception. Fifthly, the existing rules of budgetary discipline would apply to net costs in the same way as they did to net expenditure.

This would not be enough to avoid dangers to the control of expenditure. The additional conditions to be met to avoid dangers to the control of expenditure were described as follows. 'The budgets should be integrated in a cost framework based on cautious assumptions; the budget deficit should continue to be allowed to vary as a result of fluctuations in tax revenue, provided the budget deficit ceiling has not been reached. The switch to cost ceilings would mean that more fluctuations than at present would occur in the cash-based budget deficit. Fluctuations would also occur if shifts took place under the cost ceilings from current expenditure to capital expenditure and vice versa. A precondition for a smooth changeover would therefore be that there is a large enough difference between the budget deficit provided for in the coalition agreement and the ceiling to be agreed under the coalition agreement to absorb these fluctuations. Moreover, that value will have to be sufficiently below the EMU ceiling of 3% of GDP to restrict the risk of censure in connection with the excessive deficit procedure.' So far for the rather technical analysis of the ministry of Finance.

2.4. Parliamentary Opinions on the Subject

In 1997 this analysis with the possible solution just described, was sent to Parliament. Remarks against and in favour of the solution were given. And a new conclusion was drawn.

Let us start with the assumed advantages. The cost system could contribute to a 'neutral' decision between current expenditure and capital expenditure. Budgetary integration of an extra capital expenditure would be simpler than it is at present, because the full amount would not immediately have to be made available in the cost budget, but rather a multi-annual series of smaller amounts for depreciation and interest. The cost system could at the same time encourage sound management decisions on the existing capital goods stock of central government, because the associated costs would be visible in the budget. And finally, a link between the state balance sheet, and budget and accounts would lead to a consistent overall approach and a clear demarcation. Just as in the private sector there is a connection between balance sheet and profit-and-loss account.

On the other hand the following arguments against the solution were given. An important argument against was that the concept of capital expenditure is not equivalent to expenditure conducive to sustainable economic growth. For instance, expenditure on education and research cannot be classified as capital expenditure except for buildings and equipment owned by central government. On the other hand, some capital expenditure, such as government offices, does not have a particularly positive effect on growth. Expenditure on the physical infrastructure, too, is capital expenditure only if it results in infrastructure that is owned by central government. Investment contributions to other government authorities and to companies not owned by the state fall outside the concept of capital expenditure as a result of the ownership criterion, which is implied in the adoption of the Economic System of Accounts demarcation. This consequence was described as a specific disadvantage in the decision-making framework of the Economic Structure Enhancing Fund (FES).

The second argument against the solution was that the cost system would create two different steering systems for budgetary policy. The Maastricht Treaty and the Pact for Stability and Growth require separate objectives and conditions for the cash-based and transaction-based budget balance. In addition, the general introduction of the cost system would assign central importance to costs rather than to cash expenditure. Although this could be taken into account by means of an extra safety margin in the budget balance target and/or a separate assessment of the cash required by capital expenditure, it would not make budgetary policy simpler or more transparent.

The third argument against was of a very practical nature. A smooth, general switch to the cost system would require a major modification of the budget classification system and the budget records. The government said it had rejected temporary, less radical solutions on account of the risks they entail for financial management. In view of the fairly limited benefits to be obtained from a general switch, major changes are seen as manifestly disadvantageous. This was seen as especially true when one would consider that the modification costs are not purely incidental: the cost system is undeniably more complex than the current system. In addition it was mentioned that in the next years, priority would have to be given to preparing accounting systems for the introduction of the euro and the computerization problems concerning the year 2000.

2.5.   Recent Considerations about the Subject

On the basis of the given arguments in 1997 government proposed to Parliament that on the aggregate level of central government the present cash based system of budgeting and reporting be maintained. So, no 'Big Bang' transition to the accrual system was considered. On the other hand in the same policy document government announced measures to propagate the use of the more result-oriented management model supported by full accrual accounting and budgeting for individual government bodies wherever possible.

The thinking behind this approach as described in the policy document is that efficiency and effectiveness can be improved by making visible the products (output) delivered by a government service and the related costs. Determining the costs of government activities and attributing them to products or services is expected to facilitate decisions on resource deployment. For instance, it allows the cost of providing public services to be charted. By monitoring movements in the cost per product, or by comparing them with costs in comparable organizations, management is rendered more transparent and an insight can be gained into efficiency and effectiveness. As a result, steering can be modified too. Agreements can be made between different tiers of management on product costs. Certain forms of market forces can be introduced by creating relationships between suppliers and customers, and costs can be passed on to buyers. This requires a transfer from the budget of the supplier to that of the customer. This promotes cost awareness on the part of both the supplier and the customer.

A more result-oriented management model means that the organizations themselves can determine the combination of input factors (personnel and equipment) used to produce their products. Steering on the input side must therefore change: the organization must be able to make transfers between the individual cost types within the total agreed output budget. This will make integrated management possible. The government expressed as its view that working with the accrual system instead of expenditure makes the use of this management model even more beneficial.

Firstly, a full accrual system allows better cost-price calculation. If expenditure is attributed to products without further adjustment, capital expenditures cause fluctuations from one year to the next that are of no relevance to the assessment of efficiency, and this impedes comparisons with other organizations. It would also mean the use of annually fluctuating prices if 'costs' are passed on. Secondly, with integrated management, the organization itself determines the optimum mix of input factors, and shifts can take place between current expenditure and capital expenditure. Steering should therefore focus on the cost level rather than cash effects. Thirdly, the full accrual system has the advantage that the cost level is partly determined by capital expenditure costs from the past. These depreciation costs are derived from the balance sheet, and interest attribution occurs too. This means that the organization is constantly forced to consider whether a capital good should be retained or sold, leading to efficient capital goods stock management. This incentive does not exist in general in the current commitments/cash system. It also means that the sale revenue from a capital good is credited to the organization concerned.

A cost-oriented system means that the budget, too, can be drawn up in cost terms and this naturally means that the financial statements are also drawn up on a cost basis. As a result, cost-based steering (assessment and authorization) will be able to take place up to the level of Parliament. Agencies already use this more result-oriented management model, linked to the income/expenditure system. In the government's view, it is worth examining whether this model can be used more widely. So government announced it intended as part of the procedure for inter-ministerial policy studies, to carry out an overall management study in various major executive services which are not agencies. The aim should be to ascertain whether the introduction of a more result-oriented management model, linked to the full accrual system, would benefit the management of these services. In addition to these intentions government announced the already mentioned loan facility for the smooth operation of part of government working in the accrual system and said it would consider the possibility for government services to adopt the accrual system without naming themselves agencies.

Parliament decided to postpone the debate on the document until the results of the announced inter-ministerial studies would be available. The studies themselves led mostly to the conclusion that a system of result-oriented management with the accrual system would be the optimal solution for the respective services. This means that in the next few years the count of services with this system will rise.

It is not certain what the future will bring on this topic. Clearly one of the arguments against the total transition to the accrual system as described in 1997 will not hold for long. By 2002 we will have overcome the year 2000 troubles and we will have introduced the euro. In addition recently critical remarks have been made on maintaining two systems next to each other in central government. Add to this that slowly but gradually some other OECD countries introduce the accrual system. New Zealand and the UK have got company of Iceland and Australia, and there are signs that one or two will follow in the near future. I think the results in those countries and the development of introduction for individual services in the Netherlands will be important factors for a new discussion. For now enough about the role of the accrual system in Dutch central government.

2.6. Renewal of the Budget and Report Structure

It's time now to devote some attention to the second subject. That is the content of recent government proposals to renew the budget and report structure. In the Netherlands the state budget is made up of budget documents for each ministry separately. Those documents have to pass the legislature just as any other bill. Each minister has to defend his own budget in the two chambers of Parliament. Also each minister has to draw an annual report on the outcome of his budget. The Minister of Finance produces accompanying overview documents, and is responsible for overall co-ordination of the budget process. In May 1999, mister Zalm, the Dutch minister of Finance, presented to the president of our Lower House of Parliament, a policy document with the title 'From policy budget to policy report'. This document explains why the budget document structure and the report structure need reshaping, and what the results should look like. Originally the proposal for the budget structure and the proposal for the report structure stems from two different initiatives. The first initiative originated from the staff of our Lower House of Parliament. They organized a working conference on the speeding up and the improvement of annual reporting on the budget outcomes, in which members of Parliament and of the National Court of Audit and the minister of Finance participated. The general impression of all participants was that the time was right to organize more political attention for the reports. This resulted in an agreement on a new time frame for the end of the budget cycle, and the start of an informal working party on the subject of quality improvement of the annual reports. The new time frame agreed upon is, that the annual reports have to be presented to Parliament by the middle of May and that Parliament will finish the discussion with government on the reports before the parliamentary summer recess. The finishing of the discussions in Parliament before the summer recess is important, in order to ensure the attention wished for, because after the summer recess, all attention is focused on the policy for the next year.

The informal working party on quality improvement of the reports consisted of people working for our National Court of Audit and some ministries, and was presided by a staff member of the Lower House. The result of their work was published last year under the title: 'The annual report in the political arena'. Main conclusion was that annual reports should cover policy, management and the financial outcomes in an integrated way, focused on main issues, and fitted to the needs of Parliament. Ideally the main issues should be the policy priorities that should be listed in the process of establishing the budget. The working party recommended to introduce a management statement to cover the control of normal management issues and to limit the attention in the report for management issues to special issues in that area, like reorganizations. It was also recommended that the judgement of the National Court of Audit be included in the report and that this judgement should cover all aspects. The working party advised to fix the day of the presentation of the report to Parliament on the third Wednesday in May. The third Wednesday was chosen with a wink to the third Tuesday of September, the constitutionally established day for the presentation of the budget for the next fiscal year. The message was that rendering an account of the results should be considered as at least as important as presenting plans. Parliament, the National Court of Audit and government welcomed the proposals of the working party in general, and the minister of Finance announced that he would take care to government proposals on that basis. So far for the first initiative.

The second initiative leading to the recent publication of government proposals for a new structure for the budget document and the annual report, stems from the ministry of Finance itself. About a year ago the ministry of Finance reached the conclusion that the time was right to investigate whether a new structure for the budget-document would be better suited for the central purpose of the budget. This central purpose is that the budget of each ministry should give answers to three simple questions. What policy goals does government want to achieve, what actions is government going to undertake to achieve those goals, and what may those actions cost. Interviews with users of the existing documents brought to light that they considered them to be difficult to read. Answers to the central questions could not, or only with great difficulty be found, they said. One parliamentarian confessed to use the press-briefing document instead of the budget document, while preparing himself for the debate in Parliament. The budget documents appeared to have grown too thick and too little focused on the three simple central questions. The growth process of the existing documents is in itself perfectly understandable. Most additions were the result of questions from parliament. Once an addendum with a new subject was added, it appeared difficult to get rid of it in the next year. Moreover the basic structure was highly focused on control of public expenditure in answer to the fiscal stress mentioned earlier. Relatively little structured attention was devoted to the relation with the policy goals and activities.

The main elements of the recent government proposals are:
the budget document will be structured as follows:
- the budget law;
- a readers guide;
- the policy paragraph;
- the management paragraph;
- the agency paragraph;
- the in-depth-addendum.

Let us explain the most important elements. Time fails to go cover all. The policy paragraph will become the heart of the document. It will consist of a policy agenda and the policy line items. The policy agenda will in brief present the proposed policy priorities for the coming year, and the way by which the minister proposes to realize his goals. In addition the policy agenda will contain a summary of the financial effects of the proposed policy measures for the next fiscal year and at least the four years following.

The policy line items in the policy paragraph will represent the most important change in the budget structure. In the new structure each policy line item in the budget will be focused on a separate operational policy goal. Information for each item should answer the already mentioned three central questions: what policy goal does government want to achieve, what actions is government going to undertake to achieve that goal, and what may those actions cost. At present there are different line items for program expenditure and running cost expenditure. In the new structure all expenditure and income related to the actions to reach a specific policy goal will be brought together in one policy line item. As a consequence it will be possible within the constraint of the attainment of a specific policy goal to shift between the different types of expenditure without prior consent of Parliament. It will suffice to render account of the choices in the annual report. The major challenge in the transition process towards the new budget structure is going to be the definition of the policy line items. Clearly Parliament will want to have a say in that process, as the result will have an impact on the extent to which the parliamentary vote can directly alter the direction of government spending. The ministries may experience even more radical changes. It is quite likely that in some cases the organizational structure will have to be adjusted to ensure the focusing on the attainment of the explicit policy goals. And at least the process of defining the appropriate operational goals, and of sorting out the activities and the expenditure and income related to those, will be time and energy consuming. We all know the rich literature on the difficulties of measuring the quantity and quality of government output.

And nevertheless government decided that it is worthwhile to make a major effort to reach the optimum in this area. The ministry of Finance is preparing itself to help the other ministries in this process as much as possible.

Essentially the structure of the annual reports of the ministries will follow the structure of the budget as just described. The annual reports will focus on answers to three related questions. Did government reach its goals as set in the budget, did government complete the actions as planned in the budget, and did the costs of the actions remain within the limits as set in the budget? Government decided also to follow most of the other proposals of the working party mentioned earlier. The judgement of the National Court of Audit will be included in the reports and lengthy paragraphs on management issues will be replaced
at least partly by a management statement.

2.7.   Implementation of these Plans

It is not just a matter of regrouping already existing information. Real work has to be done on several subjects:
-    The redefinition of the budget line items on the basis of operational policy goals.
-    The definition of meaningful output, activity and outcome indicators.
-    The definition of the scope of the management statement.
-    The adjustment of information systems to cope with the new information needs.
According to the timetable presented to Parliament, the 2002 budget is scheduled to be the first budget in the new structure. So it has to be ready in September 2001. As a consequence the first annual report in the new structure will appear on the third Wednesday of 2003. This may seem far away. But this schedule implies that little more than a year is available for basic preparations, because the budget preparation process for the year 2002 starts in the fall of the year 2000. This is why government announced that it will report in May next year on the progress of the project and whether the timetable will hold.

The last question to enter into is, whether there is a relationship between the two topics covered in this presentation. There is in two ways. Firstly, it is clear which topic has priority now. That is the new budget and report structure. Secondly, once we have successfully managed that project, it might be argued that we have a new argument to make the overall transition to the accrual system. Cost-information is superior to expenditure-information, in relation to outputs. A few countries, notably New Zealand and Australia, have even made the two steps at once. The Dutch government is ready make to make the first.

THE DUTCH PROVINCIAL AND MUNICIPAL ACCOUNTING SYSTEM

Cees Schouten

3.1. Accountability in an Administrative and Social Context

The first rules governing financial 'reporting' obligations imposed by central government on the municipalities in the Netherlands date from 1800. In that year rules were introduced that obliged municipalities to account in May of each year for the local receipts and expenditure in the presence of representatives of the local citizenry. They were also required to produce a brief statement of property, debts and possessions. Since 1800 the rules have been regularly changed and adapted in keeping with the spirit of the times. It follows that today's rules bear no resemblance to the original rules. The role of financial reporting too has therefore changed considerably over time.

In this paper we will concentrate on the changes to the accounting rules in 1985 and 1995. In consequence of these two sets of changes, the present Dutch municipal and provincial accounting rules are to a large extent based on the rules that apply to the private sector and are thus an application of accrual accounting. These far-reaching changes are the result of the social and economic developments that have taken place in the last few decades and, as a corollary, the increasingly exacting demands made on local authorities. The modern view of the role of government differs fundamentally from that which held sway, for example, in the 1950s.

This proposition brings us to the essence of this paper, namely that, as a result of the present view of the role and duties of government, financial reporting can no longer be regarded simply a matter of 'bookkeeping' and should instead be seen as administration. This means that we will place the accounting rules in a broader context in this paper. The rules, and in particular the changes to the rules, are a reflection of the changing ideas about the duties that government should take upon itself, how it should perform these duties and how it should communicate with the public. We will also extrapolate from this evolving line and look into the future. The present debates and developments provide an indication about the future development of the relationship between administrative and financial management.

This paper is arranged in the following way. Section 3.2. provides a survey of the position and role of municipalities and provinces in the Netherlands. Section 3.3. examines how views on the role of government in general and the local authorities in particular have changed in the 1980s and 1990s. Attention will also be paid to the developments in the administrative management of the local authorities that have led to an improvement of the financial management during the first half of the 1990s; the so-called PMI project (BBI in Dutch). The changes to the accounting rules are described in section 3.4. Although the accounting rules are admittedly based on accrual accounting,

19

A. Bac (ed.), International Comparative Issues in Government Accounting, 19-37.
© 2001 *Kluwer Academic Publishers. Printed in the Netherlands.*

there is and must be scope for tailoring the financial reporting rules specifically to the needs of the municipalities. However, what constitute the distinctive characteristics of municipalities and how they might influence the reporting requirements was and is a topic of discussion. Section 3.5. identifies some present and future developments that are of importance to both municipal financial reporting and administrative management. The last section contains some final remarks.

3.2.   Municipalities and Provinces in the Netherlands

This section describes the position and importance of the municipalities and provinces in the Netherlands. It examines the statutory basis of the local authorities (i.e. the provinces and municipalities), their scope and duties as well as their income and how they obtain it. As we shall see, the municipalities especially play an important role in the Netherlands. The duties and finances of the provinces are of much more limited scope than those of the municipalities. This is why this paper will confine its attention to the municipalities. Many of the aspects that will be dealt with, for example the accounting rules, are in fact the same for the provinces as for the municipalities.

3.2.1. STATUTORY BASIS OF MUNICIPALITIES

The Netherlands has three tiers of government: central, provincial and municipal. There are 12 provinces and 538 municipalities in the Netherlands. The Dutch municipalities are of extremely varied size and composition. For example the number of inhabitants of municipalities varies from 1,003 (Schiermonnikoog) to 721,000 (Amsterdam) and the area covered ranges from 179 (Bennebroek) to 49,365 (Noordoostpolder) hectares. Table 3.1. provides a breakdown of the municipalities by size.

Municipalities 1999 by number of inhabitants		
<5,000		20
5,000 - 10,000		105
10,000 - 20,000		187
20,000 - 50,000		168
50,000 - 100,000		33
100,000 - 150,000		15
150,000 - 250,000		7
>250,000		3

Table 3.1.: Dutch Municipalities by Size

The role of the municipalities is laid down in the Constitution. The 1848 Constitution, which - despite some changes - still largely corresponds to the present Constitution in terms of the political organization of the country, forms the basis for the present Dutch constitutional structure. This Constitution provides that the Netherlands is a decentralized unitary State. Generally speaking, this means that the central government is responsible for determining general policy. The central government fixes the framework within which other government bodies discharge their duties. The provinces have a supervisory and coordinating role. The municipalities are charged mainly with performing duties that have a more immediate impact on the public.

The Position of Municipalities

Municipalities have an independent position in the Netherlands. This is recognized in the Constitution. The Constitution states that the municipalities are competent to regulate and administer their own internal affairs as they see fit and discharge their duties in their own interest. Municipalities may therefore assume responsibilities of their own volition; municipalities are autonomous. The actions of the municipalities are limited only by statutory rules adopted at provincial or central government level. However, there are also duties in respect of which the municipalities have an obligation to cooperate. The Constitution also provides that municipalities may be required by or pursuant to Act of Parliament to provide regulation and administration in order to implement the policy of other tiers of government. The contrast between the two types of duty, i.e. those assumed by the municipality itself (autonomous duties) and those whereby the municipalities help central government to implement policy (joint administration) has become less marked as time has passed. Many duties have been imposed on municipalities by or pursuant to Act of Parliament, but in a way which allows the municipalities much latitude in the manner of implementation and in how priorities are set and the money is disbursed (subject, of course, to the statutory rules). At the same time, the policy freedom of the municipalities in areas in which they are supposedly autonomous is sometimes limited. In other words, there is a kind of a sliding scale ranging from full autonomy at one end to joint administration at the other.

Democratic Legitimacy

Municipalities are independent entities that have their own democratically legitimate government. The municipal council elected by the inhabitants of the municipalities chooses from among its members the executive councillors who, together with the burgomaster (a Crown-appointed mayor), constitute the executive of the municipality. Matters of general administration come under the authority of the municipal council and the day-to-day administration is the responsibility of the burgomaster and executive councillors, irrespective of whether the duties in question involve matters of autonomy or joint administration. The powers of the municipal council, i.e. general administration, include in any event the adoption of municipal legislation (bye-laws), the adoption of the budget, and supervision of the (financial) policy pursued by the burgomaster and executive councillors, among other things by approval of the annual accounts.

The municipalities play an important role in the Netherlands. They form the administrative tier closest to the citizen, and municipalities are primarily responsible for many matters that affect members of the public in their daily life. Decisions regarding the budget can therefore have a major impact on the inhabitants of the municipality. The main items of municipal expenditure are: spatial planning and housing, social provisions and social work, general administration and public order, education, traffic and culture. The contact between municipalities and their inhabitants is often more intensive than the contact of the other tiers of government with the public: the involvement and participation of citizens can take place more easily at this level. For example, local people often have a say in traffic safety plans and building plans in the vicinity of a residential area.

3.2.2. FINANCES

Municipalities also play an important role financially in the Netherlands. In 1998 municipal expenditure accounted for approximately one third of total public spending in the Netherlands[1]. Central government expenditure too accounted for about one third, as did the expenditure of the social funds. Figure 3.1. gives an indication of the ratios of public spending as a percentage of the gross domestic product (GDP) of the three separate groups in 1998.

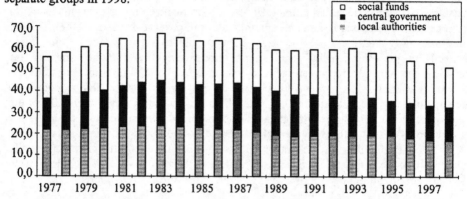

Figure 3.1.:   Public spending of Central Government, Local Authorities and Social Funds as a Percentage of GDP, 1977-1998
Source: *Miljoenennota* 1998, p. 2258

The municipalities have three kinds of income: the general grant from central government (municipal fund), the specific grants from central government, and their independent sources of revenue. The transfers from central government form by far the largest source of their income. Figure 3.2. gives the breakdown of these three sources of income in their entirety in 1998. The specific grants, which account for almost half of their income, are payments for duties which the municipalities undertake in the context of joint administration. The general grant and the independent revenues are general resources, in other words funds that the municipalities can spend as they see fit, but within the limits of the law.

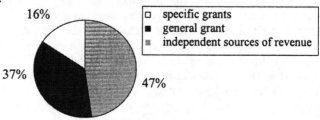

Figure 3.2.:   Sources of Income of the Municipalities, 1998
Source: *Miljoenennota* 1999, p. 255

---

[1]   The municipal expenditure also includes expenditures on joint administration tasks.

The amount of independent revenues of municipalities in the Netherlands is relatively modest. This is because it was considered socially unacceptable in the late 1920s that the level of tax and the quality of services should vary widely from municipality to municipality. The quality of the roads, the fire service and primary education differed greatly. Several important municipal taxes were therefore abolished in 1929. By the late 1980s the municipalities' independent revenues accounted for less than 10% of their total income. As figure 3.2. shows, this figure has now climbed again to 16%, mainly caused by higher costs of environmental protection. The municipalities' own revenues consist mainly of taxes and levies. Property tax, sewerage charges and refuse collection charges are the most important.

When a large part of the municipal taxes (including municipal income tax) was abolished in 1929 the Municipal Fund was established. This Fund is replenished from national taxes. Since the new 1997 Allocation of Finances Act especially, the fund has been distributed among the municipalities by means of a cost-oriented system of allocation. Like the individual revenues, the general grant from the Municipal Fund forms part of the general resources of the municipality. The importance of the Municipal Fund has increased again since the late 1980s. After the Second World War, there was a trend towards centralization. This is reflected in the sharp increase in the importance of the specific grants. In 1987 the specific grants accounted for almost 70% of income. Although there has been a trend towards decentralization (also see section 3.3. below) since the 1980s, the specific grants remain important as Figure 3.2. shows. The decline in specific grants has come about largely as a result of the transfer of specific grants to the general grant. The total municipal income in real terms was only slightly lower in 1998 than in 1987.

3.2.3. DEMOCRATIC LEGITIMACY AND FINANCIAL REPORTING

Municipalities in the Netherlands play an important role in the contact between government and citizens. Although Dutch municipalities have only very limited powers of taxation when compared with municipalities in many other countries, they play an important role, particularly in policy matters. They perform a large part of government functions and account for one third of public spending. Half of the expenditure is allocated by municipalities to autonomous functions. In performing their functions Dutch municipalities often have more powers than their counterparts in other West European countries, even in cases where local taxes in those countries are of a more substantial volume than in the Netherlands.

The political primacy rests with the municipal council, which is elected by the local citizens. Municipalities have their own democratic legitimacy. This is why the greatest importance is attached to careful consideration of decisions and the rendering of account. Municipal financial reporting plays a crucial role in the taking of decisions and in rendering account for these decisions. A transparent and professional administration is in the interests of the proper functioning of democracy. This is first of all because of the knowledge of the financial position of municipalities (see section 3.4.) and, second, because of the account rendered by the administrators to the citizens (see section 3.5.). Before we discuss the accounting system of Dutch local authorities, we will consider the view on the role of government in general and of the municipalities in particular. The evolution of this view also affects municipal financial reporting.

3.3.   View of the Role of Government

3.3.1. BACKGROUND TO NEW VIEW OF THE ROLE OF GOVERNMENT

As in most other West European countries public spending rose considerably in the Netherlands in the 1970s and the first half of the 1980s. As a result, the public spending ratio reached 66.6% of GDP in the Netherlands in 1983. This ratio was one of the highest of the Western countries. In view of the high burden of taxation and social charges, measures to cut public spending were taken from the early 1980s onwards. As a result of these substantial cuts, public spending was reduced to 50.9% by 1998. In figure 3.1., already an indication is given of the public expenditure of the central government, local authorities and social funds. Figure 3.3. shows the burden of taxation and social charges as a percentage of GDP from 1977 to 1998. This burden has decreased only slightly.

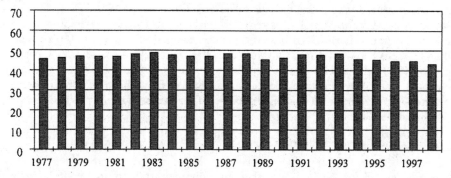

Figure 3.3: Burden of Taxation and social Charges as a Percentage of GDP, 1977-1998
Source: *Miljoenennota* 1998, p. 260

The high burden of taxation and social charges resulted not only in spending cuts but also in a different view of the role of government. This different view was also a product of the increasing complexity of society and the functions and functioning of the legislation. These were found to hamper effective government policy.

In the following section we will discuss in broad outline how this view of the role of government (particularly municipal government) evolved in the 1980s and 1990s. Afterwards we will examine the PMI project, in which the administrative management of municipalities takes precedence. This project is in essence a consequence of the new view of the role of the lower authorities.

3.3.2. THE 1980s AND 1990s

Increasing Autonomy and Decentralization
The need to cut spending meant that more attention had to be paid to efficiency and effectiveness. The aim was to achieve a slimmed-down government that confined itself to its core tasks. A number of large operations were designed among other things to bring this about. Deregulation, increasing autonomy, privatization and the retreat of the public sector (rolling back the frontiers of the State) were major operations which were started in the 1980s and were intended to lead - and did lead - to a different type of government.

Privatization, deregulation and increasing autonomy have also taken place intensively in the municipalities in the Netherlands. This can take the form, say, of contract management. A far-reaching form of increasing autonomy is a non-governmental organization in which the organization itself has a large degree of autonomy but the municipality retains ultimate responsibility for the formulation and implementation of policy. These developments require new and more business-oriented forms of financial control and reporting. Performance agreements, performance measurement, cost prices, financial implementation information and accounting information, planning and control: some of these are new requirements for financial reporting and others are existing requirements that are now applied more strictly.

The developments coincided with a major operation of great importance to the municipalities, namely decentralization. As already mentioned in section 3.2., the percentage of specific grants has fallen substantially since the 1980s while that of both the general grant and individual revenues has risen. This shift reflects the decentralization as municipalities now have less money for the functions that they perform by way of joint administration and more money for those functions which they perform autonomously (or largely autonomously). Figure 3.4. shows how the specific grants and general grant and the independent revenues changed in the period from 1987 to 1998.

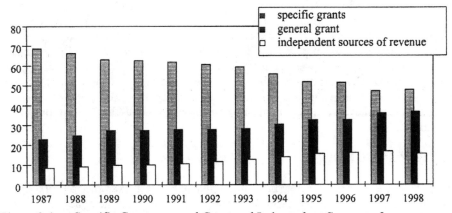

Figure 3.4.:   Specific Grants, general Grant and Independent Sources of revenue as a Percentage of total Income, 1987 - 1998
Source: *Miljoenennota*, various Issues

The decentralization process coincided with the privatization and deregulation operations, which were intended among other things to cut public spending. In addition, both the central government and the municipalities believed that the latter could carry out their duties better and more efficiently. Although the shift of duties from the central government to the municipalities was accompanied by a transfer of funds to the general grant, this was therefore reduced on the assumption that efficiency could be improved. The cuts in the municipal budget combined with the increase in duties mean that municipalities are now exposed to greater financial risks. Here too, municipal financial reporting has become more important from the point of view of decentralization and must therefore be placed on a still more professional footing.

A responsive and Pro-active Government
The market orientation and emphasis on efficiency led not only to a realization that government should confine itself to its core tasks but also to a different view on how the government should perform its tasks. In addition to this development, citizens are acting more and more like consumers in their relations with government: there is a 'market' for the authorities in which members of the public can be both citizen and customer. A market for the authorities means that it is becoming increasingly important for the authorities to adopt a customer-oriented approach. Less bureaucracy and more responsiveness are the watchwords. This is particularly essential for the municipal authorities because the municipality is closest to the citizen. Responsiveness entails open and active government that gives pride of place to the citizen and a customer-oriented approach. A responsive government provides information, anticipates developments and reacts adequately. And it co-ordinates issues and priorities of the community at large and those responsible for running the municipality. The view that the authorities should be pro-active takes this reasoning one stage further. This means that the citizen need no longer always ask for something and need no longer always fill out forms in order to get what he or she is entitled to. Instead, the authorities come to the citizen, for example by automatically linking databases (taking account of privacy rules) and spontaneously send the citizen information about the schemes to which he/she is entitled. Information and communication technology is a major factor in the ability of the authorities to play such a role. More and more municipalities are therefore capitalizing on the new information and communication technology in order to approach the citizen actively. The automatic implementation of schemes and the streamlining of the supply of information to citizens can enhance the efficiency of the authorities. After all, automatic implementation means that fewer application forms and questions are received. A pro-active approach by the authorities can therefore benefit efficiency. Clearly, however, the reverse is also true. Transparent and consistent financial reporting and a well-developed planning and control cycle are essential if the municipality is to discharge its duties to its citizens effectively.

3.3.3. THE PMI PROJECT

As a result of the ever greater demands on municipalities, for example to work more efficiently and effectively, increasing attention was paid to their administrative management. Municipalities were found to lack sufficient modern administrative instruments. This is why all kinds of measures were taken in many municipalities to improve this situation. Ultimately this led to the PMI project. PMI means Policy and

Management Instruments for municipalities (the Dutch acronym is BBI). Under the PMI project a framework for systematic administrative (financial) management was developed for municipalities.

The aim of the PMI project was to strengthen the position of the municipal council, to allow better control of the organization and to enhance customer-orientation. For the purposes of implementation of the framework PMI distinguishes between phases based on the budget cycle. Important steps in the process are, for example, the translation of political wishes and desires into concrete policy plans, interim management and administration reports, development of the annual report and annual accounts as policy instruments and development of instruments for measuring effectiveness.

The PMI project, which lasted from 1990 to 1995, was very successful. Almost all Dutch municipalities applied and are still applying the PMI ideas (or aspects of them). Tilburg is a well-known example - also recognized internationally - of how things can and should be done. Nonetheless, the impact in many municipalities has in the end proved to be limited (see, for example, Ter Bogt and Van Helden, 1999, and Van Helden and Ter Bogt, 1998).

The innovations and improvements brought about by the PMI occurred mainly in the economic field, to a lesser extent in the administrative area and to an even smaller extent in the area of relations between government and citizen. However 'technically perfect' innovative processes and instruments may be, they still require administrative backing if they are to be adequately applied and integrated in the day-to-day practice of the administration. It should be noted in this regard that the positive effects of PMI have occurred mainly in relation to the municipalities as organizations. Other possible reasons why the PMI project had less impact than expected are the sheer size and extremely varied nature of the project and the fact that it may not have lasted sufficiently long to enable the ambitious administrative aims to be fulfilled. Recently, the Ministry of the Interior and Kingdom Relations restarted a number of projects for the purpose of strengthening the financial function of the municipalities. Incidentally, these projects deal with aspects of the financial function and are of a more practical orientation. The accounting rules play a major role in these projects, as they also did in the PMI project.

3.4. Accounting Rules

The accounting rules for municipalities and provinces specify the criteria to be met by the budget and accounts. The budget has many functions. For example, approval of the budget by the municipal council serves as an authorization for the plans of the municipal executive (burgomaster and executive councillors). In addition, the budget plays an important role in decisions on the allocation of resources. The municipal budget has a function in macroeconomic terms too. The budget shows how the municipal finances can influence economic processes. The annual accounts are important, first of all for the purpose of rendering account and, second, for the measurement and evaluation of performance. In short, municipal financial accounting plays an essential role in the functioning of a municipality not only as an organization responsible for the performance of certain functions but also as a democratic organization. Article 3 of the present accounting rules therefore provides that 'The budget, multi-year budget, annual accounts and notes provide, in accordance with generally accepted accounting standards, such information that it is possible to form a sound opinion of the financial position and of the income and expenditure'.

In this section we will deal with the last revisions of the accounting rules in 1985 and 1995. Two views on the basic criteria of the accounting rules played a role in both revisions. First of all, there is the tendency of local authorities to operate increasingly on commercial lines (see section 3.3.). As a result, the criterion that municipalities should comply with the guidelines for commercial accounting has become increasingly important. The 1985 accounting rules therefore took a big step in this direction, and a further step was taken when the 1995 accounting rules were introduced. This process has not yet stopped. Even now there is a debate on whether the rules should not be brought even more into line with the Civil Code. The financial reporting rules of the private sector are contained in Title 9 of Book 2 of the Civil Code (referred to below as CC2).

The second criterion explicitly adopted in the revisions of the accounting rules is the unique character of municipalities - for example the fact that they take social considerations into account when deciding on the allocation of resources This is termed specificity (of local authorities) in the remainder of this paper (see section 3.4.3.) Commercial and financial considerations therefore often play a less important role than in the case of enterprises. In addition, the budget of the municipalities has a constitutional basis, (see section 3.2.). It follows that political and legal principles may be in competition with commercial and financial considerations. However, specificity may never excuse a lack of clarity. On the contrary, the democratic legitimacy of municipalities means that the financial reporting must be transparent and reliable.

There is a clear tension between the two criteria. This tension is a central element of the present debate on the accounting rules. A description of the debate is given in section 3.4.3. First, however, the 1985 and 1995 accounting rules are discussed in sections 3.1. and 3.2.

3.4.1. THE 1985 REVISION: THE FIRST STEP

The 1929 accounting rules were still in force until the 1985 revision. Although they had been repeatedly modified since the Second World War, they had never been revised in their entirety. There were two main arguments for a comprehensive revision in 1985. First, there was the need of the municipalities to respond to the developments concerning the function, role and position of municipalities as described in section 3.3. Methods and techniques derived from the private sector were of importance in this connection. Second, there was a need for more and different information from the municipalities for macroeconomic purposes.

The 1985 accounting rules represented a drastic change for they entailed a switch from cash based accounting to accrual accounting. However, the system introduced in 1985 was by no means identical to the guidelines for annual financial statements that applied to the private sector. Besides introducing accrual accounting the revision also made other changes designed to improve information about the financial position. The multi-year budget and the notes to the budget are important examples of this. As a result of the introduction of the concept of the multi year budget (albeit non-obligatory) the municipalities were encouraged to take account of long-term considerations when making decisions. The notes to the budget were intended to increase the transparency of policy and policy aims.

To facilitate the collection of macro-economic information, the rules stipulated that income and expenditure had to be classified according to the nature of the municipal involvement. These classifications are known as functions, such as education and housing. Simultaneously expense and income categories were introduced, e.g. interest and tax revenues. They too were intended to facilitate the gathering of macroeconomic data. In addition, these categories were intended to improve the internal control of municipalities, as the categories were based on the subdivision of income and expenditure customarily employed in the private sector.

3.4.2. THE 1995 REVISION: THE SECOND STEP

A further set of new accounting rules came into force as early as 1995. The main reason for amending the accounting rules again in 1995 was the entry into effect of the new Local Government Act and Provincial Government Act on January 1, 1994. As a result of these new Acts various technical alterations had to be made to the accounting rules.[2] However, there were also other reasons for revising the rules, in particular the continuing evolution of local authority operations along commercial lines and the PMI process (see above).

As already mentioned, the specificity of municipalities played an important role in the new accounting rules. However, the rules represented a further step in the direction of business-oriented financial reporting. This section will examine both the CC2 aspect and the specificity aspect of the accounting rules.

Changes in the Direction of CC2
Most of the changes made in 1995 involved further modification of the statement of income and expenditure and the balance sheet to bring them more closely into line with CC2. Once again, a few of the changes were also intended to improve the information about the financial position. For example, it now became obligatory to include a risk statement.

The Balance Sheet. Until 1995 the profit and loss account was supplemented by a capital statement. The capital statement was essentially a relic of the old cash-based accounting rules. When the accounting rules were altered in 1995 the capital statement was abolished and the balance sheet was introduced. The transition from capital statement to balance sheet was presented as a procedural matter and not as a fundamental change (Besluit comptabiliteitsvoorschriften 1995, Klop; 1994). It was reasoned that the difference between the balance sheets of two successive years is the same as a capital statement. In addition, the introduction of the balance sheet was accompanied by a rule

---

[2] One consequence is that since 1995 the accounting rules for municipalities and provinces have been the same.

making it obligatory for municipalities to produce a financing and investment statement too. By submitting this statement with the budget, the municipal council is still able to authorize investment decisions.

Not everyone was in favour of introducing the balance sheet and abolishing the capital statement. Some people considered that the capital statement was a clear and informative instrument (Borderwijk; 1993, Hofman; 1994). However, the advantage of a balance sheet is that it corresponds to the practice of the private sector. The use of common terminology is conducive to clarity both for municipal accountants and controllers and for local administrators. Another argument against introduction of the balance sheet was the concern felt by some people as to whether the municipal council could still obtain sufficient information about the separate investment decisions. As mentioned above, this problem was solved by making it obligatory for municipalities to have a financing and investment statement. The last and most important argument against the balance sheet was that although it is useful for an income-earning organization it has little merit for an organization such as a municipality whose main function is to spend income. The balance sheet and notes are important to an income-earning organization because they provide a clear and systematic picture of the extent of the assets and liabilities and their composition. This information is less important for a municipality because its object is not to generate profit. Nonetheless, a municipality can obtain interesting information from a balance sheet, namely about the income that has not been spent; in other words, about the financial position of the organization.

Whether a balance sheet actually provides information about the financial position depends on what information it contains about assets and liabilities. At present, this information is of unclear value in many municipalities. The valuation of assets, the manner of calculating depreciation, the reserves and provisions are three subjects that are often currently not regulated in such a manner that the balance sheet actually provides a clear picture of the financial position. Some of the problems involved are discussed in a subsection of 3.4.2.

The Risk Statement. To obtain a clear picture of the financial position of municipalities, it is therefore of great importance not only to have a true valuation of the assets and liabilities but also that there should be adequate information about events and risks not revealed in the balance sheet. Since 1995 it has therefore been obligatory for municipalities to submit a risk statement with the budget. This is a new instrument that is a further step in the direction of a system designed to allow better assessment of the financial position of the municipalities. The risk statement is intended to allow for the inclusion of internal and external risks that cannot be quantified. This is why the balance sheet makes no mention of the risks described in the risk statement. Provisions have to be made for quantifiable risks. Although many municipalities are aware of the importance of the risk statement and of risk management in general, the risk statement is an instrument which municipalities still seem to have difficulty in applying in an adequate manner. Various measures to develop risk management have been taken by the municipalities themselves, by the authorities that supervise the municipalities and by the Ministry of the Interior and Kingdom Relations.

Differences owing to Specificity

The 1995 accounting rules still differ in some respects from the CC2 provisions. It is debatable whether some of these differences are really necessary and whether they do not tend to obscure the information contained in the municipal accounts. As long ago as 1997 a report was published by the Netherlands Institute of Chartered Accountants (NIVRA) on the subject of fixed assets in municipal accounts. The report was highly critical of the valuation of assets, the depreciation policy of municipalities and discretion allowed by the accounting rules in these areas.

Two examples are given below of problems that are frequently cited. Both concern subjects in respect of which the accounting rules are in principle the same as those of CC2, but permit exceptions owing to the specificity of municipalities.

Possibility of Net Valuation of tangible fixed Assets. Under the Civil Code only gross valuation is permitted. In the case of net valuation of assets, the contribution of third parties (e.g. central government subsidy) is set off directly against the assets. It follows that assets are undervalued on the balance sheet. In the case of gross valuation the total amount of the assets is shown on the balance sheet, and any contribution by third parties is treated as a special-purpose reserve. Although the end result is in principle the same, net valuation allows the municipality greater flexibility in the short term since the contribution is not transferred to reserves. In due course, however, a sum must be transferred to reserves for replacement. The disadvantage of net valuation is that it is less clear what funds will be needed in the future. This increases the risk that too little will be set aside to the reserve for replacement and thus poses a threat to the continuity of the level of service provided to the citizens.

Result-dependent Depreciation. The accounting rules provide that the depreciation of fixed assets should be on the basis of the diminution in value. However, result-oriented depreciation is permitted if this is desirable for administrative reasons. The Civil Code does not allow result-oriented depreciation. Generally speaking, result-dependent depreciation makes it more difficult to obtain a true idea of the financial position of the municipality: since the assets are not valued on the basis of expected economic life, this affects both the financial position and the information about the reserves needed for future replacement. Result-oriented depreciation may be properly used where the future value can be determined administratively. This applies, for example, to assets that have not been designated for replacement in the future. A square, park or even a building need not necessarily have the same function in a few decades' time. In such cases, there is less need for depreciation on an economic basis.

3.4.3. PRESENT DEBATE ON CC2 AND SPECIFICITY: A THIRD STEP?

The increasing tendency of the municipalities to operate on lines for the private sector and the introduction of the obligation to adopt accrual accounting represent a break with the past. This is in itself may be a reason for examining the adequacy of the accounting rules and how they are applied in practice. In addition, there are signs (for example the NIVRA report) that the process of improving financial reporting has not yet been completed. It is, of course, debatable whether it ever could be.

The main problem identified by the NIVRA report (and which also emerges in the above examples) is that there is a substantial continuity risk in various respects and also a lack of transparency. The lack of transparency in municipal financial reporting seems to be a product of the departures of the 1995 accounting rules from CC2. Although the reason given for these departures was the specificity of the municipalities, no explicit definition of this specificity is given in the accounting rules. This leads to the following questions. Are the departures on account of the specificity of municipalities actually necessary? And, if so, what is the precise nature of the relationship and are the rules geared to take account of this relationship? The Ministry of the Interior and Kingdom Relations has started a project designed to provide an answer to these questions. The discussion below is based on this project and reflects the stage it has now reached.

Specificity and Financial Reporting Rules
The main distinctive characteristic of municipalities from the point of financial reporting is that they are spending organizations. Enterprises try to generate profit by producing goods and services, in other words they endeavour to acquire income. By contrast, municipalities do not seek to make a profit and have the object of looking after the welfare of the local population. To achieve this object, they are mainly concerned with the disbursement of income. They obtain this income from central government and from taxes, levies and charges. A possible effect of this characteristic of municipalities on financial reporting is that the balance sheet may serve a different purpose. The balance sheet is often seen not as a statement of the financial position but as a settlement of accounts with the inhabitants of the municipality. Often municipalities see no point in providing the public with information about the financial position. It may, after all, be difficult to justify an increase in property tax if this is necessary mainly for reasons of business administration. Municipalities are therefore inclined to arrange the balance sheet in such a way as to show why increases in taxes and levies are necessary.

Other distinctive characteristics of municipalities - for example the wide range of functions that municipalities are required to perform, the fact that Dutch municipalities cannot in principle become bankrupt, and the primacy of politics in decisions on functions and policy - seem to influence above all the organizational structure (an enterprise might well adopt a very different structure and simply hive off functions). However, the need for different guidelines for financial reporting has not been clearly demonstrated. For example, the fact that Dutch municipalities cannot become bankrupt may influence the depreciation periods. Municipalities may well, for instance, continue to use personal computers that would have long been completely written off by businesses operating in the private sector; after all, businesses cannot afford to use outdated equipment since their prices then become non-competitive. These arguments do not apply to municipalities. As long as the PCs do the job, there is no need to replace them. The only rule about the depreciation periods is that they must be in proportion to the diminution in value of the assets. In other words, although the depreciation periods used by municipalities may be longer than those used in the private sector, this does not mean that the manner of depreciation and hence the accounting rules should be different.

Reconsideration of Specificity
In short, the influence of specificity seems to be limited in terms of impact. CC2 should apply to the municipalities and provinces too, unless the spending nature of

municipalities necessitates a different approach in respect of specific points. It follows that the accounting rules and their application should perhaps differ less from CC2 than is at present the case. Or, to put it another way, specificity played a relatively important role in the 1985 accounting rules. This role was much reduced in the 1995 rules and could be reduced still further in the future. At present, there would seem to be a 'transitional period' in this respect.

Although the trend may still be towards CC2, it is important that the specificity of municipalities should not be overlooked. If this specificity justifies departures from the CC2 rules, such departures should be possible. However, such departures should be explicable to administrators and public alike and an alternative must be provided. Specificity is not an excuse for less clear guidelines. On the contrary, the transparency of municipal reporting should take precedence. The authorities should operate on the lines for the private sector where this is feasible and efficient, but should not allow this to undermine the principles of democratic accountability to the municipal council and citizens.

3.5. Future Developments

3.5.1. FINANCIAL REPORTING AND ADMINISTRATIVE MANAGEMENT

Before the demands made of a modern government body were examined from the administrative angle in section 3.3. and the rules for the budget were described in section 3.4. What is common to the two sections is that municipalities are increasingly having to operate on lines for the private sector, which makes great demands on the clarity, consistency and reliability of the information. Partly as a result, administrative and economic developments are going hand in hand more and more often. For example, the word accountability originally meant simply a duty to account: public officials were required to show how public funds had been administered. Now, however, the term has the much broader meaning of stewardship; not only officials but also and above all the municipal executive (burgomaster and executive councillors) should render account for their actions to the municipal council and hence to the inhabitants of the municipality.

Owing among other things to the ever wider and more complex range of functions of municipalities, administrators too are attaching more and more importance to a clear and well-organized budget and accounts, particularly in respect of the implementation of policy and its effects. At the same time, the local inhabitants are demanding more and more value for their tax money and are claiming the right to information about income and expenditure. It is to be expected that this trend will continue. In a democratically functioning municipality the legitimacy of the administration becomes ever more important. In recent years it has been mainly a matter of accountability: the will and desire of the administration to render political account for - in the present case - the financial policy. Local people desire this too, not only as clients but also most certainly in their capacity of citizens. In this section we will briefly examine the concept of accountability and the instruments that can support it.

3.5.2. CHANGING NATURE OF ACCOUNTABILITY

Nowadays accountability tends to be interpreted more broadly in local government circles in the Netherlands. Indeed, the terminology has changed: *'verantwoording'* is now used instead of *'rekenschap'* to express this more active form of rendering account. This is a logical step after the PMI process, which led above all to improvement of the internal municipal administration. Improvement of the management process is a precondition for the next step: the further improvement of relations between administration and citizen. A pro-active approach to accountability plays an important role in this. It is no longer sufficient to produce an auditor's report that the figures give a true and fair view. Nowadays, the process of rendering account is a kind of two-way traffic: between the municipal executive and the municipal council and, thereafter, between the municipal council and the citizen. The municipal executive wishes its actions to be checked by the council, and the council by the citizen. The essential point - which is important to the issue of legitimacy - is that the person rendering account can demonstrate reliability and responsiveness. The concept of reliability denotes the extent to which the control exercised by the municipality is in keeping with expectations. And the concept of responsiveness refers to the extent to which the municipality is receptive to stimuli from its environment and responds to them (see section 3.3).

3.5.3. INSTRUMENTS

This new-style accountability entails the possibility of public debate. What is crucial to any such debate is the availability of transparent, correct and timely information that enables people to form a reliable impression of the financial position of the municipality. Transparent information is of particular importance in the administrator-citizen relationship. The public wish to know whether they are getting value for money. The administrator wishes to show that this is indeed the case. This imposes greater demands on the financial reporting. We will illustrate this by reference to two instruments.

The Annual Report
Municipalities have the duty to render account for the policy they have pursued. This means that the policy in question must be evaluated. Such evaluation involves assessment of both the financial and non-financial aspects of the policy. At the same time, lessons for the future can be learned from the evaluation. The annual report is an instrument that is ideally suited to rendering account, first of all to the municipal council and, second, to the citizens too; an annual report can do justice to these elements of the accounting.

The 1995 accounting rules were therefore amended by order of August 25, 1997 in such a way as to impose an explicit duty on the municipality to prepare an annual report. This means that not only an annual account but also an evaluation is required. Such an evaluation necessitates answers to questions such as what was the policy and to what extent was it achieved, and these answers should preferably be supported by performance data.

In view of the functions of the annual report, i.e. the rendering of account with regard to both financial and non-financial data and the expounding of a policy for the future, the annual report should contain the following elements:
- the aims of the municipality in the short, medium and long term
- the data on resources and performance, i.e. whether the past aims have been achieved and the productivity and quality of performance
- the operational performance too is important, for example information about the number of people used for a particular job, how the organization is structured, how the process of planning and control is organized and whether these arrangements are suitable now and in the future in the light of expected changes.

These three elements of the annual report should not only be described but also, wherever possible, evaluated. Evaluation entails analysis of the aims of policy and whether they have been achieved. It is extremely important in relation to all three elements, in particular because the instruments used sometimes yield unexpected results or have unforeseen and undesired side-effects. Evaluation can lead to adjustment of existing instruments or of the aims. Often evaluation occurs to some extent implicitly, but explicit evaluation - and hence the formulation of the aims too - may be important, for example with a view to changes in the composition of the personnel and the administration.

Acceleration of Annual Account and Report
At present, the municipal council must have dealt with the annual accounts and the annual report by September 15 and the budget by November 15. As there is only two months between these dates, the emphasis is on the budget. In addition, many municipalities prepare a spring budget memorandum covering various aspects of policy. The annual report therefore has only a limited added value. Municipalities could try to emulate the private sector and central government and speed up the process by which the annual accounts and annual report are dealt with by the council. If the annual report were to be completed by around March 15 and dealt with by the council in, say, May, the findings in and regarding the annual report could be included in the budget. It is essential that the process by which the annual report is dealt with by the council be speeded up because even an annual report that meets all the other criteria has little added value if it is not dealt with shortly after the end of the financial year.

3.6.   Final Remarks

Social and economic developments have led to a different view of government. Nowadays, government authorities and hence municipalities too are expected to be efficient, effective and market-oriented and, at the same time, to take as much account as possible of the citizen. In addition, municipalities are expected to have their own democratic legitimacy, and hence to retain the characteristics of government bodies. In other words, much is expected of municipalities and these expectations will not diminish in the future. The evolution of the financial function is assisting municipalities in the process of adapting to their new role. Transparency of financial reporting is a central feature of the financial function. Both the market and customer orientation of the municipalities and the democratic legitimacy and new-style accountability require first and foremost clear and reliable financial reporting. It does not in fact make any difference in this connection whether CC2 is followed more closely or whether the significance of the specificity of the municipalities is reflected more clearly in the accounting rules. However, the rules should be modified in such a way that they promote the clarity of financial reporting as far as possible and allow the municipalities the scope to operate both as government bodies and as market-oriented undertakings.

The significance of the changes - past and future - in the field of financial reporting should not be underestimated. These are changes that have a far-reaching impact on the organization of the municipalities and on the manner in which they are administered. It is precisely because the financial reporting can and must help the municipalities in the way in which they give effect to their new role than it is more than mere bookkeeping. It is essential in this regard that there should be a basis of support in the administration for changes in the field of financial reporting. As we saw in the case of the PMI project, such support is crucial to the success of innovations that go beyond the municipality as an organization. With a view to future developments it is of paramount importance that innovation in the field of financial reporting and the financial function in general should be decided not only by officials but also by administrators.

References

- Bac, A.D., Knoop, C.J.F. en van Zanten, J.H. (1991) *Gemeentelijk financieel beheer,* Leiden/Antwerpen.
- ter Bogt, Henk J. and Van Helden, G. Jan (1999) *Accounting change in Dutch government,* paper presented at the seventh Conference on Comparative International Government Accounting Research, 24 - 25 June 1999, Tilburg, the Netherlands.
- Borderwijk, P. (1993) *Niks veranderen, de kapitaaldienst moet blijven,* in: Binnenlands Bestuur, 17/9/1993, 31.
- Cornelisse, P.A., Haselbekke, A.G.J. en Ros, A.P. (1994) *De overheid in Bedrijf,* Houten.
- van Helden, G. Jan and ter Bogt, Henk J. (1998) *The application of businesslike planning and control in local government,* Paper presented at the EIASM International Converence on Accounting for the New Public Management, Venice, Italy, September 17–19.
- Hoff, J. (1986) *Waarom gemeentelijke comptabiliteitsvoorschriften?,* in: Financieel Overheidsbeheer, nr. 1, 3-7.
- Hofman, J.A. (1994) *Commissie GCV/PCV zet eigen geloofwaardigheid op het spel,* in: BMI Magazine, Januari 1994, 3-8.
- Hop, Jan Herman (1996) *De Comptabiliteitsvoorschriften 1995,* mei 1996 (scriptie).
- Kaag, M.M. (ed) (1983) *Privatisering en deregulering: van verzorgingsstaat naar waarborgstaat,* 's – Gravenhage.
- Koopmans, L., Wellink, A.H.E.M., de Kam, C.A. en Woltjer, H.J. (1995) *Overheidsfinanciën,* Houten.
- Klop, P. (1994) *Nieuwe comptabiliteitsvoorschriften geven duidelijk beeld van financiële positie gemeenten,* in: B & G, December 1994, 26-30.
- van Leeuwen, L, van Graafeiland, J.A., Groenveld, K, Gijzel, B.R.A., Koopmans, L, Sterks, C.G.M., Uhl, G.J.S. and Vos de Wael, A.B.I.M. (1985) *Gemeenten tussen rijk en markt,* 's-Gravenhage.
- Ministerie van Binnenlandse Zaken (1994) *Besluit Comptabiliteitsvoorschriften 1995,* Den Haag.
- Ministerie van Binnenlandse Zaken (1996) *Grondwet voor het Koninkrijk der Nederlanden 1996,* Den Haag.
- Ministerie van Binnenlandse Zaken (1993) *de nieuwe gemeentewet,* Den Haag.
- Ministerie van Binnenlandse Zaken en Koninkrijksrelaties (1999) *Bewegend Bestuur 1999,* Den Haag.
- Ministerie van Financiën (1998) *Central Government - Local Authorities,* Den Haag.
- Ministerie van Financiën *Miljoenennota,* Den Haag, various issues.
- NIVRA-rapport (1997) *Vaste activa in de gemeenterekening.*
- Van der Schaaf, S. (1996) *Verschillen tussen titel 9 BW 2 en CV 1995 verklaarbaar!,* in: *De Accountant,* nr. 10, juni 1996.

CHAPTER 4

THE FINANCIAL MANAGEMENT SYSTEM OF THE CITY OF TILBURG

Pieter G. van der Poel

4.1. Introduction

The concern controller of the municipality of Tilburg is officially responsible for the management model and the means policy of this city. It gives great pleasure to be able to tell something about the current state of affairs in this field.

First of all, I shall tell you a little about the aims of this address. In order to give you an idea of the context, the position of Tilburg both as a city and as an organization will be described. Then I shall tell something about the essence of the Tilburg Model as it developed during the years 1985 to 1995. After that, we will have a look at the essence of the Permanent Development Process, which started around 1995. Finally, after giving you an insight into the current situation, a few general conclusions and recommendations will be given.

The aim of this lecture is to give an insight into the guiding or management philosophy of the municipality of Tilburg and to show how that philosophy has been put into practice through the years. It will give an insight into the effects this management philosophy has had for the citizens of our city. Finally, a number of critical factors for success and a number of conditions for further development will be mentioned.

Tilburg is the sixth biggest city of the Netherlands. It has around 190,000 inhabitants which makes it just about the same size as Groningen. Amsterdam, Rotterdam, Utrecht, The Hague, and Eindhoven are bigger than Tilburg. Tilburg's growth as a city was largely due to the textile industry. This branch of industry ran into serious problems during the sixties when textile products from Third World countries began to glut the world market. The result was that the entire textile industry in the western world - and therefore also in Tilburg - collapsed in a very short time. The financial and social problems that ensued put a great strain on the local administration. That administration, however, discharged its duties admirably. Partly thanks to the favorable economic climate in the Netherlands, Tilburg is once again one of the most vital large cities in the Netherlands.

The struggle to get the municipal finances back into shape also led to Tilburg developing itself as a forerunner with respect to the design and working of the local administration. An indication of this is the membership of Tilburg in the international network for better government, called the Cities of Tomorrow. This membership was gained thanks to the city's nomination for the 'Carl Bertelsmann Preis 1993'. Tilburg is also the first tilted government body in the Netherlands. Since 1997, Tilburg has based its organizational structure on the logic of the citizens instead of on the logic of its own production

39

A. Bac (ed.), International Comparative Issues in Government Accounting, 39-52.
© 2001 *Kluwer Academic Publishers. Printed in the Netherlands.*

processes. And lastly there is the wide range of publications that has appeared about the Tilburg Model. At the beginning of 1999, for instance, Mr. Joost Mönks obtained his doctorate from the University of Geneva with a thesis entitled 'Towards performance oriented and participatory public administrations', in which the developments in Tilburg are analyzed and commented upon.

4.2.   Essentials of the Tilburg Model

The next paragraph will explain a number of essentials about the Tilburg Model as it developed in the period from 1985 to 1995. In the first place, something about the philosophy. In the mid-eighties the idea that the government should not only strive towards rightfulness but also towards efficiency gained more and more support. Of course, this development was primarily the result of the enormous financial and economic problems confronting Tilburg at that time and the extremely high local taxes that ensued from that. During the middle of the eighties, Tilburg was one of the three most expensive cities in the Netherlands. During that time the idea was born that the principles of good commercial management could also be applied to governments. Among the examples that inspired the city council at that time about how this could be achieved were a number of American models, including that of the Pentagon.

The idea that business-like management is also applicable in government organizations led to an attempt being made to define areas of policy in terms of suppliable products. This did not only concern well-known items such as passports, but also products like 'management and administration of public education'. In addition, an attempt was made to describe those products in more detail in output terms, such as the pupil intake figure, the pupil outflow figure, the number of students with and without a diploma, etc. At the same time, the relevant costs were integrally assigned to those products. These measures make it easy to see exactly what the municipality provides in the way of services, at what cost, and at what percentage of cost-effectiveness. This system also makes it possible to identify and control the financial economic and administrative risks per product. A further consequence of the ideas on business-like management is that responsibilities are redistributed. The responsibilities of the council regarding policy - the decision of what products and services should be provided in what quantities - are emphatically differentiated from the executive responsibilities of the management for the implementation of the policy. In Tilburg it is the heads of department who are accountable to the audit committee for the manner in which policy has been implemented, and not the political accounting officer. In addition, the executive responsibilities have been drastically decentralized, right down to the product level. The product holder is fully responsible for all managerial aspects in connection with his product. This approach implies a substantial de-staffing. Tilburg has by far the smallest Concern Staff department of all the large cities; 35 persons including the secretaries of the Aldermen.

The decentralization of responsibilities, which was revolutionary for its time, was supported by a well-balanced control armamentarium. The principle of self-control played a leading role in this respect. The various departments and services were fully equipped for carrying out their tasks in a proper manner. That means that they got their own departmental controller, their own accounting officer, their own P&O functionary, their own information advisors, and so on. In the context of each department's individual responsibility a report obligation was imposed on that department. The management report instrument was developed for this purpose. Departments must report three times a year about deviations from the budget. They must indicate how any such deviations should be interpreted in terms of policy, what corrective measures the director has undertaken in terms of conduct of business, and what corrective measures he recommends that the council must take if policy issues are concerned.

It was crucial, in this context, that the Anglo-Saxon model of controllership was simultaneously introduced. The controller is the person who must ensure that the administrative provision of information complies with the set of standards of quality, i.e. timely, complete, correct, reliable, etc. As far as that is concerned, the controller has the authority to bypass the directorate, just as the concern controller has the authority to bypass the city manager. This is done in order to ensure that the council has a clear insight into the state of affairs at the executive level at all times.

4.3.   The Audit Committee's Role

The control armamentarium is further complemented by the advent of the audit committee. This committee normally inspects the annual report on behalf of the city council. In Tilburg, the audit committee has gradually developed into a local auditor's office. In other words, the committee does not restrict itself to inspecting the annual accounts but also carries out investigations on a permanent and independent basis into the functioning of the council and the functioning of the municipal organization. The subjects to be investigated are determined by the city council. Important investigations that have been carried out during the past few years, for instance, are the study on information protection and privacy and the investigation into the policy with respect to putting work out to tender. This last study was concerned with the efficacy of the labour market policy. The audit committee is authorized to call in external expertise and to hear members of the council, officials and other witnesses. The working method of the committee is first to investigate all the facts. On the basis of these facts the committee then comes up with conclusions. The conclusions are submitted to the Mayor and Aldermen for comment. After the Mayor and Aldermen have given their response, the committee formulates conclusions and recommendations on behalf of the city council. The committee restricts itself to the facts and the conclusions ensuing from those facts. Interpretations or political judgements are emphatically avoided. That dimension falls under the exclusive rights of the council.

All fractions in the city council are represented in the audit committee. Thanks to the clear role awareness and the meticulous method of working, the committee has always been able to reach unanimous conclusions and over the past years it has developed into an authoritative body.

4.4.   Preventive Departmental Investigations and Concern Control

The last major control instrument is the preventive departmental investigation. Preventive departmental investigations entail that each department is investigated once every four years as to the quality of its business conduct. The investigations are carried out by an external agency that is commissioned by the city council.

The investigations deal with issues such as the strategic orientation of the department, the administrative organization, the staff policy, the satisfaction of the workers, the relationship between the department and the council, the relationship between the department and other departments, etc. A preventive departmental investigation gives a picture of the vitality of the business conduct and of the quality of management. The preventive departmental investigation leads to the drafting of a plan for improvement. This is also an instrument designed to support a continual improvement in the way business is conducted. Preventive departmental investigations do not infrequently lead to the conclusion that a department head is not functioning as he should. It is not uncommon for a department head to fall as a result of a preventive departmental investigation.

In the sphere of planning, the so-called Perspective Memorandum was introduced. In the Perspective Memorandum the city council outlines its vision with respect to the administrative and financial developments in the long term. The Perspective Memorandum is then worked out in more detail in a budgetary context in terms of the consequences for the coming year.

A few words about the positioning and the duties of concern control. Concern control includes all the means functions of the municipality. Concern control has three main tasks: firstly, the development of the management philosophy - call it the development of the Tilburg Model. Secondly, taking care of a well coordinated input and application of that management philosophy. What we are concerned with here is the development and upkeep of the policy unity, for example the communal ICT architecture, the financial policy, or the guidelines for drawing up a budget, management report, or annual report. The third main task is the mirror function, ensuring that the control armamentarium is functioning properly with the result that the quality of the administrative provision of information is safeguarded on a permanent basis. This task is given shape by means of controlling memoranda arising from departmental productions as well as by means of consolidated reports to the council. Concern control starts with the reports as submitted by the departments, asks questions, but never instigates an inquiry on its own.

The Tilburg Model has prevented a financial economic débâcle in Tilburg. The city has never had to go begging to the State because its finances were in bad shape. This by contrast with a number of other cities. The second effect of the Tilburg Model is the fact that the local taxes have decreased systematically. Tilburg is currently number thirty five on the list, which makes it the cheapest big city in the Netherlands. A third important effect is the quality of the housing conditions. The basic quality in Tilburg, on average, is reasonable. There are no serious downs as far as impoverished neighbourhoods or run down industrial estates are concerned. Finally, the establishment climate for the business community has improved dramatically. In comparison with other big cities, the vitality of the business community in Tilburg, on average, is fair to good. That was a very different story during the sixties and seventies.

4.5. Objections to the Original Tilburg Model

There were also a number of objections to the original Tilburg Model, however. First of all, there was the increasing distance between the management and the council. This was caused by the relatively large degree of autonomy the directorates had in connection with the integral responsibility they had for their own conduct of business. In a certain sense a process of technocratization was taking place in the council. In this context, the principle of integral management was leading to a relatively pronounced division among the municipal departments. Officials belonging to one department did not regard the officials of other departments as their colleagues. For the citizens the result was that they were often sent from pillar to post. At the same time, the city council was repeatedly confronted with contradictory recommendations. An example: a negative report by the department for Environmental Affairs concerning the development of industrial estates alongside the motorway was followed within a few months by a positive report from the Public Works department about the same subject. The above-mentioned disadvantages led - partly as a result of the social criticism they caused - to a further refining of the management philosophy in 1995. We will enter into that in more detail a little later on.

Before that, it is necessary to point out two critical factors for success in connection with the development of the Tilburg Model. These were, a widely supported feeling of urgency in connection with improving the way business was conducted on the one hand, and the leadership factor on the other. As far as the feeling of urgency is concerned, we refer back to the high local taxes and the disastrous financial situation of the municipality mentioned earlier. At the same time, the leadership at both executive and official level was characterized by an external orientation, by the ability to correctly estimate the value of concepts that fell outside the own way of thinking and to remould these concepts to suit the context, added to this was the courage to take fundamental decisions and to implement them.

These critical success factors also proved instrumental for the further development of the model. The general criticism that the Tilburg Model was really only an internally oriented planning and control model and that, on top of this, it excluded the political administration, caused a new feeling of urgency. At the same time, the original type of leadership was strengthened, rather than weakened, due to the fact that the success of the Tilburg Model had also formed and attracted enterprising accounting officers and managers.

4.6. Recent Developments

Let us now have a closer look at the developments that have taken place since 1995. These developments are known by the name POP. The letters POP stand for Permanent Organizational Development Process. The POP should be seen as the next stage of development of the Tilburg Model. The essence of the management philosophy has been retained but the POP has added something to it. Two things in particular: in the first place, the transition from supply management to demand management. We came to the realization that we could no longer take our own way of thinking, our own products and services, and our own methods of production as point of departure for the administering of the city, but that we needed to base our activities on the citizens and their way of thinking instead. We usually refer to that process simply as thinking inwards from the outside. It is interesting to note that, here again, Tilburg took the liberty of borrowing ideas from the business community. The second important enrichment of the management philosophy is the transition from thinking like linear engineers to thinking in terms of developments and mutually influential systems and processes. Here Tilburg is taking advantage of a social trend drawing inspiration from the concept of a learning organization.

The concept of demand orientation led us to the idea of distinguishing between three forms of citizen. The term 'citizen' in this sense should be taken to include businesses and institutions. We identify the citizen as the representative of a shared interest. Think, for example, of a representative from an environmental organization, an employers' organization, or a shopkeepers' association. Secondly we see the citizen as an inhabitant of his district or neighbourhood, and thirdly the citizen as a customer of municipal services. We then got the idea of also distinguishing between three forms of municipality geared to the three forms of citizen I have just mentioned. Opposite the citizen as a representative of a shared interest we put the interactive municipality. The citizen as an inhabitant is met by the participating municipality. And finally the citizen as a customer is faced with the service-providing municipality. We realized that this division in fact defines three different domains or playing fields for the government. In each of those playing fields the municipality has a different mission and a different role. That inspired us to structure the municipal organization according to the distinctive forms or roles of the municipality. Finally, we formulated a mission per type of service which positions the municipality within the three different domains.

As a result of all this, we now have a City Affairs department which represents the interactive municipality and focuses on the representatives of shared interests for the purpose of developing a basis of support for strategic choices at city level. The participating municipality is represented by the department District Affairs, which focuses on the inhabitants of a district or area in order to support them and help them live together in a responsible way. The service-providing municipality is represented by the Public Affairs department, the Municipal Businesses division, the Fire Brigade, the Municipal Cleansing department, and the department of Social Workshops. These departments focus on providing good and inexpensive services. It goes without saying that the principles of good business-like management are particularly applicable to these last types of department. It is worth noting that these departments represent more than 80 % of the staff complement of the municipal organization! This last group of departments has been given the order to provide their products and services in conformity with the market. That is easily measurable, for instance by benchmarking. As regards the Public Affairs department, Citizens Charters are currently being developed.

As an aside, I should like to point out that the executory services that are provided for the municipal organization as a whole - such as administration, legal affairs, staff services, engineers' office, information and computerization - have all been grouped together under the Municipal Businesses division. This division functions as a contracting department for the other departments. We are developing an internal market for this which is controlled by service provision agreements and a free truck system.

4.7. The main Ideas of POP

If one takes the logic of the citizen as starting point, one will discover that the needs of the citizen are almost by definition integral needs. The citizen in his role as customer really does not want a building permit. He wants to build and he wants to arrange all the matters that are linked to that, such as buying the land, being issued with a permit, registration in the resister of population, information about local taxes, and so on, quickly and if it is at all possible preferably at a single counter. If one wants to meet the citizen in this wish one will have to turn the whole organization upside down. The staff will have to learn to think in a demand oriented way, work processes will have to be redesigned, the provision of information will have to be drastically adjusted. And certainly not least importantly, the system of control will also have to be reviewed. Clearly, this will take years of work! And a similar story about the development of integral policy focused on the citizen as inhabitant and, respectively, as representative of a shared interest would be possible.

The concept of demand orientation cannot be supported by a divided official apparatus. Departments and services are becoming increasingly aware that they need each other more than ever. As a result, the will to agree on shared frameworks is also undergoing a phase of rapid development. These frameworks are developed and agreed on in intra-municipal consultative structures. At the top of these is the Management Consultative Body; the team of directors. Under mandate from the City Council, the Management Consultative Body supervises the unity of policy and means. The Management Consultative Body gets advice from intra-municipal theme groups for the development of strategic policy. The Controllers' Consultative Body supervises the unity of the means policy under mandate from the Management Consultative Body. The Controllers' Consultative Body is advised by an intra-municipal P&O consultative body, the consultative body of the Accounting officers, the consultative body of the Information Consultants, and the intra-municipal development team Tilburg Model. In practice the primacy of the integral management at departmental level was supplemented by the primacy of the unity of policy and means at intra-municipal level. The Concern Staff department plays a specific role in this context due to the fact that it supplies the chairmen and secretaries for all the intra-municipal consultative structures.

The POP is a comprehensive and long-lasting process. Nonetheless, a number of significant results can already be mentioned. Municipal services are obtainable for the citizens at a single counter. The single counters are decentrally located. The Public Affairs department has set up so-called city-shops in the former villages of Udenhout and Berkel-Enschot, as well as in the new housing estate Reeshof. All counter services can be obtained at these shops. This includes such matters as employment counselling, social security payments, taxes, citizen affairs, building and environmental permits, public information, etc. The city-shops are extensively visited and the citizens appear to be very content about their functioning. The District Affairs department has formed integral area teams. These teams are involved with the development of integral district development plans in dialogue with inhabitants, businesses, and institutions. Interrelated social, economic, and physical aspects in this connection are researched and developed. The first indications are that problems at district level can be dealt with more effectively and with a broader basis of social support by using this approach. The POP has also led to strategic policy at city level being handled more interactively and integrally than before. This should ultimately lead to increased effectiveness and a stronger basis of social support. We will return to this topic when we discuss the Large Cities Policy. The fact is that the method of working described is also connected with the relationships between the various government levels and the way in which those relationships are controlled.

Just like any other development, however, the POP also has its drawbacks. The intensity of the organizational developments have indisputably resulted in a temporary production loss. In addition, the workers are under considerable pressure. The traditional official, in particular, is being confronted with quality demands to which he cannot always comply. We are trying to minimize loss of personnel by means of a modernization drive among the work force.

The ideas about demand orientation and integrality also lead to other forms of planning. As from last year, Tilburg has been developing a City Vision with a planning horizon of around ten years. During the preparatory phase, a first attempt was made to involve the population and representatives from the interest groups in an interactive way. This development, by the way, is emphatically in line with the State's Large Cities Policy. The State links greater policy freedom on the part of the large Cities in the form of extra financial means and deregulation to two requirements: being tuned to the objectives of state policy and broadly-based support from the population. The last requirement to be achieved by means of interactive policy preparation and co-financing by social partners, including the province. In that connection, a long-term investment program is currently under development which will provide an insight into which measurable effects, performance and programs contribute to the realization of the City Vision, as well as which parties contribute to this and to what extent. On the basis of the long-term investment program, the municipality will be entering into a covenant with the province and the State at the end of this year. As far as controlling is concerned, the State and the municipalities are working on a monitoring system in order to measure the intended effects and performance. In addition, a two yearly self-analysis by the municipalities is foreseen in combination with an independent audit committee to be appointed by the State.

4.8. Conclusions and Recommandations

Let us wind up with a few general conclusions and recommendations, which will be put in the form of a number of propositions.
1. The quality of the public administration can be substantially improved by application of management concepts from the business community.
2. In view of the specific function of the public administration, however, the application of business-like managerial concepts demands a differentiation of the public domain.
3. At local level, the public domain can be divided into three areas or playing fields:
   a. policy-making and implementation at city level (City Affairs);
   b. policy-making and implementation at area level (District Affairs);
   c. public service provision.

4. In each playing field the municipality has a specific mission and role. Specific laws and management mechanisms are also applicable.

5. In the field of public service provision - and this concerns over 80% of the organization - business-like management is optimally applicable. With the use of specific instruments, such as benchmarking, Citizens' Charters, and service provision agreements, marketing activities can be developed and/or stimulated.

6. Brussels, The Hague, and the Association of Dutch Municipalities should give strong support to the comparability among municipalities, among other things by setting standards in connection with the provision of information.

7. In the fields of policy-making and implementation, business-like concepts lead to quality improvements in the form of greater integrality when the principle of demand orientation is applied.

8. The realization of marketing activities is not an option in the case of policy-making.

9. In the fields of City Affairs and District Affairs, far-reaching improvements in quality can be realized by means of interactive policy development aimed at defining effects and performance.

10. Effect and performance management calls for drastic adjustment to the management armamentarium. One could think in terms of the development of

    a. monitoring systems;
    b. covenants between governments and covenants between governments and social partners;
    c. program management and control;
    d. self-analysis and external audits.

11. A municipality that professionalizes its conduct of business builds on its credibility and trust. These are the most valuable conditions for a well-functioning democracy.

References

- Literature about the Tilburg Model ® : Internet: http://www.tilburg.nl

- Arntzen, H.L. (1986) _Managementrapportage; een opkomend overheidsinstrument,_ Bestuur nr. 4, april 1986.
- Arntzen, H.L. _Managementrapportage; een ingeburgerd overheidsinstrument?._
- Arntzen, H.L. (1992) _Sturen en laten sturen,_ BMI-magazine, december 1992.
- Arntzen, H.L. (1982) _De gemeente in ontwikkeling: naar een betere beheersing en effectiever sturing,_ Openbaar Bestuur, 1992, 2.
- Arntzen, H.L. (1994) _Oude wijn in nieuwe zakken?,_ O&S signaal, 1994/1.
- Arntzen, H.L. en C.A.T. Schalken (1994) _Het stadsmarktonderzoek: een brug tussen bedrijfsmatig werken en bestuurlijke vernieuwing?,_ Openbaar Bestuur, 1994, nr. 6.
- Baten, L. (1994) _Tilburg, eine Stadt macht Gewinn,_ Neuß Grevenbroicher Lokal Zeitung, 29 Oktober 1994.
- Baten, L., (1995) _NGZ, Forum: Die profitable Amtsstube,_ Neuß Grevenbroicher Lokal Zeitung, 23 Januar 1995.
- Besseling, E. en Pranger (1995) _Gemeenten en bedrijven: verschillen en overeenkomsten in reorganiseren,_ Werkcollege organisatie en leiding 1, Faculteit der economsiche wetenschappen en econometrie, Vrije Universiteit Amsterdam, April 1995.
- Bordewijk, P. (1994) _Begroting Tilburg maakt pretenties niet waar,_ Binnenlands Bestuur 41, 14/10/1994.
- Bordewijk, P. (1995) _De rivaliteit tussen ambtenaar en politicus,_ Intermediair, 27 oktober 1995, 31e jaargang nummer 43.
- Broek. P. v.d. (1994) _Schaduwkanten aan het Tilburgs Model,_ Univers, 15 december 1994.
- Broekhuizen, A. (1982) _De nieuwe zakelijkheid; Tilburg bereikt de grenzen van de verzakelijking,_ BB Management, nr. 7-8, 27.11.1992.
- Carl Just Von (1994) _Die Holländer machen es vor; so saniert man eine Stadt,_ Blick Schweiger Tagezeitiung, 13 juli 1994.
- Conijn, F. (1994) _Burger is koning; maar het verzet tegen bedrijfsmatig werken van gemeenten groeit,_ Elsevier, 3 september 1994.
- _Das Unternehmen Stadtverwaltung tilgt die Defizite,_ Berner Zeitung, 2 November 1992.
- _Das Modell Tilburg: Klienten geben ihrem Konzern beste Noten,_ Demokratische Gemeinde, 6/92.
- _De BV Tilburg: een stad als concern,_ Vrij Nederland, 25 december 1993.
- Dijkstra, W.J.A. (1994) _Risico's van het Tilburgse model,_ Openbaar Bestuur, oktober 1994.
- Driessen, C. (1994) _Gefürt wie ein Konzern; Das Niederländische Tilburg macht Millionengewinne,_ Frankfurter Rundschau, 7-7-1994.
- Faßbender, Von H. (1994) _Der Konzernstab sitzt im Rathaus, Tilburg: Eine Stadt macht gewinn,_ Dürener Zeitung, 30-07-1994.
- Forster, H. (1992) _Spar-Modell Tilburg: Die Stadt als Unternehmer,_ Neue Zeitung, November 1992.

- *Gemeindemanagement, Im Tilburg wurde die Verwaltung wie ein Konzern organisiert,* Wirtschaftswoche, nr 14 27 März 1992.
- Geurts, J. (1993) *Aan de Moederborst van het Tilburgs Model,* BMI-magazine, november 1993.
- Geurts, J. (1993) *Bestuurlijke vernieuwing te koop; een reportage over de ontwikkeling van een nieuwe haute cuisine,* Tilburg Magazine, maart 1993.
- Geurts, J. (1993) *Tilburg als voorbeeld van de presterende democratie,* Tilburg Magazine, september 1993.
- Geurts, J. (1994) *Meetbare Beleidsdoelen nieuw instrument voor politieke sturing,* Binnenlands Bestuur, 9 december 1994.
- Grit, K. (1994) *Economisering en representatie; over de opmars van het economisch denken en economen aan de hand van een case-studie naar de gemeente Tilburg,* doctoraalscriptie, faculteit der Wijsbegeerte, Rijksuniversiteit Groningen, juni 1994.
- Groenendijk, R. *Van legitimatie naar oriëntatie,* NGI-magazine, jaargang 7.
- Groot, H. de (1995) *De praktijk van doelmatigheids- en effectiviteitsonderzoek: Tilburg,* hoofdstuk 7 van Doelmatig & Doeltreffend decentraal bestuur, Academic Service.
- Haselbekke, A.G.J. en A.P. Ros (1991) *Where there's a will there's a way: performance measurement by dutch local governments,* Seirbhis Phoibli, Vol. 12 No. 2, Nollag.
- Haselbekke, A.G.J. (1995) *Public Policy and Performance Measurement in The Netherlands,* Public Money & Management, volume 15 nr.4, oct-dec.
- Haselbekke, A.G.J. (1995) *Sturen op prestaties en effecten; illusie of werkelijkheid?,* Overheidsmanagement, december 1995.
- Horsten, H. (1993) *Bestuur Tilburg voorbeeld voor Kiel en Bern,* De Volkskrant, 17 april 1993.
- Huijgevoort, van J.A.A. (1985) *Van Traditionele gemeentesecretarie naar eigentijdse bestuursdienst,* Bestuur nr.5 mei 1985.
- Huijgevoort, van J.A.A. (1992) *Politiek bestuur en ambtelijk management,* Studieselectie, januari 1992.
- Huijgevoort, van J.A.A. (1989) *De gemeentelijke controllingfunctie,* BMI-magazine, december 1989.
- Huijgevoort, van J.A.A. (1989) *Contractmanagement, een nieuwe stijl van sturen,* Studie selectie, januari 1989.
- Huijgevoort, van J.A.A. (1992) *Marketing bei der Kommune Tilburg,* Internationales Design Zentrum, Berlin, September, 1992.
- Iersel, van J. (1995) *Financieel beeld gemeenten blijft onduidelijk,* B&G, april 1995.
- Iersel, van J. (1989) *Naar een gemeentebalans zonder comptabiliteitsvoorschriften,* Financieel Overheidsmanagement 1989, 3.
- Iersel, van J. (1990) *De rekening als beleidsinstrument,* BMI-magazine juli/augustus 1990.
- Jukema, J. (1995) *In vogelvlucht..., Impressies van de organisatieontwikkeling binnen gemeentelijke hoofdstructuren,* Stafburo Eilandgroep Curaçao, Willemstad, september 1995.
- Kleinfeld R. en A.F.A. Korsten (1995) *Konzernstadt: Neue Steuerungsmodelle in den Kommunalverwaltungen,* Stadt Krefeld, 19 Juni 1995.
- Klienten geben ihrem Konzern beste Noten (1992) *Das Modell Tilburg,* Demokratische Gemeinde 6.

- Knapen, M. (1993) *Gemeenten herontdekken burger als bron van informatie; Het Tilburgs Model behoeft ogen en oren*, Univers, 13 mei 1993.
- Korsten, A.F.A. (1995) *Verwaltungsmanagment in niederländischen Gemeinden auf neuen Wegen: Das Tilburger Modell oder Tilburg als neues Mekka der öffentlichen Verwaltung?*, Krefeld, 19 Juni 1995 (in Kleinfeld R. en A.F.A. Korsten, Konzernstadt: Neue Steuerungsmodelle in den Kommunalverwaltungen)
- Krämer, R. (1992) *Das Tilburger Modell der Verwaltungsorganisation und Verwal tungsführung*, Schaab & Co, Düsseldorf.
- Krosse, J. (1994) *Tilburgs Model schaamlap voor falen*, Het Brabants Dagblad, 22 september 1994.
- Kuipers, B. (1992) *NV Tilburg; spuitje olie*, Management Team, 27 januari 1992.
- Langerwerf, C.A.J.M. (1994) *Model voor schaalgrootte*, Balanceren tussen schalen en kwaliteit, Andersson en Bron (redactie), VNG-uitgeverij, december 1994.
- Lantinga, H. (1993) *Kommunalverwaltung mit Struktur einer Holding-Gesellschaft*, Verwaltungsorganisation 27.
- Lantinga, H. (1994), in *Handboek Financieel Gemeentebeleid, onderdeel A 100 Financieel Management*, Samson Tjeenk Willink, juni 1994.
- Lantinga, H. (1995) *Het organisatiemodel van de stad Tilburg*, Uit: Praktijkgids management lokale besturen, afl. 18 (juni 1995)-257, SECT 7/1.
- Leeuwenkamp (1995) *De synergie van citymarketing en corporate communication: Ervaringen in Tilburg*, City management & marketing, nummer 1, 1995, Samson Tjeenk Willink.
- Matinus, J. (1992) *Politiek econoom of economische politicus?*, Controllers Magazine, nr. 6, nov./dec. 1992.
- Mattauch, C. (1994) *Profitable Amtsstube*, Wochenpost nr. 26.
- Möncks, J. (1999) *Towards performance oriented and participatory public administrations*, thesis, Universiteit van Genève.
- Mix, U. M. Herwijer (Hrgs.) (1996) *10 Jahre Tilburger Modell; erfarahrungen einer öffentlichen Verwaltung auf dem Weg zum Dienstleistungscenter*, SachBuchVerlag Kellner, Bremen.
- Nipkau, N. (1994) *Tilburg macht's möglich; Führerschein in 165 Sekunden*, Wir in Europa, nr. 79 Augustus 1994.
- Pekdemir, U. (1994) *Tilburgs Model; Hoe ging de gemeente Tilburg tewerk bij de reorganisatie van hun diensten?*, Pen & Pc, Stadsdrukkerij Antwerpen.
- Pekdemir, U. en I. Zaat (1996) *Managementrapportage: een zinvol instrument bij overheidsorganisaties en gesubsidieerde instelling*, Budgettering in de welzijnssector, VUGA, band 2, F7.
- Poel, P. v.d. (1995) *BBI is nog te autistisch; de driedemensionale burger en het Tilburgs Model*, BMI-magazine, jaargang 7 november 1995.
- Quix, F. (1993) *De gemeente als bedrijf; Enterpeneur Krosse verkoopt Tilburgs Model*, Magazine van Bedrijfskunde Groningen, nr 6, jaargang 13, augustus.
- Roels, E. (1992) *Het Tilburgs Model alleen kosmetisch?*, Overheidsmanagement, 1992, II.
- Roser, T. (1996) *Eine Stadt als Konzern; Das niederländschen Tilburg gilt asl erfolgreiches Modell für das Moderne Management von Verwaltungen*, FrankfurterRundschau, 17. Mai 1996, nr. 114.   •

- Roser, T. (1996) *Die Firma Stadtverwaltung macht neuerdings Gewinne; Die niederländische Stadt Tilburg arbeitet wie ein Konzern*, Stuttgarter Zeitung, 24. Mai 1996.
- Roser, T. (1996) *Tilburg: Eine Stadt wird als Konzern gefürth; Management statt Bürokratie*, Der Bund, 14. Juni 1996, 147. Jahrgang nr. 137.
- Savelkoul, H.J.N.F.L. (1995) *Beter Sturen met producten?; een onderzoek naar de invloed van produktbegroting en contractmangement op de politieke sturing van ambtelijke organisaties*, Faculteit economische wetenscahppen, Open Universiteit, maart 1995.
- Schalken, K. (1993) *Burgeronderzoek als ogen en oren voor het Tilburgse Model*, doctoraalscriptie, Katholieke Universiteit Brabant, april 1993.
- Schrijvers, A.P.M. (1988) *(Financiële)sturing van een grote gemeente*, Bedrijfskunde, jrg. 60, 1988/4.
- Schrijvers, A.P.M. (1989) *Kan de gemeenteraad doeltreffend van beleid wel controleren*, BMI-magazine maart 1989.
- Schrijvers, A.P.M. (1989) *Als we maar kengetallen hadden, zou de politieke sturing gemakkelijker gaan*, BMI-magazine april 1989.
- Schrijvers, A.P.M. (1989) *De controlling- en secretarisfunctie binnen een gemeente*, BMI-magazine, juli 1989.
- Schrijvers, A.P.M. (1991) *De financiële beheersing van een grote gemeente; de ontwikkeling van het Tilburgse Model*, De Accountant, nr.7 maart 1991.
- Schrijvers, A.P.M. (1991) *Contractmanagement; een bedrijfskundig en bedrijfsecono- misch sturingsmodel*, Openbaar Bestuur, 1991, nr.1.
- Schrijvers, A.P.M. (1989) *Beleids- en beheersinstrumentarium van de gemeente Tilburg*, Management in Overheidsorganisaties, (red. van A.J.G.M. Bekke ... et al), Samson Uitgeverij, augustus 1989.
- Schrijvers, A.P.M. (1993) *The management of a larger town*, Public Administration, vol. 71 nr 4, 595-605.
- Singeling, B. (1994) *Financiële communicatie; marktonderzoek geeft nieuwe impulsen*, COMMA, 11.
- Stoof, J. (1994) *Het Mekka van de presterende overheid*, BB Management, 25/08/1994.
- *Tilburg is wakker geworden*, NRC, 12 december 1993
- Tops. P.W. en G.J.C. Hartman (1988) *De wisselwerking tussen ambtelijk en politiek management*, Bestuur nr. 12, december 1988.
- Tops P.W. e.a. (1992) *De Tilburgse gemeenteraad, gezien door de gemeenteraadsleden*, Katholieke Universiteit Brabant, sectie bestuurskunde, juli 1992.
- Tops P.W. (1991) *Lokale democratie en bestuurlijke vernieuwing in Tilburg*, Eburon.
- Verbon, H.A.A. een J. van Bussel (1994) *Het 'Tilburgse model'*, uit: P.A. Verheyen (red.), Non-profit in bedrijf, Kluwer.
- *Videofilm tekst 'op zoek naar het Tilburgs Model'*, KPMG, augustus 1995.
- *Vorbild Tilburg*, Wirtschafswoche, nr. 13 20.3.1992.
- Vugt, G.W.M. (1992) *Tilburgs subsidiëringssysteem welzijnssector succesvol*, B&G, november 1992.
- Vugt, G.W.M. (1992) *Budgetsubsidieriëring Tilburg; aan een nader oordeel onderworpen*, Kontakt, juni 1992.
- Vugt, G.W.M. (1993) *Toepassing van nieuwe sturingsconceptie in de welzijnssector*, Openbaar Bestuur, januari 1993.

- Vugt, G.W.M. (1993) *Outputsturing door budgetsubsidëring blijkt goed te werken,* Trendbeeld, mei 1993.
- Vugt, G.W.M. en Weggemans T.J. (1994) *Van experimenteel tot instrumenteel,* Tijdschrift voor de Sociale Sector, januari 1994.
- Wansink, H. (1993) *Een stad is geen bedrijf,* Intermediair, 19 februari 1993.
- *Wege zum Dienstleistungsunternehmen Kommunalverwaltung, Fallstudie Tilburg,* Kommunale Gemeinschaftsstelle für Verwaltungsvereubfachung (KGSt) bericht nr. 19, 1992.
- Wolf A. de, J.v. Iersel (1995) *De gemeente Tilburg en doelmatigheid,* hoofdstuk 10 in Doeltreffend omgaan met doelmatigheid, redactie: Verhoog W e.a., Kluwer Bedrijfswetenschappen.
- Wolters, G.J. (1993) *De Tilburgse reorganisatie; kwaliteit van de processen,* Trendbeeld.
- Wolters, G.J. (1994) *The Tilburg Model; Management and Control in Local Government,* Bertelsmann Foundation Publishers, Volume 2, Güterloh.
- Zaat, I.J.L.M., *Budgetfinanciering gebaseerd op prestaties,* BMI-magazine.

CHAPTER 5

A COMPARISON OF JAPANESE AND AUSTRALIAN SECOND TIER GOVERNMENT PERFORMANCE REPORTING

Mark Christensen and Hiroshi Yoshimi

5.1.   Introduction

In recent years a rapidly growing body of literature has developed around the theme that public sectors across a wide variety of countries are changing. Within this literature has been a category of contributions examining changes in performance reporting and measurement but little of it has considered comparison across countries. Comparative public administration theory and methodology is challenging (Heady, 1996; Moon & Ingraham, 1998; Peters, 1988; Peters, 1990) and so the literature is not extensive. This paper adds to that literature by examining recent changes in Australian and Japanese public sector performance reporting by 2nd tier governments.

Public sector performance reporting is an important topic in many respects. Firstly, good reporting by the public sector to various stakeholders is crucially important to the operation of an informed democracy since voters should be able to form informed opinions as to the performance of governments when they cast votes. Secondly, performance reporting by any management (public or private sector) is the important fourth function in addition to the three 'classic' functions of planning, doing and controlling. Thirdly, performance reporting has undergone significant change in a number of public sectors and as such it forms an area of interest to analysts of public sector change in general.

Section 5.1. of this paper establishes a theoretical framework within which to consider performance reporting in the wider area of public sector accounting. Section 5.2. provides a case study report of two recent developments in Australian and Japanese 2nd tier performance reporting and so provides the information on which section 5.3. can consider the differences which emerge between Australia and Japan. Section 5.4. explores some of the factors capable of explaining the observed differences and so leads to section 5.5. some tentative conclusions as to what light the experience of Japanese and Australian performance reporting can throw on New Public Management.

5.1.1. A THEORETICAL FRAMEWORK: NEW PUBLIC MANAGEMENT AS A RESEARCH AGENDA

By arguing for a 'new global paradigm' in public sector management, Osborne and Gaebler (1992) sowed the seeds for a growing body of literature which examined the phenomena known as 'New Public Management' (NPM) or managerialism. The

A. Bac (ed.), International Comparative Issues in Government Accounting, 53-70.

literature on NPM[1] is now quite wide and includes official exhortations to adopt various elements of NPM, academic considerations of the advantages and disadvantages of NPM and various texts dealing with specific elements of NPM techniques.

This paper considers the impacts of public sector performance reporting as one of NPM's techniques. This is done within the context of a 'crisis of confidence with performance measurement' (Williams, 1998: 21) which calls for further research at both a supra-organizational level (such as in this paper) and at an individual organizational level.

The usefulness of NPM as a theoretical framework for this cross-country examination of public sector performance reporting is twofold. Firstly, the NPM literature provides a broad contextual base upon which performance reporting can be considered and research hypotheses identified. Secondly, NPM changes have been pervasive but have not followed a strictly consistent path across nations (Olson, et al., 1998; Rhodes, 1998) thus analysis of public sector performance reporting as an NPM technique will add to the available data related to this issue. The literature has advanced since Hood described the discussion as 'close to being a data free zone' (1995: 98) but there is still need for additional data in order to test theories in this field (Humphrey & Guthrie, 1996). This Section will now describe the NPM theoretical framework adopted by this paper.

NPM forms a research agenda by establishing a framework from which to consider a range of public sector management issues. By the mid 1990s a number of authors had identified features of public sector change loosely called 'managerialism' (Halligan & Power, 1992; Mayne & Zapico-Goñi, eds, 1996; Parker & Guthrie, 1993; Wanna, O'Faircheallaigh & Weller, 1992). However, by 1995 these various features were being drawn together into a framework that is of use by this paper. The framework described by Hood (1995) involves different conceptions of public accountability with different patterns of trust and distrust leading to altered requirements of and responses from public sector accounting systems. Hood notes that public sector systems of administration may be considered in terms of two cardinal elements, namely, their degree of distinctiveness from the private sector and the extent of rules operating to maintain buffers against political and managerial discretion. Using these two cardinal elements of public sector administration, 7 underlying doctrines can be identified as shown in table 5.1.

Hood argues that doctrines 1 to 4 from table 5.1 involve NPM techniques aimed at reducing the distinctiveness of public sector administration compared to the private sector. Similarly, he argues that doctrines 5 to 7 involve NPM techniques aimed at reducing public sector rules and so increasing the discretion available to public sector managers. It is possible to be too forensic here. That is, the separation of the seven doctrines into the two cardinal elements of distinctiveness and discretion can be

---

[1]   For a cross section of the literature on NPM or its elements see for example Aucoin (1990), Considine & Painter (1997), Common et al (1993), Farnham & Horton (eds) (1996), Flynn (1990), Guthrie (1995), Halachmi & Bouckaert (eds) (1996), Hirst & Khilnani (eds) (1996), Hood (1995), OECD (1998), Olson et al (eds) (1998), Parker & Guthrie (1991), Parker & Guthrie (1993), Pollitt (1993), Public Services and Merit Protection Commission (1997), Pusey (1991), Zifcak (1997).

somewhat artificial and in fact can partly obscure the often observed inter-related aspects of various NPM features.

Doctrine	Operational significance	Some accounting implications
1. Unbundling of the PS into corporatized units organized by product	Erosion of single service employment; arms-length; devolved budgets	More cost center units
2. More contract-based competitive provision, with internal markets and term contracts	Distinction of primary and secondary public service labour force	More stress on identifying costs and cost structures; cost data become confidential and cooperative behaviour becomes costly
3. Stress on private-sector styles of management practice	Move from double imbalance PS pay, career service, unmonetized rewards 'due process' employee entitlements	Private-sector accounting norms
4. More stress on discipline and frugality in resource use	Less primary employees, less job security, less producer-friendly style	More stress on the bottom line
5. More emphasis on visible hands-on top management	More freedom to manage by discretionary power	Fewer constraints on handling of contracts, cash, staff; more use of financial data for management accountability
6. Explicit formal measurable standards and measures of performance and success	Erosion of self-management by professionals	Performance indicators and audit
7. Greater emphasis on output controls	Resources and pay based on performance	Move away from detailed accounting for particular activities towards broader cost center accounting; may involve blurring of funds for pay and for activity

Table 5.1.:   Doctrinal Components of New Public Management (Hood, 1995: 96)

This paper argues that Doctrine 6 ('explicit formal measurable standards and measures of performance and success') which is of central interest here, has a strong relationship with Doctrines 2, 3, 4, and 7. The use of performance measures is what makes it possible to establish and enforce contracts with specific service levels. Further, performance measurement emerging from Doctrine 6 facilitates implementation of private sector management styles of practice, increased stress on resource usage and a greater emphasis on output controls. It is difficult to envisage how Doctrines 2, 3, 4, and 7 can be more than rhetoric without the measures of performance that are core to Doctrine 6. In fact, a great deal of the controversy surrounding NPM relates to the difficulty of the explicit performance measures to adequately underpin Doctrines 2, 3, 4, and 7 thus, the counter-argument proceeds, exposing the pure rhetoric of NPM (eg. Considine, 1990: 175-176; Painter, 1998; Trosa, 1997; Considine & Painter, 1997; Guthrie, 1998a; Guthrie, 1998b; Guthrie & Parker, 1998; Olson et al., 1998; Rhodes, 1998).

5.1.2. RESEARCH METHOD

Lüder (1992) provides a critique of research methods applied by various scholars in their analysis of causal factors hypothesized to impact on the adoption of altered accounting methods in a number of public sectors. Since changes in public sector performance measurement are an example of accounting system change, Lüder's analysis of research methods is useful to this paper. Most of the research methods reviewed by Lüder are of a quantitative empirical nature and he expresses three specific concerns about them (Lüder, 1992: 106-107):

1. the relationship between accounting system change (as a dependent variable) and the various tested independent variables is not monocausal but is multicausal;
2. it is frequently very difficult to directly measure the independent variables (such as 'political competition', 'professionalism', 'user socioeconomic status' and so on);
3. it is questionable as to whether accounting system change is a binary variable since there are variations of change rather than simply 'on' or 'off'.

Lüder's concerns are supported by others (Cheng, 1994: 64; Covaleski & Dirsmith, 1990: 555) and they heighten this paper's view that a quantitative research method alone is not suited to its research interests. Instead, it is necessary to apply a qualitative research method with the objective of determining if identified observations are consistent with elements of a theoretical explanation of the broader phenomena. However, since 'cause and effect, or accounting change and organizational impact, tend to be loosely linked or even nonexistent with respect to manifest relationships and involve many additional forces, research focus should remain on the social context and the interpretations of actors as opposed to a priori theories or the research methods employed' (Covaleski & Dirsmith, 1990: 548 - 549).

The social context and interpretations of actors provides a framework from which to view accounting change. In order to understand accounting practice, such as public sector performance measurement, 'we must start by recognizing that accounting provides a structure of meanings which are drawn upon in organizations, but which are themselves the outcome of organizational activities. ... It is necessary to locate practice in its historical, as well as its economic, social and organizational contexts. Case studies are particularly suitable for this type of research. They allow the researcher to adopt a holistic orientation and to study accounting as part of a unified social system. ... Such studies do not provide the type of predictive theory which is sought by positive theorists. But social scientists would argue that accounting practices are socially constructed and can therefore be changed by the activities of the social actors themselves. Nevertheless, it is still possible to construct social theories of accounting; viz. explanatory theories which will help to understand the social structures which shape current practice. It is here that case studies have an important role in the research process. Descriptive, illustrative, experimental and exploratory case studies are all potentially useful, and explanatory case studies are essential.' (Scapens, 1990: 268)

The research method adopted by this paper is to provide two descriptive case studies of performance reporting in Australia and Japan and to use NPM as a theoretical framework to explain observations from this case. As will be shown, NPM is inadequate as a full explanation and so we complement it with additional themes.

Accounting can be considered in isolation of its context or it can be viewed as having an impact on (and being impacted by) specific contexts (Hopwood, 1985). Broadbent & Guthrie identify the former approach as being 'the technical approach ... (which) assumes that accounting is a powerful force for change and perceives the context within which it exists as unimportant' (1992: 6). In preference to the technical approach some researchers have retained a technical focus but have included as variables in their analyses the specific contexts of change; Broadbent & Guthrie (1992) describe this approach as 'technically contextual accounting' (1992:11) and they provide a most useful review of 'alternative' accounting research that has adopted this approach. This paper adopts a technically contextual view of accounting in its case studies on Australian and Japanese performance reporting.

A technically contextual view of accounting helps to demonstrate that accounting has played an important role in the two cardinal elements of NPM. Firstly, accounting information was necessary to identify assets, liabilities, revenues and expenses which are arguably the core concepts of the private sector and so if identified for the public sector, can reduce its distinctiveness. Secondly, accounting information was necessary to measure results so that the explicit can replace the implicit as is required if levels of trust must be reduced. As an example, the introduction of program budgeting allowed accounting information to show the inputs (expenses) used by each of the programs which were previously embedded in agency budgets. Further, as annual reports were produced to recount a year's activities which were funded out of a program budget, accounting information was used to attest to the activities. So strong was the role of accounting information (or so weak was the role of non-accounting information) that it has been accused of capturing the debate (Guthrie, 1995b: 42).

Whilst accounting might have captured the debate it has been attacked as being 'not particularly informative' (Harris, 1995: 10) with respect to inner budget (non-trading government) organizations. Attacks have also been aimed at accounting as being inadequate for State owned enterprise reporting (Guthrie, 1994: 95-97). As a result in 1991 the Australian Accounting Research Foundation noted: *'financial information is only a sub-set of the information necessary to allow an adequate assessment of a Department's performance'* (1991: 87-88). Thus the picture emerges of significant deficiencies in the usefulness of accounting technologies that have been an integral part of the underlying philosophy behind recent public sector reforms (Miller, 1996).

This paper takes a broad view of performance measurement as advocated by the US General Accounting Office (GAO) to describe performance measurement as regular collection and reporting of data on: inputs (money, staff and materials), workload or activity levels, outputs or final products, outcomes of programs, and productivity (efficiency cost per unit of output or output per unit cost) (GAO, 1992: 2).

Performance reporting is thus any on-going collection and *disclosure* of information which can be of use in the judgement of whether a program has achieved its objectives. The disclosure is necessarily public rather than being limited to the agencies that generate the performance information or limited to a central agency.

5.2.   2ⁿᵈ Tier Performance Reporting in Australia and Japan

Australia and Japan both have a government structure based on a federal, state or prefectural and local governments. This paper will describe case studies of performance reporting by governments at the State (in Australia) and Prefectural (in Japan) levels.

5.2.1. AUSTRALIAN PERFORMANCE REPORTING: THE NSW CASE

Almost all States in Australia have devoted increased resources and rhetoric to performance reporting since the 1980s. However, within these developments a recent change deserves most attention and is the subject of this case study: the publication by the New South Wales Government (NSWG) of service efforts and accomplishments statements (SEAs).

SEA reporting has been advocated in the USA since 1990 when Hatry et al, completed a research report for the GASB and subsequently a number of authorities have advanced the concept (for two sources of some commentaries see the Special Edition of International Journal of Public Administration, 1995; and, Halachmi & Bouckaert, eds., 1996). NSW embarked on SEA reporting in 1996 in a special project initiated and conducted by the Office of the Council on the Cost of Government (OCCG, 1996: 34-36). Inspite of experience in developing program statements and publishing performance indicators (albeit somewhat limited in nature), NSW agencies were not able to fully explain a 20% increase in real spending over the eight years to 1996 and so OCCG decided to devote resources to the SEA reporting project (McDonald, 1996: 2). SEA Statements were designed to address the main performance reporting deficiency: inadequacies in the 'ability to report on their accomplishments, in terms of outputs and, particularly, outcomes' (OCCG, 1996: 34).

The 13 SEA reports, of which 10 have been published, do not report agency performance but they cover separate policy areas dealing with the accomplishments achieved (outcomes), activities undertaken (outputs or 'service efforts'), resources consumed (inputs) and efficiency measures (unit costs of outputs and outcomes). In addition to numerical measures being reported, the SEA reports also provide contextual information which assists interpretation of the performance measures.

The move away from agency related performance measures meant that a more complete picture could be presented (OCCG, 1997d: 72). Thus performance indicators are 'set in a broader context which defines and delimits the role of the NSW Government activities in a particular industry or sector' (McDonald, 1996: 3); also, data discontinuities resulting from agency changes are avoided (Walker, 1998: 116). However, this advantage came at the cost that agencies had difficulty to think in terms of policy areas rather than their limited activities (OCCG, 1997c: 44) and there were resultant complex negotiations, for example 'in one case 25 agencies had an interest in the development of outcome indicators for one policy area' (OCCG, 1997c: 43). The resultant complexity of the SEA Statements and their mismatch to the bureaucratic boundaries of NSW delayed production of SEA reports and caused some to be too long (Walker, 1998: 122) and to be based on poor data (OCCG, 1997d: 71).

The other reasons for delay in the release of SEA reports seem to be
- given the public release of SEA reports, agencies were very cautious thus making the Council prepare initial draft reports using publicly available information to promote action (OCCG, 1997c: 43), and
- extensive and meaningful SEA contextual information meant that the performance indicators reported are more comprehensive than earlier efforts which tended to merely 'decorate a budget document' (Greiner, 1996: 16).

Inspite of difficulties in preparing SEA reports OCCG compiled 1,700 SEA outcome and output indicators which compared to 870 indicators previously published in the NSW Budget Papers (OCCG, 1997c: 44). Not all these indicators have been published but the comprehensive nature of SEA reports is nevertheless a strength.

A review of the SEA reports presents evidence of their 'work-in-progress' nature. 3 reports (school education, transportation and environment) remain to be published even though they are complete; input measures account for 31% of all measures; outcome and output measures are subject to warnings of possible data problems in each report; the data is not audited and has been criticized for its inadequacies (Walker, 1998: 121); and, as an indication of potential for improvement, proposed future measures amount to 37% of reported measures.

The published SEA reports are but a small part of the achievement of the OCCG SEA project. The more important results from this on-going project are:
- 'in several cases ..(they have).. led to a fundamental re-examination of agencies' roles and functions' (OCCG, 1997c: 43) as well as understanding their roles in the whole of government delivery of service (Walker, 1998: 120);
- use by Treasury and the NSWG of SEA indicators (OCCG, 1997c: 45);
- enhanced coverage of indicators; for example, in prior Budget Papers the relatively few performance indicators meant each indicator covered $104 million in health policy area expenditure whereas the SEA indicators will represent an average of $26 million (OCCG, 1997c).

In summary of the SEA project's achievement: 'What started out as an attempt to meaningfully report government activity to stakeholders has expanded into a program to lead substantial reform of the performance monitoring regime within agencies' (OCCG, 1997d: 71). The performance monitoring regime can be likened to the 'balanced scorecard' view of performance reporting as advanced by Kaplan & Norton (1992). Whilst a typical SEA report does not have Kaplan & Norton's four headings, it presents diverse information which is capable of providing insights into customer, financial and internal views of the performance being reported. Further, the diversity of information addresses the inadequate predominance of accounting information in NSWG performance reporting (Walker, 1998: 117 for example cites one performance document with 'about 300 performance indicators' of which only 3 related to services and most of the others being accounting based).

The diversity of information in SEAs includes accounting and non-accounting performance measures and is necessary in order to achieve a high rating in terms of usefulness (PSMPC, 1997; Hatry, et al, 1990; Greiner, 1996). Within this diversity is essential non-accounting information that complements and completes typically cost based accounting information. As noted by the (USA) Federal Accounting Standards Advisory Board 'performance measurement requires both financial and non-financial measures. Cost is a necessary element for performance measurement, but is not the only element' (FASAB, 1997: 335). Both OCCG and the PSMPC have found deficiencies in the abilities of the NSW and Commonwealth public sectors to measure costs accurately (OCCG, 1998a: 14), however, it is apparent that once these technical difficulties are reduced, SEA reporting will significantly improve the usefulness of available accounting based performance information.

The NSW SEA project is in its early days with 'mixed success' (OCCG, 1998a: 4; Walker, 1998: 122) and it is 'anticipated that with improved data these indicators will be modified, replaced and augmented over time' (OCCG, 1997a: 9). The real test will be if improvements in performance reporting are on-going in the face of a series of dangers. There is a danger that agency managers may alter their work practices so as to artificially report improved performance as a result of the closer scrutiny achieved by SEA reporting (Halachmi, 1996: 79). Equally, there is the danger that the NSW Government may not sanction publication of SEA reports that do not show successful performance - especially in an election year. This was an initial reaction in the USA when eight major State and Local Government associations objected to the GASB regarding SEA reporting (Halachmi, 1996: 90). An additional danger is that if the OCCG championing of SEA reports wanes, so too will the efforts of agencies in maintaining their SEA measures (the importance of a high level 'champion' in SEA reporting is recognized by Greiner, 1996: 18).

Against the risks faced by SEA reporting must be placed the significantly increasing pressure for performance reporting from the community and special interest groups.

5.2.2. JAPANESE PERFORMANCE REPORTING: THE HOKKAIDO CASE

In Japan, the 2nd tier of government is based around prefectures. The 3rd tier of government is based around cities, towns or villages[2]. However, some of the largest cities usually with a population of over one million population have special rights of prefectures.

These governments have both an elected assembly of representatives and a government office. Both assembly members and the head of the government are directly elected by

---

[2]   Tokyo is not a city, but 23 wards which consist of Tokyo metropolitan area have their own
     rights which are like as other cities. Tokyo metropolitan government is one of prefecture
     which include the 23 wards and other cities, towns and villages.

residents.[3] This system was introduced in Japan after World War II as an adaptation of the US government system. However, most tax revenue is still collected by the central government as it was before the War, so the 2nd and 3rd tier governments in Japan have limited original tax sources. Consequently, both sets of governments receive budgetary allocations from the central government.

Japan is divided into 47 prefectures and Hokkaido is one of these prefectures. Japan consists of four main islands, of which Hokkaido island is the northernmost. Hokkaido prefecture covers all of this island so the Hokkaido Government governs the largest land mass of any 2nd tier government. Hokkaido is mostly agricultural land and as such it is a relatively poor area in Japan.

Hokkaido has an extreme climate with periods of intense cold which have caused it to be the last land area to be opened in Japan. Since the Meiji era, large amounts of money have been invested in Hokkaido by the central government. However, even now, Hokkaido continues to receive more central government funds and dedicated projects such as roads, dams or other social infrastructure. In 1998, the budget of the Hokkaido government was around 3.5 billion yen and so was the second largest Japanese prefectural government budget after Tokyo.

Prefectural government budget decisions in Japan are made by elected assembly members. Under such a system the government has a responsibility to report its performance mainly to its assembly. However, there have been serious problems experienced in the acquitting of this responsibility.

Firstly, even if it is sometimes considered that a performance report to the assembly is important, the direct reporting or disclosure of performance information to its residents is not so important. For example, there are no documents labelled 'performance report' available from the Hokkaido government. Whilst the Hokkaido government has an 'administrative information office', which discloses most published documents available for the public, free copies of these documents are limited and most documents must be photocopied at a cost to the user. Most documents are copies of the originals which were submitted to the Hokkaido Assembly and so they are not easily understood by the general public. Some books or brochures are available free of charge, but such free brochures are limited. For example, the Hokkaido Government publishes *Zaisei Jokyo (Financial Status)* semi annually. In the preface of this publication, the Governor of Hokkaido noted 'this *Zaisei Jokyo* is published in June and December in every year to inform residents of the current financial status of Hokkaido', but only ten copies are available in the administrative information office. As a result, most Hokkaido residents cannot get this brochure; indeed, most don't even know of its existence.

Secondly, once a project has had its budget determined, it has been very difficult to review or reconsider its effectiveness. In Hokkaido, large sums have been invested in many development projects. Some of them are obviously not effective, but there has been no system to stop or reconsider the projects.

---

[3] The head of local government is called a governor in prefecture, a mayor in city or town, a head in village.

To cope with this situation, the Hokkaido Government decided to introduce 'Time Assessment' from 1997. According to the Hokkaido Government (1997), 'Time Assessment calls for the checking, re-evaluating and, if necessary, drastically changing measures and, based on an objective time scale'. This assessment tries to re-consider projects that have not been in progress for a long time. In 1997, the Hokkaido Government selected 9 projects for Time Assessment. By early 1999, 8 of the 9 projects were either stopped or abandoned because of the time assessment process. As an example, the Hokkaido Government decided to stop the construction of Shihoro Heights Road in 1999 in accordance with the result of its Time Assessment. This construction project faced difficult geography and it was pointed that it would seriously damage the environment by running through the Taisetsu Mountain National Park. The reason for the suspension of this project was its low expected effectiveness compared with its high cost and adverse environmental impact.

Time Assessment would appear to be based on a performance measurement process, but its method is not apparent. It is carried out by a Government investigation team but it seems that its reports are based mainly on public or mass media opinions rather than a numerical index. Future Time Assessments are capable of significant improvement by development of a performance measurement process.

The importance of Time Assessment for the Japanese experience of performance measurement is that the government and the public became to recognize that accountability is one of the key concepts to pursue. Accountability has not been a common word or concept for the Japanese people (Van Wolferen, 1994). Through the Time Assessment, at least the Hokkaido Government and its residents realize the importance of the concept and this can be seen as part of a broader realization (Kokubu, et al, 1998: 149). A further significant development is that the Japanese central government is paying attention to Hokkaido's trial, and is trying to introduce Time Assessment.

Future changes in performance reporting are likely to be the adoption of external auditing use of Time Assessment and the development from next year of 'Policy Assessment[4]' as a process of qualitative appraisal of funded project priorities. Both these developments will improve the quality and extent of accountability by the Hokkaido Government and so they form part of Hood's 6th Doctrine within his NPM framework.

---

[4]   This system was trialed in 1998 using the experience of Time Assessment to expand the performance measurement process in each annual budget. Its purpose is to classify every funded project into 4 priority categories using qualitative factors on both departmental and whole-of-government bases. On the basis of the 1998 trial 199 projects (20.3 billion yen) were stopped or abandoned, 108 projects (15.9 billion yen) were reduced in scale, 193 projects (123.5 billion yen) were altered in scope, but 2,113 projects (1,958 billion yen) were continued and 101 projects (14.9 billion yen) were expanded.

5.3.   Differences in Performance Reporting

The two case studies of performance reporting presented here demonstrate some interesting points of comparison. The comparisons consist of similarities and differences. The main similarities are:

- both the Japanese and NSWG developments have been in the context of broader changes to public administration which have demonstrated a lower level of trust by both governments and citizens;
- there has been a recognition in both Japan and NSWG that performance reporting needed improvement;
- whilst not over stating the case, the power of bureaucrats has been reduced in both countries as performance reporting changes have been implemented; in the case of Japan (Moon & Ingraham, 1998: 88) perhaps less than in the NSWG context but this has been from a more powerful starting point;
- in the NSWG case there has been only relatively minor publicity and hence little use of the published SEAs reports whilst the Hokkaido Time Assessments have been limited in their number so it is reasonable to expect that there has not been significant change in the level of public confidence in performance reporting;
- at least to date, there has not been explicit linking of the performance reporting developments in either country to the doctrines of NPM as suggested by Hood (1995). The absence of linkage might result from the newness and incomplete nature of both developments but it could also mean that the rhetoric related to improvements in accounting related performance reports is not to be realized (Miller, 1996).

Perhaps the differences between Japan and NSWG performance reporting are more enlightening than the similarities. The differences that can be observed, and will be further discussed in section 5.4. are:

- extent of performance reporting effort: the NSWG experience is one in which greater effort has been expended than in the case of Japan. The full SEAs project in the NSWG has extended for 2 years and it has required significant resource input whereas the Hokkaido effort is only at an embryonic stage given the large number of projects capable of being subject to Time Assessment;
- motivation for changes in performance reporting: in the case of the NSWG experience there has been a motivation for change from within the bureaucracy[5] whereas in Japan the bureaucracy has been resistant to change and reluctantly drawn along by public demand;
- role of central agencies in promulgating changed performance reporting: in the NSWG context there was competition between central agencies for a main role in improved performance reporting whereas in Hokkaido central agencies have not been important;
- degree of accountability discharge resulting from performance reporting: the discharge of accountability in the NSWG context is more comprehensive (although still incomplete) than in Japan where the limited number of projects reduces the scope of accountability discharge.

---

[5]   However, it should be noted that change in the NSWG context has been driven by an accounting professor who has taken a part-time Chairmanship of a central agency.

5.4.   Explanatory Factors

The case studies present evidence for and against the view advanced in section 5.1. of this paper, that NPM-type change is dependent upon performance reporting changes and that NPM provides an explanatory model from which to understand changes in performance reporting. The evidence in support of this is mostly from the NSWG case study:
- linking future performance reporting to the budgetary cycle: for example, the OCCG comments that 'significant longer term benefits of the SEAs project will be its contribution to the development of performance measures as budgetary tools' (OCCG,   998a: i-ii; PSMPC, 1997);
- explicitly linking performance measures to organizational change as a central coordinating agency policy (Pierce & Puthucheary, 1997);
- emphasis given in performance measures to accounting based information (Walker, 1998: 117; OCCG, 1997a);
- unbundling the public sector is facilitated by production of performance measures that go beyond organization unit but relate to government purpose (eg. the Law, Order and Public Safety SEA Report measures performance of activities undertaken by some 16 agencies; OCCG, 1997a).

Evidence against the argument that performance reporting changes act to underpin other NPM changes is from both the NSWG and Hokkaido cases:
- whilst accrual accounting has been introduced as predicted by the NPM model, it has not produced more useful performance measurement information (OCCG, 1996; Guthrie, 1994; Guthrie, 1998a);
- instead of accountability requirements being discharged, there has been a tendency to label information as 'commercial in confidence' to withhold performance measures related to contracting out (and other information) from the public (ABC, 1998; Harris, 1998; Zifcak, 1997);
- as the public sector has been unbundled into corporatized units, performance reporting has not been standardized (or even overly useful) for these corporatized units (Guthrie, 1994);
- the failure to audit performance measures in either NSW or Hokkaido (Guthrie & Parker, 1998) does not reflect support for Hood's 6th doctrine;
- performance measures have inconsistent uses: published measures are not the same as used in contract-based competitive provision (Harris, 1998) and different measures of the same concept are used for different audiences without justification (OCCG, 1998a: 14);
- the underdeveloped nature of performance measures in NSW and especially Hokkaido reflect at least a retardation behind other NPM changes and thus cannot be said to be a prerequisite to those changes.

On balance the comparison of the two case studies shows that the NPM view is not capable of fully explaining the observations. It does hold some explanatory power but it needs complementing from additional views of this complex area. Three views worthy of consideration are contingency theory, governance views and the role of epistemic communities. Proof of the validity of these views is beyond the scope of this paper but some conjecture is posed here to encourage further research.

The Contingency Model of Accounting Innovation posits that the interactions between four modules explains change: stimuli, structural variables of information users, structural variables of information producers, and implementation barriers. On the face of both the NSWG and Hokkaido cases there is support for the Contingency Model in that the differences can be attributed to more favorable conditions in NSW for both structural variables of information producers, and lower implementation barriers. Nevertheless, the unknown is the extent to which these modules interact and so the predictive ability of the Contingency Model is limited.

One factor which the Contingency Model specifically incorporates in its stimuli and in its structural variables is the role of professional bodies. A refinement of this factor has recently been posited by other authors in their argument that epistemic communities can be an important part of a 'middle range' theory to explain public sector accounting change (Laughlin & Pallot, 1998). The concept of an epistemic community can be extended from Haas' more limited view (1992: 3) to include structures such as the large management consulting firms. These firms have been active in advising governments in the adoption of NPM changes and as such are contemplated as being an important explanatory factor. For example, Saint-Martin's (1998) three-country study explains variety in NPM changes as a result of differing influences exerted by management consultants. In the same way the greater influence of management consulting firms in NSW may explain why it has advanced its performance reporting beyond Hokkaido's. Clearly, this is not fully explanatory but it does seem to be informative.

A third complementary view to be added to NPM is that of governance. The dominant feature of the governance model is that networks now control public policy partly because of the crisis ridden delegitimated role of the State (Peters, 1998). Such a model has similarities and differences to the NPM model and it can be found to be consistent with selected parts of both the Contingency Model and a view on the role of epistemic communities. Indeed, the NSW and Hokkaido cases support the governance view as a explanation of both change and stability. In the NSW case the power of networks extending beyond the State (and including epistemic communities such as international management consulting firms) has been strong; in contrast, networks between the bureaucracy and business in Japan has been stronger than other networks and so their inclination to resist change has proven to be a barrier which has retarded change. However, as shown by the Hokkaido case, such resistance is limited and is becoming less important as accountability expectations rise.

The three explanatory views added to NPM are seen in the light of the case studies to be plausible and certainly deserving of further research effort.

5. 5. Conclusion

Performance reporting has changed in both NSW and Hokkaido at the same time that other NPM changes have been observed. However, there are sufficient differences in the observations to conclude that NPM alone cannot fully explain the path taken in the performance reporting developments. There is apparent worth in adding contingency theory, the role of epistemic communities and governance to our toolbox but additional work is required before we can be confident of the strength of these tools in explaining complex matters such as the role of performance reporting in public sector accounting change. In applying additional explanatory factors it is important to recognize that NPM paths are varied across the many countries experiencing change in their public sector accounting. The variety of paths is best understood by considering the context of the governmental traditions of each relevant public sector.

References

- Aucoin, P. (1990) Administrative Reform in Public Management: Paradigms, Principles, Paradoxes and Pendulums, *Governance*, Vol. 3, No. 2, 115-137.
- Australian Accounting Research Foundation (1991) *Financial Reporting by Government Departments*, Discussion Paper No. 16, Australian Accounting Research Foundation, Melbourne.
- Australian Broadcasting Corporation (ABC) (1998) *Shrinking Democracy*, On-line, available: http://www.abc.net.au/rn/talks/bbing/stories/s13971.htm, [Access date: 1999, January 7].
- Broadbent, J. & J. Guthrie (1992) Changes in the Public Sector: A Review of Recent 'Alternative' Accounting Research, *Accounting, Auditing & Accountability Journal*, Vol. 5, No. 2, 3-31.
- Cheng, R. (1994) A Politco-Economic Model of Government Accounting Policy Choice, *Research in Governmental & Nonprofit Accounting*, Vol. 8, 39-68.
- Considine, M. (1990) Managerialism Strikes Out, *Australian Journal of Public Administration*, Vol. 49, No. 2, 166-178.
- Considine, M, & M. Painter (eds.) (1997), *Managerialism: The Great Debate*, Melbourne University Press, Melbourne.
- Common, R., N. Flynn, & E. Mellon (1993), *Managing Public Services: Competition and Decentralisation*, Butterworth-Heinemann, Oxford.
- Covaleski, M.A. & M.W. Dirsmith (1990) Dialectic tension, double reflexivity and the everyday accounting researcher: On using qualitative methods, *Accounting, Organizations and Society*, Vol. 15, No. 6, 543-573.
- Farnham, D. & S. Horton (eds.) (1996) *Managing the New Public Services*, Second Edition, MacMillan Press, Basingstoke.
- Federal Accounting Standards Advisory Board (FASAB) (1997) *Federal Financial Accounting Concepts and Standards-Original Statements - Volume 1*, FASAB, Washington.
- Flynn, N. (1990) *Public Sector Management*, Harvester Wheatsheaf, Hemel Hempstead.
- Greiner, J. (1996) Positioning Performance Measurement for the Twenty-First Century, in Halachmi, A. & Bouckaert, G. (eds.) (1996).
- Guthrie, J. (1994) Measuring the Financial and Non-Financial Performance of Public Business Enterprises, in Guthrie, J. (eds.) (1995).
- Guthrie, J. (eds.) (1995) *Making the Australian Public Sector Count in the 1990s*, IIR Conferences, North Sydney.
- Guthrie, J. (1998a) Accrual Accounting in the Public Sector?, *Financial Accountability and Management*, Vol. 14, No. 1, 1-19.
- Guthrie, J. (1998b) Australian Experience of Output Based Budgeting: A Critical Reflection, *Australasian Evaluation Society 1998 International Conference Proceedings Vol. 2*, October.
- Guthrie, J. & L. Parker (1998) A Quarter of a Century of Performance Auditing in the Federal Australian Public Sector: A Malleable Masque, *ANZAM Proceedings*, November.
- Halachmi, A. (1996) Promises and Possible Pitfalls on the Way to SEA Reporting, in
- Halachmi, A. & Bouckaert, G. (eds.) (1996).

- Halachmi, A. & G. Bouckaert (eds.) (1996) *Organizational Performance and Measurement in: The Public Sector: Toward Service, Effort and Accomplishment Reporting*, Quorum Books, Westport, CT.
- Halligan, J. & J. Power (1992) *Political Management in the 1990's*, Oxford University Press, Melbourne.
- Harris, A. (1995) Reporting on Performance: Financial and Non-Financial Information, in Public Accounts Committee (1995), *Proceedings of the Seminar on Annual Reporting in the NSW Public Sector: the Best is yet to Come*, Report No. 92, Parliament NSW.
- Harris, T. (1998) Called to Account: Contracting & Responsibility, *Australian CPA*, Vol. 68, No. 12, 40-43.
- Haas, P. (1992) Introduction: Epistemic Communities and International Policy Coordination, *International Organization*, Vol. 46, No. 1, 1-35.
- Hatry, H., J. Sullivan, J. Fountain, & L. Kremer (eds.) (1990), *Service Efforts and Accomplishments Reporting: Its Time Has Come*, Government Accounting Standards Board, Norwalk Connecticut.
- Heady, F. (1996) *Public Administration: A Comparative Perspective*, Marcel Drekker, New York.
- Hirst, P. & S. Khilnani (eds.) (1996) *Reinventing Democracy*, Blackwell Publishers, London.
- Hokkaido Government (1998). *Zaisei Jokyo (Financial Status)*, No. 101, June 1st, Sapporo, Hokkaido (in Japanese).
- Hokkaido Government (1997) *Special Issue 'Time Assessment'*, On-line, available: http://www.pref.hokkaido.jp/soumu/sm-thsho/index-e.html, [Access date: 1998, December 4].
- Hopwood, A. (1985) The Tales of a Committee that Never Reported: Disagreements on Intertwining Accounting with the Social, *Accounting, Organisations and Society*, Vol. 10, No. 3, 361-77.
- Hopwood, A. (1994) Accounting & Everyday Life: an Introduction, *Accounting, Organisations and Society*, Vol. 19, No. 3, 299-301.
- Hood, C. (1995) The 'New Public Management', in the 1980's: Variations on a Theme, *Accounting, Organizations and Society*, Vol. 20, No. 2/3, 93-109.
- Humphrey, C. & J. Guthrie (1996) Trends & Contradictions in Public Sector Financial Management Developments in Australia & Britain, *Research in Governmental & Nonprofit Accounting*, Vol. 9, No. 2, 30-49.
- Kaplan, R. & D. Norton (1992) The Balanced Scorecard – Measures that Drive Performance, *Harvard Business Review*, Jan-Feb, 71-79.
- Kokubu, K. et al (1998) A Runner a lap Behind in the Race for Public Sector Financial Management Reform: The Japanese Case, in Olson, O., J. Guthrie, & C. Humphrey (eds.) (1998).
- Laughlin, R. & J. Pallot, (1998) Trends, Patterns and Influencing Factors: Some Reflections, in Olson, O., J. Guthrie, & C. Humphrey (eds.) (1998).
- Lüder, K. (1992) A Contingency Model of Governmental Accounting Innovations in the Political-Administrative Environment, *Research in Governmental and Nonprofit Accounting*, Vol. 7, 99-127.
- McDonald, S. (1996) *Service Efforts and Accomplishments? Leading the Way in Improving Performance Measurement Within the NSW State Government*, Address to

the Australian Society of Certified Practicing Accountants, (NSW Division), On-line, available: http://www.occg.nsw.gov.au/seaspe.pdf, [Access date: 1999, February 3].

- Mayne, J. and E. Zapico-Goñi (eds.) (1996) *Monitoring Performance in the Public Sector: Future Directions From International Experience*, Transaction Publishers, New Brunswick.

- Moon, M. & P. Ingraham (1998) Shaping Administrative Reform & Governance: An Examination of the Political Nexus Triads in Three Asian Countries, *Governance: An International Journal of Policy and Administration*, Vol. 11 No. 1, 77-100.

- Miller, P. (1996) Dilemmas of Accountability: The Limits of Accounting, in Hirst, P. & S. Khilnani, (eds.) (1996).

- New South Wales Council on the Cost of Government (OCCG) (1996) *First Report*, Sydney: Council on the Cost of Government.

- New South Wales Council on the Cost of Government (OCCG) (1997a) *Reports of Service Efforts and Accomplishments in the NSW Government*, On-line, available: http://www.occg.nsw.gov.au/publicat/serefort/SEACONT.HTM, [Access date: 1999, February 23].

- New South Wales Council on the Cost of Government (OCCG) (1997b) *Service Efforts and Accomplishments in the NSW Government*, On-line, available: http://www.occg.nsw.gov.au/publicat/serefort/SEACONT.HTM, [Access date: 1999, February 12].

- New South Wales Council on the Cost of Government (OCCG) (1997c) *Third Report*, Council on the Cost of Government, Sydney.

- New South Wales Council on the Cost of Government (OCCG) (1997d) *Fourth Report*, Council on the Cost of Government, Sydney.

- New South Wales Council on the Cost of Government (OCCG), 1998a, *Fifth Report*, Council on the Cost of Government, Sydney.

- New South Wales Council on the Cost of Government (OCCG), 1998b, *Fisheries: Service Efforts and Accomplishments Executive Briefing*, Council on the Cost of Government, On-line, available: http://www.occg.nsw.gov.au/exfish.htm, [Access date: 1998, February 27].

- Olson, O., J. Guthrie, & C. Humphrey (eds.) (1998) *Global Warning: Debating International Developments in New Public Financial Management*, Cappelen Akademisk Forlang, Oslo.

- Osborne, A. & T. Gaebler (1992) *Reinventing Government: How the Entrepreneur Spirit is Transforming the Public Sector*, Addison Wesley, Reading, MA.

- Parker, L. & J. Guthrie (1993) The Australian Public Sector in the 1990s: New Accountability Regimes in Motion, *Journal of International Accounting Auditing & Taxation*, Vol. 2, No. 1, 59-81.

- Painter, M. (1988) Public Management: Fad or Fallacy? *Australian Journal of Public Administration*, Vol. 47, No. 1, 1-3.

- Peters, G. (1988) *Comparing Public Bureaucracy*, The University of Alabama Press, Tuscaloosa.

- Peters, G. (1990) The Necessity and Difficulty of Comparison in Public Administration, *Asian Journal of Public Administration*, Vol. 12, No. 1, 3-28.

- Pierce, J. & N. Puthucheary, (1997) Using Performance Measures to Drive Change within the Public Sector, paper presented to *Performance Measures for Government Conference*, 12 March, Sydney, Online, available: http://www.treasury.nsw.gov.au/, [Access date: 1999, January 20].

- Public Services and Merit Protection Commission (PSMPC) (1997) *Beyond Beancounting: Effective Financial Management in the APS - 1998 and Beyond*, Commonwealth of Australia, Canberra.
- Rhodes, R. (1998) Different Roads to Unfamiliar Places: UK Experience in Comparative Perspective, *Australian Journal of Public Administration*, Vol. 57, No. 4, 19-31.
- Saint-Martin, D. (1998) The New Managerialism and the Policy Influence of Consultants in Government, *Governance: An International Journal of Policy & Administration*, Vol. 11, No. 3, 319-356.
- Scapens, R. (1990) Researching Management Accounting Practice: The Role of Case Study Methods, *British Accounting Review*, Vol. 2, 259-281.

  Trosa, S. (1997) The Era of Post-Managerialism, in Considine, M, & Painter, M. (eds.) (1997).
- United States General Accounting Office (1992) *Program Performance Measures: Federal Agency Collection and Use of Performance Data*, Report GAO/GGD-92-65,
- United States General Accounting Office, Washington.

  Van Wolferen, K. (1994) *The False Realities of a Politicized Society,* Mainichi-Shinbunsha, Tokyo (in Japanese).
- Walker, R. (1998) Service Efforts and Accomplishments: Law, Order & Public Safety, in Standing Committee on Law & Justice (1998), *Proceedings of the Conference on Crime Prevention Costs & Benefits*, Report No. 11, Parliament NSW.
- Wanna, J., C. O'Faircheallaigh, & P. Weller (1992) *Public Sector Management in Australia*, Macmillan, Sydney.
- Williams, B. (1998) Performance Measurement and the Search for Meaning, *Evaluation News and Comment,* Vol. 7, No. 2, 20-22.
- Zifcak, S. (1997) Managerialism, Accountability and Democracy: A Victorian Case Study, *Australian Journal of Public Administration*, Vol. 56, No. 3, 106-119.

CHAPTER 6

CENTRAL GOVERNMENTAL ACCOUNTING OF EGYPT AND THE NETHERLANDS: SIMILARITIES AND DIFFERENCES

Hassan A.G. Ouda

6.1. Introduction

No doubts that the nature and the structure of the accounting system in the governmental entities differ from one country to the other, whereas this depends on the regulations, the restrictions and the procedures which are applied in every country. As a result, it is difficult to find uniform GAAP that can be applied in different countries or to set standard procedures, which can serve all the countries in the same degree. Notwithstanding there are differences among the governmental accounting systems; these differences will be more apparent between the developed and developing countries.

This paper will give an overview of the central governmental accounting systems of Egypt and the Netherlands. Egypt and the Netherlands are using different governmental accounting systems, whereas Egypt is using the fund accounting system and the Netherlands is using the cameralistic accounting system. Moreover, the legal and the political system in both countries are different, and the Netherlands is one of the developed countries while Egypt is among the developing countries. In addition, the paper is structured as follows: In the first and second sections, a short overview of the central government accounting systems of both the Netherlands and Egypt is given. Herein, the following points are tackled: Legal framework for the central government accounting; accounting system of the central government; bases of accounting and measurement focus; and financial reporting and auditing. Thirdly, the aspects of similarities between the two central government accounting systems are discussed. Fourthly, the aspects of differences between both systems are discussed. Finally, the paper discusses the reasons underlying the similarities and differences among the government accounting systems.

6.2. Central Governmental Accounting of the Netherlands

6.2.1. LEGAL FRAMEWORK OF THE CENTRAL GOVERNMENT ACCOUNTING

The central government accounting regulation has been laid down in the Accounts Act of 1976 (Bac, 1998). This act has replaced the Accounts Act of 192 6. In the course of years the Accounts Act of 1976 has been adapted six times, the last adaptation was in July 10, 1995. According to the Dutch public system, the Minister of Finance is carrying the responsibility for the central government Accounts Act. Unlike the central government, the Minister of Internal Affairs carries the responsibility for the decentral government Accounts Act (by law).

A. Bac (ed.), International Comparative Issues in Government Accounting, 71-90.
© 2001 *Kluwer Academic Publishers. Printed in the Netherlands.*

The Accounts Act of 1976 (including the latest [sixth] adjustment of July 10, 1995) comprises the regulations of the central government budget. These regulations deal with different aspects of the budget such as budgetary year, whereas this coincides with the calendar year, and estimates, herein, the budgets include estimates of the commitments, expenditures and receipts. Moreover, the budget regulation comprises other aspects such as structure, compilation, timetables and the amendment of the budget. Also the Act of 1976 deals with the regulation concerning the financial and non-financial management of the central government. This includes management of the central government budget, herein, different Ministers are designated to manage different budgets. Moreover, the regulation of the management of cash and non-monetary assets, bookkeeping and auditing, and the recording of the commitments, expenditures and receipts are tackled in this Act.

In this Accounts Act, the supervisory function of the Minister of Finance was further elaborated, whereas the Minister of Finance exercises a supervisory function in respect of budget implementation (Accounts Act, section 35), this function includes making assessments in the light of general financial policy. Moreover, the Minister of Finance determines the information to be supplied to him for the purposes of the supervisory function and he exercises a supervisory function in respect of the structure of the financial records and the audit process involved in budget implementation. In addition, this Act tackles the regulation of the Court of Audit: whereas this includes the membership and internal procedures of the Court of Audit, and the role and the task of the Court of Audit within the central government. The Court of Audit is playing an essential role within the central government. In this respect, it is scrutinising the Ministers financial management and associated annual financial statements, and the financial records kept for the said management and statements.

The Accounts Act also deals with the regulation of the central government financial statements: these financial statements comprise the accounts of commitments, expenditures and receipts and the trial balance as at December 31 relating to these accounts, accompanied by explanatory notes. In addition, the Accounts Act comprises the regulation of Agencies. This includes the agency budget, accounting system, and financial statements. So the Netherlands has a legal framework for the central government accounting that comprises the regulations which are required for organizing, managing and controlling the budget process; determining the role and the task of the Ministers and the Ministries within the central government; and discharging the accountability for the resources which are entrusted to them.

6.2.2. ACCOUNTING SYSTEM OF THE CENTRAL GOVERNMENT

Dutch central government accounting system is organized and operated as a cameralistic accounting system. The cameralistic accounting system is a non-balancing method that is because it is a single-entry system. As a result, its internal control is not strong and its scope is limited. According to the cameralistic accounting system, the subject of the administration is the cash (het inkomen), under this system receipts are reported as being earned in the accounting period in which they are received in cash. Expenditures are deducted from receipts in the accounting period in which cash is disbursed in their payment. As a result, net income is the difference between revenue receipts and expenditures disbursements. Moreover, no adjustments are made for prepaid, unearned, and accrued items. In addition, no difference is made between current expenditures and capital expenditures. So the cameralistic accounting system gives a survey about a certain period in which the receipts and the expenditures have really occurred. And it only takes into account the changes in cash position and nor claims and debts nor stocks and changes in assets.

The cameralistic accounting system in the Dutch central government is developed from the single entry to double entry and from cash based-accounting system, which is applied in 1976 according to Accounts Act of 1976, to the cash-obligation based-accounting system. The latter was a result of introducing the obligation basis in the administration of the central government in 1987.

Furthermore, Dutch central government has attempted to use the accrual based-accounting system within the central government through the establishment of several agencies.

According to the Dutch government accounting system, the financial statements of the central government entities must be seen in connection with the budget, whereas the budget system/basis has fundamental influence on the establishment of the accounting system, which will be used to administrate the budget. These financial statements are budget execution (implementation) statements, which are based on a cameralistic accounting system. Moreover, the cameralistic accounting system is called budget bookkeeping. By the budget of the central government, the cash-obligation basis is used. As a consequence, the cameralistic accounting system is a cash- obligation based-accounting system. This is a two-fold system consisting of two elements as follows:
-   a commitments (encumbrances) accounting system (obligation basis);
-   an expenditures and receipts accounting system (cash basis).
The two elements should be kept with the budget registration (this includes: the multi-year estimates/available budget amounts of commitments, expenditures and receipts) in a close relationship to each other, in order to make it possible to provide information about available budget space concerning commitments and expenditures. Furthermore, the commitments and expenditure bookkeeping should be kept in close relation to each other in order to give insight in the existing commitments. The two elements of the cameralistic accounting system should be established and kept with a ledger account system. Requirements of the efficiency and the control determine the way of the establishment. There should be opened at least one ledger account c.q. subledger per budget section.

In the commitments bookkeeping system the following ledger accounts can be distinguished (see the regulations of departmental budget administration):
-   commitments account inside the budget framework, in which the commitments are chargeable to a budget section;
-   commitments account outside the budget framework, in which the commitments may be recorded in accounts outside the budget framework if the settlement takes place with another sector of the central government or with a third party.

Also in the expenditures and receipts bookkeeping system of a department (Ministry) the following ledger accounts can be distinguished:
- expenditures and receipts ledger account inside the budget framework (for the expenditures and receipts which are debited or credited on the budget section; there is a separate ledger account for every expenditures and receipts budget section);
- expenditures and receipts ledger accounts outside the budget framework (those are ledger accounts on which by exception expenditures and receipts are recorded. These should not be debited or credited on the budget, because they can be settled with third parties. These accounts are also called third parties accounts;
- financial accounts such as the accounts of cash money (liquide middelen) and current account with the central head bookkeeping (rijkshoofdboekhouding [RHB]) which is kept at the Ministry of finance;
- closing accounts with cash keepers, these are the accounts, which show the current-account-relation with independent administration of the services belonging to the department.

The accounting system of the central government is formed by the whole of the central head bookkeeping (RHB), which is kept at the Ministry of Finance, to which are attached the decentral receipts and expenditures bookkeeping which are kept at every department (Ministry). The department receipts and expenditures bookkeeping are connected to the central head bookkeeping (RHB) by current accounts, which are included in every bookkeeping and the central head bookkeeping (RHB).

In connection with the cameralistic accounting system a numbers of extra- accounts are kept. These are supportable accounts, which are kept in connection with and as complementary on the other parts from the cameralistic accounting. This means that the extra-accounts report on the financial assets and liabilities are not comprised in the cameralistic accounting system. Herein one can think about debtors, creditors, guarantees, stocks, rights, shares and advanced money (voorschotten). The extra-accounts are needed because the control of accounts is often stretched over a period larger than one budget year. While the concerned accounts inside the budget framework are closed per calendar year, the settlement of the items such as creditors, debtors, guarantee, etc. and the management of shares are stretched out over more years. Moreover, the operations in the extra-accounts are not recorded according to the double entry system.

In addition, if one part of a ministry is granted the status of agency, the budget and the financial statements are based on an accrual basis. The characteristics of the accounting system of the agency are largely coinciding with those of the commercial accounting system. As a consequence, the financial statements are consisting of the profit and loss account, and the balance sheet on which all assets (including physical assets) and liabilities (including accrual liabilities) of the agency are mentioned.

6.2.3. BASES OF ACCOUNTING AND MEASUREMENT FOCUS

The accounting bases determine the elements to be recognized in the financial statements. The measurement focus determines what is being measured. Different types of measurement focus include total-economic resources concept, total financial-resources concept, current financial resources concept and cash flow and cash balances concept. In the Netherlands the *cash-obligation basis* is used. This means that the central government accounting system is organized to measure the flow of *current financial resources*. It measures cash and obligations by recognizing transactions and events, which have occurred by year-end and are normally expected to result in a cash receipt and/or disbursement within a specific period after year-end. Furthermore, the total-economic resources and total financial resources can not be measured according to the accounting bases of the Dutch central government accounting system. Whereas the total economic resources can only be measured through the using of accrual accounting, and the total financial resources can only be measured by the use of modified accrual accounting.

6.2.4. FINANCIAL REPORTING AND AUDITING

One of the main objectives of the financial reporting for government accounting is demonstrating the accountability. Financial reporting should assist in fulfilling government's duty to be publicly accountable and should enable users to assess that accountability by providing the relevant information.

According to the Dutch Accounts Act, each Minister is accountable for the management of financial affairs and the use of financial resources entrusted to him. In other words, he is fully responsible for the budget, which he manages. This budget is connected with financial statements. These financial statements are important means by which each Minister demonstrates his accountability.
By submitting the following documents the accountability of the Ministers is discharged:
1. provisional accounts;
2. financial statements of a Ministry;
3. financial statements of central government;
4. state balance sheet.

1. Provisional accounts
   By March 1 of each year, the Minister of Finance submits to the State-General the provisional accounts for the preceding year. These accounts give a survey about the realized amounts of expenditures and receipts. Moreover, these accounts should be seen as a discharge of the rough accountability, and not to start discussion about the budget polices and results. So these accounts are nothing more and nothing less than a provisional summary of the actual expenditures and receipts.

2. Financial statements of a Ministry
   According to Accounts Act (section 65) the Ministers, each in respect of the budget which he manages, should draw up the following financial statements:
   - the accounts of the commitments, expenditures and receipts, accompanied by explanatory notes;
   - the trial balance as at December 31 relating to these accounts, accompanied by explanatory notes.
   These financial statements should give insight in the financial position of the Ministry concerned at the end of the fiscal year. Moreover, it should help in making evaluation of the budget policy and budget management, which are pursued during

the budget year. In order to fulfil the above mentioned objectives, the accounts of commitments, expenditures and receipts indicate for each budget sector, besides, the actual amount, also the original estimates and the various changes to the estimates made by Act of Parliament. The explanatory notes to the accounts provide for each budget section an explanation of the policy pursued. The trial balance of a Ministry comprises besides the monetary assets integrated in the cameralistic accounting system, also the financial assets and liabilities that are not included in the cameralistic accounting system. The above-mentioned accounts and trial balance before to be submitted to the Minister of Finance should be accompanied by an auditor's report.

3. Financial statements of central government
   After the Minister of Finance has received the financial statements from all Ministers, he draws up the financial statement of the central government as a whole. This is an aggregation of the financial statements of the Ministries and comprises the accounts of central government expenditures and receipts, accompanied, if necessary, by explanatory notes and the central government trial balance as at December 31 connected with these accounts. Further, the Minister of Finance forwards by May 15 of the year following the budgetary year to the Court of Audit the following documents:
   - the financial statements of the ministries with the related auditor's report;
   - the comments that the documents referred to may prompt hem to make;
   - the central government's financial statement.
   The Court of Audit draws up for each financial statement a report of the Audit it has conducted. In this connection, the Court of Audit examines whether commitments, expenditures and receipts have been made in accordance with budgetary legislation and other statutory provisions and whether in general the requirements of order and control have been met. Next, the Court of Audit draws up a statement of approval relating to the central government financial statement. After the Final Acts have been accepted by the Parliament, the accountability of the Ministers is discharged and the financial management of the budget implementation concerning the previous financial year is closed (Van Boven, 1995).

4. State balance sheet (Staatsbalans)
   Notwithstanding, the cameralistic accounting system and the accounting basis which are used by the Dutch central government do not enable to draw up the balance sheet, the State balance sheet is prepared by the central government. As from 1996, the preparation of the State balance sheet takes place according to European basis/system of national and regional accounts (ESR-95). The annual preparation of the State balance sheet has the purpose of giving insight into the composition and size of the net worth of the central government, the change in the net worth elements during the last year, and the causes of increasing and decreasing the net worth balance. This balance sheet is prepared at the end of the fiscal year using the trial balance of the central government, on which the financial assets and liabilities are mentioned, and using the statements of ministries regarding the goods under their control.

   The balance of the assets and liabilities represents the net worth. This figure does not represent the wealth of the State because there are several assets, which are financed by the central government budget such as tangible and intangible infrastructure assets, which are not included in the State balance sheet. Moreover, this balance sheet does not give a fair view of the financial position of the central government (van Boven, 1995).

6.3. Central Government Accounting of Egypt

6.3.1. THE LEGAL FRAMEWORK OF THE CENTRAL GOVERNMENT ACCOUNTING

Before 12-04-1981, there was no legal framework for the government accounting in Egypt. The government accounting was subjected to financial regulation of the budget and accounts. This regulation is a group of instructions and periodical books issued by the Ministry of Finance during different periods. This regulation was not formulated in a form of law and, of course, did not have the power of law. As a consequence, the accrued revenues that should be collected during the budgetary year are delayed and the earmarked appropriations for the governmental units are not precisely followed and most of the governmental units have expended more than their appropriations. This, in turn, has led to an increase of the budget deficit. Therefore, there was an imperative for enacting the Government Accounting Act NR. 27 of 1981. This Act aims at:
- setting the basic regulations of government accounting in central government units, local government units and public services bodies instead of using a huge number of instructions concerning the rules of expending, collecting and control;
- supporting the financial control on expenditures, whereas the Ministry of Finance is authorized and empowered to exercise a pre-expending and post-expending control on the operations of the government sector;
- providing the required information for the decision-making process in respect of economizing the expenditures, developing the resources through setting the regulation of follow-up the budget for the country and disclosing its results and reporting on the budget performance;
- making guidelines for the government accounts that result in uniformity of definitions and terminology and codification of accounts which leads to the use of computers;
- making a combination between the cash basis and the accrual basis that is applied on the investment budget according to the Act of establishment of the National Investment Bank.

The Government Accounting Act NR 27 of 1981 comprises three parts as follows:
- Part 1: is concerned with determining the objectives of the government accounting and where it should be applied. The objectives of government accounting according to the Act 27 of 1981 are:
  - fulfilling pre-expending financial control and an internal monitoring system regarding the financial means of the governmental units which are subjected to the Act 27 of 1981;
  - economizing the expenditures;
  - controlling the obligations of the governmental units and following-up the redemption of it;

- demonstrating the implementation results of the general budget of the country and finally;
- furnishing the required information for determining the financial positions and decision making.

Moreover, this part deals with the government accounts whereas these accounts are divided into budget accounts, assets and liabilities accounts. Also this part deals with the governmental units that are subjecting to the Government Accounting Act. These units are central government, local government and public services bodies.

- Part 2: this part regulates the rules of expending and collection of the estimated expenditures and revenues.
- Part 3: this part includes general rules. For instance, the accrued compensations and salaries of the civil servant can be added to the general treasury if the civil servant does not ask for them within five years from the accrued date.

6.3.2. ACCOUNTING SYSTEM OF THE CENTRAL GOVERNMENT

The accounting system of the governmental entities is considered to be the main instrument required to carry out the financial operations that are performed by these entities and for which the general budget is prepared in the form of dedicated appropriations associated with the governmental expenditures and revenues of the country. The government accounting system of Egypt means, according to the Government Accounting Act NR 27 of 1981, a group of regulations and restrictions that governmental entities have to follow in the implementation of the general budget for the country and in recording and classifying the financial operations which are carried out by those entities. Further on, it includes the rules of pre-expending financial control and the internal monitoring system, and demonstrates and analyses the results that are expressed by the financial positions and financial statements of the governmental entities in order to give fair view of them.

The government accounting system of Egypt is uniform for the whole governmental sector (includes central and local government). This system is organized and operated on a fund basis. This means that the fund accounting system is used in governmental entities. A fund is defined as an independent fiscal and accounting entity with a self-balancing set of accounts recording cash/or other resources together with all related liabilities, obligations, revenues, and equities which are segregated for purpose of carrying on specific activity or attaining certain objectives in accordance with special regulations, restrictions, and limitations (NCGA, 1968). This means that the concept of allotted funds is consistent with appropriations of the governmental entities (Saraya, 1998). The appropriations, that are allotted in the general budget for purpose of carrying on specific activity or attaining certain objectives, are earmarked funds to expend on those objectives and activities within the limits of regulations, restrictions and Acts which are applied in Egypt. Then the fund is a synonymous for appropriation. In some countries the appropriations are divided into categories: general fund, special revenues fund, working capital fund, special assessment fund, bond fund, trust and agency fund.

In Egypt, the appropriations are divided into two categories:
1. fundamental appropriations: these are the appropriations that are adopted according to the Budget Act and their value is estimated in the beginning of the financial year;

2. additional appropriations: these are the appropriations that should be added to the fundamental appropriations in order to encounter contingent circumstances after adopting of the budget. These appropriations are further segregated into *supplementary appropriations* to cover any deficit in any item in the general budget and *exceptionally appropriations* that should be approved by the People's Council to encounter specific circumstances.

According to the Act 27 of 1981, the government accounts are categorized into four categories (Government Accounts Guideline):
1. budget accounts: these comprise the accounts of expenditures and resources according to the budget classification. Whereas the budget is divided into current budget and capital budget, further, the capital budget is divided into investment budget and capital transfer budget;
2. assets accounts: these include the accounts of fixed and current assets and the balances of current deficit;
3. liabilities accounts: this represents the obligations of the governmental entities for third parties and among each other;
4. intermediate accounts: these are the accounts that are used for control purposes and they should be cancelled as soon as their purpose is fulfilled.

The ingredients of the government accounting system of Egypt are:
1. control agency of government accounts;
2. documents of government accounting;
3. books and records of government accounting;
4. periodical reporting and financial reporting.
The first three elements can further be explained as follows:

1. Control agency of government accounts
   The Ministry of Finance is responsible for controlling the government accounts in all government entities included in the general budget: Ministries, local units, public bodies, and financing funds. This control is performed through appointment of a group of its officials by the government entities. The officials exercise the supervisory function on the accounting units of the governmental entities; control the implementation of the budget and audit its expenditures and revenues accounts and submit the financial statements to the Ministry of Finance.

2. Documents of government accounting
   Government accounting system of Egypt relies on a group of documents that have to be used by all government entities that are subjected to the general budget Act, whatever activities are performed by these entities. These documents are considered to be enough to furnish an objective evidence for recording the financial operations in the framework of line item budget (traditional budget). These documents are used to record in accounting books and records; they are an important source of information and they undertake a control role on the operations of the governmental entities. These documents are categorized into:
   - documents of original entry by which the financial operations can directly be recorded in journals and ledger accounts;

- supplementary documents which are enclosed in the documents of original entry in order to enhance the operations of those documents.

These documents are divided, according to the nature of government operations, into expenditure documents and revenues documents, store documents, and others.

3. Books and records of government accounting

The government accounting system of Egypt requires that all governmental entities included in the general budget should use a unified group of books and records of accounting, controlling and statistics. Further, it is not allowed for these entities to use new books of accounts, to make adjustments for these books, to open new forms or to use the forms for purposes other than predetermined. These books and records of government accounting are segregated into three parts as follows:
- part 1: journal books;
- part 2: ledger books;
- part 3: statistical and controlling books.

The first two parts represent the fundamental accounting books that, in turn, represent the main structure of the government accounting system. The journal and ledger books are used according to the double entry system. Part three: comprises a group of statistical and controlling books which are used to furnish the required data that can not be provided by the accounting books. These books do not use the double entry system.

The aforementioned three parts will be tackled as follows:
- part 1: journals books: these books include a group of books which are used to record the financial operations of the governmental entities based on the double entry system. These books are:
  - general journal book for expending forms (NR 244);
  - general journal book for reconciliation;
  - cash book.
- part 2: ledger books: these comprises:
  - budget accounts: these are separated into ledger book of expenditures item and ledger book of revenues items;
  - general current accounts: such as, book of cash account, book of cheques, book of bond, book of remittance and others;
  - current accounts under reconciliation: these comprise the ledger books of debt current accounts under reconciliation and of credit current accounts under reconciliation;
  - regular accounts: government accounting uses some of regular accounts to furnish additional accounting information about the contingent rights and obligations. For example, accrued accounts for the government (debt) and account of prepaid amounts (debt);
  - others.
- part 3: statistical and controlling books:
  The government entities use statistical records besides the accounting books to follow-up some certain aspects that are not available in the accounting records. Furthermore, the main reason behind the use of these books is to compensate the

lack, which emerges as a consequence of using the cash basis as an alternative of the accrual accounting. These books are:
- encumbrances records;
- records of rent contracts of places and land;
- records of contractors contracts;
- records of accrued debt of the government;
- statement of daily trail balance. This statement represents the daily trial balance of financial operations of governmental entities and it is divided into two sides: credit and debt. The debt side should equal the credit side at the end of the day.

6.3.3. THE ACCOUNTING BASES AND MEASUREMENT FOCUS

By virtue of the Government Accounting Act NR 27 of 1981, the cash basis is applied on the current budget with respect of expenditures and revenues and the accrual basis is applied on the investment budget. The application of the accrual basis on the investment budget means that the operations associated with the capital projects should be recorded on basis of what is actually achieved as soon as this achievement is fulfilled whether it was accompanied by the payments or not. On the other hand, the government expenditure on purchases of fixed assets is treated as a current expenditure (they are considered as assets to be consumed in the current fiscal year). Moreover, the cost of such assets is not depreciated or allocated as an expense over their useful live.

Furthermore, the cash basis is not applied on all items of the current budget, especially; the items that have given rise to obligations to a third party such as salaries and contracts of contractors. Whereas the accrued obligations are charged on the current budget year, despite the fact that they will be paid out in the following year. This means that the current budget year is debited by the accrued obligations, which credit a trusts account at the end of the year. In the following year, these obligations will be paid out of the trusts account. Apart from what is above mentioned the government accounting system of Egypt and its periodical-and financial reporting is organized to measure the *monetary position of the government*. This means that the measurement focus according to the aforementioned is on the cash balances and changes therein.

6.3.4. FINANCIAL REPORTING AND AUDITING

The financial statements are considered as an output of the accounting system of the governmental entities. These statements have a certain form and content which are determined by law. This depends heavily on the regulations and restrictions of each country. Further, these statements should be submitted to the different parties. In Egypt, these parties are the Ministry of Finance, Central Accounting Agency, and People's Council (Ahmed & Kamal, 1999). The main objective of the financial statements is to determine the compliance with the budget regarding the appropriations and revenues, which are adopted, and to indicate whether these appropriations and revenues were obtained and utilized in accordance with legal and contractual requirements. According to the articles No. 53, 56 and 57 of the Executive Manual of the Government Accounting Act No. 27 of 1981, all governmental entities are required to submit the following financial statements to the Ministry of Finance:

1. approximate monthly follow-up reports of revenues and expenditures;
2. monthly reports of revenues and expenditures, as well as the balances of financial accounts;
3. quarterly reports of revenues and expenditures, as well as the balances of financial accounts;
4. the end-of-year final account.

These financial statements will be dealt with as follows:

1. Approximate monthly follow-up report of revenues and expenditures
   This report should be submitted on the fourth day of the following month and it comprises the value of revenues and expenditures that are recorded in the accounting books until the last day of the month.

2. Monthly report of revenues and expenditures
   Since the approximate monthly follow-up report is quickly prepared in order to enable the Ministry of Finance to get a rough view of the financial positions of the governmental entities at appropriate time, it is prepared before closing the accounts. Further, this report does not include the balances of financial accounts.

   As a consequence, the monthly report is prepared to show the actual financial position of the governmental entities, moreover, it encompasses the opening and closing balances of the treasury (fund) and the balances of the credit and debt accounts. Furthermore, attached with this report is a statement that shows the still existing amounts of credit and debt current accounts which exceed one thousand pound and which are included in the credit current accounts under reconciliation and debt current accounts under reconciliation. The governmental entities forward this report to the Ministry of Finance in the tenth day of the following month.

3. Quarterly reports of revenues and expenditures
   This report should be presented every three months and it comprises the expenditures, revenues and the balances of the financial accounts of this period. In addition to that, it includes the expenditures, revenues and the balances of the financial accounts of the preceding three-quarters. Further, it should be forwarded to the Ministry of Finance on the tenth day of the following month. As for the last quarter report that will be sent according to the time, which is fixed by the Ministry of Finance this usually is two months after the end of the financial year.

4. The end-of-year final account
   This final account is prepared after the end of the financial year in order to show the actual expenditures and revenues and the surplus or deficit if it exists. The actual expenditures and revenues are compared with the adopted expenditures and revenues in the budget in order to demonstrate to what extent the government entities have complied with spending mandates and the financing of activities. In addition, the final account encompasses the obligations of the country to third parties and its rights by third parties at the end of the financial year. The final account is prepared in the light of the periodical book that is issued by the Ministry of Finance. On the other hand, copies of all the aforementioned financial statements should be sent to the Central Agency for Accountancy (CAA). The Central Agency for Accountancy is an

independent auditing body that reports directly to the People's Council, it carries out the continuous and final audits of the records, accounts, and financial statements of all governmental entities and enterprises owned by the government. Adopting the financial statements by the People's Council results in the accountability of the Minister of Finance and other governmental entities being discharged.

6.4. Aspects of Similarity between the two Central Government Accounting Systems

It is obvious from the overview that there are some aspects of similarity between the central government accounting systems of Egypt and the Netherlands.
These similarities are:
1. Both central government accounting systems have a legal framework
   This contains the regulations, restrictions and limitations which are considered as an imperative to attain an effective control on the expending of appropriations and collection of revenues; to strengthen the internal monitoring system; to avoid the expenditures which have no real justification; to follow-up the budget implementation and disclose its results and reports on its performance. Since the main objective of the government accounting system is to demonstrate the accountability, it will be difficult to demonstrate this accountability in the absence of the legal framework that sets forth the ingredients and the limits of that accountability. For instance, the government accounting of Egypt had no legal framework until the beginning of 1981, and this has resulted in serious distortions and extravagance. Obviously this has led to an increase in the budget deficit and the delay of the development plans and the privatisation program. Worthwhile, the Netherlands has the precedence in setting a legal framework for the central government accounting in comparison with Egypt. Whereas the first Government Accounts Act for the Netherlands was in 1927.

2. Both systems are using the line item budget (traditional budget)
   The traditional government budget is an aggregation of line items or inputs such as rent, maintenance, salaries, expenses, and the like. So this budget system stresses inputs rather than outputs, it provides data on what government consumes instead of data about what government does or about purposes for which money is spent. Moreover, the appropriation for each input such as salaries, rent, etc. does not indicate the relationship between expenditures and results and this prohibits the formulation and execution of economically meaningful budgetary policy (Ouda, 1997). The only use of the traditional budget without moving to or making a combination with other budget methods such as program-performance budgeting is considered as a main obstacle in developing the two government accounting systems.

   The Netherlands has attempted to apply performance budgeting in central government in accordance with the Budget Act 1976. This Act contains the regulations according to which performance budgeting should be applied wherever this is possible and useful. But this attempt has failed. The main reasons behind this failure were (Bac, 1994):

- shortage of personnel;
- lack of interest for the instrument in the services and in official and political top-management;
- lack of an analysis of the information needed;
- insufficient stimulating and co-ordinating by the steering group.

However, we see that the substantial reason underlying the failure of the application of the performance budget in the central government was the adoption of the cash basis instead of the accrual basis, whereas the nature and the requirements of the performance budget is consisted with the implication and concept of the accrual basis.

In Egypt, according to Budget Act No. 53 of 1973, the government entities are required to set their activities in the form of programs. This means that these entities should prepare program budgets for their activities, this in addition to the current and capital budget. This was an initial step to switch from the traditional budget to the program-performance budget. However, up till now this attempt did not assist in switching to program-performance budgeting.

3. The cash basis is considered as an overriding accounting basis by the two government accounting systems
   The use of cash basis by both systems is the result of the fact that the traditional budget is used by the two systems. The nature and the requirements of the traditional budget are consistent with the implication and concept of cash basis. Furthermore, the use of the cash basis has led to serious distortions and the miss of important information.

4. Both systems are using the double entry system
   As pointed out earlier, the cameralist accounting system which is used by the central government of the Netherlands is a single entry system. But this system is developed from single entry to double entry. On the other hand, the fund accounting system, which is used by central government accounting of Egypt, is originally a double entry system.

5. Both systems are segregating the government accounts into two categories
   These are budget accounts and others than the budget accounts. In the Netherlands the budget accounts encompass the estimates of commitments, expenditures and receipts. The other accounts are called Extra-accounts; this includes the accounts of debtors, creditors, shares, guarantee, advanced money, and stocks. On the other hand, in Egypt, the budget accounts includes the estimates of expenditures and revenues. The other accounts comprise the assets accounts, liabilities accounts, and intermediate accounts.

6. Fixed assets are not capitalized by the two systems, hence, depreciation is not recognized
   This is a natural consequence of using the cash basis by both systems. Whereas there is no difference made between the capital expenditures and current expenditures and all expenditures are considered as costs of a given year.

6.5. Aspects of Differences between the two Systems

In addition to the aforementioned similarities there are some aspects of differences between the two systems as follows:

1. Both systems are using different accounting systems

   The cameralistic accounting system is used by the central government of the Netherlands (see section 6.2.2). This system is not divided into separate funds and the accounting system is considered as a whole. Further, a program called in Dutch 'Operatie Comptabel Bestel' supplemented this system. This program has assisted in improving the cameralistic accounting system. But in principle, this system is primitive; it is subjected to constant changes. This system has three variants:
   a. old cameralistic: Herein, only the real made receipts and expenditures are recorded;
   b. the new cameralistic: As well the real made receipts and expenditures as the anticipated and deferred entries are registered;
   c. the improved cameralistic: This is the new cameralistic system supplemented with the accrual accounting (Volmer, 1992). The Dutch central Government is using the second variant. Moreover, this system has a limited scope and its internal control is not strong. Inherent to the system, it is not possible to prepare a balance sheet because the system does not support it.

   The fund accounting system is used by the central government of Egypt. This system is divided into different funds, each fund is considered as a separate accounting entity, a complete self-balancing group of accounts should be established and maintained for each fund. This group should include all general ledger accounts and subsidiary records necessary to reflect compliance with legal provisions and to set forth the financial position and results of financial operations of the fund. In Egypt, the classification of the appropriation is departed from, within a certain limit, what other countries for instance USA and UK adopt. Whereas the appropriation is divided into two categories: Fundamental appropriation and supplemented appropriation. Moreover, the fund accounting system provides, in comparison with the cameralistic accounting system, detail information and its control system is strong.

2. Both systems are using different accounting bases

   In the Netherlands, the cash-obligation basis is used by the central government accounting system. We see that the contents and implication of this system have almost the same contents and implication of modified cash basis. While the cash basis recognizes the transactions and events only when cash has been received or paid (IFAC, 1991), the obligation basis records transaction when goods and services are ordered and thus represents obligations incurred by government. On the other hand, the modified cash basis measures the cash and obligations by recognizing transactions and events which have occurred by year-end and are normally expected to result in a cash receipts and/or disbursement within specific period after year-end (IFAC, 1993). So it can be concluded that the cash-obligation basis is a synonymous for the modified cash basis. Hence, the modified cash basis is applied by the central government accounting system of the Netherlands with the exception of the agencies, which are using accrual accounting.

In Egypt, the budget is divided into a current budget and a capital budget. The cash basis is applied on the current budget and on capital transfer budget, while the accrual basis is applied on the investment budget. Unlike, the Netherlands, the part of a Ministry, which is granted the status of agency, its budget and financial statements are based on the cash basis.

3. Different measurement focus

The central government accounting of the Netherlands is organized to measure the *flow of current financial resources and changes therein*. This means that this system is organized to furnish information about cash flow during the period, those obligations that must be met within a short period from reporting date and current cash balances and receivables available to meet these obligations.

Unlike, the central government accounting of Egypt is organized to measure the *monetary position of the government*. In other words, it measures cash flows and balances (changes therein). This means that this provides information on cash receipts, cash disbursements and cash balances. Furthermore, it furnishes information on what is actually achieved from the capital projects as a consequence of the application of accrual accounting on the investment budget.

4. Different control and auditing system

In Egypt, the Ministry of Finance is the main body that is responsible for the internal control system on the government entities. Its officials who are appointed at all the government entities perform the internal control. The officials are authorized to control the financial operations associated with the budget implementation process of these entities. In addition, there are other bodies participating in the control and auditing process. These are:
- Central Agency of Accountancy: this is responsible for the external auditing;
- Central Agency for Organization and Management: this is responsible for determining the governmental entities needs of human resources. This affects the appropriation of wages. This means that it is controlling the appropriation of wages by the government entities;
- Control Agency of Administration: this agency aims at pursuing the fraud and stealing of the public money, hence, it is participating in financial control on the public money;
- Ministry of planning: this Ministry prepares the development plan for the country, it performs the control task on this plan, whereas it follows-up the carrying out of the capital projects in accordance with appropriated costs and determined timetable.

Notwithstanding, the budget implementation process is controlled and scrutinized by many people, who act as 'multiple checks', the control and auditing process is neither efficient nor effective.

Unlike Egypt, in the Netherlands each Ministry has its internal control system. This is addressed to daily and operational procedures concerning the financial management. It also aims at avoiding the mistakes and irregularity (Kraak, 1997).

In addition, there is an internal Audit Department (DAD); this is given the task of auditing the financial management and the financial statements thereon. The Audit Department should prepare an auditor's report about the budget implementation process of the Ministry concerned. Moreover, the Court of Audit is an external auditing agency. However, the Netherlands has less control and auditing bodies than Egypt, but it does not mean that the control and auditing process of Egypt is more efficient and effective than that of the Netherlands.

5. Different financial reporting
   There are many differences between the two countries regarding the financial reporting. These differences are concerned with the contents of the financial reporting; numbers of statements and the reporting date. The financial statements are only submitted at the end of the financial year to the Dutch Ministry of Finance. The statements comprise:
   - provisional accounts;
   - financial statements of a Ministry;
   - financial statements of central government;
   - state balance sheet.

Unlike, in Egypt, some financial statements should be submitted monthly and quarterly to the Ministry of Finance. In addition, the final account should be submitted at the end of the fiscal year. These statements encompass:
   - approximate monthly follow-up reports of revenues and expenditures;
   - monthly reports of revenues and expenditures, as well as the balances of financial accounts;
   - quarterly reports of revenues and expenditures, as well as the balances of financial accounts;
   - the end-of-year final account.

6.6. The Reasons underlying the Similarities and Differences among the Government Accounting Systems

Since the environment of the government accounting has been influenced by different factors, there is no standard or uniform government accounting system that can be used by all countries. On the other hand, there are some countries, which use the same government accounting system; for instance, Germany, the Netherlands and Austria use the cameralistic accounting system. But the contents and ingredients of this system are somewhat different in these countries. Also there are some countries that use different government accounting system; for instance Egypt uses the fund accounting system and the Netherlands uses the cameralistic accounting system, notwithstanding, there are some aspects of similarities. So the differences and similarities can be found whether the same or different government accounting systems have been used. Further, the degree of similarity and difference is variable. This depends on different factors. Herein, we pose the following question:
Why might government accounting systems be similar or differ among the countries?

We see that the following reasons or factors underlie the aspects of the similarities and differences among the government accounting systems:

1. political system;
2. legal system;
3. degree of the development, culture and consciousness of the people;
4. qualification of the staff that is required to develop and implement the government accounting system;
5. the language influence;
6. the colonialism influence.

These factors can be explained *in short* as follows:
1. Political system
   The nature of the political system whether it is democratic or dictatorial has a substantial influence on the development of the government accounting systems, hence, on the similarities and differences of these systems. Moreover, the formation of the political system whether this is a coalition or not can affect the government accounting systems. However, how can the government affect the government accounting? So if the government does not like to report bad news, it will change the rules used to measure and report financial information.

   For instance, one government would like to measure the monetary position of the country, while others would like to measure the flow of current resources, total financial resources or economic resources. This relies heavily on to what extent the government would like to disclose the truth, whether it is positive or negative, for its people's and to be responsible for its actions.

2. Legal system
   The degree of the flexibility of the legal system affects the government accounting systems, hence, their similarities and differences. So if a certain government wants to develop or to make some changes of the government accounting system, these changes can not be made without legal supporting. If the legal system is inflexible, this will result in delaying or not making these changes. On contrary, if the legal system is flexible changes are possible. Then, the flexibility and inflexibility of the legal system affect the similarities and differences among government accounting systems.

3. Degree of the development, culture and consciousness of the people
   Whenever the people are developed and have a high degree of their consciousness, they will be able to elect their real representatives and to hold them accountable for the resources entrusted to them. On the other hand, the representative will take into consideration that their people have reached a degree of consciousness that enables them to measure or evaluate the performance of the government. Therefore, the government should choose the appropriate rules used to measure and report the financial information that are consistent with the degree of the culture and consciousness of their people.

4. Qualification of the staff that is required to develop and implement the government accounting systems
   The lack of qualified accountants is critical for government accounting changes. This also assists in making the differences and the similarities of the government

accounting between the developed and developing countries. Whereas it has been noticed from the experience of different countries that the personnel with qualified knowledge in government accounting are scarce (Ouda, 1999). Especially developing countries face a serious shortage of qualified trained accounting personnel. That explains why most of the developing countries are still using the cash basis and traditional budget in their government accounting systems. Therefore, most of the government accounting systems of the developing countries are in somewhat similar.

5. The language influence

It has been noticed that most of the Anglo-Saxon countries are using the fund accounting system in their government sector. On the other hand, most of Roman-Germanic countries such as Germany, the Netherlands, Austria, etc. are using the cameralistic accounting system. This means that the language can affect the aspects of the similarity and difference of the government accounting systems among the countries.

6. Colonialism influence

The colonialism influence can add one more reason for why a certain country uses a fund accounting system or a cameralistic accounting system. Most of the colonialism countries have imposed their accounting system on the occupied countries. For example, Egypt was a colony of England; therefore, the Egyptian government accounting system has been based on the British fund accounting system.

References

- Ahmed, A. Kamal, A. (1999) *Government and National Accounting,* Cairo University Press, Cairo.
- Bac, A. (1993) *Government Accountancy in the Netherlands,* De Accountant NO. 3/ November.
- Bac, A. (1998) *Accounting for European Union in the Netherlands,* 4Th Biennial CIGAR Workshop 10-11-1998, Birmingham.
- Bac, A. (1994) *Performance Measurement in the Dutch National, Provincial and Local Government,* Pual Haupt Publishers, Berne, Stuttgart, Vienna.
- Bestebreur, T. Kraak, A. (1997) *Modern Financiële Management bij het Rijk, De Rijksbegroting Belicht.*
- van Boven, P. (1995) *De Rijksoverheid, Externe Verslaggeving in de theorie en de praktijk,* onder de redactie van Hoogendoorn.
- Dutch Government Accounts Act: Including the latest adjustment of July 10, 1995 (Stb. 1995, 375).
- Egyptian Government Accounting Act NO 27 (1981) Public Body of Press, Cairo.
- Government Accounting Auditing and Financial Reporting: National Committee on -
- Government Accounting U.S. (1968).
- IFAC (1991) Financial Reporting by National Governments: Issued by the International federation of Accountants.
- IFAC (1993) Elements of the financial statements of the National Governments: Issued by the International federation of Accountants.
- Noval, Z. (1989) *Government Accounting in Theory and Practice,* Ain Shams, Cairo.
- Ouda, H. (1997) *Comparative Government Accounting Study: Egypt and the Netherlands,* Master Thesis: Erasmus University Rotterdam.
- Ouda, H. (1999) Benefits and Costs of the Application of Accrual Accounting in the Public Sector, Non-published Paper.
- Regeling Departementale Begrotingsadministratie (1993) Ministerie van Financiën.
- Saraya, K. (1998) *Government and National Accounting,* Alexzandria, Alexzandria University.
- Volmer, F. (1992) *Enige Beschouwingen met Betrekking tot de Gemeenterekening.*

CHAPTER 7

ACCOUNTING AND DEMOCRATIC GOVERNANCE: A COMPARATIVE STUDY OF ONE NORWEGIAN AND ONE RUSSIAN COUNTY

Anatoli Bourmistrov and Frode Mellemvik

7.1. Introduction

Accounting is a social construction which can be found in all types of organizations, e.g. private and public. It cannot be isolated from its context, e.g. the social processes operating in and around organizations (Mellemvik et al., 1988; Hoopwood, 1983). In this sense, accounting is context influenced and vice versa (see e.g. Grønhaug et al., 1997; Garrod & McLeay, 1996). Through the process of interaction with its context accounting becomes institutionalized (Bergevärn, 1995).

Local governments are public institutions which operate in a specific context, i.e. institutions which combine reflection and action as basis for legitimation (Brunsson, 1985 and 1989). From one side, these institutions are supposed to be democratically governed, i.e. the expression of political ideas and decisions and talk about future actions are important for the electorate. From another side, these organizations are responsible for production of public services to the local population. These two sides are supposed to be closely interlinked - actions are reflected in accounts and ideas are reflected in budgets.

Accounting is meant to connect dimensions of the past and the future (Mellemvik & Olsen, 1996). Interpretations and explanations of past experiences are said to be given by accounts (Meyer, 1986). Accounts are in this way important because they (March and Olsen, 1995; p. 46) ' ... make actions imaginable and consequences interpretable by ... [defining] the meaning of history, the options available, and the possibilities for action. Accounts are used both to control events and to provide reassurance that events are controllable'. Accounting can also help to fill the gap between the worlds of decisions and actions (Høgheim et al., 1989; Olsen, 1997). Thus, accounting is not only important as an instrument of formal registration of the past, but as an instrument which allows learning to be introduced into financial management processes.

Politicians are seen to be major users of municipal accounting information (Brunsson & Jönsson, 1979; Olson, 1983). Accounting is meant to function as a tool for politicians in their decision-making and for other governance purposes. The rise of the 'new' public management and 'new' public financial management reforms could be, for instance, understood, as a respond to the fact that municipal accounting techniques had became so complicated that politicians could not understand the accounts (Olson et al., 1998). Politicians in general do not have and are not meant to have accounting competence, i.e.

91

A. Bac (ed.), International Comparative Issues in Government Accounting, 91-122.
© 2001 *Kluwer Academic Publishers. Printed in the Netherlands.*

especially not detailed knowledge about accounting techniques. Rather they have competence in governance.

The relation between municipal accounting and governance has therefore been characterized by tensions, e.g. accounting is supposed to be used for the political governance but is too complicated to be useful for politicians. The recent development of 'new' public management may even be regarded as a way of trying to overcome these tensions. The problem is, however, that the solutions found in 'new' public management mostly are copies of business companies, i.e. organizations that are not meant to be democratically governed. If accounting should contribute to democratic governance, it is important that politicians could easily understand the accounts, and that the accounting information reflects what is relevant for the politicians.

There has not been much accounting research in the area of exploring nature of these tensions between democratic governance and accounting. That is why, in this paper we discuss the interrelationships between accounting and democratic governance in two local governments, one in Norway (Nordland county) and one in Russia (Lenigrad county).

In order to discuss the interrelationship between accounting and democratic governance we have structured our paper in the following way. Firstly, we will discuss how to understand accounting and democratic governance from different perspectives. Secondly, we will describe method and methodology of our study. The formal political and accounting systems of Nordland county and Leningrad county will be described in the third part of the paper. The paper ends with a discussion and analysis of interrelationships and tensions between accounting and democratic governance.

7.2.   Frame of Reference

In this frame of reference we will discuss the concepts accounting and democratic governance as well as interrelationships between these concepts based on different theoretical approaches found in the contemporary research literature.

7.2.1. ACCOUNTING

Accounting can generally be characterized as having several important features, and could be studied from several perspectives. Because we focus on accounting and democratic governance we firstly will emphasize that accounting is about relations, i.e. it reflects relations between the principal and the agent. Accounting is about giving accounts for some actions to someone. The intended function of accounting is to be a language which facilitates the reduction of uncertainty in a principal-agent relation in order to improve accountability, stewardship, control and decision making (Mellemvik et al., 1988). In this sense, accounting reflects relationships between different parties with different interests, i.e. according to Ijiri (1975) these parties could be described as the principal (*accountor*), agent (*accountee*) and accountant.

A second element of accounting that is important when studying accounting and democratic governance is that accounting is a language which is meant to allow communication between the parties involved, e.g. between politicians and administration. Accounting has its own means of communication, e.g. verbally through texts. Accounting textbooks underline that accounting is a language. As to any other language, accounting can be given some general characteristics. Any language is a system of written symbols, like several conceptual words, quantities and numbers associated with economic transactions, which might be arranged in a pattern matter through the rules of grammar and used for the purpose of communication (Hawes, 1972). Through the rules of the accounting 'grammar' the accounting 'sentences' are formed, e.g. numbers and texts are combined. Through such a process the text receives its qualitative features. The intended reader (the principal) of the text constructed by the accountor is meant to receive information about the past actions of the accountee. The accounting language is, however, constructed on an analytical view of the world (Mellemvik et al., 1988). There is no uncertainty in the 'grammatical' technology, e.g. double-entry record keeping clearly based on certain causal effects of the single transaction (Ijiri, 1975). In this sense, the accounting language is built on a logic of consequentiality. Levitt & March (1988) showed that this kind of logic is applied when behavior can be described as driven by preferences of actions and expectations of their consequences. Intentions and the calculations of different choices are major characteristics of this logic.

Though the grammar of accounting is solid and consequentiality oriented, the text of the accounting report - as all kind of texts - is given for interpretation. To guide interpretations of accounting texts rules of accounting presentation are formalized, i.e. norms and standards are created to guarantee the quality of the text. However, these norms and standards reflect different traditions, i.e. the accounting language is characterized by different dialects, accents and pronunciations. It is for sure not harmonized between nations or organizations. Moreover, different users of an accounting report might even interpret the same report in different ways (e.g. Macintosh, 1985; Mellemvik, 1997).

Such consideration leads us to a third element of accounting that is important when studying accounting and democratic governance, i.e. accounting is a social construction and cannot be isolated from its context. In this sense, accounting is context influenced and through the process of interaction with its context accounting became institutionalized. At the societal level such institutionalization processes can be described as interaction between accounting practices and accounting norms and standards (Nobes, 1991; Hopwood and Page, 1987; Watts and Zimmerman, 1979). Institutionalization might proceed through different mechanisms, e.g. through coercive, mimetic and normative processes (DiMaggio and Powel, 1983) and through hierarchical and ideological learning (Bergevärn et al., 1995).

7.2.2. DEMOCRATIC GOVERNANCE

Democratic governance is a complex concept combining two other complex concepts - democracy and governance. Democracy has a direct meaning of a form of government in which the people rule, i.e. it originates from Greek *demokratia* where *demos* represents people and *kratos* - rules. However, there exists a great variety of different models both in theory and in practice of what is democracy (Held, 1987). The contemporary understanding of democracy is associated with the existence of at least the following features:

1. government legitimacy is based on a claim of doing what people want;
2. political representatives are elected regularly from a number of several alternative candidates;
3. all adult population can participate in secret elections, and
4. freedom of speech, press and assembly exists (e.g. Powell, 1982).

Through the elections, different democratic bodies or political institutions (with high or low autonomy) are formed with the intended function of making decisions for related constituencies. These bodies can be formed at different governmental levels which interact in different ways, e.g. counties and municipalities. In this way democracy is linked to representation and structure between representatives and bodies.

Another important aspect of democracy is about continuous interaction between individuals, organizations and ideologies where sometimes conflicting aims are pursued, e.g. interests of majority and minority groups are conflicting. In this interaction, information represents an important factor for setting up ways of handling conflicts (Brunsson & Jönsson, 1979). In this way democracy is about processes which require information openness.

Governance can be identified as a synonym to the word government, i.e. a process or activity of governing (Finer, 1970). There exist, however, other understandings of the phenomena (Rhodes, 1997), e.g. corporate governance (where governance is about giving *overall directions*), the new public management (where governance is seen as *steering*), self-organizing networks (where governance is defined in relation to *management of networks*). What is common, however, to all such views is that the governance generally is about to take care of interests of many, about the future and a model of handling decisions.

The concepts of democracy and governance are combined when one talks about democratic governance. The governance part of the phenomena stands for models of finding solutions or a way of handling problems (e.g. reforms, decisions) in the future in the interest of many. The democracy part stands for representation, a structure of the representative bodies in the society, information openness and participation, e.g. the decisions should be made openly in the interests of many by elected representatives.

Democratic governance is, thus, built much on a logic of appropriateness, i.e. the logic which involves consideration of future actions' legitimacy and matching procedures to the situation (Levitt & March, 1988). March and Olsen (1995; 1989) point out that this logic is reflected in existing rules, identities and roles, which define what is acceptable, right, appropriate and desirable in the society. Thus, the future action might be determined by a conception of necessity and appropriateness in connection to existing rules.

7.2.3. ACCOUNTING AND DEMOCRATIC GOVERNANCE

Evidently, there are many tensions between accounting and democratic governance. For instance, accounting is about the recognition of clear principal-agent relations (e.g.

shareholders-manager). Democratic governance, however, emphasizes several principal-agent relations between different kind of principals, e.g. electorate-politicians and, in its turn, politicians-administration. The question is then what principal accounting focuses on in organizations characterized by democratic governance?

Accounting technology is certain and based on a logic of consequentiality. On the contrary, democratic governance is based on a logic of appropriateness. The question is then how a language based on a logic of consequentiality is applied in context of actions and behavior based on a logic of appropriateness?

Accounting often implies that some authorized norms have to be applied. The question is then who determines norms and rules for the accounting language that have to be used by democratically governed institutions?

Such questions indicate the complexity of issues involved into the discussion of tensions between democratic governance and accounting. In the following section we will present how we have approached the study of relations between democratic governance and accounting.

7.3. Research Methodology

In order to explore the stated purpose of the paper, i.e. to discuss the interrelationships between accounting and democratic governance, we used frame of reference to construct, structure and analyze our empirical descriptions. The research purpose of the paper is exploratory with focus on interpretation and understanding.

7.3.1. RESEARCH SETTING

Two counties, one in Russia (Leningrad *oblast'*) and one in Norway (Nordland *fylke*) and their political/administrative and accounting systems were used as our research setting. There are at least two different reasons for this choice. First of all, we as one Russian and one Norwegian researchers know these counties very well. There are similarities and differences between these counties which give an opportunity to study interrelation between accounting and democratic governance in two different contexts. Norway has a relatively long history of representative democracy (since 1834). On the contrary, representative democracy in Western understanding in Russia is a relatively new phenomena which was introduced in 1990 after the 70 years of totalitarian Communist Party leadership. Counties in both countries have different functions in the governmental hierarchy. Public sector accounting is also expected to develop differently in these two countries.

Secondly, this paper is a part of a bigger project. According to policy of Norwegian Ministry of Foreign Affairs, one of the important elements of the activity program for Eastern Europe is assistance in the development of democracy. Representatives of Nordland county have initiated a project which intended to give assistance to its sister county in Russia. The main idea of the project is to transfer theoretical and practical competence which Norwegians have within fields of democratic governance and financial management. This study, at its beginning stage, was seen as a preliminary work towards identifying relevant areas for the cooperation.

7.3.2. DATA

In order to explore the state research purpose of the study, we collected, analyzed and presented data on democratic governance and accounting system in two counties. Some data was easily accessible and openly published, for example, norms on local governmental accounting. To obtain some, however, it was necessary to work in achives and to use personal networks, e.g. personal characteristics of politicians. We have also conducted several interviews (e.g. face-to-face and telephone) especially in order to verify that our understandings and interpretation of information were correct.

Based on a theoretical frame of reference we have operationalized and, consequently, collected data on concepts of democratic governance and accounting system in the way shown in table 7.1. For each county, we presented general characteristics like size, population, number of municipalities. After that, each county's political and accounting systems have been given characteristics, presented in the table.

Representation highlights the questions of how elections are made and who is elected into local governmental bodies, i.e. descriptions of system of elections as well as charac-teristics of politicians, like sex, age, occupational background. Autonomy concerns the organization and its independence of other organizations. For local governments autono-my is associated with self-government and the degree of independence from the state. The interconnection between functions and tasks of the county, its municipalities and the state was an important dimension to describe. Through descriptions of the formal politi-cal and administrative structure, we could picture how the political and administrative institutions are organized and how these institutions are interrelated. Finally, we tried to present and analyze information on how often politicians are gathered into assemblies and meetings, how many cases are and nature of cases discussed.

Characteristics of **Democratic Governance**	Characteristics of **Accounting**
- *Representation* (e.g. election system, characteristics of politicians)	- *Relations* (e.g. for whom the accounting reports are prepared)
- *Autonomy and structure* (e.g. functions of local government, interrelation with state and municipalities, number of political/administrative institutions within local government)	- *Language and communication* (e.g. the frequency of report's presentation, contents of annual reports, technical accounting system)
- *Information* (e.g. number of council meetings, number of cases discussed, nature of cases and decisions)	- *Institutionalization* (e.g. ways in development of new systems, practices and norms)

Table 7.1.:   Characteristics of Democratic Governance and Accounting

When characterizing accounting in a local government, we have focused on descriptions of the following characteristics: relations, communication, and institutionalization. Relations deal with who is *accountor* and who is *accountee* in the local government. Communication and language characteristics included frequency of reports presentation, the qualitative characteristic of reports as well as some descriptions of the accounting technical system. We, however, mainly analyzed annual reports in the following qualitative dimensions: number of statements included, nature and type of statements, content of statements, means of information presentation (verbal/graphic). We have also been interested in general characteristics of accounting system, e.g. how economic transactions are generally recorded and summarized. Finally, we also discussed the institutionalization of accounting by referring to development in local governmental accounting norms and practices and their interactions.

7.4.   The Case of Leningrad County (*Oblast'*), Russia

Leningrad county is situated around the City of St. Petersburg in North-West Russia. The size of the total territory is 85.900 km^2 which is populated by 1,7 millions of inhabitants. County's administrative-territorial division comprised 17 regions and 6 cities of county's subordination. However, since the beginning of local governmental reform and approval of the Municipal Code in 1995, 29 municipalities[1] were established in 1996 according to the preferences of the local population. The size, population and financial potential of such municipalities vary, however, much more considerably than before the process of transition started.

In a new Federal structure, the county is one of 89 rightful subjects of the Russian Federation. Its rights, functions and obligations are regulated by the Russian Constitution (1993), Federal Treaty[2] (1993) and Statute of Leningrad county (1997). The legal and functional relations as well as division of responsibilities between county and its municipalities are determined by the Statute of Leningrad county and Statutes of each of the municipality.

7.4.1.   FUNCTIONS OF COUNTY GOVERNMENT

These laws define what kind of responsibilities, or what we also refer to as functions, governmental authorities should have at different governmental levels, i.e. the state, subjects of the Federation (e.g. counties) and municipalities. From the texts of these documents, the county should perform several functions. First of all, the county government is seen as an agent of the state power in the Russian Federation, e.g. it has to provide correspondence of all locally issued norms and laws to the Constitution and Federal Laws. It is also supposed to participate in the development and realization of some Federal programs. Secondly, government in the county plays the role of *guarantist*, e.g. on behave of the state power the county should protect human rights and freedom of the citizens on the county territory; guarantee the acceptable level of living for citizens introduced by the Federal standards. Thirdly, a county has some functions which emphasize its autonomy, e.g. the right to approve county's own laws, to develop and utilize county's natural resources, to make international economic contacts.

To perform such functions, on the county's territory, '... both state government and local self-government are executed' (The Statute of Leningrad County, 1997; Article 3, p. 2).

---

[1]   In Russia they are called municipal formations (*municipal'nie obrazovaniya*).
[2]   The Federal Treaty is a special agreement between authorities of all subjects of the Russian Federation and the Federal authorities.

The state power is executed by the population through, first of all, the forms of direct democracy (i.e. referendums and democratic elections), secondly, through the functioning of the representative councils and the administration, and finally, through the courts. Local self-government is guaranteed through formation of municipalities in rural and urban regions, where issues of local importance in jurisdiction of local authorities are considered.

Thus, the duality of governance in Leningrad county is a major characteristic where both state governance and local self-governance are emphasized. These two forms of governance are interactive. From one side, self-governance assumes the local autonomy for county and municipalities by handling local issues in their jurisdiction. County and municipalities are having authority only over the issues of local importance and tasks which are given to them by the state. From the other side, county government acts also as an agent of the Federal authorities when e.g. implementing Federal programs.

There are many different activities that a county usually is responsible for, e.g. financing of professional schools, large hospitals, public transportation, majority of fire departments (Wallich, 1993). However, through the system of fund transfers, county government might influence the level of public services produced in a particular municipality.

7.4.2. REPRESENTATION

Through the process of free democratic elections deputies of the representative council as well as the governor of the county are elected for the period of four years. The elections in the Russian Federation are basically conducted based on both majoritarian and proportional election systems. At the national level, for example, the proportional election party-system is used when elections of 225 deputies of 500 into the State *Duma* are conducted. In this case, the number of representatives for each party in the *Duma* is determined on the basis of votes each party received. Another 50% is elected according to the majoritarian system (Lukin, 1997).

At the level of subjects of the Russian Federation, the laws of a particular subject should specify what kinds of election system are chosen, e.g. majoritarian or proportional. In Leningrad county, the majoritarian system is used. Applied to the elections into the county representative council, 50 electoral districts are determined in the county. Several candidates are proposed in each district but only one would be elected as a representative from that district. The right to propose a candidate is given directly to the electorate, i.e. the candidate can be proposed by the people from the place of work (enterprise, organization), study (university) or living (see e.g. Kutaphin & Fadeev, 1997).

There are more than 70 different officially registered parties in the Russian Federation (Lukin, 1997). However, at the county and municipal levels it is not obligatory to be a member of one or another party to be elected into the representative council. Moreover, if some politicians are members of one or another party, this fact is not stated in any of the records kept. We have analyzed characteristics of politicians, elected into the county's representative council in 1997. These characteristics are occupational background, sex and average age.

Figure 7.1. shows the occupational background. As one can observe, the majority of deputies are represented by managers of private enterprises (38%), for example, directors of different limited companies and partnerships. Some of them are partially owned by the county. Top and middle level managers of public organizations, like state enterprises, heads of public organizations, even leaders of trade unions, represent 22% of all deputies. Professionals, like doctors, teachers, economists, military officers represent 20%. The same percentage of representative is represented by non-professionals (e.g. deputies which currently are not having any other occupation than deputy).

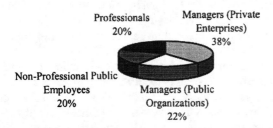

Figure 7.1.:   Occupational Background for Politicians in Representative Council of Leningrad County

The number of deputies with higher education among members of the representative council is very high, i.e. 96% of all deputies are having at least one higher education. The list of the deputies shows that male deputies are extremely dominating, i.e. there is only one women out of 50 deputies. The average age of members of the representative council is 50 years.

7.4.3. POLITICAL/ADMINISTRATIVE STRUCTURE OF LENINGRAD COUNTY GOVERNMENT

The political/administrative system of Leningrad county is represented by elected and appointed representatives working in several governmental bodies. There are three major elements of the political/administrative structure: the representative (legislative) council (*zakonodatel'noe sobranie*), governor of Leningrad county (*gubernator*) and the administration (*administratsia*). The structure of county authorities and interrelationships between them are shown in the Figure 7.2.

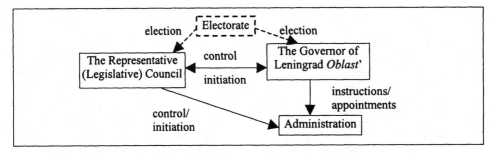

Figure 7.2.:   The Structure of the Government of Leningrad County

The representative council of Leningrad county is comprised of 50 representatives which are elected from all electoral regions of the county. The number of representatives has changed in 1997 from being 25. The structure of the representative council consists of eleven permanent committees and other structural elements, which are shown in Appendix 7.1. The work of the representative council is led by the Chairman of the representative council who is elected for four years. He introduces the structural committees of the council and govern their activities.

The governor has the highest position in the Leningrad county government. He is also chief administrative officer of the administration. He has the right of introduction of new county laws. His obligations are different, e.g. to represent Leningrad county inside and outside of its region, to govern the work of administration, to introduce by his own decisions the top positions in the administration, to be fully responsible for the functioning of the administration. He controls the obedience of the Statute of Leningrad county and of human rights and freedom of citizens. Thus, he and the administration play mostly guarantist and agent roles. The governor in Leningrad county can be seen as a 'managing director' of the public institution called 'Leningrad county'.

There are several functions which are prescribed to the representative council e.g. making local legislation, the right to take legislative initiative in the *Duma* of the Russian Federation, determination and control of the use of the resources and ownership, approval of budget and execution of control over the budget implementation. Such functions underline the autonomy of the representative council. The representative council, thus, has a function of post-action control of the 'managing director', i.e. the governor.

The major function of the representative (legislative) council, however, is to approve different kinds of laws. The representative council is working in sessions (meetings) where politicians discuss different cases which are usually approved as county laws. Not all cases discussed, however, result in approval of laws (*zakoni*), e.g. some laws can be returned for further handling and processing. Any law might be discussed in three trials and finally approved or dismissed. Any decision of the council other than law can be regarded as enactment (*postanovlenie*). Some cases are just of informative nature, i.e. more oriented towards presentation of information than a case for decision. For example, during the year 1998, there were organized 17 meetings of the representative council. 441 cases were discussed and resulted in approval of 68 laws and 300 enactments. In addition, 2 laws were dismissed, 35 were in the process of discussion and 3 were returned for further preparation and handling.

In summary, the governor has a relatively high degree of power mostly in all fields. The governor manages the financial resources of the Leningrad county. His function can be summarized as law initiation in the representative council, appointments and issuing instructions for the administration. His decisions and actions are regulated and controlled by the representative council. The decisions of the representative council, which are approved in the form of laws, are obligatory for implementation. The actions of administration are also accountable to the representative council. Thus, the representative council has mostly a control function and a function of initiation for the administration. By approving laws and decisions, the representative council makes a kind of 'frame' for the work of the administration and the governor.

7.4.4. ACCOUNTING SYSTEM OF LENINGRAD *OBLAST*

Accounting Norms
Norms for Russian local governmental accounting, in accordance with the old Soviet tradition, are still very detailed regulated and control oriented (see e.g. Bourmistrov & Mellemvik, 1999), which was generally the case of countries with centrally planned economies (e.g. Chan, 1996; Jaruga & Nowak, 1995). In a centrally controlled norm system such regulations are often based on instructions and standards from the Federal Ministry of Finance. The major intention with strong central regulation is to make the processes of comparison and generalization of accounting information for the central authorities easier, i.e. to lower the cost of handling such information (see e.g. Ash & Strittmatter, 1992).

What do such instructions and standards regulate? The answer would be almost everything. Some norms are old (issued during the Soviet time and still in force), some relatively new. Norms regulate the bookkeeping procedures, charts of accounts, forms of all reports, timing of reports (monthly, quarterly and annually). The norms usually regulate in detail what should be regarded as a transaction, how it should be recorded and how this transaction should be handled in accounts.

Moreover, all reports and statements are printed in a standardized form and distributed among the departments of local government before the end of the year. The instructions of the Ministry of the Financed are issued each year which regulate accounting reporting (i.e. forms and structures of reported statements) for particularly this year.

It is compulsory for all organizations and especially accounting and financial departments to abide by the decisions and instructions, e.g. the chief bookkeeper has a personal responsibility for conformance of all norms.

Characteristics of Accounting System
The accounting system in the Leningrad county can be characterized as budget accounting, i.e. accounting is considered as a tool which is used to control and monitor the budget implementation. The bookkeeping system has both actual and memorial accounts for that purpose. In this system, the budgeted amounts and actuals are continually compared to each other. The main objective of accounting is, thus, to control that payments made are not higher than appropriated and all revenues are collected as planned.

The accounting system mainly operates with cash receipts and payments (i.e. on the cash bases). The major purpose of the county government is to collect and disburse cash. Accruals are not recorded at the level of county, rather in the balance sheets of particular organizations financed from the county budget. When consolidated, the value in the end of the year for main balance sheet items are summed and reported in the special statement 'Note about fixed assets and materials of organizations financed from the budget'. In this sense, there is no comprehensive balance sheet.

Other accounting reports rather balance sheet are considered to be important by the Ministry of Finance for statistical and control purposes. Mainly two statements are prepared and communicated by the financial department of Leningrad county consequently monthly, quarterly and annually. These reports are
1. balance of budget implementation (*balans ispolnenia budgeta*), and
2. statement of budget implementation (*otchet ob ispolnenii budgeta*).
The balance of budget implementation is a kind of balancing statement where opening balance of cash, year's revenues and expenditures as well as cash closing balance are presented. The statement of budget implementation is actually the statement of income and expenditures, where those are listed in details, according to the items of budget classification. Both county's own accounting reports (*sobstvenno-oblastnoy otchet*) and consolidated reports including both county and all municipalities are prepared by the financial department of Leningrad county.

Accounts Reporting at the End of the Year to the Representative Council
Each month and quarter the mentioned above accounting reports are presented to the county's chamber of auditors for auditors' consideration (12 times/year!). However, as one official said in an interview, these reports are given to the representative council *only when it is found necessary by members of the representative council*! There are two exceptions from this rule, however. The first one concerns the accounts reporting at the end of the year. The second one is in case when the budget should be adjusted during the year. In the second case, the accounting report is prepared to the permanent budget committee. It shows what has been actually received in income and what kind of expenditures have occurred since the beginning of the year and the proportions of these amounts compared to initially budgeted.

We have mainly analyzed these documents which are presented at the end of the year to the council. Last year accounts are approved in form of law. Mainly five documents are prepared for consideration by the members of the representative council (totally placed on 60-80 pages). These are:
1. the proposal for the law about the accounting report of budget execution;
2. explanatory notes to the accounting report of budget execution;
3. statement of the budget implementation (only statement of income and expenditures are included; the balance of budget implementation *is not*);
4. conclusions of the legislative committee, and finally
5. the enactment of the administration concerning the results of the budget implementation.

The proposal for the law about the accounting report of budget execution is a draft of the law which should be approved. This document states only total amounts of income and expenditures, and excess of income over expenditures (or deficit).

Explanatory notes to the accounting report of budget execution give short explanation of why particularly this situation within income and expenditures has occurred during the year. This report is filled with different kinds of information, especially tables. The document gives characteristics to the budget implementation in static perspective (when the actuals are compared to the budget) and in dynamic perspective (when the increase (decrease) in income and expenditures are considered in comparison to the subsequent year). The explanations are given why there is a difference between planned and actual performance.

This document is very close in its context to the enactment of the administration concerning the results of the budget implementation. The enactment shortly summarizes the explanatory note and signed by representatives of the administration and the governor.

The conclusion of the legislative committee is prepared to secure that the prepared law is not violating the current national and local legislation.

The proposal, explanatory notes and conclusions of the legislative committee are kind of juridical texts, while the statement of income and expenditures is of a financial nature.

The structure of the statement of budget implementation (statement of income and expenditures) is shown in Appendix 7.2. In this statement, the Russian concepts income (*dohodi*) and expenditures (*rashodi*) are used. However, these income items are cash-inflow and expenditures are cash-outflows. The structure of the statement is mainly in conformity with norms (e.g. the norm on the budget classification). The major elements are total income, total expenditure, excess of income over expenditures (or deficit, in opposite case) and specification of how the deficit is financed. In the statement, expenditures are classified according to the functional budget classification[3] (i.e. functions performed by the governmental entities). However, in notes to the statement, some expenditures are given according to the economic budget classification, i.e. according to economic consideration, especially for operational and capital purposes (e.g. purchase of goods and payments for services, interest payments, capital investments, subsidies). Some balance sheet items are also given, e.g. receivables and creditors.

The statement presents information about the planned amount according to budget or adjusted budget, actuals to the end of the year and the variation between planed and actual amount for each item.

The annual report is presented personally by the governor who also writes introductory comments on the budget execution.

7.5. The Case of Nordland County (*Fylke*), Norway

Nordland county (*fylke*) is situated in Northern Norway. It is one of 18 Norwegian counties. The size of the total territory is 38.327 km^2 with approximately 240.000 inhabitants. There are 45 municipalities in an administrative-territorial division of the county.

---

[3] The Federal Law 'On Budget Classification of The Russian Federation', N115-f3, approved 15.09.1996.

7.5.1. FUNCTIONS OF COUNTY GOVERNMENTS

Counties in Norway could be regarded as large municipalities, i.e. there is one common law regulating the activities of both municipalities and counties. The main difference, however, is that in counties the public services should be produced on the large territory, covering several municipalities. Usually, the county's authority has responsibility for public services which can be run more effectively at the county level due to e.g. economy of scale effect (Fevolden et al., 1994). The counties operate, thus, at a regional level which is differentiated from the local level of municipalities. The main activities of counties are connected to regional high schools, hospitals, transportation, communication and culture (Mellemvik & Pettersen, 1998).

There is a clear and relatively stable division of responsibilities between the state, counties and municipalities in Norway. However, the formal state-county structure describes a principal and agent relation, i.e. the state is the principal and the counties are regarded as its agents. Counties have to perform public services in the ways which are defined by the centrally issued laws and regulations. There are many kinds of regulations, e.g. norms and standards, supporting and guiding documents, as well as claims on different kinds of evaluations. These laws, rules, norms and instructions are used by the state to regulate counties' activities, even though the last Local Governmental Act of 1993 as all former Norwegian local governmental acts officially have guaranteed local government independence.. In this sense, the state delegates responsibilities to the counties and monitor how these services or functions can be performed.

The state can also regulate and influence the activities of counties through transfers of central funds. It is argued that it is done mainly to provide equal opportunities for citizens of all counties. Counties, however, are more dependent on central fund transfer than municipalities (see e.g. Fevolden et al., 1994; Mellemvik & Monsen, 1993).

In addition, there is in each county a state representative, the district governor, who is a link between the central state and local governments. The district governor is appointed by the central government. The main function of the governor is to evaluate the legality of all decisions made by both county and local municipality councils. If a decision violates central laws, the governor will suspend that decision.

Recently, especially with association of the 'new' public management reform, the state regulation has shifted at least a little from regulation of processes to regulation of results. Mellemvik & Pettersen (1998) show however that Norway is hesitant in following the international trends associated with new public management.

7.5.2. REPRESENTATION

The county council representatives are elected for four years. A proportional election system is in use in Norway, i.e. the number of representatives from each party is determined on the basis of votes each party received during the elections. Nine parties are represented in Nordland county council, see Figure 7.3. The highest representation is hold by the Norwegian Labor Party (34%), the Center Party (17%) and the Conservative Party (15%).

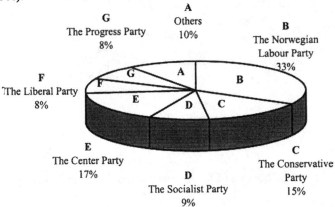

Figure 8.3.:   Party Representation in Nordland County Council

Figure 7.4. shows the occupational background of the politicians in Nordland county. The majority of politicians (47%) are professionals, e.g. doctors, teachers, drivers, nurses, etc. Politicians with a background of executive and middle managers of public and private enterprise represent 23%. Only a few politicians (11%) are self-employed, like farmers and entrepreneurs. 50% of all deputies are woman. The average age of the deputies is 50 years.

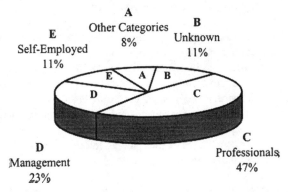

Figure 7.4.:   Occupational Background for Politicians in Nordland County Council

7.5.3. POLITICAL/ADMINISTRATIVE STRUCTURE OF NORDLAND COUNTY

The political/administrative system in Nordland county is build up by several bodies. The structure of the county's authorities and interrelationships between them are shown in Figure 7.5. The main bodies are Nordland county council (*fylkestinget*), the Nordland executive board (*fylkesutvalget*) and administration (*administrasjon*).

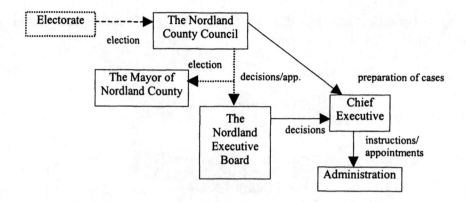

Figure 7.5.:   The Structure of the Government of Nordland County

Nordland county council consists of 53 members who are elected politicians. The council has the highest authority and makes decisions and approvals on behalf of the county. Council politicians are working on sessions and plenum sittings where decisions are taken and political issues are discussed.

The politicians in Nordland county are also working in 6 permanent committees, an infrastructure committee, a health and environmental committee, an industry and business committee, an education and competence committee, a culture and adolescence committee, a protocol and control committee. The main task of these committees is to prepare cases for political discussions and decision-making.

The Nordland executive board consists of 13 members elected by the county council. Parties represented in the county council are also represented in the board. The main function of the board is according to the Municipal Act of 1993 to prepare proposals for long-term economic plans, the year budget and taxation policies. However, it is the county council that might determine the area of the board's functioning. The executive board of Nordland county is responsible for day-to-day affairs of the county. Meetings of the board are usually held every 14th day. The cases discussed vary greatly, e.g. health, education, commerce. However, cases which need more comprehensive political discussions have to be discussed and decided in the council.

The political leadership of the county is represented by the county's mayor. He is elected by the council's members on the first council meeting. The mayor's major function is to lead the meetings of both the council and the board. At the same time, the mayor officially represents the county and is empowered to sign documents concerning the county's affairs. The major can also be empowered by the county council to make decisions which are not of the matter of great importance[4].

The administration of Nordland county is led by a chief executive, and he and his administration are responsible for preparing issues for political decision-making. The

---

[4]   See e.g. Lov om Kommuner og Fylkeskommuner, Ch. 2, §9, art. 5.

chief executive has to be appointed by the county council. He is the top leader of the county's administration. The chief executive can be empowered by the county council to make decisions in cases of an administrative nature.

The main task of the administration is to secure that all cases which are discussed by the elected political organs are cleared up and that their approvals and decisions are implemented. The work of the administration is organized in 6 departments, education, culture and recreation, transportation and communication, health, trade and commerce and dental service.

The major functions of the county council is to make decisions. While the executive board is responsible for day-to-day affairs, the main tasks of politicians in the county council are to develop policies and long-term strategies. The council is working in meetings where politicians discuss different cases which are usually prepared by the administration, committees or executive board.

During 1998 the county council had 5 meetings were 129 cases were discussed. The type of cases discussed varies much. 43% of all cases presented to and discussed by the council are informative in their nature, e.g. orientation about public services situation and new central laws. 30% of all cases can be characterized as planning activities, e.g. discussion of budget, strategic and operational plans and programs for different sectors. 24% of the cases were some kind of evaluations of past actions, e.g. the accounting report of the past year and evaluation of implemented programs, and decisions made by the executive board and the administration. The remaining cases (3%) concerned elections and appointments to governmental bodies and organizations.

7.5.4. ACCOUNTING SYSTEM OF NORDLAND FYLKE

Accounting Norms
In Norway, municipal accounting is regulated by centrally issued laws. The Norwegian Parliament has delegated the responsibility to give detailed accounting norms to the Ministry of Local Governments and Regional development. All municipalities have to adapt to these accounting norms because they have the power of the law. This way of regulating local governmental accounting reflects the view of the state on municipalities as the state's agents. The state is monitoring the economies of all municipalities and counties.

Bergevärn et al. (1995) showed that local governmental accounting norms have emerged from the norms own history, rather than from local practices in counties and municipalities action systems. The latest issued norms of 1993 allow local governments some degree of freedom in choosing accounting system and accounting procedures as long as all transactions can be converted to the system required by the norms. However, the norms require four statements to be prepared by all local governments:
1. operating statement (*driftsregnskap*);
2. capital statement (*kapitalregnskap*);
3. fund statement (*bevilgningsregnskap*), and
4. balance sheet (*balanseregnskap*).

Though three of these statements have many similarities with statements that had to be prepared also according to former norms, these 'new' statements include more 'business-like' concepts as surplus, deficit, revenue, operating statement, fund statement. The fourth statement - the balance sheet - is a blue print of that statement prepared for an enterprise.

The technical bookkeeping system was not changed in 1993. A very much complicated bookkeeping system has still to be applied by Norwegian local governments. This system builds on a mixture of cash-based and accrual-based accounting.

Accounting Reports presented to the County Council
Accounting information is discussed by the council about each fourth month. The main accounting report is called 'Evaluation of Accounting and Results'. It is prepared as a feedback report from the chief executive to the county council on the utilization of the resources, implementation of activities and development in resource productivity in relation to the budget. The major purpose, stated in the document, is to give basis for decision-making in respect to next year's long-term plans and budgets by presenting an overview over the present economic situation and volume of service production.

This report is structured in two major parts:
1. an overview of the county's economy which gives total budgetary performance and changes in the budget, and
2. comments on performance in different sectors (administration and departments). This report consists of 147 pages totally.

The structure of the report is following:
1.1. Budget, adjusted budget, accounting and variance (for income and expenditures).
1.2. Adjustments in the budget summarized. Allocations to funds.
1.3. Budget implementation for each sector with tables, charts and short verbal analysis.
2.1. Operational statement (see appendix 7.3.1.). Besides the statement there are comments on revenue, expenditures, loan interests and repayments. Tables and charts are also applied.
2.2. Capital statement (see appendix 7.3.2.).
2.3. Balance sheet (see appendix 7.3.3.).
2.4. Evaluation of liquidity. Assessment of working capital and 'liquidity reserves'.
2.5. Fund Statement (see appendix 7.4.).
2.6. Summary including evaluation of total performance.

7.6. Analysis: Political and Accounting Systems Compared

The characteristics of the political and the accounting system in the two counties reveal many differences and similarities. In this section we would like to summarizes and analyze these differences and similarities.

7.6.1. DEMOCRATIC GOVERNANCE

When it concerns democratic governance, we can observe considerable differences in all characteristics we have studied, i.e. structure, nature of autonomy, representation and information demand (see table 7.2.). In the political/administrative system of Leningrad county, the governor plays an important role as a separate political institution which is not the case in Nordland county. The fact that the governor of a Russian county is directly elected by the electorate makes his positions in many cases independent of the council. The council, however, is supposed to limit, monitor and control actions of the governor and the governor's administration. In Nordland county, on a contrary, the council has a much stronger position than the major who is elected out of the council members. There is in fact no independent governor in Nordland county.

Characteristic	Leningrad *Oblast'*	Nordland County
Structure	The Strong Governor	The Strong Council
Representation	'Male Management Elite'	'Professional Advocates'
Autonomy of Local Government	'Responsible'	'Decentralized Liberalism'
Information demand	'Immunity oriented'	'Initiation oriented'

Table 7.2.:   Characteristics of Democratic Governance. Comparison between Nordland and Leningrad Counties

Characteristics of 'representation' are very different in these counties. The only similarity is average age. The politicians in both counties are middle aged people, about 50 years old in average. Their occupational and educational backgrounds represent different groups of the society. In Leningrad county male managers are dominating in the representative council. In Nordland county politicians are people mainly representing several kinds of professions. In Leningrad county, 50 politicians are supposed to represent an electorate of 1,7 millions, while in Nordland county 53 politicians represent a population of 0,24 millions. 'Representation' in Nordland county is, therefore, 7 times higher than in Leningrad county. In this sense, the electorate representation in Leningrad county forms an elite. In Nordland county the council politicians reflect more different interests and in this way could be characterized as advocates. These differences might be explained by the differences in the election system, e.g. in Russia people vote for the 'personality' of a particular politician while in Norway people elect parties and their representatives.

Autonomy or 'the search for autonomy' is an important characteristic of any local government (Goldsmith, 1994). Clark (1984) identifies three types of local governmental autonomy (high, medium and low) based on primary principles of self-government and local independence, i.e. the power of *initiation* and the power of *immunity*. Initiation is about the freedom of local government to define its own goals and tasks. The power of immunity is determined by constrains imposed on local government by the central government. Any local government can be characterized in these two dimensions. Particularly, by having both powers of immunity and initiation local governments have high autonomy. On the contrary, when a local government does not posses powers of immunity and initiation the autonomy is low and the local government can be characterized as 'Weberian bureaucracies' (Goldsmith, 1994).

These two counties, can be characterized having medium autonomy, i.e. the central government constrains work of local governments both in Russia and Norway. However, the reasons for the medium autonomy classification are different. In Leningrad county the local government (both council and governor) has little power of initiation, i.e. the county government is constrained by national and local laws in the choice of tasks it might perform. However, at the same time, the county government seems to be immune from the central government concerning how tasks devoted to the county are performed. Moreover, Leningrad county approves its own laws concerning implementation of tasks. According to Goldsmith (1994) such governments are called 'Representative and Responsible'. The Leningrad county government fits 'responsible' characterization, because it has to take care of many predetermined tasks and public services. However the representation in case of Leningrad county is mainly limited to the male management elite. In this sense, it is questionable whether the council could be characterized as a 'representative' one.

Nordland county, on contrary, seems to have substantial power of initiation, i.e. the Municipal Code gives much autonomy to the county in defining what tasks the county could take care of. The county could in fact do whatever it would like to do as long as it does not violate any national laws. The central authorities, however, constrain local governments in the ways of how services and activities that the local governments have to take care of, might be performed. Particularly, it is done by regulating local governmental activities through number of centrally issued laws and regulations. In this sense, Nordland county can be characterized in terms of 'decentralized liberalism' (Goldsmith, 1994), i.e. the strong Norwegian state has decentralized many tasks to the county and in this way allowed the county liberty and local autonomy. In Norway local autonomy has been important for local governments for more than 150 years. Already in 1836 when Norway was a part of the Swedish Kingdom, the Local Government Act declared that Norwegian local governments were independent of the Swedish king. The tensions between the central state and local governments did, however, survive the dissolution of the union with Sweden. Even the current Norwegian king addressed the importance of local government autonomy when he in 1995 criticized central government politicians for being too eager in focusing on state-wide issues in instead of local problems and local opportunities: 'Without doubt local government autonomy is an important part of our democracy. I will honor all those who through many years have devoted most of their time to local politics. Maybe the media before the [last] election could have focused to a larger degree on such people and their local problems. That may have helped to re-establish the dignity and honor of local government elections. Central politicians will have enough opportunities to present their primary aims and political ideologies' (H.R.H. King Harald's speech to Parliament, November 15, 1995).

We can expect that the freedom of defining its own tasks (initiation) and the degree of constraints imposed by the central government (immunity) will influence what kind of information local council demands for its functioning. In the case of Leningrad county, which mainly approves different kind of laws, information demand is 'immunity oriented', i.e. the local council discusses cases and makes decisions on future actions through approval of rules (norms, laws, standards) and, thus, making institutional constraints. In Russian local governments such decisions are even named and stated as 'laws' and not as decisions.

Contrary to that pattern, politicians in the council of Nordland county, constrained in power to defining ways of implementation, discuss cases and make decisions on future actions through approval of task-oriented programs, plans and strategies. In this sense, they demand information which is in it nature 'initiation oriented'. These decisions on local level are in Norway never referred to as laws because the law is a concept that is only applied by the national Parliament.

7.6.2. ACCOUNTING

Table 7.3. reports the main characteristics of accounting in these two counties. The main difference seems to be how the principal-agent relations are understood, the difference that reflects the political/administrative structure of the county. In Leningrad county this relation is more complicated than in Nordland county. 'The strong governor' of Leningrad county is a principal for the administration, but, at the same time, is an 'agent of people'. He is in some cases also an agent for the council, especially when he has to legitimate his and the administration's actions by presenting accounting reports and making explanations to the council. In this case, the principal-agent relation is blurred, i.e. it is difficult to say who is the principal and who is the agent without referring to a particular situation. Moreover, this blurred principal-agent relation can be understood as a kind of 'competition' between two principals (the council and the governor). For both of them it is important to show that they are responsible and powerful. In Nordland county it is a more pure and straightforward principal-agent relation where the council is the principal and the administration is the agent.

Characteristic	Leningrad County	Nordland County
Relations	(P)Council? (P) Governor? (A)Governor? (A)Administration?	(P) Council (A) Administration
Communication	Regularly and when requested	Regularly
Language	'Cash Flow' Oriented	'Results' Oriented
Technical System	Numbers Oriented Budget Accounting	Numbers Oriented Allowance Accounting
Institutionalization	Coercive Hierarchical Learning	Hierarchical Learning

Table 7.3.:   Characteristics of Accounting. Comparison between Nordland and Leningrad Counties

When we compare the formal for procedures of presentation of accounting information, they seem to be much the same in Leningrad and Nordland counties, i.e. accounting reports are presented before the councils regularly 2 - 3 times a year. However, in Leningrad county accounting information could also enter the council discussion more irregularly. Councils' politicians can request accounting information when they need it and, thus, question the legitimacy of 'the strong governor's' actions. In Nordland county, information to the principal (council) would be prepared and reported by the agent (the administration) only according to the formal procedures.

When we compare the accounting languages of the two counties, we find that different accounting concepts and accounting statements are used. The accounting language in Leningrad county is cash oriented. Even though the accounting statements are filled with concepts like income and expenditure, they report cash inflows and cash outflows. In Nordland county the accounting language is much more a mixture between cash and accrual accounting and the language also has many similarities with the enterprise accounting language. The language focuses on concepts that are close to 'results' of economic activities, e.g. operational surplus or deficit. All accounting statements could be interpreted according to 'enterprise-accounting', e.g. there is a balance-sheet that is a blueprint of the balance-sheet prepared by Norwegian enterprises. The fund flow statement is also much inspired by such statement in the private sector. However, the mixture of cash and accrual based accounting makes accounting information confusing (Mauland & Mellemvik, 1999).

The difference in languages used does not imply, however, difference in the technical accounting systems. In both counties, the budget accounting system is used, i.e. accounting is considered as a tool which is used to control and monitor the budget implementation by continually comparison of budget items and actuals. In Norway, the accounting report has changed name from 'budget accounting' to 'allowance accounting'. This change of name might reflect an influence from the private sector where budget are more closed and usually not reported together with the accounting statements. In spite of this change there have been no substantial change in the accounting techniques in Nordland county.

Finally, the national ministries have important influence on local governmental accounting in both countries. This influence of the state seems, however, to be stronger in Leningrad county, i.e. the county has to follow all norms of the Ministry of the Finance. The same is true for the Norwegian county, but the county could develop whatever accounting reports they wanted as a supplement.

7.7.   Summary and Conclusions

The purpose of this exploratory study was a discussion of the interrelationships between accounting and democratic governance in two local governments in two different countries. Based on our study, this discussion can be summarized in relation to three questions we have raised based on this study's frame of reference. These questions focus on three dimensions of tensions between accounting and democratic governance.

7.7.1.   PRINCIPAL RELATIONS INFLUENCE ACCOUNTING PROCEDURES AND THE DEMAND FOR INFORMATION

The first question was what principal accounting focuses on in organizations characterized by democratic governance? Accounting is meant to function in relations between principals and the agents. However, our study showed that several relations might exist involving different kinds of principals (and, thus, agents) reflecting on a common and at the same time complicated political and administrative structure. The political and administrative structure affects communication. When the principal-agent relation is straightforward (as in the Norwegian county) communication between bodies involved seems to be regular and frequency of reporting formalized as a standard operating procedure. However, in the case of 'blurred' principal-agent relations (e.g. two principals) communication becomes irregular. The confusing situation is that there are two principals. As in all democracies the elected politicians are only substitutes of the real principal (the electorate). When there are two or more principals there is an opening for competition for power and responsibility. This competition makes the frequency of reporting to be determined in other ways than through formalized operating procedure. The 'controlled' principal (e.g. governor) has always to be prepared to give accounts for his actions to the 'controlling' principal (e.g. the council), i.e. formal procedures are only needed for formalized accounting rule-oriented control. The political control of the representative principal is done continuously by another representative principal. Accounting communication, thus, becomes symbolic in both cases, i.e. in order to follow procedures, in the first case, and to challenge another principal, in the second.

We also found that principals in democratically governed institutions demand different kind of information depending on the institution's relations to other institutions which they are dependent on. Both local governments studied search for local autonomy, immunity and/or initiation. When the search is immunity oriented it is important to define borders (i.e. laws), making the local government less dependent on others. Agreement about future actions are then build into the a set of local rules. When the search is initiation oriented, local decisions, where agreement about future actions is compressed into new strategies and plans, are important.

7.7.2. THE ACCOUNTING LANGUAGE DOES NOT PORTRAY THE POLITI-CIANS

The second question was how a language based on a logic of consequentiality is applied in contexts of actions and behavior based on a logic of appropriateness? First of all, the understanding of representative democracy is different in these two counties. In Leningrad county, the local council is governed by directors of private and public enterprises. On the contrary, Nordland county council is populated by professionals. This difference might be explained by differences in democratic traditions. In Russia, democracy is quite a new phenomena which is associated with the changes in the Russian society at the end of the 1980s. The council, thus, is populated by representatives who reflect ideas and institutions that where more or less unacceptable in the communist regime, e.g. private enterprises. These representatives do therefore fit well into the picture that when democracy is developing, institutions that were regarded nearly as illegal now are regarded as builders of the society. In Norway, on the contrary, the representative democracy has a strong tradition which has been developed during decades. Professionals, reflecting different and conflicting interests might, thus, be regarded as important promoters of democracy.

Different accounting models are applied in these two counties. Surprisingly, we observe a kind of contradiction between the characteristics of political representation and the accounting language used. Directors in Leningrad county uses some kind of complicated household oriented accounting language, i.e. accounting reports are strongly cash orientated. Professionals in Nordland county have to use something that has similarities to enterprise accounting. Why will directors used to enterprise accounting reports apply complicated cash oriented accounting reports? And why will professionals who are not meant to be experts in accounting accept enterprise-alike accounting reports? We do not know much about politicians real use of accounting information. These seem, however, to be a mismatch implying that enterprise oriented politicians do accept cash oriented accounting, and that politicians with a background from public sector accept enterprise oriented accounting. Both these accounting models are however complicated, and maybe the case is that when these models are complicated it is difficult to argue against.

In Russia, local governments have gained higher autonomy than they had during the Soviet time. However, accounting systems for local governments are much the same as they were 20 years ago. On the contrary, local governments in Norway have for more than 150 years been more or less autonomous. Though local governmental accounting in Norway has not changed much each decade, it has changed in the 1990s. In this sense, we have two situation where, in the first case, the organization changes, but its accounting system does not. In the second, the organization does not change much, but its accounting develops. We concluded, thus, that accounting and organizational development might be independent of or at least not linked closely to each other. Contradictions observed between politicians' characteristics and accounting information in the two counties we studied, thus, can be understood as a part of such missing link between organizational and accounting changes.

7.7.3. ACCOUNTING NORMS DO NOT REFLECT DEMOCRACY

In understanding why contradiction exist between politicians' characteristics and accounting information, the third question is relevant. The question was who determines norms and rules for the accounting language that has to be used by democratically governed institutions? We observed strong state regulation of accounting in both counties. In Russia, this regulation is more detailed and still coercive, while local governments in Norway have some flexibility after fulfilling central rules and norms (e.g. through supplementary statements). The central rhetoric in both countries emphasizes local autonomy, but the state still regulates and often by coercive methods local governmental accounting. In this sense it is easy to conclude that accounting norms are in these two countries developed through other than democratic processes, i.e. accounting norms do not reflect democracy.

Such a situation might be given an understanding if we consider central-local relations. The position of the state is very strong in both these two countries. Through the continuos quest for autonomy, local governments create much uncertainty for the central state. In this situation, the central government needs stabilizers. Local governmental accounting could function as such a stabilizer, and in that way reduce uncertainty for the state. By using accounting for monitoring and controlling local government accounting becomes less important as an instrument to be used by local politicians for the purpose of local governance. Accounts are said to give interpretation and explanations of experiences, which make consequences interpretable and actions imaginable. The problem with local governmental accounting is that it should be interpretable both for the central and the local levels of governments. When it only can be meaningful for the central state there seem to be two available solutions at hand for the local level. Do not bother too much about accounting but let accounting symbolize that most things are under control, or introduce procedures which imply which that the actors involved have to presenting accounts continuously.

References

- Ash, E. and Strittmatter, R. (1992) *Accounting in the Soviet Union*, Praeger Publishers, New York.
- Bergevärn, L., Mellemvik, F. and Olsen, O. (1995) Institutionalization of Accounting A Comparative Study between Sweden and Norway, *Scandinavian Journal of Management*, 11(1): 25–41.
- Brunsson, N. and Jönsson, S. (1979) *Beslut och Handling - Om Politekerens Inflytande på Politiken*, Kontenta, Stockholm.
- Brunsson, N. (1985) *The Irrational Organization*, John Wiley & Sons.
- Brunsson, N. (1989) *The Organizational Hypocrisy - Talk, Decisionms and Actions in Organizations*, John Wiley & Sons.
- Bourmistrov, A. and Mellemvik, F. (1999) Russian Local Governmental Accounting: New Norms and New Problems, In *Research in Governmental and Non-Profit Accounting (forthcoming)*.
- Chan, J. (1996) Budget Accounting in China: Continuity and Change, In: J. Chan, R. Jones, K. Lüder (red.), *Research in Governmental and Non-Profit Accounting: Volume 9*, Jai Press, London.
- Clark, G. (1984) A Theory of Local Autonomy, *Annals of the Associations of American Geographers*, 74:195-208.
- DiMaggio, P. and Powell, W. (1983) The Iron Cage Revisited: Institutional Isomorphism and Collective Rationality in Organizational Fields, *American Sociological Review*.
- Fevolden, T., Hagen, T. and Sørensen, R. (1994) *Kommunal Organizering: Styring, Effektivitet og Demokrati*, TANO, Oslo.
- Finer, S. (1970) *Comparative Government*, The Penguin Press, London.
- Garrod, N. and McLeay, S. (1996) *Accounting in Transition. The Implications of Political and Economic Reform in Central Europe*, Routledge, London.
- Goldsmith, M. (1994) Changing Local Government Structures, Finance and Management, In E. Hansen (red.), *Challenges to Local Government in European Welfare Development*, AKF Publisher, Copenhagen.
- Grønhaug, K., Mellemvik, F. and Olson, O. (1997) Editorial: Accounting in a Scandinavian Research Context, *Scandinavian Journal of Management*, 13(1): 1–3.
- Hawes, L. (1972) *Pragmatics of Analoging*, Addison-Wesley, London.
- Held, D. (1987) *Models of Democracy*, Polity Press, Cambridge.
- Hopwood, A. (1983) On Trying to Study Accounting in the Context in which it Operates, *Accounting, Organizations and Society*, 287–305.
- Hopwood, A. and Page, M. (1987) The Future of Accounting Standards, *Accountancy*, 100(11):114-116.
- Høgheim, S., Monsen, N., Olsen, R. & Olson, O. (1989) The Two Worlds of Management Control, *Financial Accountability and Management*, 163-178.
- Ijiri, Y. (1975) *The Theory of Accounting Measurement*, American Accounting Association.
- Jaruga, A. and Novak W. (1995) Governmental Accounting in Transition: The Polish Experience, *Financial Accountability and Management*, 11(1):75-94.
- Kutaphin, O. and Fadeev, V. (1997) *Municipalnoe Pravo*, Urist, Moscow.

- Levitt, B. And March, G. (1988) Organizational Learning, *Annual Review of Sociology*, 14:319–340.
- Lukin, U. (1997) *Arkhangelskaya Oblast: Ekonomika i Politika na Poroge 21 Veka*, Pomor State University Publishing, Arkhangelsk.
- Macintosh, N. (1985) *Social Software of Accounting and Information Systems*, The Pitman Press.
- March, J. And Olsen, J. (1989) *Rediscovering Institutions: The Organizational Basis of Politics*, The Free Press, New York.
- March. J. and Olsen, J. (1995) *Democratic Governance*, The Free Press, New York.
- Mauland,H. and Mellemvik, F. (1999) Municipal Accounting in Norway. Central Norms Create Confusing Information at the Local Level, *Paper to be presented at the 7ᵗʰ CIGAR, Tilburg University, The Netherlands, June 24ᵗʰ-25ᵗʰ*.
- Mellemvik, F., Monsen, N. and Olson, O. (1988) Functions of Accounting - A Discussion, *Scandinavian Journal of Management*, 4(3/4):101-119.
- Mellemvik, F. and Monsen, N. (1993) 'Divergence, Exploration and Exploitation: Development of Annual Reports in Norwegian Local Governments'. *Working Paper 11*. Bergen: Norwegian School of Business Administration.
- Mellemvik, F. and Olson, O. (1996) *Regnskap i Forandring*, Cappelen Akademisk Forlag, Oslo.
- Mellemvik, F. and Pettersen, I. (1996) Norway – A Hesitant Reformer?, In O. Olson, J., Guthrie and C. Humphrey (red.), *Global Warning: Debating International Developments in New Public Financial Management*, Cappelen Akademisk Forlag, Oslo.
- Mellemvik, F. (1997) Accounting, The Hidden Collage? Accounting in the Dialogues between a City and Its Financial Institutions, *Scandinavian Journal of Management*, 13(2):191-207.
- Meyer, J. (1986) Social Environments and Organizational Accounting, *Accounting, Organizations and Society*, 11(4/5): 345-56.
- Nobes, C. (1991) Cycles in UK Standard Setting, *Accounting and Business Research*, 21(83): 265-274.
- Olson, O. (1983) *Ansvar och Ândamål - Om Utveckling och Användlingav ett Komunalt Ekonomisystem*, Studentlitteratur, Lund.
- Olson, O., Guthrie, J. And Humphrey, C. (1998) *Global Warning: Debating International Developments in New Public Financial Management*, Cappelen Akademisk Forlag, Oslo.
- Olsen, R. (1997) Ex-Post Accounting in Incremental Budgeting: A Study of Norwegian Municipalities, *Scandinavian Journal of Management*, 13(1):65-75.
- Powell, B. (1982) *Contemporary Democracies*, Harvard University Press, Cambridge.
- Rhodes, R. (1997) *Understanding Governance*, Open University Press, Buckingham.
- Wallich, C. (1994) *Russia and the Challenge of Fiscal Federalism*, The World Bank, Washington DC.
- Watts, R. and Zimmerman, J. (1979) The Demand and Supply for Accounting Theories: The Market for Excuses, *The Accounting Review*, 54(2):273-305.

Appendix 7.1.: **Structure of Representative Council of Leningrad County Government**

Source: internet page: www.lenobl.ru/struct/zs_strukt.htm

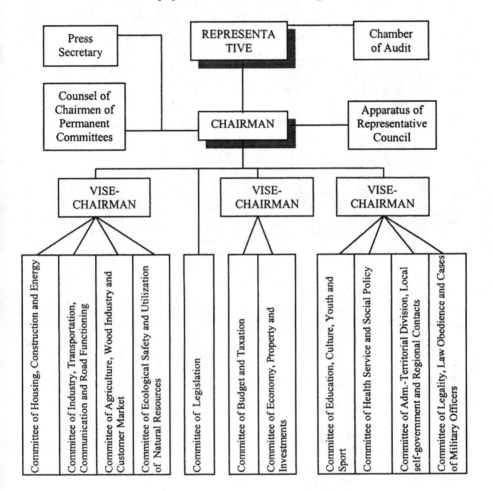

Appendix 7.2.:   The Statement of the Budget Implementation Leningrad County

Code According to Budget classification	Item	Code of the line	Adjusted Plan for the Year	Executed since 01.01. 9X	% of the exe- cution
	Income				
1000000	Tax Income (with corresponding subitems)	01			
2000000	Non-tax income (with corresponding subitems)	17			
3000000	Grants and transfers (with corresponding subitems)	33			
4000000	Income of restricted off-budget funds	41			
	Total income	45			
	Expenditures*				
0100	State and local government	02			
0500	Police, fire department and state security	04			
0600	Fundamental research and technological progress	06			
0700	Industry, power generation and construction	08			
0800	Agriculture and fishing industry	10			
0900	Environmental safety and protection of natural resources	12			
1000	Transportation, road keeping and communication	14			
1100	Development of market infrastructure	16			
1200	Housing and communal economy	18			
1300	Prevention and elimination disasters	20			
1400	Education	22			
1500	Culture, art and movie production	24			
1600	Mass media	26			
1700	National health and physical culture	28			
1800	Social policy	30			
2100	Financial support to other budgets	32			
3000	Other expenditures (subsidies)	34			
3004	Expenditures of restricted off-budget funds	38			
	Total expenditures	40			
	Excess of income over expenditures (or deficit)	42			
	(continued from previous page)				
	Sources of finance (for the deficit)				
0120	Change of cash on bank account	71			
0270	State and (municipal) bonds	73			
0400	Subsidies received from other budgets	75			
0700	Loan from banks and other commercial organizations	77			
0500	Other sources of internal financing	79			
	Total amount of sources of finance	81			

Given as a note:

Salaries of state and municipal employees (code 110100)	**100**			
Payments of social insurance (code 110200)	**101**			
Capital investments in fixed assets (code 240000)	**102**			
Receivables: - payments for communal services (code 110700)	**103**			
Creditors: - salaries of state and municipal employees (110100)	**104**			
- payments of social insurance (code 110200)	**105**			

Comment: the amount in the line 42 is equal to the amount in the line 81, with "-".

*- in addition, some of expenditure items are further classified according to economic classification. example:

code	item
0100	state and local government including: - salaries (code 110100) - purchase of equipment of long-term use (code 240100) - capital construction (code 240200)

Appendix 7.3.:   Accounting Statements (Nordland County)

7.3.1. Operating Statement

descriptions	acc. 1996	approved budget 1997	adjusted budget 1997	acc. 1997	changes in real terms 96/97 (%)	budget variance 1997 (nok)
revenue						
operating revenue excluding interests						
expenditure						
operating expenditures excluding interests						
gross operational surplus						
net interest expenditures						
repayment of loans						
total interest and loan repayments						
net operational surplus/deficit						
financial transactions						
total financial income						
total financial expenditures						
net financial transactions						
accounting surplus of the year						

7.3.2. Capital Statement

descriptions	acc. 1996	approved budget 1997	adjusted budget 1997	acc. 1997	changes in real terms 96/97 (%)	budget variance 1997 (nok)
use of capital						
need for capital						
financing						
total financing						

7.3.3. Balance Sheet

assets	1995 nok %	1996 nok %	1997 nok %	changes nok 1996/97
cash				
funds				
receivables				
inventory				
total current assets				
shares				
loans				
equipment/real estate				
total fixed assets				
total assets				
liabilities and equity	1995 nok %	1996 nok %	1997 nok %	changes nok 1996/97
total debt				
fund				
liquidity reserve				
capital account				
total equity				
total liabilities and equity				

Appendix 7.4.:   Fund Statement (Nordland County)

sources of funds	1993	1994	1995	1996	1997	changes in real terms 96/97 (%)
operating revenue						
other revenue						
total sources of funds						

uses of funds	1993	1994	1995	1996	1997	changes in real terms 96/97 (%)
operating expenditures						
investments						
total operating expenditures and investments						
interests						
repayments						
loans						
allocation to funds						
sum of use						

TRANSFERABILITY OF REFORMED LOCAL GOVERNMENT ACCOUNTING TO PROVINCIAL GOVERNMENT ACCOUNTING IN BELGIUM

Johan Christiaens

8.1. Introduction

Nowadays there is a strong tendency in Belgium to reform Non-Profit and Public Sector Organizations from cameralistic/cash accounting, which was primarily set up to measure and control the spending of budgetary means, towards business-like accrual accounting. The most important examples are: Hospitals (1987), Health Service Insurances (1990), Pension Funds (1991), Flemish Universities (1995), Flemish High Schools (1995) and Local Governments [Municipalities (1990)] and OCMWs[1] (1998).

For the moment the Belgian legislator is preparing the accounting reform of Provincial Governments and the reform of other governmental entities such as the Ministry of the Flemish Community is also taken into consideration. For provincial governments a draft of the reformed legislation particularly considering the accounting system has recently been edited. More precise regulations as to the further implementation are currently still in progress.

According to provincial officials an important motivation for reforming the provincial accounting system would be the pursued replacement of the accounting and administrative software due to the euro and the tendency to ERP software.

This paper aims at presenting a general view of the current accounting reform in Belgian provinces and the similarities and differences with the recently reformed local governments, which are municipalities and official centres for mutual welfare. After presenting the different characteristics of local and provincial governments, section 8.3. focuses on the objectives of their accounting systems. In section 8.4. the research question of this paper is discussed. The remainder is devoted to an exploratory study of the similarities and differences of the local accounting systems vs. the provincial accounting systems using an empirical study of municipalities as well as the draft of accounting legislation in provinces.

---

[1] An OCMW *(Official Centre for Mutual Welfare)* is a governmental non-profit entity providing a number of additional municipal services such as health care, care of the elderly, etc. Each municipality is related to just one OCMW and vice versa, both providing well-defined municipal services. In Belgium the OCMWs are juridically separated from the municipality, whereas in other countries such entities are part of the municipality.

A. Bac (ed.), International Comparative Issues in Government Accounting, 123-134.
© 2001 *Kluwer Academic Publishers. Printed in the Netherlands.*

8.2.   Characteristics of Local and Provincial Governments

8.2.1. NUMBERS

The Belgian local governments mainly consist of 589 municipalities, which have dealt with an important accrual accounting reform since 1995 and 589 official centres for mutual welfare (OCMWs), which are currently confronted with an accrual accounting reform. These local governments are part of 10 provinces, which are currently confronted with an accounting reform inspired by the local government accounting reform of municipalities.

8.2.2. SERVICES

Looking at the services provided by provinces, there appear to be a lot of similarities with respect to the local governments, particularly municipalities. Provinces provide services such as administration, recreation, education, safeguarding and maintenance of art patrimony, care for the environment, public works and infrastructure, sports and cultural activities similarly as municipalities. The most important exception is the police and fire department for municipalities.

OCMWs are more specialized in individualized efforts such as health care services, financial support of poor citizens, social services and care for the elderly, but provinces are also providing similar services.

8.2.3. ORGANIZATION

In terms of organization provinces as well as local governments can be related to so-called 'autonomous non-profit organizations'. Both also consist of governmental enterprises for services that are provided by means of market mechanisms. Examples of such enterprises are recreation parks with entrance fees, harbour facilities, water distribution, etc. These enterprises are not juridically autonomous, but are part of the concerned government, although their accounting systems are mostly separated from the rest of the governmental administration.

8.2.4. MANAGEMENT

Although provinces are more extensive than local governments, they have mostly a centralized accounting system. Due to their geographical spread they have to assign decentralized provincial treasurers whereas local governments are able to centralize this function.

8.3.   Objectives of Local and Provincial Government Accounting

Generally, the current accounting reforms in Belgium aim at providing complete, objective and transparent information. Business-like accrual accounting is seen by the legislator as the most important means to reach this objective. A second important objective is to improve governmental management by introducing managerial tools transferred from the profit sector.

The objectives set forward in the ongoing provincial accounting reform are the following:

- achieving one similar accounting system for all governments;
- providing complete, objective and transparent accounting information;
- conformity with double-sided business-like accounting systems;
- valuing and disclosing all assets and liabilities;
- disclosing completely the provincial contingencies;
- preparation of an integrated cost accounting system in order to obtain cost information of services provided;
- keeping the traditional decentralized tasks and responsibilities unchanged.

These objectives are fairly similar to the objectives of the municipal accounting reform in 1990 with date of implementation 1995 where the major focus is on transferring business-like financial accounting just like that hoping that the advantages of business-like accounting such as management tools, measuring performance, using cost accounting information, etc. could also be transferred automatically.

In the other form of local governments, i.e. Flemish OCMWs the reform goes even further and includes organizational (e.g. the introduction of activity-centres appointing account responsibles) and managerial changes such as the introduction of long term and short term planning system, an internal and external auditing system as well as cost accounting techniques.

For local governments as well as for provincial governments user needs are shown up to the best advantage as an important objective, but, in Belgium these needs have not been determined even after an important number of years of implementation of the changed governmental accounting systems.

As is the case in local government accounting, the reformed accounting reporting of provinces is not guaranteed for several reasons: firstly the new financial accounting system will be added without changing or adapting the role and supremacy of the budgetary accounting system, which will result in accounting conflicts. Secondly, the financial accounting system risks to be made insufficiently important: the budgetary resources do not depend in any respect on the financial accounting system. Thirdly, there is insufficient professional guidance for the implementation and the reporting. Fourthly, audit following-up the implementation and the outcomes is unexisting. Lastly, as is the case in other foreign studies (CICA, 1985; Collins, Keenan and Lapsley, 1991) one can argue that there will be a very limited use of the annual accounts by stakeholders and citizens.

8. 4. Research Question

The lack of accounting research on this topical subject, the presumed occurrence of a poor adoption and a weak harmony in reforming public sector accounting and the differing function of a central provincial government, lead to the research questions of this paper:

- RQ1 Are the concepts of the recent local government accounting reforms transferable to provincial governments?
- RQ2 What are the major areas of differences in provincial accounting systems?

In previous research there are some descriptive, exploratory studies regarding governmental accounting practices, often set up by regulatory authorities. Examples are GASB: Jones et al. 1985, CICA 1980 and CICA 1985 for American and Canadian States and local governments. Through examining the annual accounts these studies empirically describe the different types and possibilities of accounting techniques, assertions and principles (e.g. full accrual vs. modified accrual and cash; consolidated vs. fund type of statements).

Some studies concentrate on the compliance of governmental accounting practices with accounting regulations. Faber & de Jong (1988) looked at the municipal accounting reform towards accrual accounting in The Netherlands involving the investigation of annual accounts. The major findings were non-compliance to regulations and a serious heterogeneity (Faber & de Jong, 1988:38).

In this study attention is given to an ongoing accounting reform in Belgian provinces in light of earlier accounting reforms in local governments (i.e. municipalities and OCMWs).

This exploratory comparative study is firstly based on the findings of an earlier empirical study of the financial accounting reform in Flemish municipalities (Christiaens 1997, 1999). Secondly the concept of the reformed provincial accounting legislation forms the basis of a preliminary analysis and evaluation combined with an attempt to study the provincial situation using interviews with the provincial treasurers of 4 of the 10 provinces (i.e. East-Flanders, Limburg, Province of Antwerp, Flemish-Brabant).

8.5.   Transferability to Provincial Governments

8.5.1   CONCEPTUAL FRAMEWORK

Looking at the different regulating accounting legislation in municipalities, in local official centres for mutual welfare and in provinces, one can demonstrate that there is actually no adequate conceptual framework supporting the accounting and reporting objectives in Belgium.

Furthermore, the analysis will indicate that provinces are trying to take over local authority accounting concepts, whereas local government accounting is itself a unsuccessful copy of business accounting disregarding major public sector characteristics.

The fact that the reformed municipal accounting differs conceptually from the accounting systems set up for local official centres for mutual welfare leads to additional problems in the transferability to provinces. Therefore, a number of problems regarding transferability will occur. Hence, a possible negative consequence is the drifting apart of the governmental accounting systems instead of reforming convergently governmental accounting in Belgium.

Referring to the classification alternatives of Vela in his analysis of the local government accounting systems in several European countries (Vela, 1997), the reformed accounting systems can be shown in the next table.

Local Governments	Reformed Accounting System
▪ Municipalities	Budgetary Accounting → Financial Accounting - The (new) financial accounting system is linked with the remaining budgetary system and influenced by budgetary rules - Cost accounting and management accounting are not developed
▪ Walloon OCMWs	Mainly the same system as for municipalities
▪ Brussels' OCMWs	Budgetary Accounting → Financial Accounting - The (new) financial accounting system is linked with the remaining budgetary system and influenced by budgetary rules; however, the accounting standards differ from municipalities and from Walloon OCMWs as well - Cost accounting is legally foreseen, but in progress; management accounting is not yet developed
▪ Flemish OCMWs	Financial Accounting → Management Accounting - The former budgetary accounting system is abandoned and is replaced by the (new) financial accounting system including an integrated cost accounting system and budgeting - Management accounting is in progress
▪ Provincial Governments	Reformed Accounting System
▪ Provinces	Generally the same as for municipalities, more precise regulations still have to be defined

Table 8.1.:   Accounting Systems in Belgian Governments

It is important to clarify that municipalities and provinces are regulated by federal legislation whereas OCMWs are regulated by the different districts in Belgium (Flanders, Brussels' Capital and Wallonie).

Because the Walloon legislator has decided to comply with municipal accounting regulations, the accounting concepts of their OCMWs are from a conceptual point of view as good as completely in line with those of the municipalities.

Despite the fact that accounting reforms are induced by the legislator instead of being self-generative (Lapsley & Pallot, 1997), which could have been a guarantee for a more consistent approach, the reforms of the accounting system appear to drift apart.

Supremacy of Traditional Budgetary Accounting
Contrary to Flemish OCMWs the Belgian municipalities, Brussels' OCMWs, Walloon OCMWs and Belgian provinces have not abandoned their traditional budgetary accounting system, which is actually a cameralistic cash-based system primarily concentrated on the recording of authorized spending. On the contrary: in several ways budgetary accounting is dominating the new financial accounting system although the

two systems have different targets. This dominance of the budgetary accounting system creates a number of accounting differences and problems.

Apparently a diverging approach in conceptual framework is driving away the accounting standardsetting, reporting and auditing. The needs for generally accepted standards becomes more and more apparent.

8.5.2. IMPORTANT ACCOUNTING ISSUES

Community Assets
In local governments all fixed assets juridically belonging to the municipality are considered and treated *as if* they were financial economic *business assets* just like that. Therefore all the properties have to be disclosed no matter their perspective or background. However, a number of assets having only a cultural, social, artistic, historical, military background and function are actually not real business assets and their valuation in the first balance sheet can seriously be questioned. They are not at all used in a financial economic perspective; they have no economic significance. On the contrary, their inalienable presence is costing the municipality a lot of maintenance and safeguarding. Moreover, the reckless legal assumption of business assets is contrary to public sector accounting in other countries[2] and contrary to ideas and suggestions[3] of conceptual framework researchers (Pallot, 1992).

In the concept of reformed provincial accounting the legislator does not seem to have heard of the concept of public assets. One can expect that the provinces will use the same approach as municipalities.

Accounting Entity
Similarly as for local governments the concept of the provincial government accounting system is based on the *legal entity concept* instead of on an *economic* or an *ownership and control* or a *political accountability concept* (CICA, 1985:35-36). This implies that the provincial accounting system only recognizes activities carried on within its legal framework. As well as for local governments consolidation of the provincial governments is not regulated nor intended.

Some of the Belgian provinces organize high school education and since Flemish high schools are regulated by separate accounting legislation (1995) a problem of integration and harmonization will occur. To show the disparities with respect to the accounting regulations of schools, a comparison of the accounting treatment of school buildings as used by different organizations and governments is shown in table 8.2.

---

[2]   For local authorities in the UK a separate category 'community assets' was created on April 1, 1994 (Allen CIGAR 1995, p. 5.)

[3]   See also Lapsley AAAJ 1988, p. 27.

Organizations	Balance sheet existing?	Buildings disclosed as assets?	Revaluation[4]?	Depreciations?
Municipality Schools	YES	YES	OBLIGATORY	50 YEARS
Flemish Universities	YES	NO	N/A	1 YEAR
Secondary Schools	NO	NO	N/A	N/A
Private Schools	YES	YES	PROHIBITED	VALUATION RULE
Flemish High Schools	YES	YES	PROHIBITED	33 YEARS
Provincial Schools - before reform - after reform	 NO YES	 NO YES	 N/A PROHIBITED	 N/A NOT YET DEFINED

Table 8.2.:   Accounting Practices School Buildings

A third remark considering the accounting entity is the choice for one and only one accounting system in Belgian government according to their legal entity. Methods of fund accounting in which a government could be divided into several accounting entities according to their nature is unknown or disliked and thus avoided.

Stocks
Empirical research (Christiaens, 1997) has revealed that local governments, particularly municipalities are not convinced in recording stocks, although imposed by accounting legislation. It is obvious that each government does have stocks, but there seem to be different opinions as to the necessity and desirability of disclosing them.

Although it is rather early to conclude, provinces are expected to develop a suchlike behaviour as the local government as to their limited attention to stock recording.

This issue should not be overstressed, but stock accounting information would contribute to the pursued improvement of governmental management, which is one the aims of the current accounting reforms.

Art Patrimony
In local governments empirical research revealed (Christiaens, 1997) that 34.6% of the municipalities showing art patrimony applied the legal valuation rule of 'insurance value'. For these municipalities 'not-insured' implies 'not-disclosed' and this legal rule can seriously be criticized.

For provincial governments, which have also properties of art patrimony, the accounting rules are not yet clearly defined. Anyway, their conceptual framework is similar as for local governments and thus similar problems can be expected.

---

[4]   Revaluation means that the disclosed value of fixed assets can be increased according to their current value.

Audit of Reformed Financial Reporting
The implications of the accounting reforms in local governments and in provincial governments regarding internal as well as external auditing are compared in table 8.3.

Local Governments	Internal auditing	External auditing
▪ Municipalities, Walloon OCMWs, Brussels' OCMWs	No reformed internal auditing efforts	Not regulated; just Provinces as Oversight Body
▪ Flemish OCMWs	- Compliance audit by the OCMW-treasurer - Operational audit by a committee consisting of OCMW-president, treasurer and secretary	- Financial audit by an external committee consisting of officials - Comprehensive audit, particularly Value-for-money audit is not regulated
Provincial Governments	Internal auditing	External auditing
▪ Provinces	No reformed internal auditing efforts	Not regulated, just *La Cour des Comptes - Rekenhof* as Oversight Body in a limited way

Table 8.3.:   Auditing Systems in Belgian Governments

This comparison reveals that the efforts to install a reformed auditing function in Flemish OCMWs principally driven by modern auditing concepts, is set aside in the most recent ongoing reform in provinces.

On the other hand, the accounting reform in Flemish OCMWs is not at all perfect in that the function of auditing is not far-reaching and the auditor needs not to be an independent professional. Installing such a professional audit function could have been a better guarantee for the follow-up of the implementation and for the quality of the accounting outcomes.

Other Elements
The following table evidences some weak elements found in the analysis of local government accounting (Christiaens, 1997) and reveals the consequences towards provincial accounting.

Accounting elements	Municipalities	Flemish OCMWs	Provinces
Fixed assets, particularly public goods are exhaustively inventoried and recorded in the governmental accounting system irrespective of their nature, purpose and service-providing character	YES	YES	YES
Land and buildings have to be revaluated according to certain price level rates without any further conditions	YES	NO	NO
Provisions for risks and charges are incorrectly defined by regulations	YES	NO	Not yet defined
Accruals and deferrals are weakly defined and regulated	YES	YES	YES
There is a lack of attention for stocks	YES	NO	YES
The cut-off of the Profit and Loss Account is insufficiently regulated	YES	YES-NO	YES
Writing down of assets is insufficiently regulated	YES	YES-NO	YES
The *de minimis* level of recognizing purchases as fixed assets is not regulated	YES	YES	100.000 BEF
Redemptions of loans are recorded as costs and are readjusted in a separate part of the Profit and Loss Account. Therefore, they are incorrectly accounted for twice	YES	NO	NO
Credit lines are recorded as if they were assets and liabilities instead of registering them as contingencies in the Notes of the annual accounts	YES	NO	NO

Table 8.4.:   Weak Elements regarding Accounting Practices in the current Governmental Reforms

OCMWs of Brussels' Capital District and of the Walloon District are not further enclosed in this table because their characteristics are similar to those of municipalities. This table reveals that a few issues, such as revaluation fixed assets, redemptions, credit lines, ... are ameliorated towards provinces, but a number of weakly regulated items remain even after a number of years of experience in local government accounting.

8.6.   Differences in Provincial Accounting Systems

8. 6.1. CONCEPTUAL DIFFERENCES IN PROVINCIAL ACCOUNTING SYSTEMS

Regarding the homogeneity across the different provinces little is known at this moment since the legislation is not yet definite. However, based on the interviews with provincial treasurers and other officials, there appear to be different points of view in the approach of implementing the reformed provincial accounting system.

Some provinces would prefer a similar approach as in the reformed municipalities which is the system of keeping the traditional budgetary accounting system and linking it with a new form of financial accrual accounting.

Other provinces seem to be resistant to the business-like accounting reform and prefer to keep the traditional cameralistic accounting system without a serious accounting reform.

A third possibility would be a reform inspired by the accounting system of Flemish OCMWs in which the accrual accounting system is prevailing combined with a business-like cost accounting system. Driven by this new accrual accounting system, budgets and budgetary accounts are set up and are followed up.

In table 8.5. these possible accounting systems are summarized accompanied of three other possibilities which are not very well known nor accepted. In addition, some important strengths and weaknesses are presented.

Integrated accounting systems	Strengths, weaknesses
1) Traditional budgetary accounting + New financial accrual accounting (reformed accounting system of municipalities)	+ Accrual accounting is introduced and budgetary accounting is maintained - Such a linked system needs compromises - Unsuccessful combination leading to conflicts
2) New financial accrual accounting with an integrated cost accounting system and in addition a budgetary accounting system (reformed accounting system of Flemish OCMWs)	+ Accrual accounting is prevailing + Integrated system of cost accounting - Lay-out of budgetary accounting is defined by accrual accounting concepts - Overemphasis on accrual accounting
3) Cameralistic accounting system (current accounting system of provinces)	+ Tool of control of the 'public purse' - No patrimonial view - No system of management accounting
4) Maintaining of the traditional budgetary accounting system extended with a separated system of accounting adjustments and reclassifications in order to develop additionally at the year accrual accounting reports	+ Budgetary accounting is maintained + Rather easy to implement + Different reports for different purposes - Accrual accounting information supporting management purposes is not available during the year
5) Fund accounting in which the different activities of the government are separated and accordingly treated: thus different accounting systems for different activities (=funds)	+ Different approaches and different reports for different purposes + Advantages of the other systems are kept whereas the disadvantages are avoided - Need for defining the different funds - More complex to implement
6) A kind of 'Triple accounting' (?) in order to combine accrual, cost and budgetary accounting information	+ Would be an integrated accounting system - Is not yet developed

Table 8.5.:   Forms of Possible Integrated Accounting Systems

8.6.2. DIFFERENT TIMING OF IMPLEMENTATION

The interviews with provincial treasurers who will be responsible for the accounting system revealed that the objectives of the financial provincial accounting reform is not very clear. There appear to be different interpretations with respect to the goals of the new accounting system. Apparently, there is not yet a conceptual framework considering the aimed targets and consequences of governmental accounting systems in Belgium.

Furthermore, it appeared that a certain province has already started implementing the new provincial accrual accounting system before the legislator has approved definitely the concept of provincial accounting reform. The reason for this early start was the need for an information technology (IT) improvement and the search for ERP software.

One could argue that this starting of the reform 'avant la lettre' will create problems in timing, consistency and compliance with the provincial accounting reform.

The need for a user oriented conceptual accounting framework and harmonized governmental accounting regulations becomes clear. Many of the unsuccessful findings have to do with the lack of audit and the shortcomings in supporting a traditionally rather isolated sector.

8.6. Conclusions

The objectives of the recent accounting reforms are in a first perspective the creation and improvement of management tools. In a second perspective the purpose is to improve the transparency and accountability towards external users. Obviously, this reform implies a changing role of accounting.

There appears to be a lack of a conceptual framework for governmental accounting in Belgian local governments as well as in provincial governments, although important aspects of know-how exists in a number of other countries. This lack explains the problems of transferring business-like accrual accounting towards local governments which were the first as well as towards provincial governments which is happening for the moment. Both provincial and local governmental accounting are dealing with similar problems and a single approach would be desirable.

The standardsetters prescribing the provincial reform have not taken into account sufficiently the lessons drawn from the local government accounting reforms; the need for a centralized professional standardsetting body appears.

The provincial accounting system seems to be easily copied from municipal accounting which was copied from business accounting. This took place actually without user need research nor applications regarding the use of accounting data in the fields of management accounting, management control, planning and control, management tools, accountability, auditing.

Finally, the coming provincial accounting system does not seem to have been made indispensable, which might weaken the application, the reporting and the continuity.

References

- Allen, S. (1995) *Capital accounting for local government in the U.K.: an attempt to measure the effect of applying commercial accounting concepts to the local government environment*, working paper CIGAR 5 Conference, Paris, 4th-5th May 1995.
- Canadian Institute of Chartered Accountants (CICA) (1980) *Financial reporting by governments: a research study*, 223.
- Canadian Institute of Chartered Accountants (CICA) (1985) *Local government financial reporting: a research study*, 116.
- Christiaens J., *Financial accounting reform in Flemish municipalities: an empirical study of the outcomes*, working paper CIGAR 6 Conference, Milan, 5th-6th June 1997, pp. 42.
- Christiaens J., Financial Accounting Reform in Flemish Municipalities: An Empirical Investigation, *Financial Accountability & Management*, Vol. 15, nr. 1, 21-40.
- Collins, W., Keenan, D., Lapsley, I. (1991) *Local authority financial reporting: communication, sophistry or obfuscation*, ICAS and CIPFA, Edinburgh 1991, 46.
- Faber, A., de Jong, E.J. (1988) *De Gemeenterekening: theorie en praktijk van de jaarrekening volgens de Gemeentelijke Comptabiliteitsvoorschriften*, Research Memorandum No. 1988-41, Vrije Universiteit Amsterdam, 40.
- Jones, D.B., Scott, R.B., Kimbro, L., Ingram, R.W. (1985) *The needs of users of governmental financial reports*, GASB, Stamford.
- Lapsley, I. (1988) Research in public sector accounting: an appraisal, *Accounting, Auditing & Accountability Journal*, Vol. 1, No. 1, 21-33.
- Lapsley, I., Pallot, J. (1997) *The capital accounting controversy in local government - a New Zealand:UK comparison*, working paper CIGAR 6 Conference, Milan, 5th-6th June 1997, 27.
- Pallot, J. (1992) Elements of a theoretical framework for public sector accounting, *Accounting, Auditing & Accountability Journal*, Vol. 5, No. 1, 38-59.
- Vela-Bargues, J.M. (1997) *Local government accounting in Europe: a comparative approach*, working paper CIGAR 6 Conference, Milan, 5th-6th June 1997, 24.

COMPARING CAMERAL AND ACCRUAL ACCOUNTING IN LOCAL GOVERNMENTS

Norvald Monsen and Salme Näsi

Motto: 'Refining sugar is a means of raising the quality and utility of the finished product by separating out the elements of the raw material not wanted. The refining of initially classified accounting data has the same kind of objective'
(A.C. Littleton, 1953, p. 57).

9.1. Introduction

Historically the accounting models applied in the governmental and business sectors differ strongly. This difference is due to the fact that there are differences between governmental and business organizations, a point to be discussed further in the next section of the paper. In spite of these differences, however, there seems to be an international trend towards the replacement of traditional governmental accounting (e.g., cameral accounting) with business accounting (i.e., accrual accounting). For example, such a change occurred in the local governmental sector in Sweden in 1986 and a similar change occurred in Finland 10 years later. Currently there are similar changes going on with regard to state accounting in these two countries.

It seems to us as the experiences of local governmental accounting were not taken into account in the current argumentation for replacing cameral with accrual accounting in the local governmental sectors in different countries. Why was cameral accounting thinking introduced in the local governmental sector in the first place as opposed to accrual accounting thinking? What is the objective of the cameral accounting system compared to the accrual accounting system? What are the similarities and differences between the cameral and accrual accounting models? And how do these similarities and differences relate to the local governmental and business organizational contexts? Such and similar questions have not been addressed in the current debate about how to develop local governmental accounting. One purpose of this paper is therefore to compare cameral and accrual accounting thinking, and to relate this discussion to local governmental accounting.

The recent change from cameral to accrual accounting in the local governmental sector in Finland, beginning with fiscal year 1997, offers the opportunity to undertake an empirical study of such a change. The second purpose of this paper is therefore to study the accounting development of one particular Finnish local government (the City of Vaasa), and relate this empirical study to the theoretical comparison of cameral and accrual accounting which is referred to above.

The paper is structured as follows: The following section will focus on organizational metaphors, followed by a discussion of various accounting models. Thereafter, an

A. Bac (ed.), International Comparative Issues in Government Accounting, 135-157.

empirical study on the change from cameral to accrual accounting in Finnish local governments follows, with a comparison of cameral and accrual accounting information. Layout of financial statements of Finnish local governments are presented (in Appendix 9.1. and 9.2.) and used as a case example of governmental accounting reform. The paper ends with an analysis and some conclusions.

9.2.   Organizational Metaphors

Accounting is a phenomenon that should be studied in its organizational and societal contexts (see e.g., Hopwood, 1983). Before studying the development of local governmental accounting in Finland, an organizational frame of reference will therefore be presented in this paragraph.

According to Mellemvik et al. (1988), there is an interdependence between accounting and its context. Furthermore, the organizational context of accounting consists of complex and paradoxical phenomena that can be understood in many different ways:

'... our theories and explanations of organizational life are based on metaphors that lead us to see and understand organizations in distinctive yet partial ways.' (Morgan, 1986:2).

Morgan underlines that we use metaphor whenever we attempt to understand one element of experience in terms of another. One of the interesting aspects of metaphors rests in the fact that it always produces a kind of one-sided insight. However, by using different metaphors to understand the complex and paradoxical character of organizational life, we are able to manage and design organizations in ways that we may not have thought possible before (Morgan, 1986). Moreover, Morgan suggests use of the following eight metaphors for building our 'images' of organizations: organizations as machines, organizations as organisms, organizations as brains, organizations as cultures, organizations as political systems, organizations as physic prisons, organizations as flux and transformation, organizations as instruments of domination.

A detailed overview of these different metaphors may be found in Morgan (1986). For the purpose of this paper, however, it suffices to focus on the two metaphors that mostly have been used in previous studies of local governments: organizations as machines and organizations as political systems (see e.g., Brunsson, 1986; Jönsson, 1982). Organizations that are designed and operated as if they were machines are now usually called bureaucracies. But most organizations are bureaucratised in some degree, for the mechanistic mode of thought has shaped our most basic conceptions of what organization is all about (Morgan, 1986: 22). For example, when we talk about organization, we usually have in mind a state of orderly relations between clearly defined parts that have some determinate order. Although the image may not be explicit, we are talking about a set of mechanical relations. We talk about organizations as if they were machines, and as a consequence we tend to expect them to operate as machines: in a routinized, efficient, reliable, and predictable way (Morgan, 1986).

Organizations do not - and should not - always operate as machines. Politics and politicking may be an essential aspect of organizational life, and are not necessarily an optional and dysfunctional extra. In this regard it is useful to remember that in its original meaning, the idea of politics stems from the view that, where interests are divergent, society should provide a means for allowing individuals to reconcile their differences through consultation and negation (Morgan, 1986).

When one applies the machine metaphor in organizational studies, the focus is on the organization as one unit with common interests(s) and objective(s). In business organizations, the generation of profit is a common motive, and the machine metaphor fits well when studying this type of organizations. On the other hand, when the political metaphor is used, the focus is on different interests, conflicts and power relations which are present in organizations. This latter description pictures the situation in local governments, because we here find different political actors with different opinions. Consequently, the political metaphor has been used in previous studies of local governments (see e.g., Jönsson, 1982; Monsen, 1993; Olson, 1983; Brunsson, 1986, Rombach, 1986).

In the following paragraph, we will turn our attention to different accounting models. We will focus on the two accounting models that have been used in the business sector (accrual accounting) and governmental sector (cameral accounting) and relate these models to the organizational context of local governments, as we see this context by help of the machine and political metaphors. Moreover, the cash flow accounting model will also be discussed, because such an accounting model could provide a link or bridge between the cameral and the accrual accounting models. In practice, a cash-flow statement is often prepared as an additional statement to the cameral and accrual accounting statements both in the governmental and business environments.

9.3. Different Accounting Models

Financial accounting models can be categorised in many ways. Jones and Pendlebury describe in their public sector accounting textbook five different accounting techniques: budgetary accounting, cash accounting, accruals accounting, commitment accounting and fund accounting, stating that these five are not mutually exclusive and that it is possible for one organisation to adopt more than one technique simultaneously (Jones and Pendlebury, 1996, pp 139-165). Some of these techniques, like accrual accounting, are mostly used in the business sector organisations, and some others, like fund accounting, are used in the public sector.

9.3.1. CAMERAL ACCOUNTING

In the public sector, the annual budgeting system is a mean to allocate resources and to fix the level and distribution of taxes. The main purpose of a traditional governmental accounting system is to control the execution of the annual budget approved by the parliament, municipal council or an equivalent decision maker. For this control budget and accounting numbers are continuously compared and at the end of the fiscal year variances between the budget (ex-ante) and the accounting (ex-post) figures are reported. The term 'budgetary accounting', as used by Jones and Pendlebury, is a term well suited to describe accounting models used in public sector organizations, where the budget plays such an important role. Another term used for such accounting modes, is the term 'cameral accounting' (German 'Kameralistisches Rechnungswesen') (see e.g.

Walb, 1926; Wysocki, 1965; Filios, 1983 and Monsen and Näsi, 1996, for more information about cameral accounting). Because the cameral accounting system has influenced governmental accounting in many countries, including Finland, we will focus on the specific cameral accounting model, as opposed to the more general budgetary accounting model, to which cameral accounting belongs.

One of the main features of cameral accounting is the central role of cash and money management (see e.g., Monsen and Näsi, 1996). Another characteristic feature of cameral accounting is based on the central role of the budget in the public sector economy. The important task of accounting is to control the execution of the budget approved by decision makers (budgetary control). The third feature of cameral accounting - non-existence of a comprehensive balance sheet - follows from the two previous features. The focus of accounting is the budgeted expenditures and revenues and corresponding cash payments instead of profit measurement and asset calculation. Figure 9.1. summarizes these 3 important features of cameral accounting.

> **Cameral Accounting:**
> - money focus
> - budgetary control
> - non-comprehensive balance sheet

Figure 9.1.: Cameral Accounting

The term 'cameral system' is often used in Finland to refer to the set of the annual budget and financial accounts and reports which are tightly linked together as to their detailed structure and contents. The key concepts of both the budget and accounts are *revenues* and *expenditures*; the former referring to different *sources of money* (taxes, state grants, service fees and loans) and the latter to *usage of money* (listed by the nature of expenditures, like salaries, materials, rents, repayments of loans, etc., or by the function or activity, like general order and safety, health care, social services, education, general administration etc.). Based on these wide concepts of revenues (sources of money) and expenditures (usage objects of money), the cameral accounting model can be said to be money- or cash-focused.

Accounts in cameral accounting relate to the budget for a particular time period, a fiscal or financial year. Therefore, even accounts have a 'year-to-year life', rather than an indefinite life. Thus the going concern assumption which is fundamental in accounting for profit-seeking entities is not entirely applicable to public sector budgetary accounting (compare Hay and Mikesell, 1974, p. 387). The 'year-to-year life' of accounts means that the cameral or other traditional budgetary accounting systems do not generate financial data for a comprehensive balance sheet. Investments in long-term assets (e.g., fixed assets) and payments of loans and debts, for instance, are recognized and reported as expenditures and revenues for the budgetary year in question. As a matter of fact, cameral accounting whose function is limited to monitoring the execution of the budget with different sources and uses of money, can be interpreted to represent a single-entry bookkeeping system even though every single transaction in bookkeeping is recorded on two accounts, on debit and credit side (compare Chan et al., 1996, p. 14).

9.3.2. ACCRUAL ACCOUNTING

The accrual-based accounting refers to a form of bookkeeping that records not only transactions that result from the receipt and disbursement of cash but also the amounts that the entity owes others and that others owe to the entity. *The realization principle* is employed in the revenue recognition, and the matching of revenues and expenses in closing annual accounts (compare Belkaoui, 1993, p. 448-49). *The matching principle* states that expenses should be recognised in the same period as the associated revenues; that is, revenues are recognised in a given period according to the realization principle, and the related expenses are then matched against the revenues in closing the accounts. The association is best accomplished when it reflects the cause-and-effect relationship between costs and revenues (Belkaoui, 1993, p. 240, Littleton, 1953, 67-68).

The general objective of accrual accounting is to calculate the annual income (profit or loss) and display the financial position of the accounting entity at the end of the financial year. Annual income measurement is necessary in the business firm context, and therefore, business accounting is often used as a vague synonym for accrual accounting. Accrual accounting rests on the concepts of accrual, deferral, allocation, amortisation, realisation, and recognition (see Belkaoui, 1993, p. 195). By requiring the entity to provide periodic, short-term reports, the accounting-period postulate imposes accruals and deferrals, the application of which is the principal difference between accrual accounting and cash accounting. Each period, the use of accruals and deferrals is required in the preparation of the financial position of the firm in terms of prepaid expenses, uncollected revenues, unpaid wages, and depreciation expense (Belkaoui, 1993, pp. 232-233).

Accrual accounting yields an income figure but it is not absolute or objective. Accruing depreciation, stock valuations, provisions for doubtful debts, etc., are subjective judgements which make historic cost profit subjective, especially under conditions of changing prices (Jones and Pendlebury, 1996, p. 153-54). All allocations are subjective. Belkaoui refers to the A.L. Thomas text The Allocation Problem in Financial Accounting Theory (1974) with an explicit statement that all allocations which are the basis of accrual accounting, are arbitrary and incorrigible. Accrual accounting also yields a measure of capital. The idea of capital maintenance has economic significance: income is only recognised after capital has been maintained intact. Just as with profit measures, capital measures of historic cost accrual accounting are affected by changing prices. The question is, which capital maintenance concept, financial capital or physical capital should be used, and should it be measured in units of money or units of purchasing power.

Three distinct views about measuring annual income are identified (see Belkaoui, 1993, p. 189-193): the asset/liability view, the revenue/expense view and the nonarticulated view (see figure 9.2.). The *asset/liability view*, also called the balance-sheet or capital maintenance view, holds that revenues and expenses result from changes in assets and liabilities. The *revenue/expense view* emphasizes measuring of earnings of the firm as the difference between revenues in a period and the expenses incurred earning those revenues, and not the change in net capital. Assets and liabilities, including deferred charges and credits, are considered residuals that must be carried to future periods in order to ensure proper matching. The revenue/expense view is also called the income statement or matching view and represents a dynamic accounting theory (see Schmalenbach 1933[1]), whereas the asset/liability view represents a static accounting view or theory. The third view, *the nonarticulated view*, is based on the belief that articulation leads to redundancy, since all events reported in the income statement are also reported in the balance sheet, although from the different perspective. This view represents a dualistic view of accounting.

| **Accrual Accounting:** |
| - the asset/liability view |
| - the revenue/expense view |
| - the nonarticulated view |

Figure 9.2.: Accrual Accounting

9.3.3. CASH FLOW ACCOUNTING

Cash flow accounting recognises only cash inflows and cash outflows.[2] Cash flows into and out of a business enterprise are the most fundamental events upon which accounting measurements are based and upon which investors and creditors are assumed to base their decisions. Hendriksen (1982, p. 236) writes: 'Most accounting measurements are based upon past, present, or expected flows of cash. Revenues are generally measured in terms of the net cash expected to be received from the sale of goods or services. Expenses are generally measured in terms of the cash paid or expected to be paid for goods and services used by the firm. Accruals represent the allocation to the current period of expected future receipts or disbursements for services. Deferrals represent the allocation to current and future periods of past receipts and disbursements for goods and services. (...) Because of the deliberate and inherent biases created by the use of allocation procedures and historical transaction prices, there is some doubt that traditional accounting methods are adequate to report the complex economic activities of

---

[1]   The concepts of statics and dynamics (which Schmalenbach first formulated) are classic criteria for categorising theories of accounting. 'According to the dynamic view, the main function of accounting is the calculation of profits. In this process the outcome of a comparable period is taken as a measure of efficiency; profits are defined as the difference between expenses and revenues. The calculation of profits is seen as the primary task of the annual accounts; so the profit and loss account is given priority over the balance sheet. Diverging from the established view, Schmalenbach interpreted the balance sheet as an auxiliary to the calculation of profits. He viewed the individual items of the balance sheet as a collection of transitory and anticipatory quantities. In his approach the assets include, as well as money, payments to be received and expenses to be incurred in later accounting periods (advance performance).; the liabilities on the other hand, as well as the capital, comprise 'subsequent performance', i.e. money to be paid out and revenues of later periods.' Potthoff and Sieben, 1994, p. 83.

[2]   Belkaoui (1993, p. 449) writes: 'The cash-flow basis of accounting has been correctly defined as   the recording not only of the cash receipts and disbursements of the period (the cash basis of accounting) but also of the future cash flows owed to or by the firm as a result of selling and transferring the titles to certain goods (the accrual basis of accounting).'

today. One way to avoiding some of these biases is to emphasise the reporting of cash flows...'

Sterling (1979, p. 209-211) writes that "sometime ago financial analysts began talking about 'cash flow income'. They adjusted the income statement by adding back allocations such as depreciation. The resulting figure was termed cash flow income or cash flows from operations, and it was considered to be more useful than the net income figure. Most accountants reacted with alarm and pointed out that cash-basis accounting had long ago been abandoned and replaced by accrual-basis accounting because the accrual basis provided the more accurate, more useful figures." Later in his text Sterling states that at the present time many accountants - and their numbers are growing rapidly - have adopted the view that cash-flow income is the superior concept. The reasons are three: 1) cash flows are relevant; 2) the concept avoids the allocation problems; 3) it avoids the valuation problem. Sterling agrees mostly with these reasons, but he also argues that not only flows but also stocks are relevant and we must report stocks as well as flows, and therefore we are faced with the problem of valuing those stocks.

T.A. Lee (see e.g., Lee, 1986) is another researcher who has published extensively on cash flow accounting, and who has argued in favour of this type of accounting. For example, in the article entitled '*A case for cash flow accounting*' (1972), he states; 'The proposition being made in this section is that cash is *the* key resource of a company and consequently, it is suggested that investors should have a much better knowledge about a company's cash than they do at present by means of the conventional profit statements, balance sheets and funds statements.' (Lee, 1972: 28).

A pure cash flow accounting system is independent of other accounting systems, such as the accrual accounting system. However, in practice the accrual-based income statement and balance sheet have often formed the basis for preparing a financial statement showing how a company has acquired and spent its financial resources during the fiscal year. Different terms have been used for such statements, including 'funds flow statements', 'funds statements' and 'cash flow statements'.

Monsen and Olson (1996) argue that funds flow statements vary in several dimensions: the definition of 'funds' (i.e. the 'bottom line'); structure (e.g. sources and uses of funds or sectors); initial concept (e.g. net income, revenues and expenditures, or cash inflows and cash outflows); adjustments, if any (e.g. when reconciling net income to net cash flow from operations); and the location of these adjustments in the statement. Based upon their discussion, Monsen and Olson (1996) argue that we can classify funds flow statements into 3 groups: (1) Traditional Models, (2) Cash Flow Oriented Models and (3) Pure Cash Flow Models (see figure 9.3.).

Funds Flow Models:
- Traditional Models
- Cash Flow Oriented Models
- Pure Cash Flow Models

Figure 9.3.:   Funds Flow Models

The main characteristic of traditional funds flow statements or models are that they define funds as working capital and that they are divided into two separate sections, namely the sources and uses of funds. They also use net income as the starting point (i.e., initial or starting concept), and they incorporate various adjustments. These adjustments are of two types, which are called Type 1 and Type 2. Type 1 adjustments refer to non-cash expenses and revenues, for example depreciation expenses. These adjustments are required in order to reconcile net income to changes in working capital. Type 2 adjustments, on the other hand, refer to working capital adjustments apart from cash. Type 2 adjustments are included in order to reconcile net change in working capital and net change in liquid assets.

Cash flow oriented models differ from traditional models, among other things, because they define 'funds' as 'cash and cash equivalents', as opposed to 'working capital'. Moreover, they only include Type 2 adjustments (i.e. working capital adjustments apart from cash) within the statements themselves. If Type 1 adjustments (non-cash expenses and revenues) also are carried out, they are presented as a note to the funds flow statement (cp. the reconciliation of net income and net cash flow from operations which is presented as a note when the so-called 'indirect' method is used for preparing a funds flow statement for a business company). This means that the initial or starting concept in the statement itself is working capital. Furthermore, a funds flow statement showing expenditures and revenues also belong to the group of funds flow models termed 'cash flow oriented models'. Such a funds flow statement is for example used in the local governmental sector in Norway. It is a funds flow statement with no reconciliation to a net income figure, i.e. no Type 1 adjustments, because the initial or starting concept is working capital. The model ends, however, with showing net change in liquid assets after Type 2 adjustments have been carried out in order to disaggregate change in working capital to show change in liquid assets.

The third group of funds flow models are called 'pure cash flow models'. In such a model, cash inflows and outflows are reported on all lines in the model. No adjustments is required, because the initial concept is cash, all the transactions represent cash inflows and outflows, and the model ends with a cash concept (i.e. liquid assets). Figure 9.4. summarizes how the three groups of funds flow models - Traditional Models (TM), Cash Flow Oriented Models (CFOM) and Pure Cash Flow Models (PCFM) - differ in two dimensions: their initial concepts (i.e. income, working capital or liquid assets) and their fund concepts (i.e. working capital or liquid assets).

		Initial Concept		
		Income	Working Capital	Liquid Assets
Fund Concept	Working Capital	TM		
	Liquid Assets		CFOM	PCFM

Figure 9.4:   Funds Flow Models (Source: Monsen and Olson, 1986: Fig. 2)

9.4.   Change from the Traditional (cameral) Accounting Model to the Accrual (Business) Accounting Model in Finnish Local Governments

The cameral accounting model of the Finnish local governments is closer to the cash flow accounting than to the accrual accounting. The cameral accounting is money- or cash-focused: revenues refer to sources of money and expenditures to uses of money and in most cases, sources of money equal to cash inflows and uses of money to cash outflows but not exactly. Due to the annuity of the budget, accrued expenses, deferred charges and prepayments are considered even in the accounts. The matching of expenses and revenues and allocation of e.g. investment expenditures as deprecation for accounting periods do not belong to the cameralistic model. Based on the budgetary balance principle it is important that enough revenues are collected (as taxes, state grants, and service fees) to cover expenditures or uses of money for different purposes - as it is important to have enough cash inflows to cover cash outflows in cash flow accounting. The cameral system in the Finnish local governments has identified expenditures and revenues in three categories: operative expenditures/revenues, investment expenditure/revenues and financial expenditures and revenues (see Appendix 9.1.).

The new financial accounting model in the Finnish local governments was adopted from the business sector and implemented in 1997 in all (452) municipalities and (about 250) joint municipalities. The Finnish business accounting model is based on the Expenditure - Revenue - theory developed by Professor Martti Saario during the 1940s (see Saario, 1945 and 1968) and it represents historical cost accrual accounting and its dynamic, revenue/expense, income statement or matching view. The matching principle is strongly rooted in the Finnish business accounting and therefore the annual profit is primarily calculated in the income statement as the difference of revenues and expenses matched against each other.[3] The income or profit and loss account is perceived as the primary financial statement, and the balance sheet plays the role of a 'transfer account' between the two accounting periods. In practice, however, financial accounting and the balance sheet information in Finland is often interpreted from the nonarticulated or dualistic view - in case of financial statement analysis, particularly.

Change from traditional cameral accounting to business accounting in Finnish local governments was motivated by some very general reasons: to add comparability among municipalities and between different sectors (business and public) of the economy; business accounting is more known than the cameralistic public sector accounting; to improve the financial accounting information in local governments; to enable preparation of consolidated accounts etc. (see Näsi, 1995, 1996).

The two intended functions of accounting are to provide information for control and to reduce uncertainty in decision-making (see Mellemvik et al., 1988). The proper control of public money is based on two concepts: stewardship and accountability. Stewardship refers to the holding of someone else's assets by a steward. The responsibility of

---

[3]   The membership of the European Union and the accounting harmonization by the implementation of the 4th and 7th Council Directives has eroded the own, Expenditure-Revenue-theory -based accounting thinking in Finland. This has happened in two accounting legislation reforms (in 1992 and 1997).

stewardship is to demonstrate that those assets have not been misappropriated. From the stewardship point of view, the balance sheet shows the financial position (assets and liabilities) of the entity at the end of the year and the income statement the increase or decrease in net assets over the year (Jones and Pendlebury, 1996, p. 116-117). 'Accountability refers to the responsibility for your actions to someone else: ...accountability goes beyond the narrowly defined stewardship of assets to include responsibility for the performance of those assets.' (Jones and Pendlebury, 1996, p. 117) Accountability is therefore a much wider a concept than stewardship and can only partly be concerned with financial accounting information.

Balance of the economy is a central demand in the Finnish municipal legislation (1976 and 1995). But is it a question of the balance of the budget or accounts? These two elements may live their own life (see Högheim et al., 1989). Or balance of the economy measured by revenues and expenditures, or revenues and expenses, or of cash inflows and cash outflows? These are some of the many questions which keep us occupied.

Useful information for decision making in the local governmental context would mean information to balance the economy of the municipality. The balance requirement is based on *the intergenerational equity* - concept which means that every generation should finance the public services it gets or consumes.[4] The intergenerational equity - concept is operationalised by the *interperiod equity* -concept and therefore, it should be possible to measure its realization on the basis of the financial accounting information. Does the historical cost accrual accounting provide measures to analyze the balance of the economy (or finance?) for the municipal decision makers and are these measures found in the income statement or in the balance sheet? And is this information new, brought by the new accrual or business accounting, or had it been possible to provide the same information based on the cameral accounting system?

From the control point of view, financial accounting reports can fulfil the stewardship aspects of the control but the wider accountability aspects can be achieved only in a very limited way. Financial accounting reports do not say anything concerning the level of services in a municipality. Economic or financial measures can be very good but the service level may be very poor in a municipality and vice versa (cp. Meklin, 1998). A municipality can make profit on the cost of services - amount and quality.

9.5.   The Cameral and Accrual Financial Information Compared: the City of Vaasa's Accounts

The question that obviously wakes up interest among people from other countries considering a correspondent accounting change from traditional governmental to accrual accounting is whether the new accrual accounting model is an innovation in the Finnish local governments. How the accrual accounting information differs from the cameral accounting information, what are the new information contents? Does the new model

---

4   The 'traditional version of the intergenerational equity concept is based upon the 'golden rule' that taxpayers in each period should finance all current expenditure and should make a contribution to the financing of inherited productive assets commensurate with the benefits they receive from those assets. (Musgrave and Musgrave, 1973, p. 607 and Robinson, 1998, p. 31-32.)

provide more relevant information than the old system? More relevant, to whom and for what purposes?

The main function of the cameral system was to report the execution of the annual budget. Therefore, the financial information was divided into the same three parts both in the budget and in the accounting reports: operative or running part of the economy, investments, and finance. The two most important financial statements were 'Total Expenditures and Revenues' and the 'Statement of Finance'. Total expenditures and revenues were presented in three columns: as in the budget, in the accounts and the variances (+/-) both in absolute figures and in percentage of the budget. Operative expenditures were classified both in the budget and in accounts by nature, by area of agency, and area of activity. The nature or source of the money classified operative revenues. Investments were listed quite in details. In the Statement of Finance different 'result' figures were calculated, the most important and most often used the annual contribution or result 2 (see Appendix 9.1, table 1). The basic structure of cameral accounting information is presented in Appendix 9.1.

The accrual accounting information in the Finnish local governments consists of the Profit and Loss Statement and the Balance Sheet. Also the Statement of Finance is prepared as an additional statement for the accrual system. The new information produced by the accrual accounting model can be listed in three points: 1) *the Profit and Loss Statement* presented in a subtractive form and with five residues: operative, driving and annual contribution, annual result and the bottom line surplus or deficit; 2) *depreciation accounting* based on historical cost and a pre-set depreciation plan (systematically made depreciations); and 3) *the comprehensive historical cost Balance Sheet* information. The layout of the P/L Statement and the BS as well as the format of the finance statement are presented in Appendix 9.2.

9.5.1. PROFIT AND LOSS STATEMENT

The change from the cameral to accrual accounting model was technically demanding, but it is even more demanding with regard to accounting thinking. How to interpret the new financial accounting information in the local governmental context. What is the role of the annual budget and budgetary accounting compared to the accrual based financial accounting information. Does this new accounting model mean a shift from an ex-ante budgeting to ex-post financial reporting? Does the Profit and Loss Statement with several residues provide more relevant information than the statement of Total Expenditures and Revenues and the Statement of Finance for accountability purposes and for decision making and balancing the municipal economy? Does the P/L statement increase the so-called 'tyranny of the bottom line' (see Estes, 1996) in the local government? For instance, these and many other questions still wait for conclusive answers in the Finnish local governments.

9.5.2. DEPRECIATION ACCOUNTING

What is the meaning of historical cost depreciations in the municipal P/L statement? The official interpretation given in the municipal accounting guide books is that the depreciation figure is meant to cover (collect money) for re-investments and that the annual contribution figure should be big enough to cover the depreciations made systematically according to a pre-set plan. The explanation may be correct in the economy of stable money value. Even then it is reasonable to ask how to finance other than re-investments and annual instalment of debts.

It seems to be the case that there is no correct or clear-cut interpretation for the depreciation figure on the P/L statement and for the needed level of the annual profit figures underneath depreciations. Annual contribution is the 'income' figure most often discussed and compared in the Finnish local governments, but that figure was calculated in the old cameral system too (see Appendix 9.1., the Statement of Finance: Annual contribution = Result 2), and it is therefore not an outcome and merit of the accrual accounting model. According to Finnish local governmental accounting handbooks annual contribution ought to be positive and big enough to cover depreciation, i.e. the annual contribution and depreciation figures are interpreted to represent the balance measure of municipal economy. This kind of interpretation is too simplistic and lacks theoretical foundation.

In the case of the City of Vaasa, the annual contribution has been positive and big enough to cover the depreciation, and also the annual result has been positive in 1997 and 1998. But does this now mean that the economy of the City of Vaasa has been in balance in these two years? It seems to us that the answer is 'no', because the amount of debt has increased in huge amounts in both the two years (see Appendix 9.3.).

9.5.3. HISTORICAL COST BALANCE SHEET

The municipal version of cameral accounting in Finland contained the balance sheet based on current value accounting. It was not produced as an elementary part of the cameral accounting system but as a 'by-product or outcome' of the bookkeeping system. Not only valuation but also other accounting problems, i.e. measurement, extensiveness, and periodization problems are solved differently in the accrual accounting than in the cameral accounting balance sheet. The historical cost accounting balance sheet of accrual accounting includes more extensively all the assets of a municipality than the old, current value balance sheet which contained only building land, buildings, machinery, and other similar assets, but did not contain roads, streets, parks, bridges etc. infrastructure assets. Even though the new balance sheet is more extensive in its scope than the old one, the total value of assets (total of the balance sheet) in the historical cost accounting is approximately 40% lower than the total of the current value balance sheet of the cameral accounting in the Finnish municipalities. The question of course is not, which of the two balance sheets is correct and which is not, but which provides more useful information in the local governmental sector. Does the historical cost balance sheet fulfil the stewardship control better than the current value balance sheet? What is the meaning of the equity figure calculated as a residue on the basis of the balance equation (equity = assets – debt) on the balance sheet? A part of the equity (a certain nominal amount of money) is nominated to be the so-called basic equity which should stay untouched on the balance sheet from one year to another.

9.6. Summary and Conclusions

As pointed out earlier, there is an interdependence between accounting and its context. Moreover, different metaphors can be used when studying organizations. Of particular interest when studying the change from cameral to accrual accounting in local governments, is the application of the political and machine metaphors, because these metaphors have been used when studying local governmental and business organizations.

Accrual accounting refers to a form of bookkeeping that records not only transactions that result from the receipt and disbursement of cash but also the amounts that the entity owes and that others owe to the entity. Thus, the realization principle is employed in the revenue recognition, and the matching of revenues and expenses in closing the annual accounts and in profit measurement (the matching principle is the central concept in the revenue/expense or the income statement or the matching view of accrual accounting particularly). The matching principle states that expenses should be recognised in the same period as the associated revenues; that is, revenues are recognised in a given period according to the realization principle, and the related expenses are then matched against the revenues to calculate the annual profit.

Because a business firm's expenditures and revenues generally relate to each other, we find a causal link between the expenditures and revenues. The reason to sacrifice expenditures is their ability to create revenues, and by sacrificing increased expenditures, increased revenues can be expected. In this way, a business organization consists of cause-effect relationships and resembles a 'profit making' machine. It is in such a machine-like organizational context where accrual accounting with its matching principle traditionally has been applied, and where the purpose of accounting is to measure the profitability of the economic activities conducted during the accounting period. In other words, the general objective of accrual accounting parallels the business firm's objectives to earn revenue from customers and to keep the costs smaller than revenues (see Littleton, 1953, p. 68).

A local government, however, represents an organization that is very different from the machine-like business organization. We do not find an unambiguous objective in governmental organizations, because politicians from different parties represent different interests and opinions of the inhabitants. Hence, different political parities have - and should have - different objectives, resulting in ambiguous and conflicting objectives for the governmental units as organizations. Due to this political dimension, the political metaphor has been used in previous studies of local governments. In this context, the annual budget is used to allocate money for different purposes and to estimate the collection of money from different sources. Cameral accounting records actual transactions and compares budgeted and actual figures to follow up the execution of the budget. The cameral accounting system was tailored to fit into the political environments.

Moreover, the monetary process of the governmental unit is more complicated than the corresponding process of a firm (see Monsen and Näsi, 1998). Firms earn most of their money as sales revenues from their customers and spend their money for purchasing production factors. Besides payments based on the input-output process transactions, i.e. payments for production factors and fees received for goods and services delivered, taxes, state grants and other money transfers play an important role in the governmental monetary process. This means, among other things, that a direct link between services and revenues is largely missing in the governmental context, and so is the link between expenses and the monetary value of the output. Matching of revenues and expenses and profit measurement are therefore even more arbitrary in the governmental context than in the business firm context.

In the political systems, objectives are many and ambiguous and the uses of money as well as sources of money are of several kinds. Consequently, the political governmental context differs strongly from the 'profit making machine'-like business context, and therefore a different accounting model was developed centuries ago for use in governmental organizations: cameral accounting. As we have pointed out above, this is a particular kind of accounting thought with a strong money focus; it is not based upon the matching principle as it is applied within accrual accounting thinking in the business context. Neither is it based upon the realization principle, which also is difficult to apply in the governmental sector for many types of transactions, such as taxes and state grants. Grounded by these arguments we do not see much sense to handle political systems as 'profit making machine' - entities for profit calculation.

In addition to the money focus, two other important features characterize cameral accounting: budgetary control and non-comprehensive balance sheet. Due to the lack of a direct link between services and revenues, the budget is used as the instrument for collecting and allocating money (taxes, state grants etc.) between and within governmental organisations to produce various services. Moreover, due to the annual focus of balancing revenues and expenditures, the cameral accounting system does not generate financial data for a comprehensive balance sheet.

Summing up, we find great differences between local governmental and business organisations. As a consequence of these differences, different accounting models, cameral and accrual accounting, have been used by local governmental and business organisations, respectively. In spite of this situation, however, Finnish local governments have now introduced an accrual accounting model, and financial information based on that model is presented in the annual accounts.[5] Finnish local governments still experience a transition period from cameral to accrual accounting and therefore the meaning and importance of different financial information - budget figures vs. actuals, the P/L statement and the Balance Sheet and the Statement of Finance figures - are not yet crystallized.

The layout for the profit and loss statement (see in Appendix 9.2.) is copied from the business P/L statement layout and contains several residues. The *operative contribution* is the first of the residues, calculated as a remainder of the operative revenues and operative expenses. This residue gives a falsified idea of matching. Charges and fees from *priced goods and services* are matched against *all* operative expenses of the

---

[5]   The Finnish system represents mainly the AFR (Accrual Financial Reporting) in the categorization presented by James Guthrie in FAM, Volume 14, No 1, 1998.

municipality. This residue, however, will probably increase the business thinking in municipalities and strengthen the idea of a municipality as a profit-making machine.

The *annual contribution* (i.e. running revenues ./. running expenditures; without investments and capital transactions) is perceived as one of the critical economic measures in the Finnish local governments. Annual contribution was calculated in the cameral accounting (as a residue in the finance statement) as well as it is calculated in the new accrual accounting model (as a residue in the P/L statement). In general, the cameral total expenditure and revenue statement together with the finance statement provided the same information as the accrual profit and loss statement; with an exception of the historical cost depreciation figure. Therefore, *the role of the historical cost depreciation figure* in financial accounts is critical and it really represents the new information produced by the accrual accounting model. It represents an allocated cost item (periodization), but what is its role, its appropriate meaning and use in the decision making and from the stewardship and accountability point of view?

Depreciations, the annual result and surplus/deficit all contribute to the idea of profit measurement; but so far without a clear-cut interpretation. What should be the level of the profit and surplus in a local government? Annual contribution, profit or surplus is needed to finance investments and annual debt instalments. But how much profit is needed from the 'economic balance' point of view (actually from the intergenerational and interperiod equity point of view)? How to define and how to measure the economic balance? What are the key concepts in the 'balance' measurement. Are they expenditures and revenues as budgeted and recorded in the traditional, money-focus cameral system, or periodized expenses and revenues of accrual accounting, or maybe pure cash outflows and cash inflows? We think that it is money that matters. Enough money has to flow in to cover the costs. Balance of economy means balance of finance. This is at least true in the smaller economic units (like families); why not in the bigger ones, like in the local governments? The money-focused cameral accounting (including the system of reservations for future investments; compare savings for bigger purchases in the family context) was quite good from the economic balance point of view. The accounting system cannot be blamed for the indebtedness of the local governments. Loans are taken by decision makers. If the cash-flow argumentation is agreed then we would ask, what do local governments benefit from 'periodizing' and from the accrual accounting system based on the revenue and expense concepts? We think that a version of cash or funds flow accounting model would provide the best basis for balancing a municipal economy. The statement of finance has played an important role in the cameral system (see Appendix 9.1.) and it is still needed as an extra statement for the accrual accounting too.

The Finnish dynamic accounting theory interprets the balance sheet as a transfer account. The layout of the historical cost balance sheet of accrual accounting (see the balance sheet in Appendix 9.2.) is copied from business sector accounting and is more comprehensive in its scope than the cameral current value balance sheet (see the balance sheet in Appendix 9.1.). The monetary values of fixed assets in the accrual accounting balance sheet are lower than in the cameral balance sheet values due to the different valuation methods, historical cost vs. current value. Which of these valuation methods or what method - if any - is most appropriate for local governments, is a topic discussed in some articles (see e.g. Robinson, 1998), but which still needs further discussions from different point of views. The historic cost is for several reasons mostly applied in the business sector, but its reliability and validity is often made questionable in the business sector too.

References

- Belkaoui, A. (1993) *Accounting Theory,* 3 Edition, Academic Press, London.
- Brunsson, N. (1986) Organizing for Inconsistencies: On Organizational Conflict,Depression and Hypocrisy as Substitutes for Action, *Scandinavian Journal of Management Studies*, 165-185.
- Chan, J.L, Jones, R.H. and Lüder, K.G. (1996) Modelling Governmental Accounting Innovations: An Assessment and Future Research Directions, *Research in Governmental and Nonprofit Accounting*, 1-19.
- Estes R. (1996) *Tyranny of the Bottom Line*, Why Corporations Make Good People Do Bad Things, Berrett-Koehler Publishers, San Francisco.
- Filios, V.P. (1983) The Cameralistic Method of Accounting: A Historical Note, *Journal of Business Finance & Accounting*, 443-450.
- Guthrie, J. (1998) Application of Accrual Accounting in the Australian Public Sector-Rhetoric or Reality, *Financial Accountability & Management*, Volume 14, No1, (February 1998), 1-19.
- Hay, Leon B. and Mikesell, R.M. (1974) *Governmental Accounting,* Richard D.Irwin, Inc. Homewood, Fifth Edition, Illinois.
- Hendriksen, E.S. (1982) *Accounting Theory,* International Edition, Fourth Edition, Irwin, Homewood, Illinois.
- Hopwood, A.G. (1983) On Trying to Study Accounting in the Context in which It Operates, *Accounting, Organizations and Society*, 287-305.
- Høgheim, S., Monsen, N., Olsen, R. and Olson, O. (1989) The Two Worlds of Management Control, *Financial Accountability and Management*, 163-178.
- Jones, R. and Pendlebury, M. (1996) *Public Sector Accounting,* Pitman Publishing, 4th Edition, London.
- Jönsson, S. (1982) Budgetary Behaviour in Local Government - A Case Study over 3 Years, *Accounting, Orgnaizations and Society*, 287-304.
- Lee, T.A. (1972) A Case for Cash Flow Reporting, *Journal of Business and Finance*, 27-50.
- Lee, T.A. (1986) *Towards a Theory and Practice of Cash Flow Accounting*, Garland Publishing, Inc., New York.
- Littleton, A.C. (1985) *Structure of Accounting Theory,* American Accounting Association, Monograph No. 5, Sarasota 1953 (13th printing 1985).
- Meklin, P. (1998) Tuliko kunnista yrityksiä? Polemiikki, Uuden kuntatiedon erikoislehti, 2/98, 10-11.
- Mellemvik, F., Monsen, N. and Olson, O. (1988) Functions of Accounting; A Discussion, *Scandinavian Journal of Management*, 101-119.
- Monsen, N. (1983) *Regnskap i politikken? Om årsrapportens funksjoner foe en kommune og dens toppledelse,* Fagbokforlaget, Bergen.
- Monsen, N. and Näsi, S. (1986) Local Governmental Accounting in Finland and Norway: A Historical Note on Cameralism, *Research in Governmental and Nonprofit Accounting*, 259-274.
- Monsen, N. and Näsi, S. (1998) The Contingency Model of Governmental Accounting Innovations: a discussion, *The European Accounting Review*, 7:2, 275-288.

- Monsen, N. and Olson, O. (1986) Silent Accounting Harmonisation: Towards the Presentation of Cash Flow Models in the Local Governmental and Business Fields in Norway, *Scandinavian Journal of Management*, 411-423.
- Morgan, G. (1986) *Images of Organization*, Sage Publications, Beverly Hills.
- Musgrave, R. and Musgrave, P. (1973) *Public Finance in Theory and Practice*, McGraw-Hill, New York.
- Näsi, S. (1995) Financial Reporting in the Public Sector, The development of local authority accounting and accountability in Finland from the 1920s to the present, Paper presented at the 18th Annual Congress of the European Accounting Association, 10-12 May 1995, Birmingham, United Kingdom.
- Näsi, S. (1996) Criteria for Choosing a Business Accounting Model in the Finnish Public Sector, Paper presented at the 19th Annual Congress of the European Accounting Association, NHH, Bergen, Norway, 2-4 May 1996.
- Olson, O. (1983) *Ansvar och ändamål - om utveckling och användning av ett konmmunalt ekonomsisystem*, Doxa, Karlshamn.
- Potthoff, E. and Sieben, G. (1994) Eugen Schmalenbach (1873-1955), in *Twentieth-Century Accounting Thinkers*, Edited by John Richard Edwards, Routledge, London.
- Robinson, M. (1998) Accrual Accounting and the Efficiency of the Core Public Sector, Financial Accountability and Management in Government, Public Services and Charities, Volume 14, No 1, February 1998.
- Rombach, B. (1986) *Rationalisering eller prat. Kommuners anpassning till en stagnerande ekonomi*, Doxa, Lind.
- Saario, M. (1945) Realisointiperiaate ja käyttöomaisuuden poistot tuloslaskennassa, Liiketaloudellisen tutkimuslaitoksen julkaisuja 6, Helsinki.
- Saario, M. (1968) Kirjanpidon meno-tulo teoria, Keuruu.
- Schmalenbach, E. (1933) *Dynamische Bilanz*, 6. Auflage, Leipzig.
- Sterling, R.R. (1979) *Toward a Science of Accounting*, Scholars Book Co. Houston, Texas.
- Walb, E. (1926) *Die Erfolgsrechnung privater und öffentlicher Betriebe. Eine Grundlegung*, Industrieverlag Spaeth & Linde, Berlin.
- Wysocki, K.V. (1965) *Kameralistisches Rechnungswesen*, C.E. Poecschel Verlag: Stuttgart.

Appendix 9.1.: Layout of Financial Statements prepared in Cameral Accounting in the Finnish Local Governments

	Accounts of the three previous financial years	Accounts of the financial year	Budget for the financial year	Difference Accounts vs. Budget
Tax revenues				
State grants				
Operational economy (net)				
Operational contribution **= Result 1**				
Interest income				
Interest expense				
Other financial income				
Other financial expense				
Annual contribution **= Result 2**				
Transfer of surplus from previous years				
Transfer of deficit from previous years				
Transfer from reserve funds				
Transfer to reserve funds				
Finance from own sources **= Result 3**				
Investments (net)				
Loans given				
Amortization of given loans				
Change of debts				
Surplus/deficit				

Table 1.: Statement of Finance

	Budget incl. changes made during the financial year	Actual accounts	Variance Budget vs. accounts	Execution-%
EXPENDITURES				
Operational expenditure				
Investment expenditure				
Finance expenditure				
Total expenditure				
REVENUES				
Operational revenue				
Investment revenue				
Finance revenue				
(incl. tax revenue				
and state grants)				
Total revenue				

Table 2.: Total Expenditures and Revenues

ASSETS	LIABILITIES
FINANCIAL ASSETS	**SHORT-TERM DEBT**
Cash	Payables
Deposits	Deferred expenditure
Accrued revenue	
Undeposit loans	**LONG-TERM DEBT**
Deferred expenditure	Budgetary loans
Receivables	Other long-term debt
Valuation items	
	ADMINSTRATED CAPITAL
Other receivables	State capital
Short-term loan receivables	Other capital
Fond special contribution	Quarantee capital
	Other capital
INVENTORIES	
	RESERVES
OUTGIVEN LOANS	Appropriations transferred
Budgetary loans	for next years
FIXED ASSETS	**EQUITY**
Work in Process	Fund equities
Land and water areas	Operative capital
Buildings	Surplus of the financial year
Constructions and machinery	
Water supply	
Harbours	
Other non-fixed assets	
Intangible assets	
ADMINISTRATED ASSETS	
State assets	
Other assets	

Table 3.: The current Value Balance Sheet

**Appendix 9.2.:   Layout of Financial Statements prepared in Accrual Accounting
in the Finnish Local Governments**

OPERATIONAL REVENUE
    Sales revenue
    Charges
    Subscriptions and allowances
    Rents
    Other revenue
    Production for own use
Operational revenue total
OPERATIONAL EXPENSE
    Wages and salaries
    External services
    Materials and goods
    Allowances
    Rents
    Other costs
Operational expense total
Operational contribution

TAXES AND STATE GRANTS
    Tax income
    State grant
    charging of VAT
Driving contribution

FINANCIAL REVENUE AND COST
    Interest income
    Other financial income
    Interest expense
    Other financial expense
Annual contribution

DEPRECIATION AND EXTRAORDINARY ITEMS
    Depreciation of fixed assets
    Extraordinary revenue
    Extraordinary cost
Annual result
Change of reserves and funds
Annual surplus

Table 1.:   Profit and Loss Statement

Income finance
    Annual contribution
    Extraordinary items
    Decrease of obligatory funds
Income finance total

Investments
    Investments in fixed assets
    Financial aid for investments
    Sale of fixed assets
Investments net
Change of long-term receivable
    decrease of loans given
    increase of loans given
    decrease of long-term
    receivable
Change of long-term receivable
Decrease of long-term debt
    Decrease of long-term debt
Need for finance
Finance with capital
    Increase of long-term debt
    Increase of other long-term
    payable
Finance with capital
**Change (decrease) of working
capital**

Table 2.:   Statement of Finance

ASSETS	LIABILITIES
Fixed assets and other long-term expenditures	**Equity**
Intangible assets	Basic equity
Intangible rights	Other own capital
Other long-term expenditure	Surplus/deficit of previous
	financial years
	Surplus/deficit of this year
Tangible assets	**Reserves**
Land and water areas	Voluntary reserves
Buildings	Obligatory reserves
Constructions	
Machines and inventories	**Valuation item**
Other tangible assets	
	Capital in our administration
Stocks and other long-term investments	State fond
Stocks and shares	Other fond
Mass promissory notes	
Loan receivables	
Other investments	
	Debt
-	**Long-term debt**
Valuation items	Loans from financial and
	insurance institutions
Assets in our administration	Loans from public sector
State assets	Other long-term debt
Other administrated assets	
	Short-term debt
	Loans from financial and
Current assets	insurance institutions
Materials and supplies	Loans from public sector
Work in process	Loans from other sources
	Prepayments
	Payables
	Other short-term debt
Receivables	
Accounts receivables	
Financial investments	
Loan receivables	
Other receivables	
Cash and money in bank accounts	
ASSETS TOTAL	**LIABILITIES TOTAL**

Table 3.: Historical Cost Balance Sheet

FINANCIAL MANAGEMENT INITIATIVES AT DIFFERENT GOVERNMENTAL LAYERS IN THE NETHERLANDS

G. Jan van Helden and Nico P. Mol

10.1. Introduction

In the Netherlands, as in many other developed countries over the world, the reforms characterized as New Public (Financial) Management have found general acclaim in government organizations. These reforms have been summarized by Olson, Guthrie and Humphrey (1998, p.18) in the following five categories, which are all of them easily recognizable in the attempts at improvement of Dutch government governance.

1. Changes in financial reporting systems, specifically the promotion of accrual-based financial statements. In Dutch local and regional government accrual accounting has been fully adopted in the eighties. In central government traditional cash accounting as yet remains being applied to core departments, but since 1994 organization units can be assigned an 'agency' status, enabling the application of accrual accounting instead.
2. Development of market oriented management systems, with some emphasis on internal and external pricing. In all layers of government full-cost pricing is being promoted wherever possible. Within government organizations transfer pricing is progressively applied (in central government specifically in transfers with the newly constituted 'agencies').
3. Development of performance measurement. Performance indicators are generally in use, in local and regional government often expanded into formal performance budgets for activities.
4. Devolvement or delegation of budgets. In local and regional government the introduction of decentralized budgeting generally followed the divisionalization of organization structure widely implemented in the past decades (as e.g. in the well-known Tilburg Model, cf. Herweijer and Mix, 1996). In central government such decentralizations are being pursued as an attempt to reduce bureaucracy by enabling organization units to some degree of self-management.
5. Changes to public sector audits, specifically aiming at value-for-money assessments. This topic is being given a lot of attention and regularly new instruments are derived from the literature to fulfill the operational audit objectives generally subscribed. However, this category may prove to be the fundamental weakness persisting in public financial management reform in the Netherlands, in local and regional as well as in central government.

This paper will focus on the reforms with respect to financial planning and control in Dutch government organizations. Both in local or regional and in central government very similar objectives of performance management have been underlying the initiatives developed in this respect. For local and regional government the so-called Policy and

A. Bac (ed.), International Comparative Issues in Government Accounting, 159-176.
© 2001 *Kluwer Academic Publishers. Printed in the Netherlands.*

Management Instruments project tried to promote this objective, in central government a Result Oriented Management Control initiative is intended to play a similar role.

The paper examines these developments, to arrive at some 'lessons learned' for the future. In section 10.2., we will characterize the layers of government with respect to relevant conditions for the intended performance based management control systems. In section 10.3. the implementation of these systems - the Policy and Management Instruments project and the Result Oriented Management Control initiative respectively - will be reviewed. Section 10.4. will finally discuss some obstacles for performance-based management.

10.2. Governmental Structure in the Netherlands

This section describes some important characteristics of the governmental structure in the Netherlands. It will focus on the following issues:
- organizational size at each of the governmental layers;
- the extent to which these layers are mutually dependent;
- an indication of the type of functions these layers perform;
- the accounting standards to be applied at each of the governmental layers.

10.2.1. SIZE OF GOVERNMENTAL ORGANIZATIONS

The governmental structure in the Netherlands consists of three layers: the central, the provincial (i.e. regional) and the municipal layer. Apart from an undivided central layer with 14 departments, there are 12 provinces and about 550 municipalities. They differ in size according to the number of inhabitants to a large extent, as is shown in tables 10.1. and 10.2. Moreover, these tables illustrate the relationship between the number of inhabitants and the number of employees of the organizations in question.

Number of Inhabitants Full-time equivalent Functions (ftes)	Lower than 750,00	Between 750,00 and 1,500,00	Larger than 1,500,00	total
less than 800 ftes	4	1	0	5
between 800 and 1200 ftes	1	2	1	4
more than 1200 ftes	0	0	3	3
total	5	3	4	12

Table 10.1.: Classification of Provinces: the Relationship between the Number of Inhabitants and the Number of Full-time Equivalent Functions (ftes).
Source: Van Helden, 1999, p. 13.

Municipal Size in Number of Inhabitants	Estimated Number of Employees (in ftes)	Number of Municipalities
1000-10,000	15-65	137
10,000-20,000	65-140	188
20,000-50,000	140-400	165
50,000-100,000	400-1000	33
100,000-200,000	1000-3500	21
larger than 200,000	3500-25,000	4
Total	156,000	548

Table 10.2.: Classification of Municipalities: the Relationship between the Number of Inhabitants and the Number of Full-time Equivalent Functions (ftes).

Sources: - estimated Number of Employees per Size Category Van Helden, 1998, p. 93;
             - number of municipalities per size category on the first of January 1998, CBS, 1998b, p. 64.

This relationship might be relevant within the context of this paper because evidently in smaller municipalities with less than about 20,000 inhabitants, the scale of the organization is only moderate: ranging from approximately 15 to 140 civil servants, expressed in full-time equivalent jobs. These organizations will probably not introduce advanced systems of planning and control. Organizational units are so small that direct personal control will be preferred to formalized control systems based on 'paper work'. Furthermore, the educational background of managers and senior staff in charge of finance are unlikely to be sufficient for the successful application of advanced methods of management control. Also, the politicians, especially those on the executive commit-tee of the council, are likely to be very involved in the details of policy planning and control. As we move up the municipal scale, both the number of organizational units and the size of each unit increases. There is then a growing distance between the political and managerial levels and the decentralization of responsibilities to unit managers becomes more important. Moreover, as direct personal control becomes more difficult, there is an inducement to develop more advanced types of planning and control.

Basically, all provinces will be appropriate for introducing these planning and control instruments because even the smallest provinces are sufficiently large in this respect. The same holds for central government where the departments (ministries) are all large-size organizations, although some autonomized units may have a relatively small scale. The total number of (civilian) employees at the central government is about 120,000 spread over 14 departments.

10.2.2. THE NETHERLANDS AS A DECENTRALIZED UNITARY

The governmental structure in the Netherlands is based on the principles of the decentralized unitary state. Unitarity implies on the one hand interdependence of the governmental layers. On the other hand, it refers to some kind of hierarchical relationships between the central, the provincial and the local level. The latter implies that the regulatory role is concentrated at the central level, or at least that provinces and municipalities are not permitted to establish regulations, which are not compatible with central laws and regulations. Another implication is that supervising authorities exist at the central level towards the provincial level, as well at the provincial level towards the municipal level (Toonen, 1998, pp. 38-39; Schouten, 1999, p. 9).

The characteristics of the Dutch unitary decentralized state appear clearly in the financial relationships between central government on the one hand and provincial and municipal government on the other hand. The unitarian element is reflected in a highly centralized taxation system. Decentralization, however, may be inferred from the relatively low share of central government expenditure. Table 10.3. presents comparisons with six other West European countries. Obviously, financial relationships between layers of government are characterized by a high degree of 'downward tax sharing'.

	Average Share central Government Taxation 1950-1990	Average Share central Government Expenditure 1950-1990
The Netherlands	96.4	64.3
Belgium	93.9	81.7
Ireland	91.1	72.3
United Kingdom	87.8	71.8
France	87.7	77.0
Germany (West)	54.7	45.4

Table 10.3.:   Financial Relations between Central and Local Governments in six West European Countries
Source: Steunenberg and Mol, 1997, p. 238

The provincial and local governmental layers in the Netherlands are strongly dependent upon central government funding. Provincial and local taxes as well as fees are only small, whereas the major part of their income comes from general grants and block grants which are supplied by central government (Van der Dusssen, 1992). Table 10.4. gives more detailed information.

Source of Income	Municipalities		Provinces	
	in milliards of Dutch guilders	in percentages	In milliards of Dutch guilders	in percentages
General Grants	22.13	36.7%	1.67	32.9%
Block Grants	28.81	47.7%	1.94	38.3%
Taxes	5.09	8.4%	1.27	25.1%
Fees ('heffingen')	4.36	7.2%	0.19	3.7%
Total	60.38	100%	5.07	100%

Table 10.4.:   Financial Relationships between Central Government and Provincial and Local Government in the Netherlands in 1998.
Source: Dutch Central Government Budget Memorandum 1999, 1998, p. 255.

10.2.3. FUNCTION CHARACTERIZATION OF GOVERNMENTAL LAYERS

The extent to which governmental functions are executive may determine the opportunities for a fruitful application of performance-based management systems. When functions are mainly non-executive (administrative), it is relatively difficult to specify adequate performance indicators. Hence, it is worthwhile to characterize the functions of the three governmental layers of the Netherlands.

Municipalities in the Netherlands perform a broad variety of functions, such as:
- welfare, culture, education, health care, sport and recreation;
- spatial planning and economic affairs;
- social services and employment programming;
- environmental affairs.

In many instances, the police, fire brigade, public transport and public utilities are transferred to larger scale corporations, which operate outside the municipal administration. Evidently, some of the municipal functions, like spatial planning, are more or less administrative, but the majority of the municipal functions can be characterized as executive.

The provincial functions show an opposite picture. Although responsibilities for roads and canals are executive, provinces mainly perform planning and coordinating functions, such as regional, welfare, environmental and water planning. These functions are administrative.

Central government takes an intermediate position in this respect. Central government in the Netherlands is primary responsible for the traditional governmental functions, like Defence, Foreign affairs and Justice. However, central government also covers nearly all other governmental functions, but mainly in a regulating sense, leaving executive parts to provinces and mostly to municipalities. Consequently, some central government functions are executive whereas others are administrative.

10.2.4. CASH-BASED VERSUS ACCRUAL ACCOUNTING

In the new public (financial) management framework accrual accounting is considered a fundamental characteristic of performance oriented management control systems. Accountability with respect to performance will refer to costs of production, to judge efficiency of activities performed. Assessment of product costs should be based upon expenses for resources consumed instead of expenditures for resources purchased. In the past decades, accounting systems for provincial and municipal government have indeed developed from cash-based into fully accrual ones (Schouten, 1999, pp. 20-23). Thus, for executive tasks in these government organizations product cost calculations may be performed and judgments on efficiency in terms of these calculations established.

However, in central government traditional cash accounting has been maintained. For core business activities in central government accrual accounting was generally considered irrelevant (and even undesirable from the point of view of budget spending control). But again the distinction between executive and non-executive tasks may be invoked to plead accrual accounting for the first category. Organization units with predominantly executive tasks (EDP services, inspection and control units, law enforcing agencies etc.) should be managed in accordance with efficiency objectives in terms of product costs.

Thus, it has been decided to allow for a certain differentiation of accounting systems in central government to accommodate these diverging requirements. Executive agencies within government will thereby be enabled to use distinct - accrual - accounting systems for their activities, linked by their cash balances to the general cash accounting system of central government. Management information with respect to these agencies can thus be adapted to their specific characteristics, but hierarchical (internal) supervision on their activities will be maintained. To prevent a proliferation of such 'autonomized' accounting systems (endangering the unity principle of government budgeting) admission criteria for this 'agency status' have been specified. Among these criteria measurability of services delivered is again considered a corner stone.

In 1994 the first four of these formalized agencies were created: the EDP unit of the Defence department, the immigration service of the Justice department, a service for plant disease control in the Agriculture department and an entrepeneurial help-desk in the department of Economic Affairs. Since then the agency status has been awarded to some twenty organization units over the whole range of departments in central government.

10.3. Application of Businesslike Planning and Control

Various financial management initiatives, which are comparable with international trends in public management (Hood, 1991; Olson, et al., 1998) were taken in Dutch government. One of the best-known of those initiatives at the municipal and provincial level is the Policy and Management Instruments project. This section will address the philosophy and impact of this project. Thereafter, this section will deal with the Result Oriented Management Control initiative at the central governmental level.

10.3.1. THE PMI PROJECT FOR MUNICIPALITIES AND PROVINCES

The Policy and Management Instruments (PMI) project was an initiative of central government in the Netherlands.[1] Its primary aim was to make local and provincial authorities familiar with new ways of governance and management. It should be emphasized that the PMI project could only stimulate rather than enforce these organizations to use new management techniques.

---

[1] The Dutch equivalent of PMI is BBI, which is the abbreviation of 'Beleids- en Beheers Instrumentarium'. Apart from BBI, some cities in the Netherlands with more than 100,000 inhabitants developed their own financial management systems. Whereas the PMI project was directed primarily to small and mid-size municipalities, the so-called Tilburg model is probably the best-known example of public sector change in large Dutch cities. The main characteristics of this model are performance-oriented management connected with divisionalisation (Schrijvers, 1993). More recently, attention was switched to customer-orientation, both by examining clients' appreciation of city services, by measuring the outcome of policy programs, and by restructuring the organization according to different types of activities, such as policy-making, production of services and front-office (Korsten, 1996).

The PMI project uses a planning and control focus: from planning, via reporting and replanning to evaluation. In this respect, various new tools of governance and management had to be developed. The presence of an output budget in which budget functions are characterized by performance indicators is often considered to be the key element of the new planning and control techniques (Houwaart et al., 1995, p. 12). Moreover, PMI uses a hierarchical system of the planning and control cycle with interconnected budgets and reports at various levels of the organization. Additionally, this project supposes municipalities and provinces to structure their organization on the basis of policy fields.

More specifically, PMI recommends to use the following planning and control instruments:
1. a medium-term plan which defines policy plans for the future rather than extrapolating financial trends from the past;
2. an output budget which specifies performance measures related to inputs for all policy fields;
3. a hierarchical planning and control system which encompasses budgets and reports on the various organizational levels;
4. performance reports which take place during each budgetary cycle, offering opportunities to manage, adjust and hold organizational units accountable;
5. the formulation of performance standards which indicate that values of performance indicators are compared with target levels, in order to improve the quality of the planning and control process;
6. auditing of relevant outcomes in order to evaluate the effectiveness of the policy plans.

10.3.2. EMPIRICAL RESULTS OF THE PMI PROJECT

Table 10.5. provides information about the existence of these planning and control instruments in an examination of eight mid-size municipalities and in an investigations of all twelve provinces. This table shows that most of the municipalities and provinces have a medium-term plan, an output budget, a hierarchical planning and control system, and performance reports. However, performance standards turn out to be rare; in fact, none of the municipalities or provinces possesses an instrument for auditing of outcomes.

Provinces and municipalities show on average a similar picture of financial management initiatives. However, this does not imply that within each of these governmental layers differences do not occur. The study of the eight mid-size municipalities, for instance, indicates that two from the eight municipalities are seriously lagging behind because they do not possess an output budget and performance reports (Van Helden, 1998b, p. 22). Moreover, a recent survey study of all Dutch municipalities indicates that the smaller the municipal scale, the lower the average usage of these instruments will be. Generally speaking, this survey confirms the results of table 10.5., in the sense that about 80% of the municipalities in the Netherlands apply output-oriented planning and control instruments (Moret Ernst & Young, 1997, pp. 106-110). Another survey of a small sample of 16 municipalities, with between 13,000 and 40,000 inhabitants found that output budgeting is used by 67% of these municipalities (KPMG, Welschen, 1997, pp. 5, 33).[2] The examination of the 12 provinces shows that mid-size and large-size provinces more intensively use performance-oriented budgeting than by small-size provinces (Van Helden, 1999, p. 4).[3]

Type of Instrument	Municipalities	Provinces
1. a medium-term plan	75%	83%
2. an output budget	75%	100%
3. a hierarchical planning and control system	88%	75%
4. performance reports	81%	92%
5. the formulation of performance standards	6%	25%
6. auditing of relevant outcomes	0%	0%

Table 10.5.:   Availability of Planning and Control Instruments in Municipalities and Provinces

Sources: -   Municipalities: Van Helden, 1998b, p. 22
                -   Provinces: Van Helden , 1999, p. 3.

10.3.3.RESULT ORIENTED MANAGEMENT CONTROL IN CENTRAL GOVERN-MENT

In central government improvement of financial management has been pursued during the last decades in a number of projects. At a general level the use of performance indicators is being promoted. In recent years attention has been focused on the provision of output and efficiency indicators in the budgets of the departments of central government. According to the 1999 Budget Memorandum, efficiency indicators are being provided for about 65% of relevant expenditures. Optimistically, the Budget Memorandum moreover concludes to some progress over the years 1998 to 1999. We may recall, however, that a very similar initiative to produce performance indicators for central government budgets had already been started at the beginning of the eighties. In the first years this initiative showed a rapid progress but nevertheless the project had to be started all over again in the nineties (Bac, 1993, pp. 310-318).

Within the departments financial management initiatives are focusing at planning and control in the so-called result oriented management control project. In this project a further development of contract management initiatives dating from the eighties is being pursued. Existing contracts with organization units had been found wanting with respect to the specification of tasks to be performed. Often organization units contented themselves with just a description of their tasks, when more accurate performance indicators were not available. In the result oriented management control project the provision of measurable output and/or process indicators is forwarded as a necessary condition for accountability with respect to the contracts agreed upon.

---

[2]   See for some case-based research on new planning and control instruments in Dutch local government: Schrijvers, 1993; Ter Bogt and Van Helden, 1999.

[3]   Some progress has been achieved in applying performance budgeting. An investigation referring to the beginning of the nineties came up with conclusion that only a minority of the provinces actually had introduced performance indicators in the budgetary process (Bac, 1993, p. 321).

To assess the impacts of this result oriented management control project we have reviewed a number of contracts for decentralized organization units in Dutch central government. In our review we have focused on government organizations of a sufficiently large size (see section 10.2.1.) encompassing units with more or less executive tasks, for which the measurability requirements stated above could be effectively met. The cases considered have been drawn from two organizations specifically: the Internal Revenue Service ('Belastingdienst') in the department of Finance and the department of Defence. The first has some 30,000 employees, the second some 70,000.

With respect to the agencies (see section 10.2.4.) a recent evaluation report was published by the department of Finance on behalf of the Council of Ministers, in which the question is addressed to what extent favourable impacts may be attributed to the agency status and the accrual accounting systems related to it.

Upon inspection of the IRS (Internal Revenue Service) and Defence contracts, the following three levels of performance management could be distinguished.[4]
1. Provision of quantified measures of performance indicators for organization units. We found such measures in all contracts considered. With respect to the IRS performance indicators do refer to volumes of tax declarations and/or tax forms issued for distinct categories of taxes, numbers of client visits and in-depth research of records, percentages of arrears in tax debt assessment and debt collection etc. For Defence units we may encounter numbers of missions to be produced (e.g. for squadrons of the air force), numbers of trainees (for instruction centers) and volumes of combat ready personnel and material (land forces).
2. Benchmarking with respect to the indicator values measured. We found this benchmarking to be most advanced whenever a number of decentralized units are performing similar activities. In the IRS we have the regional divisions enabling to benchmarking based upon mutual comparisons (as in municipalities and provinces). Detailed comparisons for these divisions do result in weighted aggregated scores for the indicators measured, from which unambiguous rankings of the divisions are derived. For many indicators specific target values have been established (e.g. maximum percentages for arrears and minimum percentages for client visits and in-depth research of records). In the Dutch Defence organization close similarities at the level of contract management are however rare, especially for primary processes. In the land forces, contracts have been drawn up for each of the only four brigades of the Dutch army. These four units moreover are only limitly comparable because of differences in tasks and mobilization levels. Benchmarking in Defence seems to be limited to secondary activities like maintenance, which are again regionally divisionalized.
3. Assessment of product costs. To evaluate production in terms of efficiency product costs should be established. Otherwise benchmarking will only imply direct comparisons of indicator values, with all possible interpretations of divergences.

---

[4]   For the IRS contracts for the Enterprise Division with respect to fiscal year 1999 have been scrutinized, provided by the IRS as representative for the service as a whole. For Defence three contracts for 1998 drawn up in accordance with the prescribed uniform format for Defence have been investigated: for 13 Mechanized Brigade, Eindhoven Air Force Base and the Royal Military Academy.

Rankings in the IRS are being constructed by weighting of individual indicators in indicator sets. Aggregated scores for regional divisions serving business clients e.g. are deduced from three sets of indicators: cash flow results (weight 10%), treatment of clients (80%) and internal control (10%). The first and last of these sets encompass only a few items (cash flow results for instance are calculated from volumes of tax obligations assessed and collected respectively). The second however, is rather complicated: 28 separate indicators are weighted in its calculation. A major obstacle to product cost assessment - notwithstanding the detailed benchmarking systems used in the IRS - however remains: in all contracts performance indicators and costs are presented disconnectedly. Neither for individual indicators nor for sets of them values realized can be linked to costs incurred to infer any judgement on efficiency of activities performed. The indicator sets provided thus do not fulfill the requirements of coherent indicator systems from which performance evaluations can be derived (Mol, 1996).

Assessment of product costs is explicitly intended in the agency model introduced in 1991. Application of accrual accounting is thereby supposed to create the necessary conditions. The agency model certainly has gained some popularity. In 1998 19 organization units in central government had been awarded the agency status, implying reform of their accounting systems to accruals. Together these agencies had a turnover of Dfl 3.5 billion and over 25,000 employees (almost 25% of central government civil service). During 1998 the agency model has been evaluated for all 14 agencies created up to 1997.

The research question pivotal in the evaluation referred to the improvement of performance attributed to the agency status. The report Continuing with Result, the Agency Model 1991-1997 (Ministerie van Financiën, 1998a) reviews to what extent performance measurement - as required for the agency status - has actually been developed and what additional improvements might be necessary to succeed in the underlying objectives of result oriented management control.

All agencies report to use quantified indicators to measure their products and services (even if for some of them not encompassing 100% of production). Thereby it is conceded however, that the indicators measured need further refinement, specifically with respect to quality characteristics. In particular, agencies generally do not report that their indicators represent outputs: the indicators are supposed to represent 'primary processes' in the agencies - but thereby they may refer to processes or inputs (hours) or even just to costs.

Assessments in the report of the impacts of the agency status on performance differentiate between two types of agencies involved. Seven of the agencies reviewed are characterized by 'quasi-market' production. They cover costs through sales revenues obtained from a number of clients. For these seven agencies clear indications of improved performance in the research period are reported. Specifically, reductions in tariffs are mentioned as evidence. However, for the other seven agencies producing on behalf of one 'principal' only (the department to which they belong or one of its directorates) such clear indications are absent. Performance measurement in these agencies does not provide evidence for whatever impacts might be attributed to the management reforms implemented there.

In the Continuing with Result report the inadequacies of performance measurement in the agencies are to some extent admitted. The report warns (1998b, pp. 49-51): 'What is crucial is to express products and services in volume and performance indicators and to allocate costs to these indicators', thereby pleading for more precise measurement requirements for the agency status in the future involving 'more or less detailed models for product cost allocation'.

As an example of the problems encountered we may consider actual product cost assessment in the Service for Penitentiary Institutions, one of the agencies reviewed. In this service cost and product information is derived from two separate systems: cost figures from a financial information system, product volumes from a capacity information system. Product costs thereby can only be calculated through a division of total costs by detention days - the most primitive 'cost allocation method' conceivable. Thus again we are confronted here with defaulting linkages of performance indicators to costs incurred.

10.3.4. CONCLUDING REMARKS

The aforementioned observations show that on average at the central, the provincial and the local layers of Dutch government performance-oriented performance systems have been introduced during the last decade. The relatively small-size organizations are somewhat lagging behind in this respect.

Our analysis of the Dutch governmental structure in section 10.2. did not indicate strong differences between governmental layers in their propensity to apply performance-based planning and control. Although the empirical results on the actually introduced planning and control systems (discussed in sections 10.3.1. to 10.3.3.) are not fully comparable, some evidence is given for similarity of these systems in the three governmental layers of the Netherlands.

However, the extent to which the systems introduced are in fact and effectively performance oriented remains dubious. Our investigations at the level of central government did show major deficiencies in the assessment of product costs: linkages of costs to products (cost objects) were only weakly established. We may doubt, moreover, if product cost assessments in municipal and provincial government is much more advanced. Specifically we may question to what extent the purported 'output budgets' actually represent targeted product costs. Performance standards and audits of outcomes (efficiency) are virtually absent (cf. table 10.6 in section 10.3.2.). Thus we might infer comparable deficiencies in the implementation of the PMI project as encountered in the strive towards result oriented management control in central government.

From this conclusion we will discuss in the last section some issues which may be relevant in the development of performance management in Dutch government organizations.

10.4. Obstacles to Performance-based Management in Practice

Generalizing from the Dutch experiences reviewed in section 3, this section will pay attention to three issues, which may impede the intended development of performance management in government. First we will address the obstacles to product cost assessments posed by cash-based accounting systems as used in Dutch central government. Second, poor quality of performance indicators may be acknowledged as a serious problem for performance management. Third, the adherence to a uniform control framework in government organizations will be criticized.

10.4.1. CASH-BASED ACCOUNTING

In the development of result oriented management control in Dutch central government the obstacles imposed by the existing cash accounting system have to be somehow circumvented. For organization units which are not being awarded the agency status performance management remains being dependent upon this system.

The advantages of accrual accounting are indeed formally acknowledged in a series of management control reviews executed by the department of Finance in 1998. Eight executive organization units - including the Internal Revenue Service - were being reviewed on the value added of accrual accounting for their activities. For all eight units this value added was acknowledged, albeit with a minority opposition for one of them and some hesitations with respect to one of the others.

However, if we look into the arguments underlying this purported value added, we may doubt if the necessity of accrual accounting for a result oriented management control as such is recognized. In the general report on the eight reviews performed - Vision on Result, published in 1998 - we encounter the following exposition on this value added (1998b, p.9, our translation): 'The favourable impacts of accrual accounting for the result oriented management control model are narrowly related to the possibilities accrual accounting offers for a calculation of standard costs for products and services. Use of expenses instead of expenditures for this model has specifically value added if expenditure and cost figures diverge. When expenditures are being allocated to products, incidental capital expenditures would cause variations among years. Such variations would trouble the view on relative efficiency and impede the development of time series of costs and cost comparisons with other producers'.

In this exposition value added of accrual accounting is linked to a divergence of expenditures and costs, which may eventually but not necessarily occur in production. Clearly, the result oriented management model is considered feasible in a cash accounting environment, whenever this divergence is absent or if it can be sufficiently cured. In many government organizations, characterized by labour intensive modes of production, expenditures (salaries) and resource costs (expenses on labour time) may in fact be equated to each other. Moreover, capital expenditure may simply be adjusted to obtain expense figures by accounting for inventories (e.g. to calculate fuel costs for transport services). For durable capital assets, expenditures may often be treated in management control as sunk costs for actual production (assets constituting a fixed 'infrastructure' for the budget period).

Along these lines contract management in the Dutch department of Defence has continued to try to embed performance management in the department's cash accounting systems. In the attempt to allocate costs to contracted outputs, as a first step the adjustment of expenditures to expense elements thereby has been carefully planned. All decentral budgets consist of three parts:[5]

1. an expenditure budget including all personnel and material resources for which the rule expenditure equals expense is supposed to apply. This part is specified in four items in a line-item format:
   - military salaries and related expenditures;
   - civilian salaries and related expenditures;
   - other personnel expenditures;
   - material expenditures.

2. A part for material resources, where resource consumption in the budget period may deviate from purchase. For this part of the budget a cost module is being developed (which however is not yet operational) to be fit into the financial information system. It should in particular include expenses on ammunition - generally the most important item in this part of the budget. In the 1998 contracts cost control with respect to this item has been notably defective. In the existing financial information systems, no linkages to the expense figures in the contracts can be established.

3. A part for transfers from other organization units. Services received from these units are being accounted for in view of the required coordination of production. However, they are in principle not controllable during the budget period: they should be agreed upon in advance. Resource costs incurred for their production remain part of the (expenditure/cost) budget of the service center, mission center budgets only specify the deliveries these units are entitled to (so-called 'drawing rights'). These deliveries are listed in enumerations of considerable length in the contracts: up to a hundred items may be specified for training facilities (distinguished in a number of categories), maintenance of weapon systems, equipment and vehicles, housing and infrastructure of several kinds etc. A general complaint with respect to this specification of 'drawing rights' understandably concerns the enormous amount of paper work involved.

These three part listings of resources bought/hired, used or received, stand apart from the enumerations of performance indicators elsewhere in the contracts. No attempt is made to engage in cost allocation by transforming the line-item format of the budget in a program format. It is not clear, moreover, how such a transformation could be accomplished. The numbers of items involved, the lack of data on the specific use of those items and the deficient linkages between the three parts of the budgets in the existing information systems would make the exercise far too complicated. Thus, in fact no cost allocation is feasible in the decentral budgets. The reconciliation of expenditure data with the intended expense information in the Defence management contracts precludes itself the assessment of product costs required to arrive at performance management as intended.

---

[5] Uniform prescriptions for all organization units have been formulated in the Defence Management Control Policy Framework ('Raamwerk Beleid bedrijfsvoering defensie'), a document regularly updated. Our exposition is based on the Winter 1998 version of this document.

As a consequence, performance indicators do not have to represent cost objects to be associated with distinct programs either. And indeed, generally they do not. Indicators for some organization unit may e.g. contain percentages available for use of certain types of equipment, labour time involved in training specific skills, values attached to outcomes of military operations practiced and numbers of personnel deployed in peace-keeping missions. Such indicators will generally not refer to identical or distinct activities. They will rather represent characteristics of overall performance, as decomposed in some relevant aspects - thereby giving an impression of what is being accomplished in the 'black box' of the unit's production processes. These characteristics might be related to overall cost levels of the unit, but they do not constitute a grouping of cost objects for cost allocation.

10.4.2. QUALITY OF PERFORMANCE INDICATORS

With respect to performance measurement in central government we expressed already some doubts in section 10.3.3. on the progress actually accomplished. Notwithstanding results reported for earlier attempts at performance measurement in the eighties (cf. Sorber, 1993), the development of output and efficiency indicators needed a restart at the end of the nineties. In municipal and provincial government more continuous progress in the development of performance indicators has been made. However, we may question the quality of the indicators arrived at.

Ter Bogt and Van Helden (1999, pp. 14-16) examined the quality of performance indicators in six divisions of two big cities in the Netherlands, ie. Groningen and Enschede. Their findings show that a majority of the indicators is input-throughput-oriented (59%), whereas a minority of these indicators is output-oriented (38%); indicators which are defined as outcomes do hardly exist (3%). This research was based on budgets of the years 1990 through 1992. The same classification of performance indicators has been used more recently by Beukert (1998, pp. 54-55) who investigated the 1998 budgets of four policy areas in the cities of Tilburg, Delft, Lelystad and Heerlen. His observations indicate that relatively more output indicators (56%) than input/throughput indicators (36%) were provided in the cities' budgets; 8% percent of the indicators were specified as outcomes. So, from a performance-oriented perspective these results show some progress in the quality of performance indicators, at least in big Dutch cities, ranging from 75,000 to 150,000 inhabitants.

It is also interesting to look more closely to the performance indicators of the mid-size municipalities which were addressed in section 10.3.2. Some general impressions will do. The text book format of an output budget - ie. the number of units supplied multiplied by the unit costs - is non-existent. On the contrary, many municipalities use a format which aims to provide a broad set of data for each of the (about 80) policy fields, such as:
- policy goals and developments;
- the types of activities which will contribute to the policy goals (mostly these activities are not quantified in a numerical sense);
- discretion in municipal policy making, indicating the extent to which a municipality can specify its own policy, or the degree to which policy is prescribed by central government (this issue refers to some kind of controllability);

- the available means expressed as Dutch guilders per year, so as a total amount of money available for the policy field in question; sometimes this total amount of money is subdivided in cost categories, such as personnel costs, capital costs and costs of subsidies;
- several performance indicators related to the policy field.

The performance indicators show - generally speaking - a rather poor quality. For example, typical indicators, such as average amount spent on cultural affairs per inhabitant, or average amount spent on road maintenance per square kilometer neither give indications about the volume of services nor about their quality. Furthermore, the denominators in such calculations - the number of inhabitants or the number of square kilometres - are not controllable. In other instances, rather heterogeneous indicators are provided, such as in the field of library services with the number of clients, the number of exhibitions, and the number of opening hours per week. In the case of policy fields where adequate indicators are hard to find, such as with spatial planning, some rather meaningless indicators are given, like the number of policy notes or plans without referring to the differences in quality between these notes or plans. Sometimes, quality indicators are provided, for example in the case of social security services where the time to take a decision on a client's approval has to meet a certain standard.

10.4.3. DIFFERENTIATED CONTROL

Both the PMI framework for municipalities and provinces (sections 10.3.1. and 10.3.2.) and the result oriented management control approach in central government (section 10.3.3.) assume that quantitative targets about outputs can be deduced from the goals of the organization and that differences between planned and realized targets indicate whether adjustment is needed. It is questionable, however, whether these assumptions are appropriate for all policy fields and in all circumstances (see also Hofstede, 1981; Kloot, 1997).

The municipalities and provinces that used the PMI framework realized that not all tasks or activities were suited to output-oriented control. Some municipalities and provinces explicitly distinguished between 'standard activities' and 'ad hoc activities'. Standard activities involve remote control by politicians, which is aimed at results and implies a lot of responsibilities for officials. It is difficult to structure ad hoc activities in advance, and politicians are usually closely involved, which means that 'results control' cannot be achieved easily.

Generally, the municipalities and provinces showed some confusion about the way in which the planning and control of ad hoc activities should be combined with their ordinary planning and control processes. For example, some of the provinces were inclined to use a separate control framework for ad hoc activities which aimed to give information about inputs, throughput times and possible effects at important moments during the project term, so-called mile stones. These moments do not coincide with the regular moments the reports on the execution of the budget are provided.

Differentiation in management control in central government encounters many hesitations, especially from concern controllers in the departments. On a general level, the introduction of the agencies in 1994 may be considered a fundamental innovation in this respect. However, too much proliferation of 'autonomized' accounting systems is being discouraged by admission criteria for the agency status (including the measurability of services delivered and the requirement of models for cost per product calculations). Generally the need to adhere to the unity principle of government budgeting is subscribed. Within the departments, uniformity seems to remain an important criterion for management control as perceived by central organization units. As an example we may refer to the three part budgets prescribed for all units within the Defence department discussed in section 10.4.1. Obviously uniformity in budget presentation can only be achieved in a line-item format: resources purchased or consumed - personnel and material - will be easily categorized, whatever the programs intended in the appropriations.

The question may now be raised why governmental organizations prefer to use a more or less uniform control framework. In our opinion, the answer to this question has to refer to the general source from which new planning and control systems are initiated. Mostly, financial departments take a leading role in this respect. Although these departments may also be pleased by a successful usage of new tools by accountable managers, they will be primary interested in the need for coordination and consolidation. The latter goals ask for uniformity. If, however, user needs were put first, probably a more differentiated approach would come up.

There might also be another reason for using a uniform control framework in government. Laughlin and Pallot (1998, pp. 385-388) emphasize the important role of what they call 'epistemic communities'. These are transnational networks of professionals with recognized expertise and competence which enable them to have an authoratative claim to relevant policy-making. These professionals pretend in a convincing way that they can contribute to solutions in policy-making. Their attitude is instrumental and they likely will provide relatively simple answers to difficult questions. Because of their backgrounds in business environments, they probably will advise governmental organizations to adopt businesslike tools and styles. More particularly, the internationally oriented consultancy firms are good examples of epistemic communities.

It is our opinion that user needs for adequate information to plan and control organization units must receive more attention. Performance-based management should put the management in the center instead of the financial expertise. Financial departments have to play a more supporting role then. Moreover, financial departments should confine themselves to specifying minimum requirements for coordination and consolidation, thus leaving room for local managers to define their own information needs. It also implies that consultancy firms should play a more polite role in achieving accounting and organizational change. Performance-based management is not a goal in itself. It should aim to deliver high quality information, to contribute to organization units which can be better controlled, and ultimately to achieve efficiency and effectiveness of governmental operations.

References

- Bac, A, D. (1993) Performance Measurement in Dutch National, Provincial and Local Government, in: E. Buschor and K. Schedler (eds.), *Perspectives on Performance Measurement and Public Sector Accounting*, Institute of Public Finance and Fiscal Law, Volume 71, St. Gallen, 309-324.
- Beukert, J.C.W. (1998) *Productbegrotingen en prestatiemeting in vier gemeenten*, Scriptie Bestuurskunde, OU, Heerlen.
- Bogt, H.J. ter, and G.J. van Helden (1999) *Management Control and Performance Measurement in Dutch Local Government*, Research Report 99A12, SOM, Groningen.
- Cabinet of the Dutch Central government (1998) *Miljoenennota 1999*, SDU, Den Haag.
- CBS (1998) *Bevolking der gemeenten van Nederland op 1 januari 1998*, Voorburg/Heerlen, 1998.
- CBS (1999*) Statistiek Gemeentebegrotingen 1999*, Voorburg/Heerlen, 1999.
- Dussen, J.W. van der (1992) Financial Relationships between Central and LocalGovernment in the Netherlands: Why are they different? *Local Government Studies*, Vol. 18, No 4, 94-105.
- Helden, G.J. van (1998a) A Review of the Policy and Management Instruments Project for Municipalities in the Netherlands, *Financial Accountability and Management*, Vol. 14, no. 2, 85-104.
- Helden, G.J. van (1998b) *BBI in de praktijk; een vergelijkend onderzoek naar de planning en control bij acht middelgrote gemeenten*, Shaker, Maastricht.
- Helden, G.J. van (1999) *Planning en control bij de provincies*, working paper, Groningen (forthcoming in *Openbare Uitgaven*, 1999).
- Herweijer, M. and U. Mix (1996) Zehn Jahre Tilburger Modell: Erfahrungen einer Offentlichen Verwaltung auf den Wege zur Dienstleistungscenter, Kelner, Bremen
- Hofstede, G. (1981) Management Control of Public and Not-for-Profit Activities, *Accounting, Organizations and Society*, Vol. 6, no. 3, 193-211.
- Houwaart, D., R. van der Linde, J. Post en K. Verduijn (1995) *Bestuurlijke vernieuwing, bedrijfsvoering en informatie; slotpublikatie Stichting BBI*, Stichting BBI, Leusden.
- Hood, C. (1991) A Public Management for all Seasons, *Public Administration*, Vol. 69, (Spring), 93-109.
- Kloot, L. (1997) Organizational Learning and Management Control Systems: Responding to Environmental Change, *Management Accounting Research*, Vol. 8, no. 2, 47-73.
- Korsten, A.F.A. (1996) 10 Jahre Tilburger Modell; Tilburg, Mekka der Öffentlichen Verwaltung?, in M. Herweijer and U. Mix (eds.), *Zehn Jahre Tilburger Modell: Erfahrungen einer Offentlichen Verwaltung auf dem Wege zum Dienst leistungscenter*, Kelner, Bremen, 21-37.
- KPMG, Welschen, P.T.M. (1997) *Onderzoek planning en control bij middelgrote en kleine gemeenten; een rapportage op hoofdlijnen*, KPMG, Utrecht.

- Laughlin, R., J. Pallot (1998) Trends, Patterns and Influencing Factors: Some Reflections, in: Olson, O, J. Guthrie, C. Humphrey (eds.), *Global Warning!; Debating International Developments in New Public Financial Management*, Cappelen Akademisk Forlag, Oslo, 376-399.
- Mol, N.P. (1996) Performance Indicators in the Dutch Department of Defence, *Financial Accountability and Management*, Vol.12, no.1, 71-81.
- Moret, Ernst and Young (1997) *Tien jaar kwaliteitsverbetering bij gemeenten*, Den Haag.
- Olson, O., J. Guthrie and C. Humphrey (eds.) (1998) *Global Warning! Debating International Developments in New Public Financial Management*, Cappelen Akademisk Forlag, Oslo.
- Ministerie van Financiën (1998a) *Verder met resultaat; het agentschapsmodel 1991-1997*, Den Haag.
- Ministerie van Financiën (1998b) *Zicht op resultaat; Uitkomsten Interdepartementale Beleidsonderzoeken naar de aansturing en bedrijfsvoering van overheidsdiensten 1997-1998*, Den Haag.
- Schouten, C.(1999) *The Dutch Provincial and Municipal Accounting System*, Paper presented at 7the CIGAR Conference, Tilburg, June 1999 (see also: Reeks Financiële Functie, 1999P1, Ministerie van Binnenlandse Zaken en Koninkrijksrelaties, Den Haag).
- Schrijvers, A.P.M. (1993) The Management of a Larger Town, *Public Administration*, Vol. 71 (Winter), 595-603.
- Sorber, A. (1993) Performance Measurement in the Central Government Departments of the Netherlands, *Public Productivity and Management Review*, Vol.17, no.1, 59-68.
- Steunenberg, B. and N.P. Mol (1997) Fiscal and Financial Decentralization: a Comparative Analysis of Six West European Countries, in J.E. Lane (ed.), *Public Sector Reform. Rationale, Trends and Problems*, Sage, London, 235-256.
- Toonen, T.A.J. (1987) The Netherlands: a Decentralised Unitary State in a Welfare Society, R.A.W. Rhodes and V. Wright (eds.), *Tensions in the Territorial Politics of Western Europe* (Frank Cass, London), 108-129.
- Toonen (1998) De gemeente in de gedecentraliseerde eenheidsstaat, in: A.F.A. Korsten en P.W. Tops (red.), *Lokaal bestuur in Nederland*, Samsom, Alphen aan den Rijn, chapter 2.

CHAPTER 11

FINANCIAL MANAGEMENT REFORM IN NEW ZEALAND LOCAL GOVERNMENT: A CENTRAL GOVERNMENT INITIATIVE OR A RESPONSE TO LOCAL NEEDS?

June Pallot

11.1. Introduction

While New Zealand's central government reforms are well known internationally, the reforms at the local level have been equally dramatic. Changes following the introduction of the *Local Government Amendment Act (No. 2) 1989* constituted the most radical restructuring of local government, its finances and its relationship with citizens since the abolition of provinces in 1876. New Zealand local government is currently experiencing a second wave of reforms, this time with a longer-term emphasis, as a consequence of the *Local Government Amendment (No. 3) Act 1996.* Further local government reform (including another round of amalgamation, corporatization of roads, and privatization of other utilities) also appears to be on the government's agenda. In each round of changes, accounting has been a crucial ingredient.

At first sight, it appears that the changes in local government over the last decade are yet another application of the model of public management developed in the New Zealand central government. That model (see Boston et al 1996; Scott et al., 1997) has attracted international acclaim for its grounding in economic theory, its consistent and comprehensive application across all sectors, and its speed of implementation. Closer examination, however, reveals that local government reform is more complex than another manifestation of the New Zealand central government model and goes to the heart of the nature and values of local government. The central-local government relationship is a dynamic one in which accounting is inextricably entwined.

Efforts to explain the purpose of, and ultimately the rationale for, local government follow one of two theoretical approaches which Loughlin (1986) refers to as a *functionalist* view and an *autonomist* view. The functionalist view sees local government as an agency of the state drawing its authority and mandate from the state i.e. local government exists to provide a predetermined range of services. This provision is evaluated primarily on *efficiency* grounds, the argument for local provision being that local agencies are better placed to respond efficiently to local demands. Different preferences are respected, information about preferences is more effectively transmitted and interpreted, and redress ought to be quicker. In short, local agencies may be expected to be more responsive to demands of citizens viewed as consumers. And if they do not respond appropriately, consumers may move to a locality where public services better meet their mix of needs (Tiebout, 1956). Prior to 1989 this has been the dominant view of local government in New Zealand, as it had been in the British system on which

177

A. Bac (ed.), International Comparative Issues in Government Accounting, 177-193.
© 2001 *Kluwer Academic Publishers. Printed in the Netherlands.*

it had been modelled (Stewart, 1996). Functionalists justify their view by reference to the fact that Parliament gives local government its legal framework.

The functionalist view is to be contrasted with the autonomist paradigm which views local government as a sphere of government in its own right i.e. local government derives its legitimacy from its effectiveness in meeting community expectations and local needs. This view is common in many European countries where the right of local communities to govern their own affairs is a constitutional right. Accordingly, local authorities have the right to take action on behalf of their communities except where it is barred by law. The selection of services is based on consultation with citizens (as distinct from consumers) and 'reflects local priorities rather than a nationally determined list' (Reid, 1999:166). *Participation,* then, is key and has an intrinsic value beyond the instrumental achievement of effective and efficient public policies. Parliament sets the legal framework but equally it does so for private sector companies and these are not viewed as agents of the state.

This paper traces the reforms of local government in New Zealand, and the role of accounting within them, in light of the underlying paradigms identified above. While much of the theory on which the 1989 and 1996 legislation is based is of an economic or accounting nature, which has a natural affinity with a functionalist view, it can be argued that the ensuing practices also provide new opportunities for the exercise of local autonomy and should also be considered in those terms. The material in this paper draws upon the legislation, published documents (annual plan, annual report, funding policy and long term financial strategy) from the various councils around New Zealand and a series of interviews held with local authority managers and politicians during September and October 1998.

11.2. Overview of Local Government in New Zealand

Since the abolition of provinces in 1876, New Zealand has had a unitary government modelled on the British system. Local authorities in New Zealand may exercise only those powers and functions specifically provided in statute. A 'power of general competence' has been discussed over the years but never enacted (Officials Coordinating Committee on Local Government, 1988, p. 58). Few functions are mandatory (resource planning, civil defence, and public health responsibilities are among the exceptions); some are taken for granted (sewage collection and rubbish disposal); others are a reflection of the collective decision-making of elected representatives in power from time to time, and might be expected to represent the preferences of citizens - housing schemes, for example (see Bush, 1992: 109). Despite the lack of a power of general competence, territorial authorities have, in practice, rarely been inhibited by the doctrine of *ultra vires* from undertaking functions. Rather, it has been the reluctance of either rate payers or central government to provide finance that has been the limiting factor. Apart from grants for road construction and maintenance, local government receives very little funding from central government; its primary sources of finance for operations are property taxes (rates) and user charges.

For most of its history the pattern has been one of a strong central government and a weak fragmented local government (Scott, 1979; Bush, 1980). Central government accounts for by far the largest share of government activity (88 percent on average from 1962 to 1997), illustrating the dominance of the centre, although there has been a slight increase in the local government share of total government activity since 1978 (McDermott and Forgie, 1999). Scott (1979) noted that in 1974, in a country with a population at that time of only 3 million, there were 991 local authorities. Approximately one third of these were territorial authorities, that is, counties, cities, boroughs and towns. The rest were *ad hoc* (single purpose) authorities ranging from electric power boards, drainage boards, harbour boards and airport authorities to tiny rabbit destruction boards. Numerous attempts at rationalization failed while the question of local government finance formed what Bush (1980) referred to as 'the endless agenda'[1]. When it came to efficiency 'the average local body was seen as ponderous, unresponsive and inefficient' (Anderson, 1993: 65).

The 1989 legislation changed all that. Almost overnight the number of local authorities (also referred to in this paper as 'councils') was reduced from over 700 to a mere 85 - 72 territorial authorities (cities and districts) and 13 regional authorities[2]. One reason this was now possible was that the central government had been on a program of such rapid change in every area of the economy and society since 1984 that New Zealanders had become accustomed to dramatic restructuring. Thus the local government changes were swept up in the overall process of reform in New Zealand

11.3. The first Wave of Reform: Amalgamation and Accountability

In December 1987, the Minister of Local Government, Dr Michael Bassett, announced a comprehensive program of reform of local and regional government based on the following principles:
- local authorities should have clear, non-conflicting objectives, including a clear separation between regulatory and service delivery functions;
- trade-offs between objectives should be made explicit and in a transparent manner, and
- clear and strong accountability mechanisms should be encouraged.

As Horner (1989) notes, these reforms were in accordance with the same principles as had informed the reforms of central government: the quest for clear linear accountability, transparency in policy formulation, and greater operational efficiency. This approach generated considerable reaction from councils as it was a radical departure from the principles which had been incorporated into the original 1974 Local Government Act.

---

[1] For example, central government was not willing to consider general revenue sharing or block grants while local government operated within an inefficient structure. Local government opposed the various attempts at structural reform (those in positions of power in smaller authorities were unwilling to give it up), leaving it weak and fragmented. The weakness of local government enabled central government politically to impose a system of subsidies and grants which was effective in implementing its own priorities (Ball, 1980).

[2] Local government in New Zealand should be regarded as an entity in which regional councils and territorial authorities have separate but complementary functions, rather than as two levels of sub-national government where on is subordinate to the other. The responsibilities of regional government are largely in the area of environmental management.

By the time the new legislation was passed, it was possible to detect 'a shift in emphasis from efficiency/rationality toward some of the more traditional values ascribed to local government' (Horner, 1989:6) Thus the purpose of local government according to the 1989 legislation is to provide:
- recognition of different communities, including their identities and values;
- definition and enforcement of appropriate rights in those communities;
- scope for communities to choose among different types of local facilities and services;
- local authority trading activities which are competitively neutral;
- efficient and effective exercise of the functions, duties and powers of local government, and
- participation of local people in the local government.

Many of the new features of local government introduced by the 1989 Act do indeed follow the model established in central government described elsewhere (Scott et al., 1990; Boston et al., 1991, 1996). For example, the elected council is 'decoupled' from the day-to-day management of the authority. The council-appointed chief executive, like counterparts in central government, is on a performance-based contract for up to five years and is the employer of all other staff. The council's job is to set 'policy' and monitor performance of the chief executive; the CE and other officers are to manage within that policy. Councils are encouraged to transfer commercial activities to Local Authority Trading Enterprises (LATEs) under provisions almost identical in wording to that covering State-Owned Enterprises at the central government level. The set of financial statements to be produced and audited are much the same as for central government departments, as is the requirement follow generally accepted accounting practice and therefore adopt accrual accounting.

Where the local government legislation differs a little from the central government formula, however, is in the requirements to consult with, and respond back to, their ratepayers and electors about their plans and performance (Department of Internal Affairs, 1992). Specifically, local authorities must include in their annual plan:
a. the intended significant policies and objectives to be achieved;
b. the nature and scope of the significant activities/outputs to be undertaken necessary to achieve the outcomes;
c. the performance targets (quantity, quality, cost) for each output;
d. the resources and indicative costs including allowances for depreciation and a return on capital[3];
e. the sources of funds, and
f. the rating policy of the local authority.
Consolidated financial statements must also be provided in the annual report.

---

[3] 'Return on capital' was later amended to 'cost of capital' so as to cover both commercial and non-commercial activities. This external reporting requirement proved unworkable, however (Audit Office, 1994) and has subsequently been dropped although local authorities use cost of capital information for internal management decision making.

The Act requires that the process of adoption follows its special consultative procedure, ensuring the availability of the draft plan, and the opportunity for submissions. Local authorities must prepare and adopt a report how they have performed. A comparison between actual and projected performance is required (s.223E), New Zealand being somewhat unusual internationally in requiring that non-financial performance information be audited (Pallot, 1999).

As a consequence of the accounting requirement to provide statements of service performance (which, according to the relevant accounting standard, means reporting on the quantity, quality and cost of outputs), many councils have put in place comprehensive annual surveys of residents. These surveys involve one-hour individual interviews with hundreds of randomly selected residents, canvassing their views on the whole range of services provided by the council. Questions are asked about the individual's frequency of use, whether the services are value for money, whether the council should change its spending priorities or the amount of spending and so forth. Initially these surveys were seen as a way of meeting the requirement to report on the quality of services and complemented technical measures (e.g. road roughness, accident rates, pH value of water) or provided an indication of quality where other measures were not readily available. They have also increasingly been viewed as a means of obtaining 'customer' or 'consumer' feedback. However, their role as a mechanism for citizen participation should not be overlooked. As one councillor put it: 'I do not believe that consultation is necessarily democratic in the sense that those people who are best able to take part in the consultation process are those who have got access to information, who can comprehend the information and have the confidence and the resources to put forward a convincing case... The advantage of the citizens' survey is that it is not like that. Because it is random, it does represent a cross section of people.' (interview, October, 1998)

In terms of delivery of services the legislation had an immediate impact on the way services such as water supply, sewage systems, stormwater and land drainage, refuse collection, commercial forestry and refuse disposal were provided (Department of Internal Affairs, 1994) and resulted in significant cost savings (Douglas, 1994; Williamson, 1994). However, it left some unfinished business. In particular, it became apparent that the annual planning and consultative process established under the 1989 legislation was too short a planning horizon given the need to speak for future generations with regard to community infrastructure services and facilities. By 1993 some of the more forward looking councils such as Christchurch (joint winner of the 1992 Bertelsmann award for best managed city in the world) had started to project expenditure for the next 20 years on a rolling basis and to impose restraints which would ensure that debt levels would remain both prudent and manageable during a period of major investment (Slevin, 1996). In the case of Christchurch the investment commenced in 1993 was largely a series of civic amenities designed to attract business and tourists to the city and boost the local economy. The restraining policy limits are embodied in published statements and financial ratios which fix, among other things, a time frame for debt repayment, net interest as a percentage of consolidated gross revenue (8 percent), term debt as a percentage of both realizable and total assets (33 percent and 12 percent), and net debt to funds flow from operations (not to exceed five times).[4]

11.5. The second Wave of Reform: looking Longer Term

In 1998, a second major wave of reform swept across local authorities as they arrived at the implementation date of the Local Government Amendment Act (No. 3) 1996. This legislation introduces what are probably the most significant financial and borrowing management provisions for local government yet seen. At the very least, it builds on the unfinished work of the 1989 reforms to local government and the sustainable environmental management responsibilities of the Resource Management Act, and it is likely that more reform is to follow concerning the Rating Powers Act 1988.

11.5.1. FACTORS LEADING UP TO THE NEW LEGISLATION

In part, the new legislation can be viewed as a further attempt to apply the model of public management developed at the central government level in local government. Most recent of the initiatives in central government had been the Fiscal Responsibility Act 1994 which included principles of managing debt to prudent levels, ensuring that operating expenses did not exceed operating revenues, preserving the Crown's net worth at prudent levels, managing all fiscal risk, pursing policies that are consistent with the predicability of level and stability of tax in future years (Richardson, 1994; Pallot, 1997a). The Act also required a number of statements to be issued to ensure transparency of the government's operations and activities. At the time this legislation was passed there was also a call from the business community to have similar legislation regulating local government activities and the government at the time had given the commitment to explore this at some stage in the future. The 1996 Amendment Act can be viewed as the government's response.

It would be simplistic, however, to characterize the latest reforms as an imitation of central government initiatives. The fact that councils such as Christchurch had initiated long term financial planning well before the 1996 suggests that local initiatives were at least as significant. Probably the most important factor was the experience of councils with the limitations of the short planning horizon in the annual planning and consultative process established under the 1989 Act. By extending the planning horizon and adopting a more strategic approach, the effects of decisions (or indecisions) made today could be understood in the context terms of the next fifteen years and beyond.

The need for a longer planning horizon was particularly important given the long life cycle of infrastructure assets which form the bulk of local authority assets. In 1993 the Audit Office had reported to Parliament that it was unable to provide assurance about the long term financial condition of local authorities because of the lack of knowledge of the condition of these assets and the absence of adequate strategic planning for service

---

[4] More recently the strategic emphasis of the council has been less on 'bricks and mortar' and more on social infrastructure aimed at reducing poverty, crime etc by acting as catalyst and facilitator of initiatives by the voluntary and business sectors of the community.

requirements in the medium to long term. To provide that assurance, the Audit Office stated that 'local authorities must have in place the means to determine future demands on their resources for repairing or replacing existing assets and long term plans or strategies to indicate the nature and scope of activities they expect to be involved in' (Audit Office, 1993: 41).

Initially, there was considerable resistance on the part of some councils to the requirement to value infrastructure assets. Old information about cost and physical condition was considered incomplete or irrelevant, meaning that councils faced the difficult, large and potentially very costly task of valuing infrastructure. They argued that the value of infrastructure was irrelevant because infrastructural assets were either not saleable or not ever likely to be sold and that the costs of valuation outweighed any benefits. Over the next two years the attitude of many councils changed. Although the legislative requirement was the main reason for valuing infrastructure assets, councils started to see some other benefits including the following:

a. It makes readers of the statements aware of the size of the public investment in infrastructure for which the council is responsible.
b. It puts into perspective the on-going cost which the council incurs in maintaining and replacing infrastructure.
c. The process of valuing requires that councils clearly identify the existence, location and condition of infrastructure assets with the result that local government managers and councillors improve their knowledge of the council's infrastructure investment.
d. Annual information about the value of infrastructure is a first step in tracking trends in infrastructure value over time and using that information to hold councils accountable for the way that they manage infrastructure (Audit Office, 1994)

By 1991, 40 of the 85 councils had valued their infrastructural assets and included the value in their statements of financial position. This number had increased to 84 by 1994. The majority (55) use depreciated replacement cost as the basis for valuing infrastructure assets. The appropriate method of reflecting depreciation in financial statements, however, was - and remains - controversial (Pallot, 1996). We return to this issue later.

The perceived need to invest heavily in infrastructure renewal in the foreseeable future also raised what had long been a contentious issue - the ability of local authorities to raise finance on the open market. The previous borrowing powers available to local government were restricted and used techniques that were expensive and inflexible (Scott, 1979). Central government approval, via the Local Authority Loans Board was required. The new borrowing provisions of the Amendment Act allow councils to improve the equity in allocating benefits of services through longer loan periods. It also allows a more prudent approach to risk management, thus potentially lowering the cost of debt to councils. Importantly, it gives local government considerably more autonomy vis-à-vis central government. Added to the fact that local government now receives virtually no funding from central government other than for roads, local councils in New Zealand have a considerable degree of financial independence.

Finally, there had been an alarming trend by large ratepayers within local authorities to review democratic rate setting decisions through the courts (Audit Office, 1998). This was an unsatisfactory state of affairs and one where the courts provided little consistency in their decisions although there was a strong tendency to require there to be a relationship between rates paid and services provided. This, combined with the Wellington City Council High Court decision that was subsequently overturned by the Court of Appeal (Salter, 1996), caused parliament to respond with the Amendment Act. Much of the Court of Appeal decision has been included in this Local Government Amendment (No. 3) Act as described below.

The 1996 Amendment has introduced significant reforms to the way councils undertake their business and fund activities. The purposes of the new legislation are to promote prudent, effective and efficient financial management by local authorities. They are required to manage their financial affairs (including debt) 'prudently' in the interests of the district of the local authority or its inhabitants and ratepayers. Every three years, starting in 1998, councils must adopt (after consultation with the community and concurrently with the annual plan) a long-term financial strategy related to a period of ten or more years. The long-term strategy is to cover expenditure (including the cost of capital) and revenue, cashflow projections, asset management, and borrowing requirements.

11.5.2. PRINCIPLES OF FINANCIAL MANAGEMENT

Section 122 of the Amendment Act sets out six principles of financial management, in an analogous fashion to the principles of responsible fiscal management at the central government level:
1. *Prudent management.* All revenue, expenses, assets, liabilities and investments are to be managed prudently, in the interests of the district of the local authority or of its inhabitants and ratepayers, and only for lawful purposes.
2. *Sustainability.* Adequate and effective provision for the expenditure needs of the local authority, as identified in the annual plan and the long-term financial strategy, must be made. This principle recognizes concerns over the unknown state of significant portions of local authority infrastructure.
3. *Consideration of options.* The benefits and costs of different options are to be assessed in determining any long-term financial strategy, funding policy, investment policy, or borrowing management policy, and in making any decision with significant financial consequences (including a decision to take no action).
4. *Lawful funding.* The identified expenditure needs of the local authority are to be funded by such lawful funding mechanisms as the local authority considers on reasonable grounds to be appropriate.
5. *Prudent debt management.* Debt shall be maintained at prudent levels and in accordance with the relevant provisions of the borrowing management policy. This principle recognizes the issue of borrowing powers as an original reason for the Local Government Act. The principle recognizes that a rational locally developed system for debt management is a superior means of safeguarding ratepayers' interests in comparison to a rigid set of numerical caps and controls established by legislation (for example a total debt to total assets ratio of no more than 40%).
6. *Balancing of books.* Operating revenues in any financial year shall be set at a level adequate to cover all projected operating expenses. This is a principle similar to that required of central government under the Fiscal Responsibility Act and this is the provision that requires councils to include depreciation/decline in service potential in

the operating expenses and hence cover these with operating revenue in the interests of intergenerational equity.

11.5.3.DEVELOPMENT OF FUNDING POLICY

The intention of the legislation is that funding decisions should be related to who benefits from the goods and services provided at any point in time and across time. From the perspective of citizens, consideration of the costs and benefits of options is a crucial part of the legislation. The term 'benefits and costs' is not confined to direct benefits or to financial costs only. Instead, it is intended to encompass direct and indirect benefits and costs (at least those of significance) and requires the application of economic as well as financial principles. It is this provision, more than any other part of the Act, which requires local authorities to review tradeoffs between activities and the different means of undertaking particular activities including direct provision, provision through a LATE or other local authority controlled structure, contracting out, long term franchising or divestment and simply acting as a purchaser. It is also important to note that this principle applies to all decisions with significant financial consequences and not simply decisions taken in developing the long term financial strategies or the other policies.

As required by the legislation, councils classify each service according to which of three types of benefits it provides: direct benefits, general benefits and control of negative effects. Direct benefits are received directly by an individual or group (e.g. a parking meter space provides direct benefit to motorists who use it). General benefits are provided to the community as a whole (e.g. street lighting improves the security of streets at night). The control of negative effects is needed to protect the community from actual or potential problems (e.g. dog control or noise control). Most services provide more than one of these three types of benefit. Section 122F of the 1996 Act specifies that costs of any expenditure should be recovered at the time that the benefits of that expenditure accrue. Section 122F specifies that as far as possible, direct benefits should be paid for by corresponding user charges, costs of controlling negative effects should be paid for by those who generate the need for such expenditure and public goods or goods which generate general benefits may be paid for by rates. Councils examine which groups (residential ratepayers, business ratepayers, rural ratepayers or non-ratepaying institutions) receive the benefits from each service and the ratio of direct and indirect benefits. The costs of providing the benefits are then allocated accordingly. The legislation permits the councils to decide whether or not this allocation of costs should be modified by issues of community interest, fairness and equity, council policy or practicality and reallocate costs if appropriate.

Such decisions should not be viewed solely in functionalist terms but also in terms of an autonomist perspective. Ultimately, the decisions described above are political and need to be resolved by political means. Councils have differed as to whether they ratified recommendations made by management, copied other councils, involved all their elected members or just a subset of them in their initial analysis. Having examined the experiences of nine councils which undertook early adoption of the 1996 legislation, the Audit Office argued that only the elected representatives can properly make many of the decisions required for the funding policy. While officers are required to produce much of the information needed for the debate, it is not appropriate for elected representatives just to sign off the final product (Audit Office, 1998: 64). Many councils held workshops of councillors at which those who participated were fully briefed on the process, the specific circumstances of each council activity, and the manner in which the activities were carried out in their own council. Conduct of the workshops helped to ensure that the interests of all sections of the community, to the extent that they are represented by elected members, were properly considered. Several councillors interviewed commented that it was the most interesting and fundamental debate they had ever had on values, purposes and priorities.

The legislation requires councils to consult with the public before finalizing their funding policy and the long term financial plan. This provides the opportunity for more direct participation by the public. The time required to comply with the special consultative procedure - in particular, the allocation of sufficient time or hearing public submissions - can be difficult to predict and control, however. Taking too much time can significantly affect an authority's ability to meet the statutory deadlines for adopting the strategy, policies and annual plan and forecasting the number of submissions that will be received is not easy. The Audit Office suggested that these problems can be alleviated if the council invests time in meeting with focus groups in the community to identify their expectations and responds appropriately to these in issuing draft policies and plans; engages in a consultation program to explain and promote the council's intentions; ensures that documents are comprehensive in detail and presented in a fashion that is readily understood by the average reader (Audit Office, 1998). Many councils appear to have followed these suggestions.

The analysis required by the Amendment Act is obviously based on theories of public economics. It requires the mixing of accounting principles with funding mechanisms and the uses of economic tools that are new to local government. It will not be surprising if the various local authorities come up with quite different benefit allocations for various similar functions given that economics is not an exact science and the theories that underpin the public good concepts have been the subject of vigorous debate in the literature for more than a century. Even if the same theories or economic models are used, different communities may exhibit different characteristics and hence alter the allocation of benefits. Add to this local government's inexperience in the use of such economic models and different interpretations are bound to occur.

11.6. Where to next?

Today local government in New Zealand is at a crossroads in terms of whether a functionalist or an autonomist approach will dominate.

Global and local trends suggest a shift from a functionalist to an autonomist view. Throughout the world, the nation state has come under challenge from two directions. The first is from increasing globalization, with capital and citizens moving freely across borders, and supra-national regulations which erode the monopoly role of sovereign states. The second is growing recognition of the plurality of societies within nation states which undermines the effectiveness of standardized policy solutions and demands instead interventions based on local knowledge and input from affected communities. Certainly the reforms have created opportunities for enhanced citizen participation, larger and stronger local councils, and greater financial autonomy through the relaxation of the borrowing regime. Councils seem to vary widely in the strategy they have adopted. Some are heavily engaged in contracting out, franchising and privatization of services. Others have chosen to focus more on empowering employees and citizens. Here, process and organizational culture may be seen as more important than structures and the challenge is to find a variety of innovative ways to channel participation.

Ironically, just as individual local authorities are starting to exert their autonomy and develop approaches and policies suited to the needs and circumstances of their individual communities, there seem to be mounting pressures for central government to impose a functionalist model. For example, the chairman of the Business Roundtable has argued: 'Local government should be drastically slimmed down... In New Zealand, local government operates within a framework laid down by central government. It is perfectly open to central government to change that framework, as it has done many times. Changes to the framework are being mooted right now in the form of the proposed roading reforms.' (Myers, 1998).

There is guarded support for the Business Roundtable's stance, and the right of central government control to define the function of local government, from the Minister of Local Government: 'I have some misgivings about the extent to which some councils, and Christchurch City would certainly be an example, may be pushing the boundaries. But I await the findings of research being undertaken before looking at what changes if any may be necessary to the role of local government.' (Williamson, 1998).

The *Electricity Industry Reform Act 1998* has the effect of preventing local authorities to from owning lines network assets as well as energy generation and retailing. This amounts to enforced privatization, whether individual local councils like it or not. On its own initiative, Papakura District Council has already 'franchised' maintenance and operations of its water supply and wastewater disposal services to a multi-national company (Audit Office,1998b). Other councils are following suit and it is possible that central government will seek to impose such an approach on all local authorities in the interests of more efficient delivery of services. Perhaps the most significant, in terms of its impact on local government, however, are central government's proposals for roading reform. As the Minister of Local Government has stated: 'Do we really need 74 territorial authorities with a population the size of a large Australian city?... With the reform package (roading reform) some of these councils' very reason for being will go.' (Williamson, 1998, cited in Reid, 1999).

Already, central government's requirement in 1990 that all councils receiving grants from Transfund contract out their road construction and maintenance operations has had a drastic impact on smaller territorial authorities. Formerly, roading was up to 60 percent of their costs and the requirement to contract out has reduced their staff levels to as few as 30 employees. The latest proposals (Ministry of Transport, 1999) go much further although not as far as those in the report of the government-appointed Roading Advisory Group (1997).

The key features of the proposed reforms are specialist road organizations and a shift from rates (property taxes) to direct funding of roads. Four to eight regionally based local road companies would take over running local roads from New Zealand's 74 local authorities and a Crown-owned company (Transit New Zealand Limited) would operate state highways and motorways. Another Crown-owned company, Transfund New Zealand Limited, would provide road funding. The principal objective of the newly created entities (following the State-owned enterprises model) would be to: operate as successful businesses; be as profitable and efficient as comparable non-public businesses; be good employers; and 'exhibit a sense of social responsibility'.

Rates would no longer be used to fund roads. Instead, roads would be financed from a Road Use Levy collected from petrol sales, vehicle licensing, usage of heavy vehicles and light diesel vehicles (at higher levels than at present). Transfund would be responsible for recommending the rates of these charges to the Minister of Transport. Individual road users and groups of road users would be given greater choice in the way they pay for their road use. They could also leave the levy system and choose an alternative way of paying for their road use. These users could enter into contracts with road providers either directly or through organizations that would establish themselves as intermediaries for this purpose. Road users that choose alternative payment arrangements would be free to rejoin the levy system. Public road companies would be able to introduce tolls on specific roads and facilities and to introduce congestion prices to restrain traffic demand on heavily used routes. The Roading Advisory Group had also advised that transponder technology would soon be available to make direct charging of all vehicles by kilometre, type of road and time of day a practical possibility.

The proposed road reforms are welcomed by some local councils who currently find roading costs an almost unbearable burden on rates. Many local authorities, however, are not keen on having these central government reforms imposed on them. The smallest councils fear they will be driven out of existence while some of the larger ones (such as Christchurch) object that commercial roading companies, keen to maximize the number of vehicles on roads, will make the implementation of public transport strategies difficult. They are also concerned about having to absorb smaller authorities and losing their sense of local community.

11.6.1. ACCOUNTING ISSUES

If roads are to be corporatized, the accounting policies adopted will be important. Indeed, if accounting encourages us to take a given presentation for granted (Hines, 1989:56) then the adoption of private sector valuation and depreciation practices may already have encouraged a commercial view of roads as the 'natural' state of affairs. An alternative view - that some assets are community property rather than government or corporate property - was rejected by the designers of the *Public Finance Act* and this has had flow-on effects for local government. Portraying roads as 'community' assets (Pallot, 1992) recognizes that they have value not only to individual users and the entities that manage them but that they form part of a common life and that the community as a whole should have some say in decisions concerning them.

Valuation of roads, as noted earlier, was initially controversial but some consensus has been reached that depreciated replacement cost is the most appropriate method. This could change if roads were to be viewed commercially. Valuations could be based on expected future cash flows. In the electricity sector, distribution assets were revalued on the basis of optimized deprival value. Electricity companies then focused on earning a commercial rate of return on those increased values and prices to consumers increased. Whether or not to include valuation of land underneath the roads is a further controversy (Barton, 1999).

Perhaps even more controversial than presentation and valuation has been accounting for depreciation. The accounting policy for depreciation of infrastructure assets has itself been contested terrain between central government and local government. The preference of local government managers (accountants and engineers) has been for decline in service potential to be measured by the difference between planned and actual renewals, making asset management plans crucial to the provision of accounting information (Pallot, 1997b). A more recent position, to overcome problems of lumpiness in capital expenditure has been a 'two-step' renewals based approach. Here the measure of change in service potential is the *long run average* of future renewals expenditure (over, say, twenty years) as indicated by the asset management plan. The 'two steps' are (1) the long-run average of estimated future renewals is expensed (as depreciation) and (2) actual renewals expenditure is capitalized. Repairs and maintenance are items that would not have been included in the renewals plan and are therefore expensed.

Central government has preferred conventional straight line depreciation as practiced in the private sector and has adopted this for depreciation of roads in the crown's balance sheet. In this it has support from the Institute of Chartered Accountants of New Zealand (ICANZ) which now operates a single standards setting regime across both the public and private sectors. In April 1998 ICANZ produced an exposure draft of a new standard on Accounting for Property, Plant and Equipment in which it advocates conventional depreciation for infrastructure assets i.e. the sum of the (straight-line) depreciation calculations for each separately identifiable component. At the same time, changes in legislation mean that local government is obliged to conform to Generally Accepted Accounting Practice as defined in the Financial Reporting Act 1993. This means standards approved by the Accounting Standards Review Board, which is oriented to the private sector, has no local government representation, and normally approves standards recommended by ICANZ. Thus there is every possibility that the approach preferred by the centre will be enforced ahead of any preferences of local councils.

A centrally imposed approach which views depreciation as a cost of service delivery has all the hallmarks of a functionalist paradigm. Viewed from an autonomist perspective, however, depreciation policy has implications for democratic or community control over the use of resources. When prices, taxes or rates are based on full costs, including depreciation, it helps to ensure that funds equal to the depreciation of an asset are not distributed and are retained in the business to maintain its asset strength i.e. capital maintenance. The question in the public sector is whether such capital maintenance decisions, particularly in the case of assets of significant public interest, should be the prerogative of managers rather than of elected representatives or the public at large. Since surplus funds can be accumulated within the organization prior to their being needed to replace capital, they can be used to finance other activities in the short term and this tends to undermine the control taxpayers or ratepayers would normally have over management (Rutherford, 1983: 87). Aiken (1994) argues that 'there can be no ultimate delegation of powers away from elected representatives with respect to the allocation and balancing of scarce resources' (p.17) and that 'the main issue with capital maintenance is the need for a *direct* (emphasis added) statement of what exactly is to be maintained and under what authority' (p.26).

An accounting approach which links depreciation calculations directly to publicly agreed maintenance objectives, in the context of publicly available asset management plans and associated financing plans, helps to avoid the risk that accounting manipulations will remove significant decisions about the allocation of resources from the realm of public debate. The financing plans force explicit public decision making about questions of intergenerational equity rather than allowing these to be determined de facto through non-transparent accounting manipulations.

The accounting controversy in New Zealand is exacerbated by the requirement in the No. 3 Amendment Act for local authorities to fund 'decline in service potential' (depreciation). As a principle of financial management, section 122C of the Act states that 'operating revenues in any financial year should be set at a level adequate to cover all projected operating expenses'. Section 122A of the Act states that 'operating expenses' and 'operating revenues' have the meaning given to them under generally accepted accounting practice. Depreciation is therefore an operating expense which has to be funded. Having required depreciation to be funded, nothing in the Act says how the funds generated can or should be used. There is also no requirement to use the funds generated for the benefit of the activity whose assets have been depreciated. The problem with the corporatization of roads is that it would remove them from the local government consultative processes for annual and long term plans altogether. Even if road users were in some way able to resist attempted price increases imposed by roading companies, based on highly manipulable depreciation figures, the question remains as to whether roads have broader social significance beyond their utility to individual motorists.

11.7. Conclusion

Local government reform in New Zealand is in many respects consistent with the model adopted at the central level, but it also reflects fundamental values such as the right of communities to govern themselves and the opportunity for individuals to develop their human potential through participation in a common life. While the first round of reforms adopted new public management principles used at the central government level, it did acknowledge the added importance of participation as a rationale for local government and created some mechanisms by which more informed public discussion could take place. The current round of reforms introduces some new initiatives, including a longer term strategic perspective and explicit judgements about the public versus private nature of goods and services. While ostensibly about better financial management, the new legislation has implications for public management more generally. It extends the scope and importance of public participation by requiring consultation not just on annual short term issues but on matters affecting the next generation of citizens as well. The new legislation governing borrowing potentially gives local authorities increased autonomy. The extent to which this autonomy can be exercised, however, may depend on the extent to which local government can withstand pressures from central government and other influential groups to minimize its role. In this context, accounting should be viewed not just as a technology for measuring the cost of services in the interests of increased efficiency, but as a process closed interwoven with community participation and control.

References

- Anderson, B. (1993) Do We Have Better Local Government?, *The Accountants Journal*, 72(10), 65-67.
- Audit Office (1993) *Report of the Controller and Auditor-General on the Financial Condition of Regional and Territorial Local Authorities*, Audit Office, Wellington.
- Audit Office (1994) Accounting for Infrastructural Assets, *Report of the Controller and Auditor General, Second Report*, Audit Office, Wellington, 32-36.
- Audit Office (1998) Experience with the New Financial Management Regime, In *Report of the Controller and Auditor-General: First Report for 1998*, Audit Office, Wellington.
- Ball, I. (1980) Central – Local government Relations: the New Zealand Experience, In D. Andrews (ed.), *International Trends in Local Government – Central Government Financial Relations*, RMIT, Melbourne.
- Barton, A. (1999) Land Under Roads – A Financial Bonanza or Fool's Gold?, *Australian Accounting Review*, 9(1), 9-15.
- Boston, J., Martin, J., Pallot, J. and Walsh, P. (eds.) (1991) *Reshaping the State: New Zealand's Bureaucratic Revolution*, Oxford University Press, Auckland.
- Boston, J., Martin, J., Pallot, J. and Walsh, P. (eds.) (1996) *Public Management: The New Zealand Model*, Oxford University Press, Auckland.
- Bush, G.W. (1980) *Local Government and Politics in New Zealand*, George Allen and Unwin, Second edition 1995, Auckland.
- Bush, G. (1992) Local Government: Politics and Pragmatism. In Gold, H. (ed.) (1992) *New Zealand Politics in Perspective*, 3rd ed., Longman Paul, Auckland.
- Department of Internal Affairs (1992) *Public Consultation in the Local Authority Annual Planning Process*, Wellington.
- Department of Internal Affairs (1994) *Territorial Authority Service Delivery 1993 -1994*, Department Of Internal Affairs, Wellington.
- Douglas, M. (1994) New Zealand Paths to Competitive Tendering, In *Introducing Competitive Tendering in Local Government in Australia* Foundation for Local
- Government Education and Development Fund, Department of Management, RMIT, Melbourne.
- Hines, R (1989) The Socio-Political Paradigm in Financial Accounting Research *Accounting Auditing and Accountability Journal*, 2(1), 251-261.
- Horner, T. (1989) Local Government Reform: Links to Public Sector Reform, *Public Sector*, 12(3), 2-10.
- Loughlin, M. (1986) *Local Government in the Modern State* , Sweet and Maxwell, London.
- McDermott, P and Forgie, V. (1999) Trends in Local Government: Efficiency, Functions and Democracy, *Political Science*, 50(2), 247-265.
- Ministry of Transport (1999) *Better Transport, Better Roads*, ministry of Transport, Wellington.
- Myers, D. (1998) Local government: Time for a New Blueprint, Speech to ACT New Zealand/Federated Farmers Local Government Reform Summit Whangarei 15 April 1998, http://www.nzbr.org.nz/documents/.
- Officials Coordinating Committee on Local Government (1988) *Reform of Local and Regional Government: Discussion Document*, Department of Internal Affairs, Wellington.

- Pallot, J. (1997a) 'Newer than New' Public Management: Financial Management and Collective Strategy in New Zealand, In L. Jones, K. Schedler and S. Wade *International Perspectives on the New Public Management. Advances inInternational Comparative Management*, Supplement 3, 125-144.
- Pallot, J. (1997b) Accounting for Infrastructure: Technical Management and Political Context, *Financial Accountability and Management*, 13 (3), 1997, 225-242.
- Pallot, J. (1999) Service Delivery: The Audit Dimension, *Australian Journal of Public Administration* (forthcoming).
- Reid, M. (1999) The Central-Local Government Relationship: The Need for a Framework?, *Political Science*, 50(2), 165-181.
- Roading Advisory Group (1997) *Roading Reform: The Way Forward* Report to the Government Wellington 12 December 1997.
- Richardson, R. (1994) Opening and Balancing the Books: The New Zealand Experience, *The Parliamentarian*, October, 244-246.
- Rutherford, B. (1983) *Financial Reporting in The Public Sector*, Butterworths, London.
- Salter, J. (1996) Rates Ruling Under Threat, *New Zealand Local Government*, 32(9), 31-32.
- Scott, C.D. (1979) *Local and Regional Government in New Zealand: Function and Finance*, George Allen and Unwin, Sydney.
- Scott, G., P. Bushnell and N. Sallee (1990) Reform of the Core Public Sector: New Zealand Experience, *Governance*, 3, 138-167.
- Scott, G., Ball,I and Dale, T. (1997) New Zealand's Public Sector Management Reform: Implications for The United States, *Journal of Policy Analysis and Management*, 16(3), 357-381.
- Slevin, G. (1996) Far Sighted Financial Planning, *New Zealand Local Government*, 32(1), 14-16
- Stewart (1996) Democracy and Local Government, In P. Hirst and S. Khilnani (eds.) *Reinventing Democracy*, Blackwell, Oxford.
- Tiebout, C. (1956) A Pure Theory of Local Expenditures *Journal of Political Economy*, 64;416-24.
- Williamson, J. (1994) The Christchurch Case Study on Competitive Tendering, In *Introducing Competitive Tendering in Local Government in Australia*, Foundation for Local Government Education and Development Fund, Department of Management, RMIT, Melbourne
- Williamson, M. (1998) Cited in Ombler, K. (1998) Have a Heart, *New Zealand Local Government*, 34(1), 14.

CHAPTER 12

ACCOUNTING AND FINANCIAL REPORTING IN SPANISH REGIONAL
GOVERNMENTS: EXPLORING SIMILARITIES AND DIFFERENCES

Vicente Montesinos, José Manuel Vela and Bernardino Benito

12.1. Introduction

Spain is a country where the Governmental Accounting system is very homogeneous at central and local level. In fact, the accounting regulations that are in force at local level follow the main orientation and guidelines of the accounting system applied at Central Government Level. This homogeneity has been a tradition in Spain, even when considering the differences between business and governmental accounting, that are rather close in their objectives, accounting principles and standards.

But the fact is that at Regional level, the accounting system that the different governments adopt is rather heterogeneous. This is due to the fact that every region ('Comunidad Autónoma', *Autonomous Community*) has the capacity to issue the standards and regulations that define its accounting and financial reporting framework. The result is that different reporting models co-exist with significant differences between them. Even if some regions have developed sound financial reporting standards, their accounting systems are usually less developed and less informative that the system adopted by central government.

The purpose of that paper is to present, using a descriptive approach, the main differences on accounting regulation among Spanish Regional Governments and to identify the divergences on accounting practices they adopt. In order to obtain empirical information, a questionnaire was filled in 1998 by head accountants in the Autonomous Communities and Central Government. According to its purpose, the paper is divided in three parts. The first one presents the main features that characterize Central Government Accounting system in order to identify, in the second part, the main differences with the accounting system adopted by the regions. The third part is concerned with the existing differences on accounting practices between the different Regional Governments, basically related with their organizational, financial and budgetary characteristics, the compliance of the regional accounting model with the provisions of Central Government accounting regulations, the accounting information system and the form and content of financial statements. Users of accounting information and their opinions considering the introduction of accounting innovations are also analyzed. The last part of the paper presents some proposals concerned with a possible harmonized accounting and reporting common framework, as a possible guideline for future accounting recommendations still to be issued and that will require a consensus effort between Central and Regional Governments in order to maintain the traditional homogeneity that has characterized in the past the Governmental Accounting system in Spain.

195

A. Bac (ed.), International Comparative Issues in Government Accounting, 195-212.
© 2001 *Kluwer Academic Publishers. Printed in the Netherlands.*

12.2. Main Characteristics of Spanish Governmental Accounting

The reform of governmental accounting in Spain started in the early eighties, as a consequence of the provisions of the 1977 General Budgeting Law (Ley General Presupuestaria). This law encouraged the reform and enforced further developments as the implementation of a first governmental accounting Chart of Accounts issued in 1981 (in force at Central Government Level since the first of January 1984). As described in Montesinos & Vela (1996) , after fifteen years since then, the reform has allowed to reach a new governmental accounting system quite advanced from a financial perspective and that has attained significant improvements in the following fields:

12.2.1. LEGAL FRAMEWORK

A unique and clearly defined legal framework that is completed by a set of accounting standards developed by a new Chart of Accounts issued in 1994 and in force at Central Government level since the beginning of 1995. Local Governments also apply a Chart of Accounts based on the 1981 Chart that was applied for Central Government. On the contrary, Regional Governments offer different accounting systems that are ruled by their own legislation and standards approved by the regional parliaments.

12.2.2. THE RELATIONSHIP BETWEEN FINANCIAL AND BUDGETARY ACCOUNTING INFORMATION

This is defined by the respective Charts of Accounts at Central and Local Government levels. As we will see later, this relationship also offers at regional level quite different solutions.

12.2.3. THE DEFINITION OF GAAP AND OBJECTIVES OF FINANCIAL REPORTING FOR CENTRAL GOVERNMENT AND LOCAL GOVERNMENTS

No common GAAP or objectives of financial reporting exist at regional level, due also to the fact that every region issues them according to its own public finance legislation.

12.2.4. THE BASIS OF ACCOUNTING

After the reform of governmental accounting at local and central levels in Spain, a modified accrual basis is used to prepare financial statements. This basis is very close to a full accrual basis with two significant exceptions:
- Capital assets, when for direct public use by citizens, are recognized as capital investments during construction and are written-off (expensed) when completed. This is the case for infrastructure, defence and cultural assets. Consequently, no depreciation expense is considered for these capital assets in the financial statement (operative statement).
- Capital subsidies are recognized using modified cash basis and transferred to income when collected or when receivable within three months or less. As a consequence of this, there are no deferred revenues to be recognized in future periods.

For budgetary reports, that are also included in the financial statements, there is no a clear definition in the law of the basis of accounting to be used, even if this basis is very close to a modified cash basis. In accordance with the General Chart of Accounts, budgetary revenues and expenditures are recognized when the administrative decisions have been adopted, independently of the time when the facts associated to them have occurred. Consequently they are not accrued. We can conclude that two basis are simultaneously used in the Spanish model: a modified accrual basis in financial accounting and a modified cash basis in the budget. As budget execution statements are included in the annual financial report with a balance sheet and an operative statement, its important to consider this difference.

12.2.5. THE MEASUREMENT FOCUS

Concerning the measurement focus adopted, the differences between budget and financial accounting are also important. Measurement foci are the criteria used to define what assets and liabilities are taken into account in order to determine the entity's financial position. The inclusion or non-inclusion of assets and liabilities in the statement of financial position depends on the measurement focus adopted in any case (IFAC, 1991, p. 2; IFAC, 1993, pp. 12-18). According to IFAC (1993, par. 073), measurement foci used for assets reporting are: current financial resources, total financial resources and economic resources. Lüder (1989, p.20; 1994, pp. 2-3) defines three types of measurement foci for net asset positions: the net-monetary-debt measurement focus, the net-total-debt measurement focus and the equity measurement focus.

In Spain, the general framework for preparation and presentation of governmental financial accounting statements sets up the economic resources/equity focus as the general rule for all the entities. In a similar way to the basis of accounting, there is a dual accounting treatment - from a measurement focus point of view - for strictly financial statements and budgetary reports. Financial statements (balance sheet and operative statement), are prepared using 'economic resources/equity focus'. There are, as pointed out before, some exceptions to this general rule: the non-inclusion in the financial statements of certain capital assets and the non-deferral of capital subsidies. As a consequence of these deviations from a pure economic resources/equity focus, a 'modified equity' focus is properly set up by general Spanish governmental accounting standards at Central and Local levels.

Budgetary reports pay attention to revenues and expenditures measured when cash is collected or paid, or when related receivables and payables have short term maturity term, normally three months or less. Budget has thus short-term financial and not economic and equity reporting purposes, and expenditures rather than expenses are recognized in budgetary reports. Expenses are included in the operative statement This is why depreciation is disclosed in this statement and not in the budget. The budgetary measurement focus is a financial one, that practically can be identified as a 'current financial resources' focus.

In what concerns Regional Governments, the diversity among the accounting standards in force in every region is again important, and an homogeneous measurement focus cannot be identified.

12.2.6. THE CONTENT OF THE FINANCIAL REPORTS.

At Central and Local levels, the content of financial reports is structured around three main types of statements: a statement of financial position (balance sheet), an operative statement, and budget execution statements.

The presentation of a balance sheet with classified assets, equity and liabilities items, provides a rationale and overall picture of the financial position of governmental entities. Other additional and more detailed financial information is included in the notes, which develop and complement the balance sheet figures and total amounts. It is important to note, as we said before, that infrastructure assets are not included after their construction is achieved.

Expenses and revenues are accrued in order to elaborate an operative statement, with some exceptions as infrastructure assets depreciation. In this account, expenses and revenues are classified by nature. Wealth and equity annual variations are thus reported in this statement, providing a very useful information for long-term evaluation of the entities' financial performance and its incidence on their future economic viability. The separated information on operative, financial and unusual items is quite useful in order to implement comparative analysis and forecasts.

Finally, the budget execution statements present the main budget execution figures for revenues and expenditures and show the budgetary result of the year, that is different from the bottom line of the operative statement. This is obviously due to the differences between the measurement focus and basis of accounting applied for budget and financial accounting pointed out above

At regional level, as we will analyze later, the situation is once again not uniform, and offers different solutions according to the region that is considered.

After the reform of Spanish governmental accounting, we can conclude that the present accounting system has an important informative dimension in what concerns financial accounting. If we analyze the development of accounting standards, in fifteen years, a conceptual framework has been defined as well as a set of Accounting Principles (GAAP) quite similar to those considered for business entities. The reform has also permitted to implement an accounting system that integrates budgetary accounting and financial accounting in the structure of the Chart of Accounts. This is very useful for reporting purposes, considering above all that the compulsory financial statements that are now issued report not only budgetary figures, but also a balance sheet and an operative statement for the overall accounting entity. As we will see now, the situation in the regions is not the same.

12.3. Governmental Accounting and the Setting of Accounting Standards in Spanish Regions

Spain has developed a reform that has followed a clear top-down orientation. Its means that the accounting model was first implemented at Central Government Level, and then extended to the lower levels of government (local level). This is why in Spain the accounting system of municipalities, reformed in 1990 following the model defined by the Chart of Accounts of 1981, is very similar to the model of Central Government (Vela, 1996), even if the new 1994 Chart of Accounts is not yet applied at local level. But the fact is that the accounting model applied at Central and local levels has not yet been fully implemented at regional level.

In Spain, there is a body with an authoritative status in the issuance of governmental accounting standards: the Intervención General de la Administración del Estado, IGAE (Office of the Comptroller General of the State). This body elaborates the governmental chart of accounts and its further developments at central and local Government levels.. While the authority in setting accounting standards is held by the IGAE for central and local governments, regional governments are autonomous for that purpose. This autonomy of the regions explains the different accounting models that can be identified among them.

Spain, as a consequence of the decentralization process initiated in the late seventies, has 17 regional governments. Even if all the regional governments have the same competencies, two groups of regions can be differentiated:
a. Regional Governments with a high level of competencies: País Vasco, Cataluña, Galicia, Andalucía, Navarra, Valencia and Canarias;
b. Regional Governments with a low level of competencies: Aragón, Castilla la Mancha, Castilla y León, Extremadura, Asturias, Cantabria, la Rioja, Murcia, Baleares and Madrid.

This decentralization process has been rather important, specially considering that in 1998, Central Administration represents a 65 % of all the consolidated expenditures of Spanish Public Administrations, while in 1986, it represented a 75 % (see exhibit 12.1.). It is also important to note that in 1998, regional governments represent a 31 % of the total public investment managed by Public Administrations and a 9,6 % of their global debt (see exhibits 12.2. and 12.3.).

Years	Total public administrations	%	Central administration (1) y (2)	%	Autonomous communities (2)	%	Local authorities (2)	%
1986	84,6	100	64,1	75.8	11,1	13.1	9,4	11.1
1987	92,1	100	68,3	74.1	13,1	14.3	10,7	11.6
1988	98,8	100	69,3	70.1	17,0	17.3	12,5	12.6
1989	116,4	100	79,7	68.5	21,2	18.2	15,5	13.3
1990	139,2	100	95,1	68.3	25,6	18.4	18,5	13.3
1991	151,9	100	102,4	67.4	29,6	19.5	19,9	13.1
1992	173,7	100	116,3	67.0	34,8	20.0	22,6	13.0
1993	189,1	100	128,1	67.8	37,9	20.0	23,1	12.2
1994	206,6	100	140,8	68.2	42,1	20.3	23,7	11.5
1995	213,3	100	143,9	67.5	44,8	21.0	24,6	11.5
1996	235,1	100	153,5	67.9	49,1	20.9	26,5	11.2
1997	248,2	100	167,0	67.3	53,0	21.4	28,2	11.3
1998	255,4	100	167,6	65.6	56,8	22.2	30,9	12.1

(1) Including Social Security and retirement Pensions
(2) Including financial debt reduction as budgetary expenses

Exhibit 12.1.: Consolidated Expenses of Spanish Public Administrations (.000 millions of euros)
Source: 'La descentralización del gasto público en España. Período 1986-1998', Ed. Dirección General de Coordinación con las Haciendas Territoriales, Ministerio de Economía y Hacienda, Madrid, 2000.

Years	Total public administrations	%	Central administration	%	Autonomous communities	%	Local authorities	%	Social security	%
1989	11,8	100	3,7	31.4	3,6	31.0	3,7	31.3	0,8	6.3
1999	14,6	100	4,9	33.7	4,5	31.2	4,3	28.9	0,9	6.2
1991	15,8	100	5,2	32.3	5,6	35.6	4,1	25.9	0,9	6.2
1992	14,3	100	4,4	29.9	5,3	37.1	3,8	26.9	0,8	6.4
1993	14,8	100	4,7	32.1	5,2	34.8	4,0	27.0	0,9	6.1
1994	15,2	100	4,6	30.6	4,9	32.2	4,9	32.2	0,8	5.0
1995	15,1	100	5,4	35.2	4,5	30.1	4,4	29.1	0,8	5.6
1996	13,7	100	3,8	28.0	4,8	35.0	4,2	30.7	0,9	6.3
1997	14,0	100	4,3	30.7	4,5	31.9	4,4	31.9	0,8	5.5
1998	16,3	100	4,7	29.3	5,1	31.0	5,6	34.0	0,9	5.7

Exhibit 12.2.: Gross Fixed Capital Formation in Spanish Public Administrations (.000 millions of euros)
Source: 'Cuentas financieras anuales de la economía española', Ed. Banco de España, Madrid, 2000.

Years	total public admini-strations	%	central admini-stration	%	autono-mous commu-nities	%	local authorities	%	social security	%	internal trans-actions	%
1986	88,0	100	79,6	90.4	2,0	2.3	5,8	6.6	1,4	1.6	-0,8	-0.9
1987	99,3	100	90,2	90.8	2,2	2.2	8,0	6.7	1,2	1.8	-0,9	-1.0
1988	101,2	100	90,1	89.1	2,5	2.5	14,1	7.9	1,4	1.4	-0,9	-0.9
1989	118,0	100	99,7	84.5	3,8	3.2	12,9	11.2	1,3	1.1	-0,9	-0.8
1990	135,6	100	117,0	86.0	5,7	4.3	13,8	9.6	1,5	1.1	-1,4	-1.0
1991	151,1	100	127,2	84.2	8,8	5.9	14,1	9.1	2,3	1.5	-1,0	-0.7
1992	171,5	100	143,5	83.7	12,7	7.5	15,6	8.2	3,5	2.0	-2,4	-1.4
1993	221,0	100	187,6	84.9	16,6	7.5	16,9	7.0	4,3	2.0	-3,1	-1.4
1994	244,8	100	205,8	84.0	20,8	8.5	17,9	6.9	7,3	3.0	-6,0	-2.4
1995	275,3	100	232,6	84.1	24,0	8.8	18,6	6.7	10,6	3.9	-7,9	-2.8
1996	312,1	100	263,6	84.5	18,6	8.9	18,1	6.0	13,8	4.4	-11,8	-3.8
1997	324,5	100	273,0	84.1	31,3	9.7	18,9	5.6	16,3	5.0	-14,3	-4.4
1998	334,7	100	282,3	84.3	32,1	9.6	18,8	5.6	18,5	5.5	-17,0	-5.0

Exhibit 12.3.: Debt of Spanish Public Administrations (.000 millions of euros)

Source: 'Actuación económica y financiera de las Administraciones Públicas' (published every year by IGAE), Madrid and Boletín Estadístico del Banco de España.

As we said before, the accounting systems and standards between the different regions are not homogeneous, specially considering that every region can issue its own accounting standards. Even if budgetary legislation is quite similar, the differences in budgetary accounting also exist. Consequently, the comparability between the accounting information provided by Spanish regions is very difficult to achieve, specially considering two main reasons concerned with:

1. the absence of a common conceptual framework;
2. the accounting standards that are applied.

The absence of a common conceptual framework of accounting for all the regions is the first reason that explains the lack of comparability of the accounting information they provide. No common recognition criteria exist, the content of financial reports is not harmonized, and even the objectives of financial reporting are sometimes different in its content and disclosure. According to those objectives, three groups of regions can be identified:

a. the region of La Rioja, were there is not a specific Finance Law that sets up those objectives;
b. the regions where the objectives of financial reporting are only set up by a basic law. This is the case of Andalucía, Aragón, Asturias, Baleares, Cantabria, Castilla la Mancha, Castilla y León, Cataluña. Madrid, Navarra, País Vasco and Valencia;
c. the regions where the objectives of financial reporting are set up by a basic law but fully disclosed by other laws. This is the case of Canarias, Extremadura, Galicia and Murcia.

Anyway, the basic objectives at regional level are concerned in general with:
- budget execution disclosure;
- situation and evolution of cash;
- disclosure of assets and liabilities;
- accountability.

The differences on the accounting standards applied also explains the lack of comparability of the accounting information provided by Spanish regions. While the standards concerned with the budget are quite uniform, the accounting standards not homogeneous due to the lack of a common chart fully applied. Nevertheless, an agreement exists for introducing 1994 Government Chart of Accounts by all Regional Government. Late in 1999 the following standards setting policies can be described in the Spanish regions:

a. regions that apply an own Chart of Accounts based on the Chart applied by the Central Government. This is the case of the majority of regions;
b. regions that apply a an own Chart of accounts not based on the Chart applied by Central Government. This is the case of País Vasco, that uses a Chart inspired in the Spanish chart for business entities;
c. regions that do not apply any Chart. This is the case of Canarias and Navarra.

The lack of a common Chart of Accounts and a common conceptual framework, explain why the accounting systems in Spanish regions are different. In order to appreciate where the differences and similarities between those systems are, the authors of this paper conducted a survey in 1988 that was addressed to all the Accounting offices in the different regions. The main objective of this survey was to analyze the divergences on the accounting practices and to identify which regions in Spain present a more informative accounting system. The main results of the survey are now presented.

12.4. Accounting Practices in Spanish Regions

The main objective of the survey developed in 1998 was to analyze the main accounting practices adopted by Regional Governments in Spain. This survey confirmed that regional governmental accounting systems are not homogeneous and that the differences among them are significant. The survey was developed sending a questionnaire that aimed to analyze the following points:

1. organizational, financial and budgetary characteristics of regional governments;
2. compliance of the regional accounting model with the provisions of Central Government accounting regulations;
3. accounting information system;
4. form and content of financial statements;
5. users and usefulness of accounting information;
6. availability and control of information;
7. accounting innovations in financial reporting.

12.4.1. ORGANIZATIONAL, FINANCIAL AND BUDGETARY CHARACTERISTICS OF REGIONAL GOVERNMENTS

The regions in Spain have organizational, financial and budgetary characteristics that are different, even if all of them approve a budget that is structured by programs. The taxes they levy, the grants from central state and their participation in some of the Central Government taxes are their main sources of revenue, even if Pais Vasco and Navarra have a specific financing system. Only three regional governments represent 50% of total regional governments, as shown on exhibits 12.4. and 12.5.: Andalucía, Comunidad Valenciana and Cataluña. Those three regions represent also a 44% of all the population of Spain.

Autonomous Communities	Surface (km2)	Inhabitants (thousands)	Regional Distribution	Density (inhab/km2)	Averadge Annual Variation 1985-1995 (%)
Andalucia	87,599	7,080.0	18.1	80.8	0.56
Aragon	47,720	1,181.0	3.0	24.7	-0.17
Asturias	10,604	1,079.2	2.8	101.8	-0.40
Baleares	4,992	744.2	1.9	149.1	1.15
Canarias	7,447	1,545.5	3.9	207.5	0.84
Cantabria	5,321	525.3	1.3	98.7	0.02
Castilla-Leon	94,224	2,490.2	6.4	26.4	-0.42
Castilla-La Mancha	79,461	1,654.1	4.2	20.8	-0.09
Cataluña	32,113	6,093.5	15.5	189.8	0.14
Valencia	23,255	3,920.6	10.0	168.6	0.43
Extremadura	41,634	1,046.5	2.7	25.1	-0.29
Galicia	29,575	2,715.3	6.9	91.8	-0.32
Madrid	8,028	5,055.3	12.9	629.7	0.49
Murcia	11,314	1,076.6	2.7	95.2	0.73
Navarra	10,391	524.4	1.3	50.5	0.14
Pais vasco	7,234	2,065.7	5.3	285.6	-0.40
La Rioja	5,045	263.2	0.7	52.2	0.09
Ceuta y Melilla	32	127.6	0.3	3,986.8	5.00
Spain	505,989	39,188.2	100.0	77.4	0.20

Exhibit 12.4.: 1995 Spanish Population and Surface by Regional Administrations
Source: 'Informe económico-financiero de las Administraciones Territoriales en 1996', Ed. Ministerio de administraciones Públicas, Madrid, 1997

Autonomous Communities	1985	1990	1992	1993	1994	1995	1996	1997
Andalucia	2,9	7,3	9,2	9,8	11,3	10,8	13,7	13,7
Aragon	0,1	0,4	0,6	0,6	1,0	0,9	1,0	1,3
Asturias	0,2	0,4	0,5	0,6	0,6	0,6	0,9	0,9
Baleares	0,1	0,1	0,3	0,3	0,3	0,3	0,3	0,4
Canarias	0,4	1,2	1,5	1,6	1,7	2,6	2,8	2,9
Cantabria	0,1	0,3	0,3	0,3	0,3	0,3	0,3	0,5
Castilla-Leon	0,3	0,9	1,1	1,2	1,9	2,0	2,5	2,6
Castilla-La Mancha	0,2	0,7	1,0	1,1	1,6	1,8	1,9	2,3
Cataluña	2,5	6,4	8,2	8,9	9,4	9,9	10,0	10,8
Valencia	0,8	3,3	4,4	4,7	5,1	5,1	5,5	6,0
Extremadura	0,1	0,5	0,7	0,8	1,1	1,1	1,3	1,3
Galicia	0,8	2,1	3,7	4,0	4,4	4,7	4,9	5,2
Madrid	0,5	1,8	1,8	1,9	2,0	2,1	2,8	3,5
Murcia	0,1	0,4	0,4	0,5	0,5	0,5	0,6	0,8
Navarra	0,4	0,7	1,4	1,4	1,4	1,5	1,5	1,6
Pais Vasco	0,8	2,6	3,2	3,7	3,8	4,0	4,2	4,3
La Rioja	0,10	0,10	0,15	0,15	0,16	0,2	0,2	0,2

Exhibit 12.5.: Consolidated Budgets of Autonomous Communities (years 1985-1997) (.000 millions of euros)
Source: 'Informe económico-financiero de las Administraciones Territoriales en 1996', Ed. Ministerio de Administraciones Públicas, Madrid, 1997.

From an organizational point of view, regional governments are also different, due to the fact that the level of competencies they have received from Central Government is not the same. Only seven regional governments have competencies on health, and some of them have adopted a rather decentralized organization creating a significant number of public corporations and autonomous entities (Pais Vasco, Cataluña and Andalucia). Nine regional governments present a consolidated budget. Due to the different level of population and competencies, regional governments offer big differences, even if the budgetary laws of all of them are quite similar. Some interesting figures are shown on the exhibit 12.6.

Autonomous communities	GDP (000 millions of euros)	GDP per capita (euros)	EU-15 real Convergence
Andalucia	68,410	9,386	60,4
Canarias	20,568	12,621	81,3
Cataluña	98,189	16,138	103,9
Galicia	29,771	10,867	70,0
Valencia	52,103	12,909	83,1
Aragon	16,564	13,980	90,0
Asturias	12,083	11,145	71,8
Baleares	15,781	20,473	131,8
Cantabria	6,300	11,970	77,1
Castilla-La Mancha	17,887	10,390	66,9
Castilla-León	29,307	11,747	75,6
Extremadura	10,187	9,522	61,3
La Rioja	3,822	14,438	93,0
Madrid	83,147	16,535	106,5
Murcia	11,626	10,503	67,6
País Vasco	30,861	14,749	95,0
Navarra	7,942	15,280	98,4
Spain	515,824	12,970	83,5

Exhibit 12.6.: GDP and Real Convergence in Spanish Autonomous Communities (year 1997)

Source: Alcaide Inchausti, 1999: 446-450

12.4.2. COMPLIANCE OF THE REGIONAL ACCOUNTING MODEL WITH THE PROVISIONS OF CENTRAL GOVERNMENT ACCOUNTING REGULATIONS

As we saw in the first part of the paper, the accounting system of Central Government is characterized by the co-ordination of two systems: a budgetary accounting system and a financial accounting system, that use different measurement foci and bases of accounting. All Regional Governments develop the budgetary system, following similar budget execution guidelines to the adopted at Central Level. But the fact is that not all the Regional Governments develop a financial accounting system (see exhibit 12.7.). This is the case of Baleares, Canarias, Cantabria, Extremadura and Galicia. The accounting system in those regions is budget oriented and uses a modified cash basis, while in the other regions development of a financial accounting system allows the adoption of a modified accrual basis.

In what concerns management accounting, it is very seldom developed, with the exception of País Vasco and Galicia. Anyway, as shown on exhibit 12.7., there are five regional governments that expect to develop a management accounting system in the future.

Autonomous communities	Budgetary Area				Financial Accounting Area				Management Accounting Area			
	A	B	C	D	A	B	C	D	A	B	C	D
Andalucia	✓				✓							✓
Aragón	✓				✓							✓
Asturias	✓				✓							
Baleares	✓						✓					✓
Canarias		✓					✓					✓
Cantabria		✓					✓					✓
Castilla-La Mancha	✓				✓							✓
Castilla-León	✓				✓						✓	
Cataluña	✓				✓						✓	
Extremadura	✓						✓					✓
Galicia	✓						✓			✓		
La Rioja	✓						✓					✓
Madrid	✓				✓						✓	
Murcia	✓				✓							✓
Navarra	✓				✓						✓	
País Vasco	✓				✓				✓			
Valencia	✓				✓						✓	
A: It is applied according to the law , B: Compulsory, C: Not applied but will be introduced												
D: Not applied and is not expected to be introduced in the future												

Exhibit 12.7.: The Accounting System of Regional Governments

12.4.3. ACCOUNTING INFORMATION SYSTEM

The accounting information system is supported by a specific software that allows to process the information concerned with the budget of revenues and expenditures, non budgetary transactions and liabilities. The design of the information system follows the model of Central Government in Aragón, Asturias and Cataluña, while other regions as Madrid, Pais Vasco or Murcia have developed accounting information systems that are very heterogeneous and present important differences. One of the main weak points of the regional accounting systems is the processing of the information related with fixed assets and the definition of appropriate accounting entities. Only Murcia and Castilla la Mancha have developed a fixed assets accounting system. The accounting entities considered are quite different and there is not a common definition of the entities that should be considered by the accounting systems. This fact stresses the problems that arise when the information provided by the different regional governments is compared.

12.4.4. FORM AND CONTENT OF FINANCIAL STATEMENTS

The annual financial reports presented by regional governments are not homogeneous, even if all of them include budget execution statements. A balance sheet and an operative statement is not always presented, specially in the case of the regional governments that have not yet developed a financial accounting system. In this case , the annual reports include mainly the information concerned with the budget and its execution.

The survey has tried to identify the degree of similarity of the annual financial reports presented by Regional governments with the annual financial report presented by Central Government. If we consider 38 statements and items that are presented in this report, and we analyze if they are disclosed by Regional Governments, the results evidence three clear facts (see exhibits 12.8. and 12.9.):

1. the annual report of Central Government is more informative according to the information disclosed;
.2. the degree of heterogeneity among the annual reports is high;
3. only six regions offer an annual report with a significant informative dimension, in similar terms as the report presented by Central Government. This is the case of Murcia, Castilla León, Valencia, Madrid, Aragón and Andalucia.

Statement and Items	Statements and items included by regional governments	
	Number	**% over total**
Balance Sheet	11	69
Economic Result Account	12	75
Budget Stettlement statement	16	100
Operative statement	9	56
Funds Flow statement	10	63
Net financial savings statement	14	88
Cash flow statement	15	94
Budgetary changes statement	16	100
Non-disposed appropriation	12	75
Functional classification of expenditures	15	94
Projects of investment executed	9	56
Administrative contracting	3	19
Granted subsidies and transfers	7	44
Agreements	2	13
Staff	2	13
Creditors not yet applied to the budget	6	38
Cash Advances	6	38
Obligations related to closed budgets	16	100
Expenditure commitments for future budgets	16	100
Net receivable total amount	15	94
Net collected revenues	14	88
Written off receivables	12	75
Returned revenues	13	81
Grants and transfers obtained	7	44
Fees, public and private prices	10	63
Net financial saving outflows	7	44
Receivables from previous years budgets	14	88
Budgetary receivables by maturity	3	19
Revenue Commitments	2	13
Revenue Commitments concerning future budgets	3	19
Expenses earmarked for specific purposes	4	25
Non financial fixed assets	4	25
Fixed assets managed for other public entities	2	13
Infrastructure assets	2	13
Financial Investments	10	63
Financial debts	15	94
Stocks	3	19
Overruled receivables	12	75

Exhibit 12.8.:   Statements and Items included in the Annual Accounts of Regional Governments (no answers are available for País Vasco)

Autonomous communities	Statements included in the annual report of Central Government that are also included in the annual report of Regional Governments with a similar content	
	Number	**% over total**
Murcia	36	95
Castilla-León	32	84
Valencia	28	74
Madrid	27	71
Aragón	25	66
Andalucía	24	63
Galicia	21	55
Extremadura	19	50
Baleares	N/A	N/A
Cataluña	20	53
Canarias	13	34
Castilla-La Mancha	18	47
La Rioja	17	45
Cantabria	12	32
Navarra	10	26
Asturias	9	24
Pais vasco	N/A	N/A

N/A: No answer available

Exhibit 12.9.:   Statements in the Annual Report of Regional Governments, in Comparison with Central Government

12.4.5. USERS AND USEFULNESS OF ACCOUNTING INFORMATION

According to the responsible persons of accounting information in the different regions, this information is useful for the users showed in figure 12.1., with the degree indicated. The users that seem more interested are those concerned with the management and execution of budget and the audit and control bodies. An it is also clear according to the results obtained in the survey, that a clear interest in budgetary information prevails.

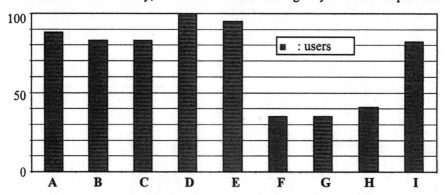

A: Political representation organs/ B: Political responsibles / C: Public entity managers / D: Budget Managers / E: Auditing and control bodies / F: Taxpayers and voters / G: Suppliers / H: Creditors / I: Financial Institutions

Figure 12.1:   Accounting Information Users and Usefulness of Information

If we consider the opinion of the responsible persons of accounting in every region, and the usefulness of financial statements, budgetary information is again considered as more relevant. The balance sheet and the economic result account is not usually considered to be very informative.

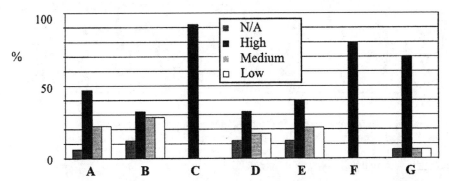

A: Balance Sheet / B: Economic Results Account / C: Budget Execution Statement / D: Operative Statement / E: Funds flow statement / F: Net financial savings statement / G: Cash statement

Figure 12.2.: Usefulness of Accounting Statements

12.4.6. AVAILABILITY AND CONTROL OF INFORMATION

Concerning the availability of accounting information, only 6 of the 17 Autonomous Communities asserted that they elaborate an economic report starting from the information included in the Financial and Budgetary General Accounts. As many users, not only politicians, are concerned by the information included in this economic report, accounting information must communicated in a clear and concise way. Citizenry is at the end of the day, the most important user, as citizens are the customers of public services, but they also pay by taxes for public activities and operations.

On the other hand, all the Autonomous Communities present their Financial and Budgetary General Accounts before External Audit Institutions. Moreover, five Communities had contracted out audits to private firms, always as a voluntary control.

12.4.7. ACCOUNTING INNOVATIONS IN FINANCIAL REPORTING

In the last part of our survey, we tried to analyze the opinions in the different regions concerning the introduction of several accounting innovations. As shown on figure 12.3., the innovations that seem more interesting for the responsible persons of accounting information are the introduction of accounting by objectives and responsibility (65% of total opinions) and the inclusion on the financial reports of value for money indicators (59% of total opinions). The innovations that seem less interesting are the inclusion of infrastructure assets in the financial statements and the introduction of a full accrual basis in the budget.

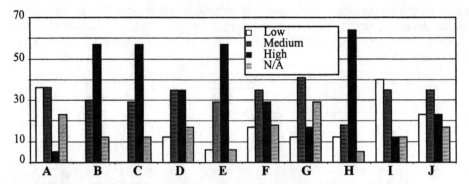

A: Inclusion of infrastructure assets / B: Consolidation of financial statements /
C: Consolidation of budgets / D: Activity based costs / E: Value for money indicators /
F: Cost accounting / G: Budget and resource accounting / H: Budget and accounting by
objectives / I: Accrual budgets / J: Full Accrual Basis statements

Figure 12.3.: Usefulness of Accounting Innovations

On another hand, if the difficulty in introducing accounting innovations is considered, the adoption of a full accrual basis on the budget, the introduction of objectives and responsibilities on budgets and on accounting, and cost accounting, are evaluated with a higher degree of difficulty (see figure 12.4.). On the contrary, the development of consolidation of financial statements and of consolidated budgets is considered to be easier by the responsible persons in developing accounting in the different regions.

If we consider both, usefulness and existing difficulties to introduce innovations, consolidation appears as the reform that in those moments seems more possible to develop. The introduction of a full accrual basis of accounting in the budget, and the inclusion of infrastructure assets on the financial reports is on the contrary, considered very difficult and not relevant.

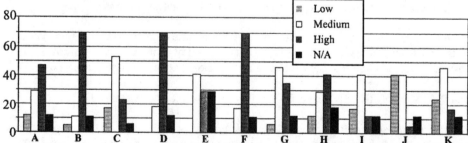

A: Full Accrual Basis / B: Accural in budgeting / C: Adjusted result with uncollectible receivables
D: Budget and accounting by objectives and responsability / E: Ressource accounting /
F: Cost accounting / G: Value for money indicators / H: Activity based costs / I: Consolidation of
budgets / J: Consolidation of financial statements / K: Inclusion of infrastructure assets

Figure 12.4.: Difficulty of Accounting Innovations

12.5. Conclusion

Accounting reforms in Spanish Regional Governments are going on more slowly than in other sectors of public administration, even important efforts are in progress, in order to implement double entry accounting in all the regions. However, the accounting system of Spanish Regional Governments is heterogeneous, diverse and not harmonized. The general situation evidences, in spite of some improvements introduced by some regions, that the accounting models have still an important budgetary orientation. The adoption of modified cash basis and of measurement focus based on financial resources is the more extended practice, even if some regional governments have adapted its reporting model to the Central Government one and are progressively introducing a modified accrual basis through the development of a financial accounting system. It is important to note that the regions that seem more concerned with the improvement of their accounting system, are usually regions that receive a significant amount of resources from the European structural funds (Objective 1 regions). This is for example the case of Murcia, Castilla León, Andalucía or Valencia, that have to report a significant amount of information to the European Court of Auditors for control purposes.

Moreover, all the Autonomous Communities present their financial and budgetary accounts before central and regional External Control Audit Institutions. Financial and budgetary reporting is not wide enough and quality of information is neither good enough for meeting the needs of citizens and other users need in a developed western society.

As a summary, it can be remarked that important efforts are made by Autonomous Communities in order implement accounting systems adapted to General Chart of Accounts, applied by Central Administration. However some agreement on an harmonization process is necessary, as there are important differences among the current regional accounting practices and central administration accounting and reporting standards. Common accounting and reporting standards are absolutely necessary, as comparability of information must be guaranteed, specially considering the process of political and administrative decentralization developed since 1978, when a democratic Constitution was adopted in Spain. In our opinion, only Central Government can enforce a consensus with the Regions in order to improve the accounting system through the introduction of a harmonized model based on the 1994 Chart of Accounts, or perhaps a new system for developing and implementing accounting standards and practices, that in any case must make possible the comparability and even the consolidation of governmental accounting information from central, regional and local public entities.

References

- Alcaide Inchausti, J. (1999) *La economía regional y provincial española de los años 1995 a 1997*, Included in *Anuario El País*. Madrid, Ediciones El País.
- Chan J.L., Jones R. and Lüder, K. (eds.) (1996) *Research in Governmental and non-profit accounting*, Volume 9, Jai Press Inc, Greenwich, Connecticut.
- International Federation of Accountants (1991) *Financial Reporting by National Governments*, IFAC Public Sector Committee Study 1. March.
- International Federation of Accountants (1993) *Elements of the Financial Statements of National Governments*, IFAC Public Sector Committee Study 2. July.
- Lüder K. (1989) *Comparative Government Accounting Study*, Interim Summary Report-Revised edition, Speyer, Hochschule für Verwaltungswissenschaften, Speyerer Forschungsberichte 76.
- Montesinos & Vela (1996*)* Governmental Accounting in Spain, In Chan J.L., Jones R. and Lüder, K. (eds.), *Research in Governmental and non profit accounting*, Volume 9. Jai Press Inc, Greenwich, Connecticut.
- Vela J.M. (1996) "Latest developments in Local Government Accounting in Spain". *Financial Accountability & Management*, Vol. 12, No.3, august 1996, 205-224.

CHAPTER 13

ACCRUALS ACCOUNTING APPROACHES IN THE UK PUBLIC SECTOR:
DIVERSITY AND CONVERGENCE

Sheila Ellwood

13.1. Introduction

Since the 1980s there have been extensive developments in financial accounting for central government departments, local authorities and hospitals within the National Health Service (NHS) in the UK. However, the developments have not been uniform - different parts of the public sector have developed their previously diverse accounting approaches over different timescales and along different lines. This article briefly sets out the accounting frameworks of three parts of the UK public sector in the 1980s together with conceptual thinking on the nature of public sector accounting at that time. It then examines how each branch of public sector accounting in the UK has developed using illustrations from the Ministry of Defence (MoD), Leeds City Council and Hereford Hospitals NHS Trust. The contextual setting is analyzed to provide an insight into why public service accounting developed in the 1990s. The final section considers the extent of convergence and diversity in accounting for public services.

13.2. An Historical Perspective

This section examines public sector accounting frameworks in the 1980s in three areas of the UK public sector - central government; the NHS and local authorities. The conceptual thinking on public sector accounting (or rather the lack of it) at this time is also summarized.

13.2.1. ACCOUNTING FOR CENTRAL GOVERNMENT DEPARTMENTS

Central government departments provide annual reports to Parliament. Until recently, accounting for central government departments in the UK was almost exclusively cash accounting. Cash accounting recognizes only cash inflows and outflows. This form of accounting is adopted by most sovereign governments. Guthrie explains the main features of annual cash accounting: This reflects the fundamental principle that no public monies should be spent in ways and in amounts not specified in annual parliamentary appropriations. Cash accounting records the cash receipts, payments and balances at the time cash is exchanged, hence cash accounting financial statements have traditionally shown sources of cash receipts, the allocation of cash expenditure and provided a comparison of actual against budgeted expenditures. Guthrie (1998) p5.

It can therefore be claimed that cash accounting is simple, relatively cheap to operate and objective. It also has close links to fiscal control and to monitoring public finance. However, it has two blatant disadvantages: it provides no measure of the worth of the

A. Bac (ed.), International Comparative Issues in Government Accounting, 213-232.

organization or its income; there is no measure of the 'true' cost of operating for period. This first deficiency is highlighted by Rutherford (1992) when he referred to the phenomenon of 'selling the family silver'. Under cash accounting, the proceeds from capital sales are shown as negative spending. Thus the accounting system does not report economic reality and is giving incorrect signals. 'On the basis of that information, the rational decision-maker can only see revenue (no costs) and the decision must be to sell' (Jones and Pendlebury, 1988, p70).

For business accounting, the accounting profession has for many years supported the view expressed by the Financial Accounting Standards board (FASB) in the USA that accrual accounting provides a better indication of an organization's present and continuing ability to generate favorable cash flows than cash accounting (Copping and Skerratt, 1997). The International Accounting Standards Board (1989) supported the FASB view that financial statements prepared on an accrual basis are more useful in making economic decisions. In the UK, the accruals concept is embodied in Statement of Standard Accounting Practice 2 Disclosure of Accounting Policies, and in the Companies Act 1995. On the other hand, accruals adjustments introduce subjectivity, accruals accounting is more costly to operate and the important link with public sector monitoring and management of liquid (cash) resources is less clear. Perrin observed the situation in the 1970s and explained the view held by the Treasury of accounting for central government departments: 'The Treasury view was that accruals accounting involving allocating costs between years on the basis of resource use rather than cash funding was incompatible with Parliamentary sovereignty and therefore unacceptable. Parliament voted cash funding year-on-year, so therefore the main control accounts, reports and accountability must be on an annual cash basis.' (Perrin, 1998) p8.

Other areas of the UK public sector had a modicum of accruals based accounting prior to the 1990s. Under accruals accounting revenue and costs are recognized as they are earned or incurred, not as money is received or paid. This approach requires cash flows to be adjusted through the introduction of debtors, creditors, stock, depreciation and so on. It can take many forms, for example, it can be based on historic cost or current value accounting. According to accounting theory, accruals accounting has considerable advantages over cash accounting by enabling measurement of goods and services consumed and income earned and, moreover, providing a measure of capital.

13.2.2. ACCOUNTING IN THE NATIONAL HEALTH SERVICE

Prior to 1991 the National Health Service adopted a partial accruals approach. Health service organizations produced detailed statements of income and expenditure, thus adjustments for debtors; creditors and movements in stock levels were brought in before the completion of annual accounting statements and the statement of balances (Balance Sheet) showed current assets and liabilities. However, spending and funding for capital items was kept completely separate. The service costs included no measure of capital consumption (depreciation) and no fixed assets were shown in the statement of balances. The omission of capital from health service accounting led to capital being termed a 'free good'. This was claimed to lead to inefficient use of capital stock. The Ceri Davies Report of 1983 for the Department of Health and Social Security portrayed poor asset management when it criticized "the somewhat casual attitude adopted by many authorities to the handling of property matters in the NHS. We believe that this attitude derives largely from the fact that property in the NHS is a 'free good'." Department of Health and Social Security 1983, p19. A further problem was the consequent poor comparability of health service costs both within the NHS and with the private sector. Mellet (1990) explained the deficiency thus 'The strength of comparisons within the NHS is weakened by the possible existence of differences in the capital/revenue mix dedicated to the same activities, as such comparisons, in the absence of capital costs, are based on the revenue element alone. Comparison with the private sector are also distorted as, in the long run, it must recover, and hence reflect in its charges and costings, both revenue and capital costs, whereas in the NHS, the consequence of the capital element may be neglected' Mellet (1990) p271.

13.2.3. ACCOUNTING FOR LOCAL AUTHORITIES

Prior to 1994/95 local authorities adopted a partial accruals approach but with some accounting entries entered in the revenue statements for capital items. As in the NHS, the accounting statements included debtors; creditors and stocks. But as Jones and Pendlebury (1984) stated: 'local authorities account for capital expenditure in a unique way. There is no counterpart in any other kind of organization, business or non-business.... The different practices adopted are reflected in different and unfamiliar terminology' Jones and Pendlebury (1984), p199.

The accounting entries for capital items were linked to capital financing. Local authorities finance capital expenditure from loans; from the proceeds of asset sales; from grants and from direct charges against local taxes. Each method had a different impact on the accounts and reported costs of the local authority's services, some in the year of acquisition, others over an extended period.

Local authorities produced detailed statements of income and expenditure and balance sheets (though not necessarily published) for each service or fund. No depreciation charges were included, however, a 'debt charge' would be included if fixed assets had been provided through loan finance. Thus the service costs included no consistent measure of capital consumption (depreciation). Fixed assets were shown in the balance sheet(s) but their valuation related to the financing method. Development of local authority accounting away from this link with capital financing was restricted by law.

Prior to 1988 local authorities were legally obliged to debit the relevant operating statements with principal and interest payments. Moreover, local authorities were not permitted to budget for an operating deficit. The situation changed in 1988 when the Local Government Finance Act set out that in place of the provision to debit debt charges to individual operating statements, local authorities must make a *'minimum revenue provision'* for the local authority a whole. This legal change enabled the introduction of a form of depreciation accounting.

13.2.4. CONCEPTUAL FRAMEWORK FOR PUBLIC SECTOR ACCOUNTING

A conceptual framework for accounting has been defined as: 'a constitution, a coherent system of interrelated objectives and fundamentals that can lead to consistent standards and that prescribes the nature, function and limits of financial accounting and financial statements' Scope and Implications of the Conceptual Framework Project, FASB (1976) p2.

By 1990, in the UK as in many other countries, there had been considerable thought given to conceptual frameworks in commercial accounting (ASSC 1975; Maeve 1981), very little comparable attention had been given to public sector accounting.

Likierman (1983) suggested six objectives and functions of public sector financial reports: compliance and stewardship; accountability and retrospective reporting; planning and authorization information; viability; public relations; and a source of facts and figures. However, he concluded 'What is published varies greatly in the relative emphasis given to each of these objectives and functions ....Indeed some published documents are effectively *only* exercises in public relations and the financial information plays a relatively minor role or is relegated to an additional, purely technical, document. On the other hand, some public bodies are required to publish only accounts and do not publish any more information to expand on them.' Likierman (1992), p12.

In the USA, a research report by Drebin et al., (1981) 'Objectives of Accounting and Financial Reporting for Governmental Units' had been commissioned for the National Council on Governmental Accounting. However, empirical studies in the UK (e.g. Butterworth et al., 1989; Likierman and Vass, 1984) largely failed to find 'individuals unequivocally external to the organization, who could be held to use financial statements for *any* purpose' Rutherford (1992). Also in 1992, Jones put forward a reason for this lack of interest: 'Why has there been comparatively much less theorizing, including theorizing about conceptual frameworks, than in commercial accounting? In the UK, the government has not needed to establish its legitimacy for many years, probably centuries: it has the power to set and enforce its financial and accounting policies and, one way or another, it has done this. It has not needed a conceptual framework. It has not even needed to explain its accounting policies, or changes in them because voters have no incentive to care and pressure groups only care about very narrow details. Moreover, for the same reasons, politicians have no incentive to become generally involved in accounting policies. Public sector accounting is therefore likely to be a matter for government officials.' Jones, R. (1992) p 262.

The UK public sector at the end of the 1980s was characterized by diverse accounting practices and there was neither an overarching conceptual framework to public sector accounting or apparently a strong interest in developing one.

13.3. Developments in the 1990s to Full Accruals Accounting in the UK Public Sector

Despite this apparent disinterest in public sector accounting, throughout the 1990s the UK public sector has experienced a concerted move towards full accruals based accounting. Areas of the public sector that had applied accruals accounting concepts except in accounting for fixed assets introduced forms of depreciation accounting and more commercial style accounts. Thus the NHS moved to introduce depreciation of capital items and company style layouts for the accounting statements and a balance sheet which included fixed assets. Local government shifted from financing charges to depreciation charges where appropriate and fixed assets included in the balance sheet on various valuation bases determined by the category of asset. However, the most dramatic changes are to be seen in central government accounting where the introduction of Resource Accounting and Budgeting (RAB) is to move government departments from cash accounting to comprehensive accruals accounting and a framework for analyzing expenditure by departmental aims and objectives.

13.3.1. 1991 INTRODUCTION OF NHS INTERNAL MARKET (FULL ACCRUALS ACCOUNTING)

The NHS White Paper, 'Working for Patients' (Department of Health, 1989) proposed the introduction of an internal market in healthcare. On the inception of the market in 1991, the health service was separated into purchasers (health authorities and family doctor fundholders) and providers (NHS trust hospitals and, initially in the first few years of the market, units directly managed by health authorities). Following the introduction of the NHS internal market, company style accounts were introduced for NHS trust hospitals. Vignette 13.1., Hereford Hospitals NHS trust highlights the main features of accruals accounting adopted by an NHS trust hospital.

Operating income in 1997/98 of £43m.

At 31 March 1998 the Trust's Balance Sheet showed:
- Fixed assets valued at £27.3m (£25.7m purchased; £1.6m donated.)
  - land 13%, buildings/ installations/ fittings 75%, equipment 13%
- Stocks £0.5m
- Debtors £1.5m
- Creditors falling due within one year £2.6m

The Accounting Policies:

Valuation of Fixed Assets (threshold £5,000 cost or more)
Land & Buildings
Valuations are carried out by the District Valuer at five-yearly intervals. Between valuations, price indices are applied to arrive at current value.
The large majority of buildings (including land, where not separable, installations and fittings) are valued by the DV at depreciated replacement cost. Exceptions - separable land, and land and buildings surplus to requirements are valued at open market value; certain non specialised buildings in operational use are valued at open market value for existing use; land and buildings held under finance leases are capitalised at inception of the lease at fair value of the asset but may be subsequently revalued by DV.
Equipment
Valued at estimated net current replacement cost using an appropriate index.
Exceptions: surplus equipment valued at net recoverable amount; assets held under finance leases are capitalised at fair value.

Depreciation [£1.7m in 1997/98: £1m buildings etc.; £0.7m equipment]
Charged on a straight line basis as follows:
Freehold land not depreciated
Leaseholds depreciated over primary lease term
Buildings, installations and fittings depreciated over estimated remaining life as advised by DV [in 1997/98 lives from 2 to 80 years used]
Equipment [including vehicles] is depreciated over the estimated life using standard asset lives [as set out in the NHS Manual] for each category of equipment. Vehicles are depreciated over 7 years.

Donated Assets
Donated tangible fixed assets are capitalised at their valuation on receipt and are valued and depreciated as above.

Stocks
Valued at the lower of cost and net realisable value. This is considered to be a reasonable approximation to current cost due to the high turnover of stocks.

Vignette 13.1:   Herefordshire Hospitals NHS Trust - 1997/98 Annual Accounts

The Hospital Trust produces accounts which follow the accruals concept with the balance sheet including fixed assets; stocks; debtors and creditors (vignette 13.1.). Herefordshire Hospitals NHS Trust Annual Report uses the Companies Act style layout for the Income and Expenditure Account, Balance Sheet and Cash flow Statement with an accompanying accounting policy statement and disclosure notes. The accounts are prepared in accordance with the Manual of Accounts for NHS Trusts, they follow commercial lines to give a 'true and fair view' and hence are generally expected to prepare annual accounts in accordance with accounting standards issued or adopted by the UK Accounting Standards Board (ASB). However, as can be gleaned from the accounting policies statement and vignette 13.1., there are a number of points of difference from generally accepted accounting practice. The Accounting Policies

Statement begins 'These accounts have been prepared under the historical costs convention, modified by the application of current cost principles to tangible fixed assets, and in accordance with directions issued by the Secretary of State for health to show a true and fair view. These accounts comply with accounting standards issued or adopted by the Accounting Standards Board, insofar as they are appropriate to NHS Trusts.' Hereford Hospitals NHS Trust, Annual Report 1997/98 p36.

Whilst revaluations of fixed assets are common in UK company accounts, the annual revaluation of assets through indexation is not. The ASB's Draft Statement of Principles (1995), which has recently been 'confirmed', submits that balance sheets should increasingly use current values , but this has been countered strongly by the accounting profession. In particular, Ernst and Young (1996) doubt the merits of any substantial move towards a valuation-based system and away from one based on historic cost. There are also examples where accounting standards have not been applied, for example, capitalization of medical negligence costs, (CIPFA, 1998). A current bone of contention is the Private Finance Initiative (PFI). Hereford Hospitals has recently signed a PFI contract. Under FRS5 Reporting the Substance of Transactions and SSAP21 Accounting for Leases and Hire Purchase Agreements, it could be argued that such arrangements should be shown 'on balance sheet'. ASB and Treasury Guidance have differed.

13.3.2. 1994 INTRODUCTION OF A NEW CAPITAL ACCOUNTING SYSTEM IN LOCAL AUTHORITY ACCOUNTING

A new system of capital accounting was introduced in local authority accounts in 1994/95. The aim was twofold: to improve the quality of external financial reporting and to help the authority manage its assets efficiently and effectively (CIPFA, 1993).

The new system was embodied in the Code of Practice on Local Authority. The Code is recognized by the ASB as a Statement of Recommended Practice (SORP). SORPs are produced by bodies recognized by the ASB as appropriate preparers of recommended practice for particular sectors e.g. CIPFA for local authority accounting. When a SORP is adopted by the ASB a negative assurance statement is displayed within the SORP indicating that it does not appear to contain any fundamental points of principle that are unacceptable in the context of current accounting practice or conflict with an existing standard.

Vignette 13.2., Leeds City Council highlights the main features of accruals accounting adopted by a local authority. The Council produces accounts which follow the accruals concept with the balance sheet including fixed assets; stocks; debtors and creditors. The Annual Report uses commercial style accounts, but not the formal layouts set out under the Companies Act. The main statements are the Consolidated Revenue Account; Consolidated Balance Sheet and Cash flow Statement which are produced together with an accompanying accounting policy statement and disclosure notes. Under the Accounts and Audit Regulations 1996 local authorities are required to prepare statements of accounts which 'present fairly' the financial position and transactions of the local authority. The SORP specifies the principles and practices required to prepare statements of accounts that comply with this requirement. However, as is apparent from the accounting policies statement and vignette 13.2., there are a number of points of difference from generally accepted accounting practice. The Accounting Policies Statement begins 'These accounts follow the appropriate accounting practices as required by the Accounting Code of Practice on Local Authority Accounting in Great Britain (1998). the code has been approved as a Statement of Recommended Practice (SORP). The accounts have therefore been prepared using the historical cost convention except in relation to fixed assets where the accounting treatment varies depending on the type of asset. Full or part compliance with Statements of Standard Accounting Practice and Financial Reporting Standards (FRS) are also identified where appropriate.' Leeds City Council, Annual Report 1997/98 p12.

Net expenditure in 1997/98 of £565m.

At 31 March 1998 the Council's Consolidated Balance Sheet showed:
- Fixed assets valued at £2060m (operational £1933m)
  Council dwellings 61.6% other land and buildings 32%, equipment 0.1% infrastructure 6.3%
- Stocks £3.8m
- Debtors £58.1m
- Creditors falling due within one year £115m

The Accounting Policies:
Valuation of Fixed Assets
Infrastructure assets e.g. highways
Assets in existence at 1st April 1994 are valued at the equivalent of any net loan debt outstanding at that date, new assets and developments are included at construction cost. Balance sheet valuations are net of depreciation (see below).
Community assets e.g. parks
Recorded at nominal [negligible] value
Operational land & properties and other operational assets
Valued on the basis of current value in existing use, unless of a specialist nature in which case they are valued on a depreciated replacement cost basis.
Non-operational assets and investment properties
Valued on the basis of open market value.

Charge for use of Fixed Assets calculated on current valuation comprise:
- a notional interest charge. 1997/98 Rate specified by Central Government for all local authorities: 8.125% for infrastructure and community assets, 6% for remaining operational assets and non operational assets.
- a depreciation charge in appropriate cases [£10.8m in 1997/98]: Property valuations undertaken by City Valuer: all have an indefinite asset life in excess of 20 years no depreciation charged on property 1997/98]. Vehicles, plant and equipment depreciated over emaining life [£3.4m].
- Infrastructure assets [£7.4m depreciation in 1997/98] depreciated :
  - if acquired after 1st April 1994, according to 30 year asset life
  - acquired before 1st April 1994, according to 15 year asset life
The authority is required to set aside a minimum revenue provision (Local Government and Housing Act 1989). If depreciation does not equal the prescribed amount a transfer to/ from the Capital Financing Reserve is made for the difference [transfer to CFR £12.1m in 1997/98].

Stocks and Work in Progress
A large element of stocks are valued at latest purchase price (due to high turnover and low inflation). Remainder are valued according to SSAP 9 i.e. at the lower of cost and net realisable value. WIP is included at cost plus any attributable profit less any foreseeable losses.The new system required: asset registers to be compiled including all the authority's capital assets; valuing and periodically revaluing all assets for inclusion in the authority's balance sheet; calculating capital charges for the use of assets, to be shown in the revenue accounts of services; and adjusting the authority's summary revenue account so that these capital charges do not affect directly the actual cash sums to be met from government grants and raised from local taxation.

Vignette 13.2.: Leeds City Council - 1997/98 Annual Accounts

As set out in vignette 13.2., the valuation of fixed assets depends on the category of asset: community assets are recorded at nominal value; operational assets are generally valued at current value, but for infrastructure assets in use prior to April 1, 1994, a pragmatic approach of valuing assets at the equivalent of any net loan debt outstanding was taken. The Council does not provide depreciation on property. Such treatment, whilst adopted by several commercial companies would have been contrary to SSAP 12. However, FRS15 issued in February 1999 acknowledges that depreciation may not be charged if it is immaterial (though such assets are subject to impairment review under FRS11).

Some accounting treatments do not comply with accounting standards. For example Leeds City Council states in its accounting policies 'As pension costs have been determined in accordance with relevant central government regulations, the City Council, the City Council does not comply with the accounting requirements of SSAP 24 Accounting for Pension Costs and the liabilities included in the Balance Sheet are therefore understated in respect of pension costs' Leeds City Council, Annual Report 1997/98 p14.

The most manifest example of local authority accounting failing to comply with private sector accounting practice is the inclusion of the principal element of repayment of external debt as an expense in the local authority revenue account.

13.3.3. 1998 RESOURCE ACCOUNTING IN CENTRAL GOVERNMENT

Central government is currently making the dramatic change from cash accounting to resource accounting and budgeting (RAB) with 'dry run' financial reports 1998/99 to be audited by National Audit Office but not 'published'. RAB comprises a set of accruals-based techniques; analysis of departmental expenditure by objectives and related to outputs; and Parliamentary approval of spending plans and authorization of expenditure expressed on an accruals basis. Under the accruals-based accounting system, each government department will produce a set of consolidated accounts, covering all its activities (including executive agencies). These accounts comprise: an operating account (revenue account) reflecting all its income and expenditure for the period; a balance sheet reflecting all of its fixed and current assets and liabilities at the end of the year; and a cash flow statement reconciling the net operating cost to the department's cash spend. To illustrate the accruals accounting embodied within RAB, vignette 13.3. highlights the main features of resource accounting as envisaged for the Ministry of Defence (MoD). Although the MoD does not have the biggest cash budget in government, it does have the largest range of assets by both number and value, as shown in the National Asset Register published by the Treasury in 1997. Assets range from fish and chip shops to Polaris submarines. Gillibrand and Hilton (1998) observed that 'The MoD asset base is such that capital charges and depreciation are likely to be at least as much as the current cash procurement budget.' Gillibrand and Hilton (1998) p23.

Seven TLB areas have net assets worth more than £1,000m (3 over £10,000m)
Seven TLB areas have annual net operating costs of more than £1,000m (4 over £3,000m)

Fixed Asset Categories (RAB Manual):
Intangible - development expenditure; intellectual property rights (IPR)
Tangible -Land & buildings
  Fighting equipment (FE)
  Plant, machinery and vehicles (PMV)
  Operational heritage assets
  Non operational heritage assets
  IT and communications equipment (IT & Comms)
  Assets in the course of construction (ACOC)
  Capital spares

The Accounting Policies:
Valuation of Fixed Assets
All fixed assets including ACOC and development expenditure, but with the exception of land and IPR are revalued annually under Modified Historic Cost Accounting (MHCA) using indexation. Land and property is revalued quinqennially.
Property valuations on different bases: open market value for existing use (OMVEU); depreciated replacement cost (DRC); modern equivalent asset valuations (MEA); net recoverable amount (NRA); nil value for certain non-operational heritage assets.
Non property fixed assets: Net current replacement cost (NCRC) i.e. the presumed method for the majority of non property assets; MEA; NRA.
Capital charges
Comprises depreciation plus a cost of capital charge (currently set at 6%)
Depreciation
Land not depreciated. Other fixed assets depreciated on a straight line basis using standard asset lives (or prescribed range).
Cost of capital
Applies to total net assets. Accounts maintained separately for each fixed asset category; stocks and for other net assets. Cost of capital charge is debited to Operating Statement and credited to General Fund.
Stock
Stock is valued at current replacement cost (CRC) unless, exceptionally, historical cost applies or the circumstances in which valuation at net realisable value is appropriate i.e. items not expected to be used/ sold in the ordinary course of business.
Debtors and Creditors
Cost recovery and income are recorded on an accruals basis and debtors are recorded in the Balance Sheet at expected recovery value. Similarly, expenditure is recorded in the period to which it relates and creditors included in the Balance Sheet.
Donated assets
Valued and depreciated as for purchased assets

Vignette 13.3.:   Ministry of Defence
                   11 Top Level Budget (TLB) Areas according to Function

The Public Accounts Committee has noted that the task of introducing RAB into the MoD is greater than for any other department and perhaps as great as for all the other departments combined (Robertson, 1999). The MoD produces accounts that follow the accruals concept with the balance sheet including fixed assets; stocks; debtors and creditors. The MoD Resource Accounting Manual purports to follow UK GAAP: 'The Resource Accounts are prepared in accordance with applicable Accounting and Reporting Standards and United Kingdom Generally Accepted Accounting Practice (UKGAAP), to the extent that it is meaningful and appropriate in the public sector context.' MoD Resource Accounting Manual, August 1998, para 2.1 (c).

However, on viewing the plethora of valuation bases prescribed in the MoD Resource Accounting Manual (see vignette 13.3.) it is difficult to recognize generally accepted accounting practice. The Manual goes on to list the accounting standards and the extent to which they apply. Table 13.1. lists the Accounting Standards which only apply 'partially' or 'as adapted'.

Accounting Standard	Application	Further explanation/ comment
FRS2 Accounting for Subsidiary Undertakings	Partially	'Requirements as to which entities are to be consolidated do not apply but consolidation principles do apply'
FRS 3 Reporting Financial Performance	Partially	'Section on disclosures in respect of historical cost profits and losses does not apply. The sections on extraordinary items, taxation and earnings per share are not relevant'
FRS 5 Related Party Disclosures	Applies as adapted	
FRS 10 Goodwill and intangible assets	Applies as adapted	See vignette 13.3. - e.g. revaluation of development expenditure
FRS 11 Impairment of Fixed Assets and Goodwill	Applies as adapted	
SSAP 9 Stocks and long term contracts	Applies as adapted	See vignette 13.3. - use of current replacement cost

Table 13.1.: MoD Resource Accounting - Accounting Standards applied partially or adapted.

The inclusion of the cost of capital charge as an expense in the Operating Statement under resource accounting (see vignette 13.3.) seems alien to UK GAAP. Moreover, the overall layout of the Operating Cost Statement (HM Government, 1994) showing the cost of resources consumed during the year appears markedly different from that set out under the Companies Act.

The Head of the Government Accountancy Service, Andrew Likierman has enunciated the original presumption set out in the 1994 Green Paper (HM Government, 1994 para 2.16) that UK GAAP would be adopted in RAB: 'The advantages of doing so, rather than having to devise a new framework, were seen to be to give a read-across to other organizations in both private and public sectors, to help in an understanding for those outside government familiar with accrual-based accounts and to work on an established framework, adapted as necessary for the particular circumstances of central government.' Likierman, A. (1998), p19.

The adherence to UK GAAP has been supported by the Treasury Select Committee: 'We recognize that the particular circumstances of the public sector will require some adaptation of UK GAAP and welcome the Treasury's assurance that it is not expected that departures from GAAP to be large or extensive.' Treasury Select Committee, (1996) para 13.

This support was reinforced by the Public Accounts Committee (PAC, 1997).

However, the list of adaptations to accounting standards, the multitude of valuation bases and the cost of capital charge could be argued to have moved resource accounting considerably from GAAP. Jones (1998) compared a typical opening sentence of a company's accounting policies statement with the equivalent sentence required by the Manual: 'These accounts have been prepared under the historical cost convention modified to account for the revaluation of fixed assets, and stocks where material, at their value to the business by reference to their current costs.' p139 Resource Accounting Manual.

Jones concluded that whilst the statement is literally true, it 'might be argued that the historic cost convention has been modified out of all recognition.' (Jones, 1998, p14).

Public sector accounting in the UK at the end of the 1990s is vastly different from public sector accounting at the end of the 1980s. However, it is still diverse, and it operates on markedly different accounting conventions (despite protestations to the contrary) from those adopted in the commercial sector. Why then have we moved away from simplistic cash style accounting to more sophisticated forms of accruals accounting often far more sophisticated than in the private sector?

13.4. The Contextual Setting

Historical changes in situations have often been assumed to be 'progressions' towards the current position, (Hopwood, 1987). However, as seen in the above UK examples, development is fragmentary. Miller and Napier (1993) point out that the rise of calculative technologies are determined in a 'piecemeal fashion' and outcomes are not associated with beginnings. Nevertheless there are some common threads both in the pressure for reform of public sector accounting and the forms of accruals based accounting developed in response to this pressure.

13.4.1. THE UK PUBLIC SECTOR MANAGEMENT REFORMS

Throughout the 1980s and the 1990s the UK government implemented a programme of reform across the public services. There was a move to differentiate across government between activities which are at the core of the public sector, and must remain so and the remaining functions which can be undertaken either within or outside the public sector. The privatization of nationalized monopoly utilities, such as British Telecom, British Gas, the UK electricity industry and the English water industry, took place after the Conservative Party's return to power in 1979 as part of a general transfer of ownership from the public to the private sector (March, 1991). For services continuing to be funded through the public sector, a key characteristic of the reforms was the separation of purchasers and providers (Le Grand and Bartlett, 1993). In addition, the services of public sector providers have been opened up whenever possible to compulsory competitive tendering, or 'market testing', against private sector organizations (and/ or other public sector providers) to ensure that they offer the best value in terms of price and quality. The Citizen's Charter (1991) aimed to raise standards of service in the public sector through the setting and publishing of service standards and more independent inspectorates. This general shift towards a more 'commercial' ethos has highlighted the need for a more commercial style of accounting, involving a move from a cash or partial accruals basis of accounting to a full accruals basis.

The National Health Service and Community Care Act 1990 reformed the structure of the NHS by introducing an internal market, whereby the responsibility for purchasing, or commissioning health care services has been separated from the responsibility for providing them. Ellwood (1996) explains that the introduction of capital charges including a return on capital in the hospital costs and consequently prices was threefold: to increase the awareness of health service managers of the costs of capital; to provide incentives to use capital efficiently; and to ensure that capital costs are fully reflected in the pricing of hospital services in order to promote fair competition within the NHS and also between NHS hospitals and private sector hospitals (i.e. 'a level playing field').

In local government, the number of local authority services subject to compulsory competitive tendering, (under which local authority direct service providers had to compete for contracts with alternative providers), expanded throughout the 1980s. Initially, only 'blue collar' activities such as refuse collection were affected, but by the early 1990s the process had been extended to cover many professional activities such as leisure management and financial services. Again such measures require improved accruals-based accounting to provide valid cost comparisons.

Similarly, in central government, the Financial Management Initiative was designed to encourage departments to produce better information on objectives, output and performance. In 1988 under the Next Steps measures, the executive functions of government (delivering services, collecting taxes, regulating, enforcing and researching) as distinct from the policy formulation functions (supporting Ministers) were to be restructured into executive agencies. Each would have a named chief executive, accountable directly to Ministers and a 'policy and resources framework' giving it clear focus and targets. By 1995, almost three-quarters of the UK's home civil service had been transferred to agencies (Talbot, 1996). A number of agencies have 'trading fund' status which enables them to manage their activities like a commercial company. Executive agencies and trading funds are required to prepare financial statements on an accruals basis along the lines of the commercial sector. Resource accounting and Budgeting takes this a stage further: 'Consolidated resource accounts would be prepared for each whole department by consolidating the accounts of each of its individual accounting units. These would comprise the 'centre' of the department and its executive agencies, including Trading Funds. Defining the boundary in this way ensures that it corresponds to the responsibilities of its principal Accounting Officer' HM Government (1994), para 2.21.

The boundary is also important, not just in terms of the reporting entity for accruals-based accounting but in terms of the wider aspects of RAB: the resource budgeting and expenditure control aspects. The accruals-based accounts were seen as providing 'a better picture of the true cost of department's activities' (National Audit Office, 1995, p3) and improving 'stewardship and accounting for assets and liabilities'. The new system under RAB of matching resources to objectives and outputs would help Parliament focus on cost and achievement. Thus RAB was seen as a logical corollary to the reforms emanating since 1982.

Thus UK public sector management reforms provided the impetus for more commercial style accounting in health, local government and central government. The specific focus was largely in obtaining improved information on resource costs enabling comparisons between service providers within the public sector and with private sector providers. Accruals accounting enabled more reliable, 'full' costs to be derived and the private sector style of accounting fitted well with the Conservative government's commercial ethos.

13.4.2. FISCAL CONTROL

Control of public sector finance has also contributed to the development of public sector accrual accounting in the UK. From its inception, it was envisaged that the change to an accruals accounting basis in central government would impact on the presentation of public sector plans (HM Government, 1994). However, the new budgeting framework could only be introduced once the new accounting systems were in place. The accruals approaches adopted in local government are also entwined with fiscal matters i.e. the minimum revenue provision to ensure finances raised are adequate to meet debt repayment. In 1997, this fiscal control aspect of resource accounting received new vigour following the Code for Fiscal Stability (HM Treasury, 1997) produced under the new Labour government which spelt out how RAB fitted with the government financial strategy. In its Economic and Fiscal Strategy Report (ESFR), the government's commitment to 'the golden rule' (that over an economic cycle, the Government will only borrow to finance public investment and not to fund current expenditure) was seen to fit well with an accruals accounting approach (HM Treasury, 1998a). Although originally it was not envisaged to produce 'whole of government resource accounts' because of the differences between various departments (HM Government 1994, para 2.24), in July 1998 the Government's proposals for publishing audited, consolidated accounts for the whole of the public sector from 2005-2006 based on GAAP were published (HM Treasury, 1998b). Given the diversity across the UK public sector highlighted earlier, the production of whole of government accounts, consolidating the accounts of a wide range of different entities across the public sector -including central government, the NHS and local authorities - clearly raises difficulties.

13.4.3. THE INTERNATIONAL PERSPECTIVE

Inevitably UK accounting is influenced by the international scene, The UK is by no means the first or only country to go down the commercial accounting route for public services. New Zealand, has had legal requirements since 1989 to: 'report in accordance with generally accepted accounting practice (i.e. on a full accrual accounting basis) in both central and local government, New Zealand has now been dealing with the issue at a practical level for a number of years' Pallot, 1997 p225.

As in the UK, the introduction of accruals based accounting followed a period of fundamental and philosophical and structural change. Pallot summarizes the key objectives as better management of publicly owned resources and a higher standard of accountability. Again, as in the UK, a wide diversity of approaches exists in relation to accounting for public sector assets, in New Zealand's case despite seven years of application.

Australian experience of accruals accounting also has its origins in a series of administrative reforms in the name of improved 'efficiency', 'effectiveness', 'respon- siveness' and 'accountability' (Guthrie,1998). Commercialization and contracting out reforms started to impact on government agencies: 'By the early 1990s a major shift in public administration had taken place in that now the focus was on cost control and the identification of 'full costs' and 'liabilities' of an agency' Guthrie 1998 p7.

Accruals accounting has also been introduced in a number of other countries such as Sweden, Finland and the USA (Hansen et al., 1998). In Sweden, as a development from the new management system of comparing outputs with resources consumed in the public sector, government agencies moved to an accruals accounting approach between 1991 and 1994. In Finland as part of the new public management reforms, accruals accounting was adopted in local government in 1997 and central government in 1998. In the USA, the federal government made a commitment to full accruals accounting following statements on federal accounting issued by the Federal Accounting Standard Advisory Board, but accruals accounting was only introduced in 1998 and the approach adopted does not capitalize military and heritage assets.

There has therefore been wide international interest in, and experience of, accruals accounting and budgeting in government. The introduction of the approach has usually been a corollary of management reforms aimed at improving efficiency. There are also international examples of whole of government accounts modelled on accrual accounting: New Zealand has produced such accounts since 1993 and in Australia, New South Wales whole of government accounts have been produced on an annual basis since 1992 and were produced by the Commonwealth (Federal) Government on a trial basis only in 1994/95.

13.5. Convergence and Diversity

There is considerable convergence in the purpose and perceived value of accruals based accounting measures for public sector services. However, diversity in accounting frameworks abounds.

13.5.1. THE PERCEIVED VALUE OF ACCRUALS BASED ACCOUNTING FOR PUBLIC SERVICES

The proposed value of accruals based accounting was set out in the UK accounting developments for the health service, local government and central government. The benefits of accruals accounting have been summarized by Evans (1995):
- better measurement of costs and revenues including comparisons between years;
- greater focus on outputs rather than inputs;
- more efficient and effective use of resources e.g. through charges for fixed assets;
- full cost of providing a service can be compared with outside suppliers;
- a better indication of the sustainability of Government policy;
- improved accountability;
- better financial management ;
- greater comparability of management performance results.

These views have been echoed internationally e.g. Mellor (1996), OECD (1993). However, there has been some concern expressed recently as to whether the practical achievements stand up to scrutiny (Guthrie, 1998; Stanton and Stanton, 1998; and Froud et al., 1998). Nevertheless there is a general consensus in favor of the move away from cash based or partial accruals accounting to full accruals for public sector services

13.5.2. DIVERSITY IN ACCOUNTING FRAMEWORKS

The introduction of accruals based accounting techniques in the UK has been espoused as adherence to commercial sector accounting practice. In the UK, commercial sector accounting operates within the regulatory framework of the Companies Acts and the accounting standard setting process. Since 1990, responsibility for the setting of accounting standards in the private sector has been vested in the Accounting Standards Board (ASB) which replaced the former Accounting Standards Committee (ASC). The ASC produced Statements of Standard Accounting Practice (SSAPs), the ASB produces Financial Reporting Standards (FRSs). Differences between accounting standards and the policies followed by NHS hospitals, local authorities and central government departments have been highlighted earlier.

The ASB has a Public Sector and Not-for-Profit Committee which assists the Board in its scrutiny of Statements of Recommended Practice (SORPs) e.g. the local authority code developed by recognized special interest groups such as CIPFA. In 1996 the Financial Reporting Advisory Board (FRAB) to the Treasury was established. FRAB's terms of reference are to 'advise HM Treasury on the application of financial reporting principles and standards in respect of central government bodies for which the Treasury has responsibility for issuing or approving directions. FRAB membership includes a nominee from the ASB (currently the chairman of the Public Sector and Not-for-Profit Committee).

The ASB itself acknowledges that it has only a limited role in the public sector. In its 'Forward to Accounting Standards' it states that 'The prescription of accounting requirements for the public sector in the United Kingdom is a matter for the Government. Where public sector bodies prepare annual reports and accounts on commercial lines, the Government's requirements may or may not refer specifically either to accounting standards or to the need for the financial statements concerned to give a true and fair view. However, it can be expected that the Government's requirements in such cases will normally accord with the principles underlying the Board's pronouncements, except where in the particular circumstances of the public sector bodies concerned the government considers these principles to be inappropriate or considers others to be more appropriate.'

Thus the ASB has very little direct role in the development of public sector accounting. In the UK, the term 'GAAP' does not have a precise meaning. In the USA. 'GAAP' stands for 'generally accepted accounting principles' and auditors state in their reports whether the financial statements 'present fairly', in conformity with general accounting principles. The common use of the term GAAP was introduced to the UK by the book *UK GAAP: Generally Accepted Accounting Practice in the United Kingdom* first published in 1989 by Arthur Young, and now published by Ernst & Young. GAAP, is explained by Ernst & Young: 'GAAP is a dynamic concept which requires constant review, adaptation and reaction to changing circumstances. We believe that use of the term 'principle' gives GAAP an unjustified and inappropriate degree of permanence....The UK's Accounting Standards Board (ASB) recognized this in its Statement of Aims, which discusses the Board's ongoing need to issue new accounting standards, or amend existing ones, 'in response to evolving business practices, new economic developments and deficiencies being identified in current practice.' We believe that GAAP goes far beyond mere rules and principles, and encompasses contemporary permissible accounting practice'.

They go on to conclude that GAAP: 'includes the accounting principles contained in accounting standards, the requirements of the Companies Act and the Stock Exchange, together with any other acceptable accounting treatments not incorporated in the official literature.'

This definition of UK GAAP is similar to that given in the Government White Paper (HM Government, 1994) i.e. 'the accounting and disclosure requirements of the Companies Act (1985) and accounting standards supplemented by accumulated professional judgement.' However the Resource Accounting Manual suggests that there is a: 'General consensus that it is founded upon ....the Companies Act....pronouncements by the Accounting Standards Board....[and] the body of accumulated knowledge built up over time and promulgated in, for example, textbooks, technical journals and research papers; for the purposes of the resource Accounting Manual, GAAP, is taken to mean primarily the first two, interpreted in the light of the last three.'

The illustrations from the NHS trust; the City Council and the Ministry of Defence clearly show that the accruals accounting approaches adopted in the public sector do not always comply with accounting standards or bear close resemblance to Companies Act requirements. 'True and fair' is now the rubric used in reporting for central government departments, the NHS and many other areas of the public sector, (although local government accounts carry a 'presents fairly' audit opinion) CIPFA, 1998. However, 'true and fair' seems to be measured quite differently from commercial companies.

On the other hand, it could also be argued that in some respects the accruals accounting adopted in the public sector is ahead of the private sector, the public sector is using techniques which the ASB wants the private sector to embrace. In 1995 the ASB published the Draft Statement of Principles (ASB, 1995), but the document was withdrawn the following year largely due to opposition from the accounting profession. A revised draft published March 1999 largely reaffirms the philosophy of the original document. The ASB believes that current values should replace cost-based measures in many cases and the balance sheet will state many items at current values. Perhaps the public sector has overtaken the private sector, it has moved from simplistic cash or partial accruals accounting to sophisticated accruals accounting based largely on current values whilst the accounting profession in the commercial sector has resisted following the lead of the ASB in this respect.

A similar diversity between public sector accounting and the commercial sector has been noted by Pallot (1998) despite New Zealand having formally adopted commercial

GAAP. Again it is claimed that in some respects, public sector accounting is more advanced than the private sector: 'Financial statements at all levels in the New Zealand government are described as being on 'modified historic cost basis' although effectively they are close to being on a current cost basis. For example, all fixed assets including infrastructure assets and heritage assets, are revalued at least every three years. The New Zealand government has therefore moved further towards current cost accounting than most organizations in the private sector in New Zealand.' Pallot and Ball, 1998 p239.

In 1992, Jones had argued that there was little interest in public sector accounting and it was therefore likely to be a matter for government officials.' In 1999, it seems that in the UK, leaving public sector accounting to government officials (or Treasury officials meeting under the guise of the Financial Reporting Advisory Board) has resulted in those government officials introducing accounting treatments which have been resisted by the commercial sector. In the public sector the treatment of less conventional assets such as fighting equipment, infrastructure assets and, of course, heritage items coupled with the absence of historical cost data has led to the introduction of various valuation approaches (but with emphasis on current value) while the commercial sector has attempted to retain (modified) historical cost.

Thus the diverse approaches adopted for accruals accounting in the public services have moved public service accounting from simplistic cash or partial accruals accounting to full accruals accounting often in a form more sophisticated or advanced than the private sector. However, the development of public sector accounting has not been driven by a clear vision of a conceptual framework for public sector accounting or strong adherence to a private sector model. Evidence from both the UK and internationally is clear that it is managerial reforms, a focus on efficiency and a belief in commercial approaches that led to major changes in public sector accounting. Accruals accounting has flourished in the 1990s but diversity in accounting practice within public services and between the public and private sectors remains.

References

- Accounting Standards Steering Committee (1975) *The Corporate Report* (ASSC, 1975).
- Accounting Standards Board (1995) *Draft Statement of Principles*, ASB, London.
- Butterworth, P., Gray, R.H. and Haslam, J (1989) Communication in UK Local Authority Annual Reports, *Financial Accountability and Management*, Summer 1989, 73-87.
- Chopping, D. and Skerrat, L. (1997) *Applying GAAP 1997/98*, ICAEW, London.
- Chartered Institute of Public Finance and Accountancy (1993) *The New Capital Accounting System; An Executive Brief*, CIPFA, London.
- Chartered Institute of Public Finance and Accountancy (1998) *The Application of a 'True and Fair View' within Public Services*, Consultation Paper, CIPFA, London.
- Clarke, K (1995) in HM Government, *Better Accounting for the Taxpayers' Money. The Government's Proposals*, Cm 2929 (HMSO, London).
- Department of Health and Social Security (1983) *Underused and Surplus Property in the NHS* (Ceri Davies Report), DHSS, London.
- Department of Health (1989) *Working for Patients*, (White Paper), DoH, London.
- Drebin, A.R., Chan, J.L., Ferguson, L.C. (1981) *Objectives of Accounting and Financial Reporting for Governmental Units: A research study, Vols I and II*, National Council on Governmental Accounting, Chicago.
- Ellwood, S. (1996) *Cost-based Pricing in the NHS Internal Market*, CIMA, London.
- Ernst and Young (1996) *Time to Decide*, Discussion Paper, E&Y, London.
- Financial Accounting Standards Board (1976) *Scope and Implications of the Conceptual Framework Project*, FASB, Stamford, Conn..
- Financial Accounting Standards Board (1978) *Statement of Financial Accounting Concpets No.1, Objectives of Financial Reporting by Business Enterprises*, FASB.
- Gillibrand, A. and Hilton, B. (1998) Resource Accounting and Budgeting: Principles, Concepts and Practice - The MoD Case, *Public Money and Management*, 18 (2), 21-33.
- Guthrie, J. (1998) Accrual Accounting in the Australian Public Sector, *Financial Accountability and Management*, 14 (1), 1-19.
- HM Government (1994) *Better Accounting for the Taxpayers' Money. The Government's Proposals*, Cm 2626 (HMSO, London).
- Hopwood, A. (1987) The Archaeology of Accounting Systems, *Accounting, Organisations and Society*, Vol.8 2/3, 287-305.
- International Accounting Standards Committee (1989) *Framework for the Presentation and Preparation of Financial Statements*, IASC.
- Jones, R.H. and Pendelbury, M. (1988) Government Accounting, Auditing and Financial Reporting in the United Kingdom, in J.L.Chan and R.H.Jones (eds.) *Governmental Accounting and Auditing: International Comparisons*, Routledge, London.
- Jones, R. and Pendlebury, M. (1984) *Public Sector Accounting*, Pitman, London.
- Jones, R. (1992) The Development of Conceptual Frameworks of Accounting for the Public Sector, *Financial Accountability and Management*, 8 (4), 249-263.
- Le Grand, J. and Bartlett, W. (1993) *Quasi-markets and Social Policy*, Macmillan.

- Likierman, A. (1992) Financial Reporting in the Public Sector, in Henley, D., Holtham, C., Likierman, A., Perrin, J. (eds.) *Public Sector Accounting and Financial Control*, Chapman and Hall, London.
- Likerman, A. (1998) Resource Accounting and Budgeting - Where are we Now? *Public Money and Management*, 18 (2), 17-20.
- Likierman, A. and Vass, P. (1984) *Structure and Form of Government Expenditure Reports: Proposals for Reform*, Chartered Association of Certified Accountants, London.
- Maeve, R. (1981) *A Conceptual Framework for Financial Accounting and Reporting*, ICAEW, London.
- March, D. (1991) Privatisation under Mrs Thatcher: A Review of the Literature, *Public Administration*, Vol 69 (Winter 1991).
- Mayston, D. (1992) Financial Reporting in the Public Sector and the Demand for Information, *Financial Accountability and Management*, 8 (4), 317-324.
- Mellet (1990) Capital Accounting and Charges in the National Health Service after 1991, *Financial Accountability and Management*, 6 (4), 263-283.
- Miller, P. and Napier, C. (1993) Genealogies of Calculation, *Accounting, Organisations and Society*, Vol.18 7/8, 631-647.
- Ministry of Defence (1998) *Resource Accounting Manual*, August 1998, MoD.
- National Audit Office (1995) *Resource Accounting and Budgeting in Government*, Report by the Comptroller and Auditor General, HC 123 Session 1994/95, HMSO.
- Perrin, J. (1998) From Cash to Accruals in 25 Years, *Public Money and Management*, 18 (2), 7-10.
- Public Accounts Committee (1997) *Resource Accounting and Proposals for a Resource -based System of Supply*, Committee of Public Accounts 9th Report, Session 1996/97, HC 167, The Stationery office, London.
- Robertson, G. (1999) The second front: targeting outputs, *Public Finance*, April 23-29 1999, 16-18.
- Rutherford, B (1992) Developing a Conceptual Framework for Central Government Financial Reporting, *Financial Accountability and Management* 8 (4), 265-280.
- Talbot, C. (1996) *Ministers and Agencies: Control, Performance and Accountability*, CIPFA Public Finance Foundation, London.
- Treasury Select Committee (1996) *Resource Accounting and Budgeting in Government: The Financial Reporting Advisory Board, Treasury Select Committee 5th Report, 1996/97*, HC 309, HMSO, London.

CHAPTER 14

ACCOUNTING FOR CAPITAL ASSETS IN THE PUBLIC SECTOR: DIFFERENCE BETWEEN ACCOUNTING STANDARDS BOARDS IN THE UNITED STATES

Josep L. Cortès

14.1. Introduction

Accounting for capital assets is one of the most controversial issues in the public sector and diverse accounting practices are adopted for reporting them around the world. It depends mainly on the basis of accounting and measurement focus adopted by governments and other public sector entities. In this paper I analyze this issue in the United States

In most countries there is only one governmental standards-setting body for all the levels, central, regional and local; whereas in the United States two public accounting standards boards coexist and there is no relation between them. The Governmental Accounting Standards Board (GASB) sets standards for state and local governments, and the Federal Accounting Standards Advisory Board (FASAB) for the Federal Government. There are differences between their standards, and the accounting for capital assets is one of them.

The accounting standards developed by the FASAB are tailored to the Federal Government's unique characteristics and special needs, whereas the GASB sets standards for all the state and local governmental entities. There are important differences between their accounting systems. The fact that the GASB accounting system is organized on a fund basis is the main one. However, in 1997 an exposure draft (ED) about basic financial statements was issued by the GASB so that governments would provide basic financial statements from both an entity-wide perspective and a fund perspective. In this paper I analyze how these two different accounting systems define, recognize and report capital assets.

The next section gives an overview of the accounting standard boards and their accounting systems, section 14.3. gives an overview of the issue of accounting for capital assets, and finally, section 14.4. and 14.5. analyze the GASB and FASAB standards respectively.

14.2. Accounting Standards Boards

In most developed countries there are public sector accounting standards-setting bodies, and a great variety of them exist: in some countries independent bodies, in others dependent from the governments. Some countries have only one body for all the levels of government, others one for each level, and in others the same body sets accounting standards for both public and private sector.

A. Bac (ed.), International Comparative Issues in Government Accounting, 233-250.
© 2001 *Kluwer Academic Publishers. Printed in the Netherlands.*

In some countries there are differences between the accounting of the different levels of government, which are due mainly to the introduction of innovations in the accounting system at different times. Sometimes different systems are chosen for each level, which is not the case of the United States.

In the United States three accounting standards boards coexist. The Financial Accounting Standards Board (FASB) sets standards for privately owned entities, the Governmental Accounting Standards Board (GASB) for state and local governments and its entities, and the Federal Accounting Standards Advisory Board (FASAB) for the Federal Government and its entities. There are differences between their standards and, even sometimes, the standards that an entity has to apply are different depending on whether it is a private, state-local or federal entity. They hardly ever work together. The accounting standards developed by them are tailored to its entities' characteristics and special needs.

14.2.1. GOVERNMENTAL ACCOUNTING STANDARDS BOARD

The GASB, which is independent of all other government and professional associations, was organized in 1984 by the Financial Accounting Foundation to establish standards of financial accounting and reporting for state and local governmental entities. It is the successor to the National Council on Governmental Accounting (NCGA), whose standards remain in effect until amended or superseded by GASB.

Fund Basis
Governmental accounting systems are organized on a *fund basis*. A fund is defined (GASB, 1997c: section 1100-102) 'as a fiscal and accounting entity with a self-balancing set of accounts recording cash and other financial resources, together with all related liabilities and residual equities or balances, and changes, therein, which are segregated for the purpose of carrying on specific activities or attaining certain objectives in accordance with special regulations, restrictions, or limitations'. But only the minimum number of funds consistent with legal and operating requirements should be established because unnecessary funds result in undue complexity and inefficient financial administration

There are three categories of funds and seven specific types: *governmental funds* (General, Special Revenue, Capital Projects, and Debt Service), *proprietary funds* (Internal Service and Enterprise), and *fiduciary funds* (Trust and Agency).

Two so-called *account groups* are also used. Fixed assets and long-term liabilities of governmental funds are accounted for through the General Fixed Assets Account Group (GFAAG) and the General Long-Term Debt Account Group (GLTDAG) respectively. They are accounting entities but not funds, because they are not fiscal entities.

Every governmental entity prepares and publishes a *Comprehensive Annual Financial Report* (CAFR). The CAFR contains the *General Purpose Financial Statements* (GPFS), and combining and individual statements for the fund types and account groups. Statistical tables are usually presented too.

The GPFS contains five basic combined statements. The *Combined Balance Sheet*, which includes columns for all the fund types and account groups; the *Combined Statement of Revenues, Expenditures, and Changes in Fund Balance*, which includes columns for governmental funds and expendable trust funds; the *Combined Statement of Revenues, Expenditures, and Changes in Fund Balance-Budget and Actual*; the *Combined Statement of Revenues, Expenses, and Changes in Retained Earnings*, which covers all proprietary and nonexpendable trust funds; and the *Combined Statement of Cash-Flows*.

Governmental fund revenues and expenditures are recognized on the modified accrual basis. Proprietary funds use the accrual basis; they employ essentially the same basis of accounting as business entities. The fiduciary funds use the modified accrual or accrual basis depending on the fund's accounting measurement objective (GASB, 1997c, sec. 1600).

The New Basic Financial Statements
In January 1997 the GASB issued an ED - Basic Financial Statements, and Management's Discussion and Analysis, for State and Local Governments[1]. It would provide basic financial statements also from an entity-wide perspective. This perspective would provide a more comprehensive view of a government's operations and financial position than is possible when information is reported only by fund or fund type. Therefore, governments would no longer report account groups. They would report general capital assets and unmatured general long-term liabilities only at the entity-wide perspective, as assets and liabilities of governmental activities.

Entity-wide financial statements would provide information about the primary government and its component units without displaying funds or fund types. There would be two financial statements, a *Statement of Net Assets* and a *Statement of Activities*. The financial statements would distinguish between the governmental and business-type activities of the primary government and between the total primary government and its discretely presented component units. The entity-wide perspective would not include fiduciary activities[2]. All information would be reported using the economic resources measurement focus and the accrual basis of accounting, as enterprise funds do today (GASB, 1997a, paragraphs 27-68).

Under a fund perspective governments would present separate financial statements for each fund category and would no longer present a combined balance sheet. However, the components of a CAFR would be an Introductory Section, a Financial Section and a Statistical Section. The Financial section would contain four components: *Management Discussion and Analysis* (MD&A); *Basic Financial Statements*, that should include the financial statements-entity-wide perspective, the financial statements-fund perspective, and notes to the financial statements; and *Other Required Supplementary Information* (GASB, 1997a, par. 7-9).

---

[1] The final statement is expected to be issued on June 30, 1999. It would be effective for years beginning after June 15, 2001 (with an extension for capitalization of existing infrastructure and for certain small governments).

[2] The ED proposes a revised definition of fiduciary activities.

14.2.2. FEDERAL ACCOUNTING STANDARDS ADVISORY BOARD

The FASAB was established in 1990 by the Secretary of the Treasury, the Director of the Office of Management and Budget (OMB) and the Comptroller General of the United States. It was created to consider and recommend accounting standards and principles for the Federal Government to improve the usefulness of federal financial reports. It is also possible to speak of a weak form of external standard-setting in the case of the FASAB (Lüder, 1992:113), where responsibility for setting standards is located within the government but there is a permanent, independent advisory body involved.

The Statement of Federal Financial Accounting Concepts (SFFAC) no. 1 points out that the role of the FASAB is different from the one of the FASB and the GASB (FASAB, 1993, par. 23-26). The FASB and the GASB set standards for general purpose financial reporting mainly to external users of financial reports. The FASAB, on the other hand, considers the information which both internal (Congress and the executive branch) and external users, need.

For the first time in 1997, the Federal Government prepared the *Consolidated Financial Statements of the United States Government* in accordance with federal accounting standards that were subjected to an independent audit. These statements consist of *Management's Discussion and Analysis* (MD&A), a *Balance Sheet*, a *Statement of Net Cost*, a *Statement of Changes in Net Position*, *Notes to the Financial Statements*, and *Supplementary Information*, which includes a Stewardship section. Four more statements are required for federal entities: the Statement of Budgetary Resources, the Statement of Custodial Activities, the Statement of Program Performance Measures, and the Statement of Financing. Fund accounting is also required for federal agencies to demonstrate compliance with requirements of legislation.

The basis of accounting used is defined as an accrual basis. However, considering that some federal government assets are not reported in the balance sheet the basis of accounting could be properly defined as a modified accrual basis.

14.3. Capital Assets in Public Sector Accounting

Capital assets in the public sector are also called physical non-current assets, public domain fixed assets, infrastructure and heritage assets, and community assets. Capital assets include assets such as roads, bridges, railways, streets, sidewalks, reticulation systems, drainage systems, dams, docks, airports, government buildings, equipment, defense assets, parks, gardens, collections of art works, historical buildings, and monuments.

Differing opinions exist on how infrastructure assets should be described. However, the differences relate to matters of detail rather than core meaning. Most definitions suggest (Rowles, 1992: 40) that infrastructure assets are public facilities, concerned with essential services, 'immovable', and necessary to sustain living standards. However, such qualities do not appear to be uniquely confined to such assets. On the other hand, the term heritage asset usually refers to physical assets that a community intends preserving because of cultural, historic or environmental associations.

Diverse accounting practices are adopted in order to report capital assets. In the private sector, capital assets are treated in the same manner as other physical assets. By contrast, in the public sector capital assets are frequently regarded as different from other physical assets. It is generally accepted that capital assets are assets, although, some may argue that these assets differ in nature from other assets. The distinction between capital assets in contrast with other assets may sometimes be arbitrary and depends on the use of the asset rather than its nature. Recognition and reporting of capital assets depends mainly on the basis of accounting and measurement focus adopted by governments and other public sector entities, so that as long as one moves along the spectrum, from cash to full accrual basis of accounting, more assets are reported in the financial statements. Under a full accrual basis all significant assets should be recognized. However, particularly when the full accrual basis is first adopted, many significant assets may be unrecognized for pragmatic reasons or because recognition criteria cannot be met.

Diverse measurement bases are also adopted, from which, historical cost is commonly used. Recognition of depreciation and maintenance of capital assets are another issue of debate between accounting standards setters.

Next I enumerate the accounting standards for capital assets in the United States.

14.3.1. GASB STANDARDS FOR CAPITAL ASSETS

GASB standards for capital assets are basically[3] National Council on Governmental Accounting Statement (NCGAS) no. 1 and GASB Statement no. 8. These standards are analyzed in detail in section 14.4.

NCGAS no. 1, which remains in effect, - Governmental Accounting and Financial Reporting Principles - contains the principles and basis of accounting and financial reporting for state and local governments. It indicates that governmental accounting systems should be organized and operated on a fund basis.

GASB Statement no. 8 - Applicability of FASB Statement no. 93, Recognition of Depreciation by Not-for-Profit Organizations, to Certain State and Local Governmental Entities - indicates that colleges and universities and other governmental entities whose private-sector counterparts are considered by the FASB to be not-for-profit organizations, and that follow the American Institute of Certified Public Accountants (AICPA) Guide should not change their accounting and reporting for depreciation of capital assets as a result of FASB Statement no. 93. However, entities that adopted FASB Statement no. 93 for financial statements before periods beginning after December 15, 1994 may continue to apply that Statement.

In January 1997 an ED about basic financial statements was issued by the GASB. Governments would provide basic financial statements from both an entity-wide

---

[3] GASB Statement no. 18 establishes standards for municipal solid waste landfill closure and postclosure care costs. SFFAS no. 6 (par. 85-111) contains standards for cleanup costs. These standards are very similar one to each other; and the estimated total cost is assigned to periods based basically on the associated asset use rather than on the passage of time. However, the study of this issue is not our matter.

perspective and a fund perspective. Under an entity-wide perspective all the information would be reported using the accrual basis of accounting. Under a fund perspective financial statements would be presented using the modified accrual or the accrual basis of accounting, depending on the fund. This ED would supersede NCGAS no. 1 and GASB Statement no. 8 among other standards.

In April 1997 the GASB issued an ED about basic financial statements for public colleges and universities[4]. These governmental entities would provide basic financial statements from both an entity-wide perspective and a fund perspective. Under both of these perspectives all the information would be reported using the accrual basis of accounting. It would supersede GASB Statement no. 8. The accounting for capital assets would be basically the same as the accounting set forth in the ED of January 1997.

These two ED and the GASB standards allow that certain public entities, as colleges and universities, and proprietary funds may apply statements and interpretations of the FASB, Accounting Principles Board (APB) opinions, and Accounting Research Bulletins (ARBs) of the Committee on Accounting Procedure issued on or before November 30, 1989, unless those pronouncements conflict with or contradict GASB pronouncements (GASB, 1997a, par. 32 and 90; GASB, 1997b, par. 7; GASB 1997c, sec. P80.104). Business-type activities, except colleges and universities, and proprietary funds may also apply FASB pronouncements developed for business enterprises issued after November 30, 1989, unless those pronouncements conflict with or contradict GASB pronouncements (GASB, 1997a, par. 32 and 91; GASB 1997c, sec. P80.105).

14.3.2.   FASAB STANDARDS FOR CAPITAL ASSETS

In its Statements of Federal Financial Accounting Standards (SFFAS) no. 6, 8 and 11, and in two different Exposure Drafts (ED), the FASAB establishes accounting and financial reporting standards for Property, Plant, and Equipment (PP&E). Section 14.5. of this paper analyzes these standards.

The SFFAS no. 6 - Accounting for Property, Plant, and Equipment - contains accounting standards for Federally owned Property, Plant, and Equipment (PP&E); Deferred Maintenance on PP&E; and Cleanup Costs. It is effective for periods beginning after September 30, 1997.

The SFFAS no. 8 - Supplementary Stewardship Reporting - establishes standards for reporting on the Federal Government's stewardship over certain resources entrusted to it, and certain responsibilities assumed by it. These resources and responsibilities do not meet the criteria for assets and liabilities that are required to be reported in the financial statements but are important to understanding the operations and financial condition of the Federal Government. It is effective for periods beginning after September 30, 1997.
The SFFAS no. 11 - Amendments to Accounting for Property, Plant and Equipment - amends SFFAS no. 6 and 8. The amendments have eliminated the category of Federal

---

[4]   The accounting standards for public colleges and universities are basically the same as the government. They have some particularities. However, the study of these particularities is not our matter either.

Mission PP&E and created a new category for National Defense. It is effective for periods beginning after September 30, 1998.

There are two EDs that affect SFFAS no. 6 and 8. The ED issued in June 1997 - Government-wide Supplementary Stewardship Reporting Standards - would amend SFFAS no. 8. The ED issued in December 1998 - Amendments to Deferred Maintenance Reporting - would amend SFFAS no. 6 and 8, it would modify the placement of this information.

14.4. Capital Assets in the GASB Standards

I am going to analyze the accounting for capital assets for state and local governments. Firstly I analyze the fund perspective and, secondly, the entity-wide perspective that will be effective in the next years.

14.4.1. FUND PERSPECTIVE

Fixed assets related to specific proprietary funds or trust funds should be accounted for through those funds in the same manner as are businesses' fixed assets. All other fixed assets, called *general fixed assets*, of a governmental unit should be accounted for through the GFAAG (GASB, 1997c, sec 1100.105-107, 1400). Anyway, fixed assets should be accounted for at cost or, if the cost is not practicably determinable, at estimated cost. Donated fixed assets should be recorded at their estimated fair value at the time received.

The outlay to acquire general fixed assets should be reported as expenditure in the governmental funds when the assets are acquired. Proceeds from sales should be reported as other financing resource or as a special item. General fixed assets are not assets of any fund but of the governmental unit as an instrument. The primary purposes for governmental fund accounting are to reflect its revenues and expenditures and its assets, the related liabilities, and the net financial resources available for subsequent appropriation and expenditure. The GASB considers that these objectives can most readily be achieved by excluding general fixed assets from the governmental fund accounts and recording them in a separate GFAAG. The GFAAG is a management control and accountability listing of a government's general fixed assets balanced by accounts showing the sources by which such assets were financed.

Reporting public domain or infrastructure fixed assets is optional. Recording information for capital assets in the GFAAG has never become common practice. When the ED is issued governments will no longer report account groups. They would report general capital assets only at the entity-wide perspective, as assets of governmental activities.

Depreciation
Depreciation of proprietary and trust fund fixed assets must be recorded to determine total expenses, net income and changes in fund equity.

Depreciation of general fixed assets should not be recorded in the accounts of governmental funds because it is neither a source nor a use of governmental fund financial resources. However, depreciation may be recorded in cost accounting systems or calculated for cost finding analyses. Accumulated depreciation may be recorded in GFAAG, but it is seldom done (GASB, 1997c, sec. 1400.116-118).

14.4.2. ENTITY-WIDE PERSPECTIVE

Under an entity-wide perspective governments would report all capital assets, except capital assets of fiduciary funds that should be reported only at the fund perspective (GASB, 1997a, par. 33-37). Capital assets would be reported as assets when acquired and depreciated over their useful lives, and should be reported in the statement of net assets at historical cost less accumulated depreciation. Donated capital assets should be reported at their estimated fair value at the time received less accumulated depreciation. The capitalized cost should include the acquisition price and all related costs necessary to prepare the capital asset for use.

However, governments would not be required to capitalize works of art, historical treasures, and similar assets, regardless of whether they were contributed or purchased, if the items are added to collections that:
a. are held for public exhibition, education, or research in furtherance of public service rather than financial gain;
b. are protected, kept unencumbered, cared for, and preserved, and
c. are subject to a policy that requires the proceeds from sales of collection items to be used to acquire other items for collections.

Depreciation
Under an entity-wide perspective accumulated depreciation should be reported in the statement of net assets. Depreciation expense should be reported in the statement of activities and is conventionally measured by allocating the net cost of the assets (historical cost less estimated salvage value) over their estimated useful lives in a systematic and rational manner. Depreciation expense may be calculated for composite groups of similar capital assets. However, governments may use any established depreciation method, including group life methods.

Alternative Methods
The GASB has tentatively agreed to consider alternative methods of reporting for infrastructure assets. Those would use *replacement cost, actual cost,* or some form of *maintenance/preservation* approach. Each approach would require a periodic condition assessment for infrastructure assets. After considering various approaches, the GASB has decided to add a project to its agenda that will consider a 'preservation approach' to accounting for infrastructure assets.

Some of the proposed preservation approaches to infrastructure asset reporting would require not only periodic condition assessments but also that a minimum acceptable condition level be established for infrastructure assets. The minimum condition level would be the level at which an asset would have to be maintained to prevent accelerated or severe deterioration. One of these approaches would require reporting of depreciation if infrastructure assets fell below that condition level. The other approach would require the reporting of the amount required to return those assets to an acceptable condition level. A third approach would require only disclosures of condition assessment and a comparison of required versus actual costs of maintenance and preservation (these disclosures would also be required for both of the other approaches).

On the other hand, the GASB recognizes that a network of infrastructure assets that is maintained and preserved can have service potential that continues for an extended period of time. Therefore, it has tentatively concluded infrastructure assets, which are a part of a network, and will not have to be depreciated if the network is managed with an asset management system and the network is demonstrably preserved. If preserved, a network of infrastructure assets can have service potential that continues for such a long period that an annual depreciation charge is not necessary. This method has been termed 'modified approach'. Governments that choose this modified approach would be required to disclose, as required supplementary information, the condition of the network of infrastructure assets, based on condition assessments performed at least every three years, for the last three assessments. Governments would also be required to disclose the estimated dollar amount needed to maintain/preserve the network of infrastructure assets at a level established by the government compared to the actual expenses for at least five reporting periods. Governments would need to disclose the condition level at which it intends to maintain its network of infrastructure assets. Like traditional depreciation accounting, operating maintenance would be expensed and expenditures that improve the quality or add to infrastructure assets capitalized. However, unlike traditional depreciation accounting, expenditures made to extend the life of infrastructure assets would be expensed under this approach.

Reporting Infrastructure Assets Retro-actively
There would be an extended implementation period of three years to report infrastructure assets retroactively (that is, capitalizing infrastructure assets acquired prior to the implementation date). The GASB would require only prospective reporting during the first three years. Infrastructure assets of proprietary funds are already required to be reported and should continue to be reported in the financial statements as the effective date of the Statement. The methods used to initially estimate the historical cost of infrastructure should be disclosed in the summary of significant accounting policies (GASB, 1997a, par. 140-142, 408-424).

If infrastructure records are inadequate or if determining actual historical cost is not practical for other reasons, governments should meet these minimum requirements:
a. inventory only those infrastructure assets that were acquired or significantly reconstructed, or that received material improvements, within the past *twenty-five years*, and
b. limit the inventory to *major* infrastructure assets and asset systems.

Roads, bridges, tunnels, storm sewers, dams, and sea walls and levees generally would be considered *major* infrastructure assets. However, other categories or types may qualify as *major* or may be included within these categories. If the cost of the asset acquired prior to the implementation date is expected to be at least 5 percent (10 percent for groups of infrastructure assets) of the total cost of all general capital assets reported in the fiscal year before the effective date of the Statement and the asset (or asset category) generally is considered to be a critical element of the overall infrastructure asset system, the asset (or asset category) may be considered as *major*.

An asset's age can be calculated from the date of the most recent major renovation, restoration, or improvement and the cost of that work can be used as its historical cost. Also a government may estimate age based on the condition of the asset or data for comparable assets. Therefore, for estimated useful lives, governments may use

a. general guidelines obtained from professional or industry organizations;
b. data for comparable assets of other governments, or
c. internal information A government also should consider an asset's present condition and how long it is expected to meet service demands.

In order to estimate the historical cost of infrastructure assets governments may use either the cost of similar assets at the time of acquisition, or the current cost of similar assets discounted for inflation since the time of acquisition. In addition to the type of asset the factors that should be considered include the asset's dimensions, the materials used, the asset's location, and its environment.

A government may choose to report infrastructure assets

a. in total;
b. in total for groups of similar assets (for example, streets and highways, as a group);
c. by individual group or system (for example, by type of street), or
d. by component of the asset category or asset system (for example, by separating roads and bridges into right-of-way land, roadways, roadway surfaces, and bridges).

But the fact of having inventoried each group, system, or component, the government may estimate its total cost and calculate depreciation of that total based on the weighted-average age and estimated useful life of the assets included. Additions that are completed in any fiscal year after the effective date of the Statement may be treated as a separate group for calculating depreciation.

4.3. NOTES TO THE FINANCIAL STATEMENTS

Although the basic financial statements would be presented for two perspectives, only one set of notes should be presented.

A Statement of Changes in General Fixed Assets is required in the current CAFR unless sufficiently disclosed in the notes to the financial statements. Under an entity-wide perspective governments should provide detail in the notes to the financial statements about the balances of capital assets reported in the statement of net assets, and the Statement of Changes in General Fixed Assets would not be required. The information disclosed should be divided into major classes of capital assets as well as between those associated with governmental activities and those associated with business-type activities (GASB, 1997c, par. 112-113).

This information should include:

a. current-and prior-year balances with accumulated depreciation presented separately from historical cost;
b. capital acquisitions;
c. sales or other dispositions;
d. current-period depreciation expense.

If collection items are not capitalized governments should disclose
a. expenditures for the purchase;
b. proceeds from sales;
c. proceeds from insurance recoveries of collection items lost or destroyed.

	Beginning Balance	Additions	Retirements	Ending Balance
Governmental activities				
Land	$ 29,484	2,020	(4,358)	27,146
Buildings and improvements	31,461	9,734		41,195
Equipment	32,110	1,544	-1,514	32,140
Infrastructure	103,975	3,820		107,795
Totals at historical cost	197,030	17,118	-5,872	208,276
Less accumulated depreciation				
Buildings and improvements	-10,358	-691		-11,049
Equipment	-9,247	-2,676	1,040	-10,883
Infrastructure	-15,301	-1,020		-16,321
Total accumulated depreciation	-34,906	-4,387	1,040	-38,253
Gov. activities capital assets, net	$ 162,124	12,731	(4,832)	170,023
Business-type activities capital assets, net*	$ 147,595	3,794		151,389
Depreciation expense was charged to governmental activities as follows				
General government	$ 275			
Public safety	330			
Public works	1.315			
Health and sanitation	625			
Cemetery	29			
Culture and recreation	65			
Community development	40			
City's internal service funds	1,708			
Total depreciation expense	$ 4,387* It is more detailed in the original			

Table 14.1.: Illustrative Disclosure of Information about Capital Assets (in thousands)
Source: GASB, 1997: Appendix E-Illustrations

14.5. Capital Assets in the FASAB Standards

I am going to analyze the accounting for capital assets for the Federal Government. Although some entities have adopted them primarily, we have to bear in mind that most standards are effective for periods beginning after September 30, 1997[5].

Capital assets are called Property, Plant, and Equipment (PP&E) which are divided into two broad categories. The first is General PP&E, where the majority of infrastructures fall into. The second category is the Stewardship PP&E. Only the General PP&E is reported in the balance sheet, and information about the other capital assets is provided in the Supplementary Stewardship Reporting.

---

[5] Before September 30, 1997 National Defense PP&E information was reported in the balance sheet and the stewardship section did not include information about heritage assets and stewardship investments.

14.5.1. GENERAL PP&E

The General PP&E category (FASAB, 1995, par. 23-45) consists of items that:
a. could be used for alternative purposes (e.g., by other Federal programs, state or local governments, or non-governmental entities) but are used by the Federal entity to produce goods or services[6], or to support the mission of the entity, or
b. are used in business-type activities;
c. are used by entities in activities whose costs can be compared to other entities (e.g., Federal hospitals compared with other hospitals).
It includes land acquired for or in connection with other General PP&E. For entities operating as business-type activities, all PP&E should be categorized as General PP&E whether or not it meets the definition of any other PP&E categories.

All General PP&E should be recorded at cost. Cost should include all costs incurred to bring the PP&E to a form and location suitable for its intended use. The cost of General PP&E acquired through donation, devise, or judicial process excluding forfeiture should be estimated fair value at the time acquired by the government. The cost of General PP&E transferred from other Federal entities should be the book value of the asset recorded on the transferring entity's books; if it is not estimable the cost should be the fair value of the asset.

Depreciation
Depreciation expense is calculated through the systematic and rational allocation of the cost of General PP&E, less its estimated salvage/residual value, over the estimated useful life of the General PP&E. Depreciation expense should be recognized on all General PP&E, except land and land rights of unlimited duration. Costs which either extend the useful life of existing General PP&E, or enlarge or improve its capacity should be capitalized and depreciated over the remaining useful life of the associated General PP&E.

Depreciation expenses are generally recognized using the straightline method over the assets estimated live, although various methods can be used to compute periodic depreciation expense so long as the method is systematic, rational, and best reflects the use of the PP&E.

Reporting Assets Retrospectively
For existing General PP&E, if historical cost information necessary to comply with the recognition and measurement provisions has not been maintained, estimates are required. Estimates should be based on either the cost of similar assets at the time of acquisition, or the current cost of similar assets discounted for inflation since the time of acquisition

Revaluation of Removed General PP&E
General PP&E should be removed from General PP&E accounts along with associated accumulated depreciation, if prior to disposal, retirement or removal from service, it no longer provides service in the operations of the entity. This could be either because it has suffered damage, becomes obsolete in advance of expectations, or is identified as

---

6   It includes roads, trails and bridges.

excess. It should be recorded in an appropriate asset account at its expected net realizable value. Any difference in the book value of the PP&E and its expected net realizable value should be recognized as a gain or a loss in the period of adjustment. The expected net realizable value should be adjusted at the end of each accounting period and any further adjustments in value recognized as a gain or a loss in determining the net cost of operations. However, no additional depreciation should be taken once such assets are removed from General PP&E in anticipation of disposal, retirement, or removal from service (FASAB, 1995, par. 39).

Disclosure Notes
The following are minimum General PP&E disclosure requirements:
- the cost, associated accumulated depreciation, and book value by major class;
- the estimated useful lives for each major class;
- the method(s) of depreciation for each major class;
- capitalization threshold(s) including any changes in threshold(s) during the period, and
- restrictions on the use or convertibility of General PP&E.

14.5.2. STEWARDSHIP PP&E

This category contains three groups, National Defense PP&E, Heritage Assets, and Stewardship Land. These assets are not reported in the balance sheet. The FASAB considers that the consumption of military assets' service potential through depreciation cannot be reliably measured and that the valuation of Heritage Assets is not objective or meaningful. Military assets have an unpredictable useful life, and Heritage Assets and Stewardship Land have virtually indefinite lives. However, the Federal Government should be able to demonstrate accountability for Stewardship PP&E by reporting on its existence and on its condition by a reference to deferred maintenance reported in the financial statements.

Information about these assets is provided in the Supplementary Stewardship Reporting (SSR), which supplements the basic financial statements. Although nowadays SSR is not audited, the FASAB expects that the OMB and the General Accounting Office (GAO) will determine appropriate audit procedures for this information.

- *National Defense PP&E* (FASAB, 1995, par. 46-56; 1996, par. 52-70) are (1) the PP&E components of weapons systems and support PP&E owned by the Department of Defense or its component entities for use in the performance of military missions and (2) vessels held in a preservation status by the Maritime Administration's National Defense Reserve Fleet.

Before SFFAS no. 11 National Defense PP&E and Space Exploration Equipment were in the same group called Federal Mission PP&E. Now Space Exploration Equipment should be treated as General PP&E.

- *Heritage Assets* (FASAB, 1995, par. 57-65; 1996, par. 43-51) include PP&E that have historical or natural significance; cultural, educational, or artistic importance; or significant architectural characteristics. Heritage Assets are generally expected to be preserved indefinitely.

- *Multi-use Heritage Assets* are heritage assets used to serve two purposes- a heritage function and government operation. Such assets contribute to the general operations of programs but the cost of these assets can not be easily assigned to heritage and operating purposes.

The cost of renovating, improving, or reconstructing operating components of heritage assets used in government operations should be included in General PP&E. Following initial construction, any renovation, improvement or reconstruction costs to facilitate government operations would be capitalized and depreciated over its expected useful life. The cost should not be depreciated over an unrealistically long life. Costs of renovating or reconstructing the heritage asset that can not be directly associated with operations should be considered heritage asset costs.

- *Stewardship Land* (FASAB, 1995, par. 66-76; 1996, par. 71-82) is land owned by the Federal Government not used in, or held for use in, general government services. The majority of Stewardship Land is 'public domain' land, that is, large areas of territory acquired by the US between 1781 and 1867, where Land is defined as the solid part of the surface of the earth. However, excluded from the definition of Land are materials beneath the surface, the space above the surface, and the outer-continental shelf resources. The materials excluded from the definition of Land will be addressed in a separate accounting and reporting standard related to them.

Reporting Stewardship Assets
Expenditures to acquire, construct, reconstruct, or improve Heritage Assets, National Defense PP&E and Stewardship Land should be reported as a cost in the period incurred. The cost should include all costs incurred to bring the PP&E to its current condition and location

The cost of heritage assets and land transferred from other Federal entities should be the book value of the asset recorded on the transferring entity's books. If the receiving entity does not know the book value, the fair value should be disclosed in notes to the statement of net cost. If fair value is not estimable, information related to the type and quantity of assets transferred should be disclosed.

However, no amounts for Stewardship Assets acquired through donation or devise should be recognized as a cost on the statement of net cost. Its fair value, if known and material, should be disclosed in notes to the statement of net cost.

5.2.1.1. REPORTING IN THE SUPPLEMENTARY STEWARDSHIP REPORT

Information about these assets is reported mainly in the SSR. Reporting at the entity level should be more specific than at the governmentwide level. There is an ED that proposes minimum reporting requirements for government-wide level.

- *National Defense* PP&E should be valued using either the total cost or the latest acquisition cost valuation method.

- *Heritage Assets* should be quantified in terms of physical units (for example, number of items in collections or the number of national parks).

- *Stewardship Land* should be quantified in terms of physical units (for example, acres) rather than in monetary terms.

The following information is to be reported:
- A description of each major category of asset.
- The number of physical units added and withdrawn during the year and the end-of-year number of physical units for each type.
- Condition, for example:
  - averages of standardized condition rating codes;
  - percentage of assets above, at, or below acceptable condition;
  - narrative information.
- A reference to the note to the financial statements if deferred maintenance is reported for the assets.

Predominant land use	US Forest Service	National Park Service	US Fish and Wildlife Service	B. of Land Management	Total	Percent
B.of Land Management land				259.0	259.0	41%
National wildlife refuge			67.4		67.4	11%
National parks		49.4			49.4	8%
National forest	153.3				153.3	25%
National grassland	3.8				3.8	1%
Wilderness area	34.7	28.0	20.7	5.0	88.4	14%
Total acres	191.8	77.4	88.1	264.0	621.3	100%

Table 14.2.: US Government Stewardship Land as of September 30,1997 (Millions of Acres)

Source: 1997 Consolidated Financial Statements of the US Government

14.5.3. DEFERRED MAINTENANCE

Federal Government and its entities should provide information about Deferred Maintenance of all their PP&E (FASAB, 1995, par. 77-84), which is maintenance that was not performed when necessary or scheduled to be, and which, therefore, is put off or delayed for a future period.

The SFFAS no. 6 defines maintenance as the act of keeping fixed assets in acceptable condition. It includes preventive maintenance, normal repairs, replacement of parts and structural components, and other activities needed to preserve the asset so that it continues to provide acceptable services and achieves its expected life. Maintenance excludes activities aimed at expanding the capacity of an asset or otherwise upgrading it to serve needs different from, or significantly greater than, those originally intended.

A line item for 'deferred maintenance amounts' should be presented on the statement of net cost with a note reference in lieu of a dollar amount. No amounts should be recognized for deferred maintenance.

Information about the classes of assets for which maintenance has been deferred and the method of measuring Deferred Maintenance used is to be disclosed. Amounts disclosed for Deferred Maintenance may be measured using condition assessment surveys or life-cycle cost forecasts, and management is permitted to split Deferred Maintenance into critical and non-critical categories. In that case the management should disclose the definition of these categories.

Table 14.3. shows an example of a Deffered Maintanance chart

Category	Method	Condition	Cost to return to acceptable condition	Critical	Non-critical
Buildings	C.A.S.	4	$ 100,000-125,000	$75,000	$25,000-50,000
Communication Eqp.	C.A.S.	4.5	$ 10,000-15,000	$2,000	$8,000-13,000
Laboratory Eqp.	C.A.S.	5	$500,000-550,000	$300,000	$200,000-250,000
Note: Condition: excellent=1; good=2; fair=3, poor=4; very poor=5; acceptable condition is fair					

Table 14.3.:   Deferred Maintenance
Source: FASAB, 1995: par. 233

The ED issued in December 1998 - Amendments to Deferred Maintenance Reporting-would amend SFFAS no. 6 and 8. It would modify the placement of Deferred Maintenance information. Now Deferred Maintenance is disclosed in the Notes to the Financial Statements, and the FASAB proposes placing Deferred Maintenance information in the SSR to emphasize the importance of the information.

14.6. Summary and Conclusions

In this paper I aimed to show an example of the meaning of having several public sector accounting standards-setting bodies within the same country. It has also been revised the definition, recognition and reporting of capital assets contained in GASB and FASAB standards, and the fact that there are differences between their accounting systems, due to the fact that the GASB sets standards for multiple type of entities and the FASAB only for one type, the federal governmental entities.

The main difference is that the GASB accounting system provides financial statements from a fund perspective (next from an entity-wide perspective too) and the FASAB from an entity-wide perspective. However, at the end, their standards for capital assets are not so different.
-   The FASAB have adopted and the GASB will adopt a basis of accounting very close to the full accrual basis, as a consequence, almost all their assets are reported.
-   In both standards capital assets are measured at historical cost and depreciation is recorded.
-   Stewardship Land, National Defense PP&E and Heritage Assets are not reported in the balance sheets of the federal governmental entities. However, as a consequence of the fact that state and local entities have not national defense, and land acquired within the past twenty-five years and some heritage assets would not be recorded, most of these assets are not reported in their balance sheets either.

Nevertheless I think the similarities are due mainly to the accounting tradition in the US rather than any cooperation.

Table 14.4 shows the main characteristics of the accounting for public capital assets in the United States.

Accounting systems	GASB Fund	GASB Entity	FASAB
Accounting basis	modified accrual/ accrual	accrual	modified accrual (very close to the accrual)
Governmental capital assets in the balance sheet	no	yes, except some heritage assets	yes, except stewardship assets
Depreciation as expense	no	yes	yes
Measurement		historical cost	historical cost
Reporting retroactively		major infrastructures <20 years actual/estimated historical cost	actual/estimated historical cost
Donated assets		fair value	fair value
Transfers from other governmental entity		book/fair value	book/fair value
Deferred Maintenance	no	no (in study)	yes, but not as expense

Table 14.4.: Public Capital Assets in the United States

References

- Federal Accounting Standards Board (1993) *SFFAC no. 1: Objectives of Federal Financial Reporting*, FASAB, Washington.
- Federal Accounting Standards Board (1995) *SFFAS no. 6: Accounting for Property, Plant & Equipment (PP&E)*, FASAB, Washington.
- Federal Accounting Standards Board (1996) *SFFAS no. 8: Supplementary Stewardship Reporting*, FASAB, Washington.
- Federal Accounting Standards Board (1997) *Exposure Draft: Governmentwide Supplementary Stewardship Reporting*, FASAB, Washington.
- Federal Accounting Standards Board (1998) *SFFAS no. 11: Amendments to accounting for PP&E*, FASAB, Washington.
- Federal Accounting Standards Board (1998) *Exposure Draft: Amendments to Deferred Maintenance Reporting*, FASAB, Washington.
- General Accounting Office (1998) *1997 Consolidated Financial Statements of the United States Government*, GAO, Washington.
- Governmental Accounting Standards Board (1997a) *Exposure Draft: Basic Financial Statements-and Management's Discussion and Analysis- for State and Local Governments*, GASB, Norwalk.
- Governmental Accounting Standards Board (1997b) *Exposure Draft: Basic Financial Statements-and Management's Discussion and Analysis- for Public Colleges and Universities*, GASB, Norwalk.
- Governmental Accounting Standards Board (1997c) *Codification of Governmental Accounting and Financial Reporting Standards as of June 30, 1997*, GASB, Norwalk.
- Lüder, K. (1992) A Contingency Model of Governmental Accounting Innovations in the Political-Administrative Environment, In: James L. Chan and James M. Patton (eds.), *Research in Governmental and Nonprofit Accounting, Vol. 7*, JAI Press Inc., Greenwich, 99-127.
- Rowles, T. (1992) *Financial Reporting of Infrastructure and Heritage Assets by Public Sector Entities*, Australian Accounting Research Foundation Discussion Paper no. 17, AARF, Caulfield.

TRANSFORMING GOVERNMENT ACCOUNTING IN JAPAN: REVOLUTION OR FASHION?

Kiyoshi Yamamoto

15.1. Introduction

For many years, accounting generally received little attention in Japanese public sector reforms. While budgeting has been the center of public finance, attention was rarely focused upon accounting. However, in recent public sector reforms accounting has become recognized as an effective tool. Transforming from cash accounting to accrual or corporate accounting is expected to improve the economy, efficiency and effectiveness of performance.

The latest law enacted separates planning and policy drafting functions from executing functions. Independent Administrative Corporations (IACs), with independent legal status outside the central government, have been established to implement the executing functions. In addition, some local governments have begun to adopt accrual accounting. Although these innovations might give an impression that the Japanese central and local governments are transforming to the 'new public management' (NPM) (Hood, 1991; Olson, Guthrie, and Humphrey, 1998), accrual accounting has been less linked to financial management in Japan than in the Anglo-Saxon countries.

This article investigates why reforms in Japanese public sector accounting have progressed in a different pattern from in other developed countries, and whether such reforms are consistent between Japanese central and local governments. The second section first describes the financial management control systems in Japan, comparing central and local governments. The third section focuses on accounting and budgeting in financial system reforms. The similarities and differences towards reforming financial management systems are examined. In the fourth section, financial system reform in the public sector is compared to other countries. In this connection, it is noted that the central government adopts an institutional approach, while the local governments take a flexible approach in their reform processes. Finally, the fifth section is dedicated to some conclusions and prospects.

15.2. Financial Management Control Systems in the Public Sector

15.2.1. BUDGET SYSTEM

The central government budget consists of the General Account budget and 38 Special Accounts budgets. The General Account is the basic account to promote the major programs of the government, while the Special Accounts are for specific projects, administering or managing specific funds.

A. Bac (ed.), International Comparative Issues in Government Accounting, 251-263.

The basic guidelines for budget formation are determined at a Cabinet meeting. Ministries and Agencies submit their budgetary requests to the Ministry of Finance (MOF) in accordance with the guidelines. After receiving the requests, MOF examines them and conducts hearings. MOF then prepares the budget draft and submits it to the Cabinet. Following approval by the Cabinet, the budget draft becomes the budget proposal which is submitted to the Diet for its deliberation and approval.

Upon approval by the Diet, the Cabinet distributes it to the heads of all Ministries and Agencies. They implement the budget under MOF control. After the settlement of accounts by the MOF, the Board of Audit (BOA) examines and confirms the accounts (see figure 15.1.).

Similarly, the local government budget consists of a General Account budget and several Special Accounts budgets. Under the present system in the local government, the assembly and the chief executive share control, while the central government operates under the parliamentary system. Accordingly, the local chief executive forms the budget draft and submits it to the assembly for its approval. The chief executive then makes a plan to execute and must do so in accordance with the plan. Following the budget execution, the chief accounting officer settles the accounts and submits them to the chief executive. Finally, the inspection commissioners audit and confirm them (see figure 15.2).

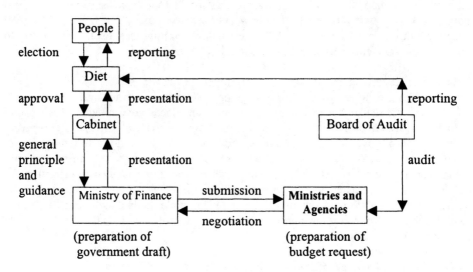

Figure 15.1.: Financial Structure in Central Government

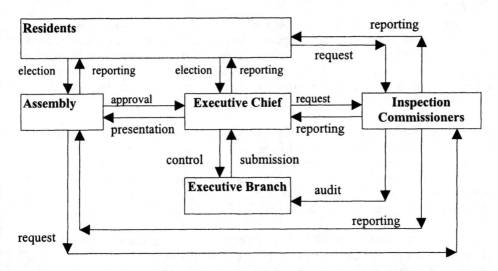

Figure 15.2.: Financial Structure in Local Government

15.2.2. ACCOUNTING SYSTEM

We analyze accounting systems in terms of financial accounting, management accounting, and auditing. For financial accounting, the general account in central and local governments are operated on the modified cash basis (IFAC, 1998) in which the books are held open for three months after year-end (March 31). Accordingly, no profit and loss statements or balance sheets are prepared.

Special accounts are divided into two types. The first does not involve preparation of profit and loss statements, as in the case of the general account. In contrast, 21 special accounts in the central government and eight in the local government, compulsory operate on an accrual basis. The second type produces profit and loss statements and basic balance sheets (100 percent in local government), with the income and expense statements on a cash basis. However, in the second type the accounting standards are different between the central and local governments. In the central government, the accounting standards and principles are defined by each special law and applied to the special account, while the special law (the Local Public Utilities Law) regulates the accounting rules and is uniformly applied to the special accounts in the local government.

Accordingly, economic resources other than financial resources are generally excluded in financial management of the public sector; fixed assets, human resources (personnel), cash and cash equivalents are separately managed. Fixed assets other than infrastructure assets are recorded in the ledger for government-owned properties. These assets are recorded in monetary terms and revalued at current cost every five years, while infrastructure assets are just recorded in non-monetary quantitative terms in their own specific ledgers.

The number of public employees is regulated by law and their wages are recommended by either the National Personnel Authority or the Local Personnel Commission. In addition, cash inflows and outflows attributable to budget executions are recorded and managed by separate accounting officers: expenditure officers and revenue officers. This system is intended to prevent corruption in the system by dividing accounting responsibility into the two functions.

Second, management accounting is underdeveloped in the public sector in contrast to the private sector in which has developed target costing or kaizen. The reason is basically attributable to the fact that government activities are financed from resources compulsory collected from the people. This hardly provides public employees with an incentive to promote efficient use of resources. However, management accounting has progressed in two areas when we use the term in a broad sense.

The first is related to human resource management which, in the public sector, is a kind of capping system. The government, whether central or local, sets a fixed number of public employees as a whole. Under the limitation, the cabinet or chief executive has discretion to allocate personnel into service departments. Consequently, the system prevents an increase in the work force and promotes reallocation of public employees into the areas having greater needs.

Secondly, the Ministry of Home Affairs (MOHA) also centrally controls local governments and implements an *enforced* benchmarking. Since MOHA has the authority to commit local allocation taxes to local governments and to approve issuance of local bonds, it may intervene in the local government for ensuring financial viability. MOHA collects a detailed series of management data on all local governments in a standardized form. Status statements of accounts or financial results are prepared and submitted to MOHA by local governments every year. Analyzing this data, MOHA obtains the standard cost by program and recommends that local governments with higher costs make appropriate reductions.

Thus, MOHA maintains an influential power over local governments, in contrast to MOF. MOF's role is considered to be a cooperative coordinator because there is a ceiling system which limits budget requests to a certain percentage of the budget of the previous fiscal year. Since the ceiling system gradually became more rigid, it works to limit increases in requests for budget funds. Now, the Japanese budget formation process begins with setting overall limits, with subsequent budget requests restricted to these limits. Consequently, the discretional power of the MOF in budget formation has deteriorated.

Thirdly, auditing is significantly different between central and local governments, although the functions of BOA and Inspection Commissioners seem to be identical. In practice, internal audits are less comprehensive except in some divisions in the central government. BOA examines government expenditures and revenues and therefore audits not only central government but also other organizations subsidized by the central government. As a result, BOA's examinations extend to local governments. In addition, BOA focuses on performance auditing while financial auditing is less emphasized. On the other hand, Inspection Commissioners largely examine financial matters in terms of regularity or compliance with financial rules and focus little on performance.

When we turn to accounting officers, they have a specific character. Public employees engaging in financial management work at the departments for a long time, while public employees in other departments are generally transferred every three to five years. Further, few of them major in corporate accounting. Accordingly, though they have the professional skills and knowledge of public finance, they rarely move to the private sector and have no qualification as government accountants. In other words, required skills vary far between sectors. Professional accountants (CPAs) do not play a significant role in the public sector because, as mentioned before, these skills are specific to the private sector or specific assets (Williamson, 1985) and not transferable to the public sector.

The foregoing comparisons between central and local governments are summarized in tables 15.1. and 15.2.

Item	Content
Financial accounting	Basically cash accounting or budgetary accounting, Partly accrual accounting in some Special Accounts
Management accounting	Underdeveloped in each organization
Auditing	Mainly external auditing, internal audits are little implemented
Management control	Divided into three parts: cash, physical assets and personnel control systems
Finance	Significantly depends on government bonds

Table 15.1.:   Similarities

Item	Central Government	Local Governments
Financial accounting	Specific standards are adopted in case of Special Accounts	Uniformly adopted through the country
Management accounting	Non-accounting measures are used for improving performance	*Enforced* benchmarking by MOHA
External Auditing	Comprehensive audits by BOA	Mainly financial audits by the Inspection Commissioners
Financial control	Devolving control by each ministry with a coordination by MOF	Centralized control by MOHA

Table 15.2.:   Differences

15.2.3. FISCAL SITUATIONS

The state of public finance in Japan has grown more serious in the 1990s in contrast to the 1980s when Japanese financial management was admired. Government deficits as a whole in Japan amount to ten percent of GDP in 1999, the worst in the G7 countries. The combined central and local government debts have reached 108.5 percent of GDP in

1999, which is the largest ratio next to Italy. As a result, the receipt from government bonds in 1998 accounted for 38 percent and 13 percent of the total revenues of General Accounts in the central and local governments respectively. The resources available for reallocation into new policies have thus decreased in the public sector despite the emergent welfare needs of the aged.

15.3.   Financial System Reforms

15.3.1. FINANCIAL ACCOUNTING

The former Hashimoto administration passed the Fundamental Law of Reorganization of Central Ministries and Agencies in 1998. One of the key features of the law is the establishment of semi-autonomous bodies in 2001 known as Independent Administrative Corporations (IACs). IACs are modeled on the Executive Agencies in the UK. They are separated from planning and policy departments of the central government and operated on accrual-based accounting. At present, the candidates for IACs are limited; public employees transferring into IACs amount to 67,000 persons, whose share is about 14 percent of total public employees except postal services and defense force in the central government. IACs will prepare balance sheets, profit and loss statements, cash flow statements and submit them to the Ministry in charge and the public according to the law.

Local governments are also taking more steps forward. Some innovative governments are introducing accrual accounting to improve accountability and performance.

The furthest is Mie Prefecture where accrual accounting is regarded as a key element in implementing public sector reform. Mie officially prepared the balance sheet of the General Account in 1998. Several other governments have prepared financial statements according to the method proposed by the Japan Productivity Center for Socio-Economic Development (JPCSED). However, accrual accounting is not adopted in recording daily transactions. It is utilized in preparation of financial statements at the end of the fiscal year. In addition, accounting practices are divergent, although the Japanese Institute of Certified Public Accountants (JICPA) published the accounting principles for the public sector in 1997 (see table 15.3.).

Item	JBCSED	Mie	JICPA
Fixed Assets	Valued at historical cost depreciated on straight line basis over 40 years other than land	Valued at historical cost depreciated on a straight line basis over 50 years other than land	Valued at historical cost depreciated other than land
Infrastructure Assets	Not recognized in balance sheet	Same as in fixed assets	Not recognized in balance sheet recognized consumption as maintenance and replacement expenses
Basis of Consolidation	- General Account - Special Accounts - Public Utilities - Government owned Corporations - Companies in which Government owns a majority of the voting shares	- General Account - Special Accounts - Public Utilities	- General Account - Special Accounts - Organizations in which government has a control capacity to dominate decision making or a dominant influence
Financial Statements	- Balance Sheet - Statement of Cash Flows from Capital Activities - Statement of Cash Flows from Operating Activities - Statement of Movements in Net Assets	- Balance Sheet - Statement of Operating Activities - Statement of Investing Activities	- Balance Sheet - Statement of Financial Performance - Statement of Movements in Net Assets - Statement of Cash Flows
Super-annuation Liabilities:	Nil	Allowance for employee Retirement benefits	Presents in the Note
Pension:	Nil	Nil	Presents in the Note
Subsidies for Capital Spending	Recognized as long term prepayments	Recognized as fixed assets	Nil
Preparation of Balance Sheet	Inventory method	Inventory method	Leading method (based on transactions)

Table 15.3.:   Comparison of proposed Accounting Principles

The diversity is attributable to three factors. First, MOHA is not interested in accrual accounting for the general account, while special accounts are operated on accrual basis because of rate setting. Second, MOHA does not have authority to develop the accounting standards. Third, the JICPA is not the standard setting body for public sector accounting.

15.3.2. MANAGEMENT ACCOUNTING

The Fundamental Law prescribes that Ministries shall carry out policy evaluation, while IACs are responsible for performance evaluation. The regulation naturally would lead to a comparison of benefits or outcomes with costs because policy makers have to ensure that the limited public resources are allocated in a manner to achieve the maximum benefits at the minimum cost. However, neither accounting by management standards nor by performance indicators are utilized. By contrast, in local governments a project evaluation system has been quickly implemented through the economy. Now two thirds have already adopted it or decided to do so. The system was also launched in Mie Prefecture in 1996. All projects over 3,200 are evaluated in terms of outcome and cost, while the cost is measured on cash basis (Yamamoto, 1997). It is remarkable to measure the outcomes for every project in quantity terms, though they are not measured in monetary terms, i.e., benefits. The projects which were rated poor in terms of cost effectiveness are abolished or have their budgets reduced.

Thus, the evaluation system could assist the chief executive and public managers to cut spending in a rational manner. Under the fiscal stress, the government must persuade interested parties including politicians who would be affected by the cut. This is the main reason why the system has spread in a short time. Further, other local governments are considering introduction of activity-based costing (ABC) into their management. It will, however, take time to introduce ABC. Since the status of public employees is secured by the law, reducing the personnel is very difficult even though ABC could show a more efficient operation with fewer employees in the public service.

15.3.3. AUDITING

BOA expanded its mandates in 1997. Amendments to the BOA law provide that BOA shall audit in terms of accuracy, regularity, economy, efficiency and effectiveness (article 20, phase 3 of BOA Law). As previously indicated, BOA has implemented performance auditing since the 1960s. However, the legal basis for it was not always evident. The amendment gives BOA a concrete base for performance auditing and even program evaluation.

The law also provides that if the Diet or Diet's committees will ask BOA to examine a specific matter, BOA may audit it and report the result to the Diet (article 30-2 of BOA Law). The new prescription might strengthen the BOA's control over ministries and agencies by linking auditing to the legislative oversight of the executive branch, while it is also possible that BOA's independence from the Cabinet would be eroded by political disputes under the parliamentary system.

On the other hand, in the local governments, external auditing started in 1999. The auditing is compulsory performed by a professional having the qualifications of CPA, lawyer or rich experience in public sector auditing in an annual contract, in every prefecture and cities having more than 300,000 population. The reform is expected to enhance visibility and strengthen accountability of the local government to the public by external checks. The inspection commissioners consist of assembly members (politicians) and the informed persons (mostly retired senior public servants in the government). Therefore, many commentators have criticized the inspection system on the ground that it lacks independence from the executive branch. In fact, the system neither could find nor prevent the corruption's in management in many local governments which appeared in 1995-96.

15.3.4. BUDGETING

The Fundamental Reorganization Law does not deal with budget reforms other than the financial management of IACs. According to the management principles draft, IACs would be operated in a different manner from the ministries.

First, IACs will be financed on an accrual basis through two types of funding: the grant for operating costs and the capital expenditures from the General Account. Second, IACs will have full discretion to use the grant for operating costs in order to achieve the objectives which are authorized by the minister in charge. In other words, the grant is a kind of lump-sum subsidiary from the central government. Third, the grant remaining unspent at year-end may carry over to the following year. Fourth, IACs may retain the operating surplus (on an accrual basis) under a certain condition. Fifth, IACs will not be allowed to incur long-term debt nor issue bonds.

Thus, the financial management is similar to the Executive Agencies in the UK and considered an operating cost control. In contrast to a flexible financial management within the government, some local governments have developed a budgeting system based upon a more systematic approach.

Mie Prefecture has adopted a matrix-type budget since 1996. The budgeting is summarized in terms of objectives and departments. It makes clear not only the interrelations between departments and objectives but also the amount of each objective at a glance. This form is expected to give primary decision makers useful information and it could make the chief executive prepare more cost-effective budgets. It would also encourage the assembly members to discuss and oversee the resource allocation more carefully, and it may become easier for citizens to evaluate the government activities.

Another approach is found in Iwate Prefecture. Its approach is more focused on the budgetary process than on the project evaluation system and is thus regarded as a budget-related performance management system. Every project is evaluated at the department, then the result is provided to the budget division. While operating and capital projects are evaluated as a unified form in the project evaluation system, this system divides the projects into two types. Operating projects are graded on four ranks in accordance with the four criteria: yearly changes of effects; comparison with the national level; linkage to the total plan; and the planned target. Capital projects are graded on 100 point scales based on necessity, emergency, comprehensiveness, cost-benefit, and feasibility. Following the provision, the budget division prepares the budget draft accounting to the gradings. Thus, the system is tightly linked to budgeting, though it is focused only little on improvement.

15.4. Discussion

Financial management reforms in Japan, as indicated, significantly differ between the central and local governments. Introducing accrual accounting and flexible financial management in IACs are made possible by the new legislation. In contrast, the innovative reforms of financial management in local governments are progressing through strong leadership of the chief executives. This leads to the varied accounting practices in the local governments which introduced accrual accounting; some local governments adopt it for preparing the balance sheets, while others try to apply it in management accounting.

Despite these differences, there are various common features. First, the reforms are oriented to the inside of the government. Though the establishment of IACs is a step toward improving performance, it is an organizational separation within the government. Project evaluation systems are basically introduced to cut spending, though they partly aim at strengthening accountability. In addition, the balance sheet does not always fairly present the fiscal condition; the net assets or equity is generally shown as a positive value in spite of large deficits. This is mainly because infrastructure assets financed by local bonds are recognized as fixed in the balance sheet although they are accompanied by the debt incurred through issuance of local bonds for their acquisition. Accordingly, in using the balance sheet, many local governments try to make public employees more cost-conscious.

Second, a market-oriented or competitive system is little linked to financial management reforms. Since the local bonds market is not competitive but operated under the approval system of MOHA, investors in the capital market have no incentive to demand financial information comparable to the private sector. Therefore, the external thrust of transformation to accrual accounting is weak although recently some rating organizations have issued ratings for local bonds. In addition, the reforms of management accounting focus on measurement of the program or project costs, while the cost is not recognized on an accrual basis. Privatization or contracting out of public services is not extended to non-industrial services although a significant part of industrial services is contracted out. Accordingly, there are few movements toward producing comparative cost data on non-industrial services. Moreover, neither asset valuation on a current basis nor imposing a capital charge is regarded as an adequate treatment in the public sector. The measurement focus is not opportunity cost (economic cost) but actual cost (historical accounting cost). This might be partly caused by the character of Japanese Bureaucracy (see, for example, Rothacher, 1993) entrenched with graduates from Tokyo University (especially Faculty of Law). Since 'unlike America, Japan places society ahead of the economy' (Drucker, 1998), economic thinking may not be readily accepted by the senior bureaucrats and the general population.

Third, accounting and auditing are not well-harmonized with budgeting. The local government, where accrual accounting has been introduced, prepares and controls the budget on a cash basis. Decision-making in allocating the funds collected is not consistent with project evaluations. The exception is the management of IACs. The grant for operating and capital activities of the IACs is to balance with the cost on an accrual basis, though the details are yet uncertain. Auditing in the central government has been more oriented to performance auditing, especially effectiveness audits. However, the focus is a post-evaluation of individual projects; even in auditing the program, the evaluation is carried out in a bottom-up approach that produces the total figure for the program from individual project investigations. This limits the program audits or program evaluations in number. As a result, the audit findings could be partly reflected in budget preparation or possibly some of the discussion. Auditing in local governments has less impact on their budgeting than BOA's audits. This is because the auditing, even in case of external auditing, focuses on detecting and preventing illegal or inadequate matters; the primary objective is to ensure that the financial management is in good order, not to improve performance. This is attributable to the fact that new external auditing policies were enacted in response to fiscal corruption (Yoshimi, 1998).

Consequently, the Japanese financial reforms are produced and advanced by external thrusts, such as demand for visibility, and improving performance and institutional design (Yamamoto, 1999a and 1999b). The reforms would produce the intended outcomes by harmonizing with institutions and their thrust. In this regard, more external thrusts are required in the central government, while institutional mechanisms need to be introduced in local government. Unless accounting standards are developed, it is difficult to compare the financial information among local governments. In addition, competitive markets in the local bonds would not work well unless the approval system for local bonds is abolished.

In the central government, it is assumed that the public, the parliament and the ministries would use the information in their decision-making, although the expanded information that IACs have to produce is expected to strengthen accountability to the public. Hence, these information users need to have a sustained interest in IACs and given understandable and reliable information. Such interest would not only work as the external thrust for improving performance and accountability but also promote the merits of its semi-autonomous nature.

15.5. Conclusion

We have discussed the similarities and differences between the Japanese central and local governments in their financial management systems and reforms. As a result, it was shown that budget-oriented management systems on the cash basis are adopted in both governments, though some innovative reforms on the accrual basis have also been developed.

In addition, financial management in local governments is a centralized system by MOHA, while ministers and agencies in the central government have a fair discretion under the coordination by MOF. On the other hand, financial management reforms in the public sector seem to be affected by the 'new public management' (NPM), though competitive mechanisms and customer-oriented factors are hardly identified. However, the development of reforms have different patterns: the organization-oriented approach with enactment in the central government, and the system-based approach with political leadership in the local government. The financial reform of central government is limited to IACs which implement the executive functions, while local governments aim at reforming their whole management systems, though accrual accounting is limited to areas such as balance sheet preparation.

The outcomes of financial reforms in Japan therefore depend on whether accrual accounting will be thoroughly adopted in the public sector, linking accounting to budgeting and management. If accrual accounting will be introduced to the public sector in a piecemeal fashion, the reform would not produce the fruitful outcomes. Because NPM works in the conditions where public services are operated with active participation of individual citizens as customers and market mechanism (Jessop, 1993); cost and quality of service are expected to function as an information signal which are equivalent to the prices in the market of private goods.

Other approaches would be needed in case of partial adoption of accrual-based financial management. In this case, some centralized control systems have to be built in the financial management system; market mechanisms or decentralized systems must be substituted for central control to avoid poor performance and ensure accountability.

Whether or not the harmonized system between central control and partial accrual-based management could be produced, as in the case of Japanese Management, should be further investigated. Japanese Management itself is a hybrid model of coordination and competitive systems, i.e., horizontal coordination coupled with rank hierarchy or tournament hierarchy (Koike, 1998; Aoki, 1990; Aoki and Dore, 1994). Therefore, it is inappropriate to discard the possibility of a 'new public management model' in Japanese Management itself.

References

- Aoki, M. (1990) *Towards an Economic Model of the Japanese Firm*, Journal of Economic Literature, Vol. 28, 1-27.
- Aoki, M. and Dore, R. (1994) *The Japanese Firm*, Oxford University Press, New York.
- Hood, C. (1991) *A Public Management for All Seasons?*, Public Administration, Vol. 69, No. 1, 3-19.
- Drucker, P. F. (1998) *In Defense of Japanese Bureaucracy*, Foreign Affairs, September/October, 68-80.
- IFAC (1998) *Guideline for Government Financial Reporting--Exposure Draft.*
- Jessop, B. (1993) *Towards a Shumpeterian Workfare State? Preliminary Remarks on Post-Fordist Political Economy*, Studies in Political Economy, Vol. 40, 7-39.
- Koike, K. (1988) *Understanding Industrial Relations in Modern Japan*, Macmillan, London.
- Olson, O., Guthrie, J. and Humphrey, C. (1998) *Global Warning Debating International Developments in New Public Financial Management*, Cappelen Akademisk Forlask, Oslo.
- Rothacher, A. (1993) *The Japanese Power Elite*, St. Martin's Press, New York.
- Yamamoto, K. (1997) *Accounting System Reform and Public Management in Local Government*, paper prepared for the 6th CIGAR at Bocconi University.
- Yamamoto, K. (1999a) Accounting System Reform and Management in the Japanese Local Government, in Caperchoine, E. and Mussari, R. (eds.), *Comparative Issues in Local Government Accounting*, Kluwer Academic Publishers (forthcoming).
- Yamamoto, K. (1999b) *Accounting System Reform in apanese Local Governments*, Working Paper.
- Yoshimi, H. (1998) *No Value for Money: Audit against the Fraud Cases in Japanese Local Governments*, paper prepared for the 2nd Asian Pacific Interdisciplinary Research in Accounting Conference at Osaka.
- Williamson, O. (1985) *The Economic Institutions of Capitalism*, Free Press, New York.

CHAPTER 16

POLISH PUBLIC SECTOR ACCOUNTING IN TRANSITION: THE LANDSCAPE AFTER EARLY 1999 STEP IN THE STATE REDEFINING

Wojciech A. Nowak and Barbara Bakalarska

16.1. Introduction

The Polish regime is still under the unique transition from centrally planned economy and monoparty political system to market economy and liberal democracy. During 1998 and early 1999 four important events were happened within The State redefining. All of them were connected with giving Poles more freedom and more responsibility for themselves and with their aspirations to return to the civilization of the West and join NATO and UE. The first was the new structure of local government, the second was the public finance structure reshaping, the third was the health service system reform and the last but not least was the pension system reform. These events triggered changes within public sector accounting system. The paper describes some of these changes and their links with international context.

16.2. Background to Recent Reforms

The reform of the administrative system of the country, which has recently been carried out in Poland, was accompanied by modernization of the public finance structure and health care and pension systems reforms. The legal aspect of all four reforms was prepared in 1998 and the reforms were introduced on January 1, 1999.

The rationale behind the reforms was giving Polish citizens more freedom and personal responsibility for their own welfare, including direct responsibility for the financial aspect of health care and provision for old age, while at the same time effecting adjustment of the administrative and public finance system to the requirements of the decentralization and devolution of public authority and gradual withdrawal of the state from financial provision for its citizens' needs, which tend to increase along with the development of liberal democracy and free market economy. Another important factor stimulating the reform processes is attempt at intensifying the already high rate of economic growth and civilization advancement. Equally important, though perhaps understated in public forum, is the need to harmonize basic aspects of political social and economic structures and functions with pertinent structures and functions in countries regarded by Poland as models to be followed in defining the country's directions of development and integrative efforts within globalization processes. After the fundamental choices made in the 1980s and '90s, the model countries are the developed Western states: in practical terms these are the members of NATO and EU, and in a broader perspective - the OECD countries.

A. Bac (ed.), International Comparative Issues in Government Accounting, 265-278.
© 2001 *Kluwer Academic Publishers. Printed in the Netherlands.*

16.3. Values and Principles

Principal values and ideas underlying the reforms introduced on January 1, 1999 include:
a. unitarian democratic state embodying the principles of social justice;
b. supporting, supplementary role of the state, limited to matters that cannot be resolved by individuals, local and professional communities or other competent invest groups;
c. decentralization of authority, which involves devolution of powers and responsibilities from central government to local self government;
d. priority of territorial integrity over sector or departmental interests;
e. regulation by the parliament of accumulation and allocation of funds for public purposes;
f. laying down the upper limit of public debt, understood as total external debt of central and local government;
g. ensuring everyone freedom in obtaining and spreading information and freedom of speech.

The changes introduced recently are grounded in the new *Constitution of the Polish Republic*, which was passed on April 2, 1997. *The Constitution* provides, among others, that:
a. public authorities act by force of law and within law;
b. political system of the state dictates decentralization of public authority;
c. inhabitants of territorial division units by law are self - governing communities;
d. local government units have legal personality and are vested with ownership right and other property rights;
e. local government perform all those public tasks which have not been defined in the Constitution and other laws as responsibility of other public authorities;
f. public funds comprise public resources which are managed through the state budget, with a central bank having exclusive right to issue money as well as formulate and implement monetary policy;
g. public levies are imposed by act of law, and public debt cannot exceed 60% of gross domestic product;
h. state budget has the form of a legal act and spans the period of one year;
i. citizens are entitled to obtaining information (including access to documents) about the activity of public authorities and persons performing public functions, with the mode of giving information being regulated by law, and in the case of the parliament - by internal regulations.

It is important to note that the new *Constitution* definitely gives priority to public finance over the state budget. This demonstrates a fundamental reorientation in the area of public finance, consisting in a transition from wishful thinking in terms of a plan to realistic thinking in terms of resources and process. In order to realize how radical a change this is, let us remind that in the period of a centrally planned economy the budget of an all-pervailing state was a main instrument for the realization of its social and economic tasks as well as a substitute for market mechanism, whereas public finance had played a secondary role.

16.4. Public Sector Redefined

Until the end of 1998 the country's administrative structure was comprised of self-governing communes as a local level and governmental voivodships being the regional part of the central government level. In early 1999 there was a fundamental reorganization: the self-governing sphere was reinforced by additional local and regional tiers - county and voivodship (still as a regional level). Therefore, although basic entities of local government are 2,489 communes, they have been combined into 16 voivodships and central administration. The number of voivodships decreased thus by 33, but newly-delineated voivodships gained dual nature, for they retained their central government character in continuing as regional units of central administration being at the same time part of self-government sphere. Voivodships have been subdivided in 308 self-governed counties comprised of communes. Besides that 65 cities have been granted the status of municipal counties. The capital city of Poland - Warsaw - is not a county. By force of an earlier special act it is a confederation of 11 communes. Each territorial entity of self-governing sphere has an elected legislative body and an executive body appointed by the legislative body. Each territorial entity also has legal personality[1] and is vested with ownership and property rights.

In terms of ownership the changes at self-governed level consist in public property generally being distributed between the State Treasury, which is a legal person[2], other state legal persons, communes, counties and voivodships (all being legal persons[3]), other local government legal persons[4], and companies with prevailing state or local government shareholdings. The general structure of the national economy after the 1999 changes is represented in figure 16.1.[5] The public sector is subdivided into the governmental sector (comprising the State Treasury, other state legal persons and commercial companies with dominant state ownership) and local government sector (comprising administrative division entities, other local government legal persons, and commercial company with dominant local government ownership).

---

[1] This concerns the capital city of Warsaw as well.

[2] Since 1990.

[3] The ownership of communes, counties and voivodships can be seen as something like local government treasury.

[4] Including these legal persons which under current legislation may be formed only by administrative division entities.

[5] When referring to profit orientation we mean profit for owners. We feel that this should be stressed because we are of the opinion that each business entity capable of continuing in operation and of development needs a certain surplus for its own.

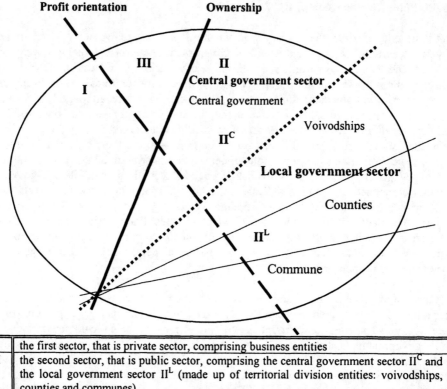

I	the first sector, that is private sector, comprising business entities
II	the second sector, that is public sector, comprising the central government sector II^C and the local government sector II^L (made up of territorial division entities: voivodships, counties and communes)
III	the third sector, that is a sector of not-for profit private entities, that is non-public not-for-profit organizations and households.

Figure 16.1.:   General structure of the national economy after the modernization of
                   territorial division in early 1999

16.5. Public Finance and Public Resources

Provisions of *the Constitution* concerning public finance are implemented through an *Act of November 26, 1999 on public finance*, which came in force on January 1, 1999. It replaced the *Budgetary Law of January 1991* previously in force. This was the next step towards overcoming the primacy of the wishful thinking philosophy of budgeting over public resources. The notion of public finance itself was specified within the *Constitution*, though not defined directly (despite devoting an entire section to this issue: Section X, Articles 216-227) which resulted in certain conceptual fuzziness. Instead a definition of public finance is found in *1998 Act on public finance*, where it says in Article 4:

Public finance comprises processes related to accumulation of public resources and their distribution, in particular:
1. collection and accumulation of revenues;
2. spending of public resources;

3. deficit financing;
4. contracting liabilities involving public resources;
5. public resources management;
6. public debt management.

From an ontological point of view, this definition of the public finance utilizes a process approach whose processes relate to public resources. The concept of public resources as used here is not defined in *the Constitution*.[6] Conceptual content of public resources, just as in the case of the concept of public finance, was considerably reduced by their definition in *the 1998 Public Finance Act* as [Art. 3 para. 1]:
'Public resources comprise:
1. public revenues;
2. non-returnable funds from foreign sources;
3. revenues of organizational entities and legal persons belonging to the public finance sector from their activities or from other sources;
4. revenues of the state budget and local government budgets from:
    a. sale of securities or other financial transactions;
    b. privatization of the State Treasury property and local government property;
    c. repayments of loans granted from public funds;
    d. loans and credits'.

The above definition of public resources uses, as can be seen, a reistic approach and has an enumerative form. Please note that this definition covers both tangible and intangible assets.

From the accounting regulation perspective it is important to note that occurrence in both definitions of receivables and payables practically rules out the pure cash basis of accounting for public finance in Poland. The method to be used should be modified cash accounting or accrual accounting, or both. The process concept of public finance implies also the need of information about states and flows, which is indispensable for management.

16.6. Public Finance Sector and the Budgetary Sphere

Public finance processes occur in the public finance sector. This sector has been defined in *the Public Finance Act* [Art. 6] as comprising:
1. public authorities and their subordinate organizational entities;
2. state legal persons and other state organizational entities whose activity is financed entirely or partly from public funds, excluding state enterprises, state banks, commercial companies and state entities being on the National Judicial Register (among others public health service institutions and insolvent debtors).

The public finance sector is divided into the governmental sector (comprising broadly understood central government with controlling bodies and the judiciature) and the local government sector, comprising entities of territorial self-government (communes, counties and voivodships), their legislative and executive bodies and their subordinate

---

[6]   The Constitution uses the notion of *finance means for public purposes.*

organizational units. It should be stressed that almost all public health care organizations and public sector entities registered by courts as insolvent are outside the public finance sector.

The Public Finance Act lays down a strict requirement that public sector entities may only have such organizational and legal forms as are specified in this *Act* or other acts. The forms, being laid down by the parliament, belong to the political sphere. The forms, which are not covered by this *Act*, include state schools for higher education and various state agencies supporting Poland's transformation. The forms laid down by *the Act* include the State Treasury and local government treasury component entities without legal personality and special purpose funds which can be legal persons. A characteristic feature of special purpose funds is the fact that within the public finance sector may operate only those special purpose funds legally established before January 1, 1999, whose revenues come from public resources, and expenditures are used for realization of appointed public tasks. In short, no new funds are to be established and the number of existing funds should be reduced in relatively short time. It is interesting to note that in the final phase of the centrally planned economy special purpose funds represented such a drain on the state budget that they were called parabudgets.

With regard to organizational and legal forms of the Treasury and municipal treasury entities without legal personality, *the Act* prescribes standardization, specifying only two basic types:
1. budgetary unit, which may be accompanied by special resources and auxiliary holdings;
2. budgetary entities.

A budgetary unit is a real being, which serves a conceptual, by definition, budget of the state or budgets of local government territorial entities. It is then a not-for-profit entity, which credits the budget it serves with its revenues and debits it with its expenditures. In American terminology it is a B-type unit. A budgetary unit may have certain funds at its disposal, which are kept in separate bank accounts:
a. on the strength of separate acts or resolutions of local government legislative bodies;
b. by virtue of inheritance, legacy or gift in monetary form;
c. by virtue of compensation or payment for lost or damaged property which a given entity obtained for utilization or administration;
d. by virtue of sale of strategic tangible resources kept as reserves for emergency.

Resources of this type are called special resources, which may be spent on:
a. purposes listed in the act setting them up;
b. purposes specified by the donor or benefactor;
c. repair or replacement of lost or damaged resources;
d. replenishment of diminished strategic reserve.

Besides special resources, a budgetary unit may set apart, organizationally and financially, earnings oriented part of its primary activity and/or all of its earnings oriented secondary activities and in this way form an auxiliary holding. An auxiliary holding covers all its costs by revenues from sale of its products (which may be budget-subsidized) and hands over half of its profits to its parent budgetary unit. It is thus a classical for profit entity within the public finance sector.

A budgetary entity is an organization linked with the state or local government budgets. It performs, non-gratuitously, specified tasks of a given budget and covers its costs by own revenues. The activity, products and investments of this type of organization may be subsidized by the pertinent budget up to a total amount of 50% of own revenues. A characteristic feature of budgetary entities is setting the upper limit on their current assets, so that periodically they have to turn over surplus assets to the pertinent budget.

The above described organizational and legal forms of state and municipal treasury component entities were initiated in Poland in 1950s. The *Public Finance Act* does not introduce anything basically new in this respect. It does however, introduce certain modifications, which are another step forward in the evolution of these forms. The most radical change was the one concerning special resources, which were limited to cash from sources listed in *the Act* and are to be spent in ways specified in *the Act*. The structure of The State and local government treasury component entities without legal personality is shown in figure 16.2. With regard to continuing in operation, it is important to say that budgetary units, auxiliary holdings, special resources and budgetary entities are set up, combined and liquidated on the strength of political or administrative decisions.

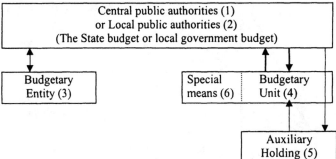

(1)	a complex entity with territorial components and the features of a not-for-profit organization
(2)	a complex territorial entity with the features of a not-for profit organization
(3)	a not-for-profit organization of type A
(4)	a not-for-profit organization of type B
(5)	a for profit organization related to B-type organization (a budgetary unit) by legal force
(6)	a special bank account for cash restricted, related to B-type organization (a budgetary unit) by legal force

Figure 16.2.: Standardized Structure of the State and Local Government Treasury Component Entities without Legal Personality

As the title of this chapter suggests, there is one more issue to be discussed, namely the concept of budgetary sphere, generally equated with the national economy recently delimited as a public finance sector. Its official scope, however, is narrower than the popularly accepted scope, which is due to the criterion of salary regulation. The budgetary sphere constitutes this part of the public finance sector where salaries and wages are regulated and (generally) funded by public authorities. Therefore currently the budgetary sphere comprises such entities as budgetary units, auxiliary holdings budgetary entities and state institutions for higher education. Graphically the relationship of the public finance sector and the budgetary sphere within the national economy is represented in figure 16.3.

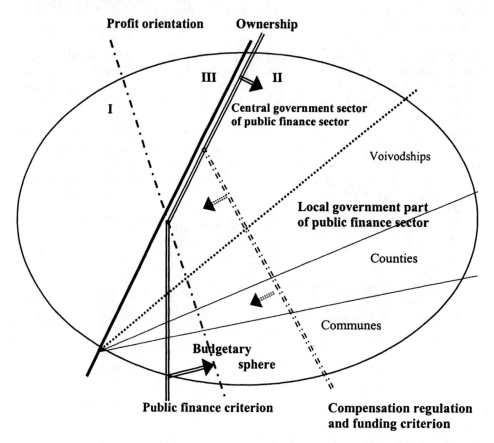

Figure 16.3.:   Public Finance Sector and Budgetary Sphere

16.6. Accounting and Financial Reporting in the Restructured Public Sector

Within the restructured public sector the hitherto general Polish principle of accounting regulation has been maintained. According to this principle accounting and financial reporting of entities outside the public finance sector are to be regulated solely by *1994 Accounting Act*[7] whereas accounting and reporting of public finance sector entities are to

---

[7]   Works in progress on its substantial revision and amendment in the current - that is 1999 - year.

be regulated respectively by *1994 Accounting Act* and *1998 Act on public finance*, with the exception for the National Bank of Poland and the State Treasury. The National Bank of Poland (which is a central bank) has been excluded from both *1994 Accounting Act* and *1998 Public Finance Act,* while the State Treasury as a whole has been entirely excluded from *1994 Accounting Act* and only partially taken into account within *1998 Public Finance Act.*

16.6.1. THE CENTRAL BANK

According to the *1997 Act on the National Bank of Poland (NBP),* accounting and reporting issues are the prerogative of its collegiate bodies, that is the Monetary Policy Board and the NBP Board. The Act provides, though, that NBP's accounting principles must be in conformity with International Accounting Standards (Art. 67) and the annual report should consist of the balance sheet profit and loss account and supplementary information[8]. The annual report of NBP is to be audited by a special commission appointed for this purpose by the Council of Ministers at the application of the Minister of Finance. After being audited, the annual financial report of NBP is approved by the Council of Ministers and then part of NBP's yearly profit is transferred to the state budget. The annual financial report of NBP is not published, but the President of the Bank is required to submit a report on activities to the parliament.

16.6.2. THE STATE TREASURY

From the accounting viewpoint, the accounting and reporting principles of the State Treasury as legal entity are regulated rather in a fragmentary way, whereas the entities controlling the property of the State Treasury fall under accounting regulations appropriate to their legal and organizational form. It means that the State Treasury companies, state enterprises and state banks fall under *the Accounting Act*, while public finance sector entities are subject to both *the Accounting Act* and *the Public Finance Act.* In respect of accounting and reporting the State Treasury as a whole is currently required to:

a. apply specific principles of fixed asset recording, laid down by the Minister of Finance (Act on Public Finance, Art. 14);

b. maintain a summary record of the property of the State Treasury by the State Treasury Minister (*1996 Act on the principles of exercising the powers of the State Treasury,* Art. 2)[9];

c. submit to the parliament (by the Council of Ministers) annual reports on the ownership of the State Treasury;

d. determine and announce (by the Minister of Finance in 'Monitor Polski', the official gazette of Polish Republic):
 - the amount of nominal debt of the State Treasury;
 - the amount of non-payable liabilities on collaterals and guarantees granted by the State Treasury;

---

[8] The structure of the balance sheet and profit and loss account is laid by the Monetary Policy Board.

[9] Such records have already served as a basis for the 1997 and 1998 parliamentary reports on the ownership of The State Treasury.

- sum of nominal debt of the State Treasury and expected disbursements on collaterals and warranties granted by the State Treasury (relative to Gross Domestic Product).

16.6.3. PUBLIC SECTOR ENTITIES NOT BELONGING TO THE PUBLIC FINANCE SECTOR

Entities belonging to this area of the public sector still apply accounting and reporting principles laid down in *the Accounting Act*, that is full accrual accounting and business reporting model. The mode of demarcation of the public finance sector has resulted in inclusion in it of all state institutions for higher education and exclusion of nearly all national health service entities. At this subchapter we would like to draw attention to the specific situation of national health service entities which, being part of the public sector, are outside the public finance sector. The specific character of their situation consist in the fact that they have to make a rapid, almost overnight, transition to the business accounting and reporting models. It must be stressed that redefining of the organizational and legal form as well as the accounting entity involves in this case the narrowing of accountability. This has significant consequences for all parties involved in financing, providing and consuming of medical services and goes against the sense of broader social responsibility prevalent in medical professions. Apart from that, significant problems have arisen connected with allocation of resources and reorganization of the purchasing system. After several months since the reform came into operation, it is already evident that financial information has a very important role in the evolution of these conflicts and problems, but this is outside the scope of the topic of this paper.

16.6.4. PUBLIC FINANCE SECTOR ENTITIES

The Public Finance Act requires public finance sector entities to apply uniform principles of accounting and to prepare reports on collection and distribution of public funds. From the accounting regulation perspective this means that unless *the Public Finance Act* provides otherwise, apply the rules of the Accounting Act and other legislation should be applied. It is important here to note the general differences introduced for public finance sector purposes. They relate to the principles of accounting, plans of accounts and reporting models.[10] The specific accounting principles relate to:
- assets and liabilities valuation;
- keeping record on fixed assets being the property of the State or local government treasuries;
- budget execution;
- financial statements preparation.

The differences in accounting principles concern mainly reporting on public finance processes and are to be reflected in respective plans of accounts. In accordance with the

---

[10] The Finance Minister is to have set by the end of the year 2000 detailed regulations implementing *1998 Public Finance Act*. Meanwhile the regulations implementing the old *Budgetary law* are in operation (see [Jaruga, Nowak, 1995] and [Jaruga, Nowak, Lisiecka-Zając, 1998].

fundamental principle of the openness of public finance to the public, *the Public Finance Act* requires the Minister of Finance to determine and announce in a relevant official gazette:

a. specific accounting principles and plans of account for the state budget[11] and local government budgets, budgetary entities, budgetary units and auxiliary holdings (including budgetary units with head offices abroad);

b. principles of accounting and plans of accounts relating to collection and distribution of those taxes, fees and other non-fax revenues of the state or municipal budgets which fall under tax authorities;

c. plans of accounts for other public finance sector entities (no special principles of accounting are planned for this group).

Plans of accounts introduced by the Minister of Finance should be conformable with *the Accounting Act* provisions and international standards. However, *the Public Finance Act* requires that:

- budgetary revenues and expenditures should be recognized when cash is received or disbursed;
- interest on payments without a fixed time-limit should be calculated and recorded not later than every quarter-end;
- all stages in the settlement of revenues and expenditures should be recorded and in the case of expenditures - also the resources involved;
- value of assets and liabilities in foreign currencies should be restated according to current exchange rates, with adjustments being made not later than every quarter-end;
- receivables and payables in foreign currencies should be valued according to current exchange rates.

It is interesting to note the requirement of consistency with international standards without referring to any particular set of standards. This gives the Finance Minister much flexibility, but also can be a source of some problems.

The receipts and disbursements as well as revenues and spending of public finance sector entities are to be classified not only according to accounting criteria, but also according to lines of activity (sections and chapters) as well as types and sources or directions (paragraphs). The latter classification is traditionally called a budgetary classification and has in Poland the nature of a legal rule set published by the Finance Minister.

One more issue to be addressed is financial reporting. Two models apply in the field under consideration. One is a business reporting model prescribed by *the Accounting Act*, and the other is the budgetary model. The former relates exclusively to public finance sector entities other than administrative division entities (communes, counties and voivodships), associations of such entities, budgetary units, auxiliary holdings, budgetary entities or special purpose funds having the character of organization. The latter relates to reporting on public finance processes and is called budgetary reporting and respective reports are called budgetary statements (generally they are the reports to

---

[11] Until the end of 1998 the plan of account for the State budget was not published.

which apply the specific principles of accounting). This model comprises several sub - models:

a. a consolidated statement on the execution of a part of the state budget;
b. a consolidated statement of the execution of the state budget;
c. a statement of the execution of local government budget;
d. a consolidated statement on the execution of the set of local government budgets;
e. reports on the implementation of financial plans of public finance sector entities other than entities of administrative division);
f. reports on public debt;
g. reports on warranties and collaterals of the public finance sector.

Specific types, forms, principles and dates of preparing budgetary statements, as well as units required to prepare such statements and their users are set out in *the Public Finance Act* or in a special decree issued by the Minister of Finance on the strength of authorization included in this *Act* and published - in consultation with the President of the Central Statistical Office - in a pertinent official gazette. Only the consolidated annual statement on the execution of local government budgets is not within the Finance Minister's competence - it is prepared by the President of the Central Statistical Office. Budgetary reports are special purposes reports, which means that they are not announced.

16.7. Financial Accounting and Reporting in the Context of Open Character of Public Finance

In *the Public Finance Act* the issues relating to accounting and reporting are under a chapter heading 'Openness and transparency of public finance'. It is stated that public finance is open, except for 'those public funds, whose sources and uses have been recognized as state secret by virtue of separate regulations or international agreements.' (Art. 11, para 3). Open character of public finance should be manifested by (Art. 11, para 2):

a. openness of parliamentary and local government budget debates;
b. openness of parliamentary debate on the execution of the state budget and debates on the execution of local budgets;
c. public announcement of:
   - amounts of subsidies granted from the state budget and local government budgets;
   - summary data on public finance,
d. disclosure of annual statements on the finance resources (sic! - not all kind of resources) and public finance sector entities activity.

Moreover, *the Public Finance Act* requires the Finance Minister to disclose on specified dates data on all financial operations of the public finance sector, in particular revenues and expenditures, liabilities and receivables, and warranties and collaterals.

Thus, public finance sector accounting and reporting systems not only should aim at ensuring due relevancy and reliability of financial information, but also contribute to the enhancement of openness and transparency of public finance. The standardization of legal and organizational forms and ways of operation of public sector entities, largely determining accounting and reporting, serves the purpose of openness and transparency, as well. So does prohibition of forming foundations by the state Treasury. In the present situation, however, openness and transparency of public finance sees to be considerably limited by poorly developed auditing, both in the external and internal aspect, and the lack of financial statement announcement.

16.8. Conclusion

When introducing the public finance bill to the parliament, the Council of Ministers stressed the fact that it had been adjusted to the intended extent of decentralization and devolution of power. According to the Council, the bill is drawn from the best models utilized by developed countries. Its chief goals were ensuring openness and transparency of public finance, full control of democratic institutions over the uses of public money, and implementation of provisions of *the Constitution of 1997* on the public finance. It was - and is - expected that the bringing of *the Public Finance Act* into operation should result in:
- consolidation of the public finance sector, which has been defined collectively as a set of central and local authority entities;
- public accessibility of comprehensible, lucid information on public finance;
- enhanced efficiency of public funds allocation;
- enhanced effectiveness of execution;
- imported control of public spending and budgetary discipline;
- achievement of compatibility with the best standards of OECD countries;
- improved organizational structures of public finance sector.

However, comparison of these goals and intentions - and the real orientation on processes and financial resources - with the concepts of managerialism and consumerism suggests that in the actual dimension *1998 Public Finance Act* may be seen rather as a subsequent than a final stage in Polish public management evolution toward New Public Management. The more so because the Minister of Finance is to have set regulations implementing *1998 Public Finance Act* by the end of the year 2000 (and, as a Polish saying has it, 'the devil is in the details'). Meanwhile the regulations implementing the old *Budgetary law* are still in operation.

References

- Buschor E., Schedler, K. (Editors) (1994) *Perspectives on Performance Measurement and Public Sector Accounting,* Haupt, Berne.
- IFAC PSC (1998) *Guideline for governmental financial reporting – Exposure draft,* International Federation of Accountants – Public Sector Committee, New York.
- Jaruga A., Nowak, W. (1995) *Governmental accounting in transition: the Polish experience,* in: Financial Accountability & Management, 11(1), February 1995, 75-94.
- Jaruga A., Nowak W.A. (1996), *Toward a general model of public sector accounting innovations,* in: Chan J.L., Jones R.H., Lüder K.G. (eds), (1996), *Research in governmental and nonprofit accounting,* Volume 9, JAI Press Inc., Greenwich, Connecticut, London, England, 21-31.
- Jaruga A., Nowak W.A., Lisiecka-Zając B. (1998) *Polish public sector accounting in transition: evidence from the mid 1990s,* in: Financial Accountability & Management, 14(2), May 1998, 105-121.
- Nowak W.A. (1998) *Rachunkowość sektora publicznego: koncepcje, metody, uwarunkowania (Public sector accounting: concepts, methods, determinants),* Wydawnictwo Naukowe PWN, Warszawa, 241.
- Nozick R. (1974) *Anarchy, state and utopia,* Blackwell, Oxford UK & Cambridge USA.
- Popper K.R. (1966) *The open society and its enemies,* 5e, Routledge, London 1995.
- Konstytucja RP (1997) *Konstytucja Rzeczypospolitej Polskiej z dnia 2 kwietnia 1997 r.,* Dz.U.RP 1997.78.483.
- Prawo budżetowe (1993) *Ustawa z dnia 5 stycznia 1991r. - Prawo budżetowe (1991 Budgetary law),* Dz.U.RP 1993. 72. 344 (wraz z późniejszymi zmianami).
- Ustawa o rachunkowości (1994) *Ustawa z dnia 29 września 1994r. o rachunkowości (1994 Act on accounting),* Dz.U. R P 1994. 121.591 (wraz z późniejszymi zmianami).
- Ustawa o finansach publicznych (1998) *Ustawa z dnia 26 listopada 1998r. o finansach publicznych (1998 Act on public finance),* Dz.U.RP 1998.155.1014.

A DIFFUSION-CONTINGENCY MODEL FOR GOVERNMENT ACCOUNTING INNOVATIONS

Alan D. Godfrey, Patrick J. Devlin and M. Cherif Merrouche

17.1. Introduction

Chan et al. (1996:10) argue that 'with the exception of Poland, our knowledge about former Soviet Union and former Eastern European countries is meager'. In the same context they suggest that: 'As things stand now, we know relatively little about: (1) how the conversion from totalitarian regimes to democracy has altered governmental accounting systems; (2) how governmental accounting systems have changed when a planned economy is changed to a market economy; (3) whether the supply and demand framework embodied in the contingency models would be applicable in those countries. When more countries are analyzed in CIGAR, we have greater confidence in the generalizability of ideas.'

The original purpose of this paper, therefore, was to respond to the above invitation and attempt to fill a gap in the literature by considering the case of Albania; a Central/Eastern European former Communist country, recently converted from a totalitarian regime to democracy and experiencing, with difficulties, a gradual transition from planned to market economy. This change is profound and includes innovations in government accounting.

In conducting our research we sought to apply recent developments of the contingency model of government accounting innovations (Chan et al., 1996). However, we found that the model, whilst useful in forming a general understanding of the innovations taking place, failed to provide sufficient insight into the organizational processes of innovation. Correspondingly, we synthesized elements of the contingency model with theories of diffusion of innovations (Rogers, 1995) to develop a new hybrid model. Section two of the paper provides a brief description of the contingency and diffusion models. Whilst, in section three, we describe the hybrid model developed from these foundations. In the fourth section, we test out the model by applying it to government accounting innovations in Albania. The final section provides a summary and conclusions of the paper.

17.2. The Contingency Model and Theories of Diffusion of Innovations

Over the last ten years Lüder's Contingency Model (1992, 1994) has been used extensively, particularly by CIGAR scholars, to analyze the possibilities for change and innovations in government accounting. The model attempts to explain why government accounting systems, procedures and practices differ from one country to another and why the speed of innovation differs among nations. At the heart of the model is the

279

A. Bac (ed.), International Comparative Issues in Government Accounting, 279-296.
© 2001 *Kluwer Academic Publishers. Printed in the Netherlands.*

fundamental assumption that innovation decisions involve interplay amongst three major players - the *public at large, politicians,* and *government administrators.*

The model states that three contextual variables - *stimuli, socio-political* factors, and *administrative* factors - are expected to influence two categories of intervening variables: *users* of government accounting information (by changing their expectations about the data they want) and *producers* of information (by changing their behaviour). This complex interaction of contextual and intervening variables influences change, positively or negatively. Whilst change itself is dependent on the impact of implementation barriers (*barriers to change*) that can directly affect the outcome of the innovations process. The Lüder model has been developed further; it has been modified slightly and applied to underdeveloped economies (Godfrey et al., 1996); it has been expanded to include some consideration of the *consequences of innovation in the real world* (Jaruga & Nowak, 1996).

Rogers (1996) identifies, through analyses of diffusion research conducted over the past fifty years, a number of approaches to the study of the diffusion of innovations. In so doing he provides a revised and updated theoretical model of diffusion. In the main, he considers diffusion from the perspective of individuals within society, although he does provide some analysis of factors impacting upon *organisational innovativeness.* A number of internal and external *organisational structural characteristics* are identified that have a bearing on the innovativeness of organizations (ibid:380).

Principally, it is this area of diffusion theory that we seek to develop within the context of the Contingency Model, although aspects of the roles of individuals within the diffusion process are critical, also, to any understanding of accounting innovations - particularly, the roles of internal and external *change agents* and *innovation champions.* Another important set of independent variables that affect the innovation process are the *characteristics of the innovation.* Previously, we have used an analysis of the impact of these particular characteristics in trying to understand the process of government accounting innovation in North Africa (Godfrey et al., 1999).

Rogers divides the innovation process into two phases; the *initiation* phase and the *implementation* phase, and each of these consist of several stages. The revised theoretical model sees diffusion of innovations not as a simple linear communication system, but as an iterative social process, where the uncertainty associated with change is clarified over time through a convergent process of social construction. The following section discusses these issues more fully in developing an integrated theoretical approach to the study of government accounting innovations.

17.3. A Diffusion-Contingency Model

What we have called the Diffusion-Contingency Model (hereafter, the Model) is illustrated in figure 17.1. It is based on the assumption that government accounting innovations in a country are the result of an iterative process whereby the interaction of political, administrative and social actors is conditioned and filtered by the organisational structural variables of the government (as an organization), which in turn affect the government's organisational innovativeness. Decisions to initiate, and to implement, an innovation are further constrained by characteristics of the innovation itself. The Model, therefore, attempts to represent a complex situation where the organisational characteristics of government, which signal the level of innovativeness of the government, intertwine and interplay with characteristics of the innovation itself to determine the success or failure of both the innovation-initiation and the innovation-implementation processes.

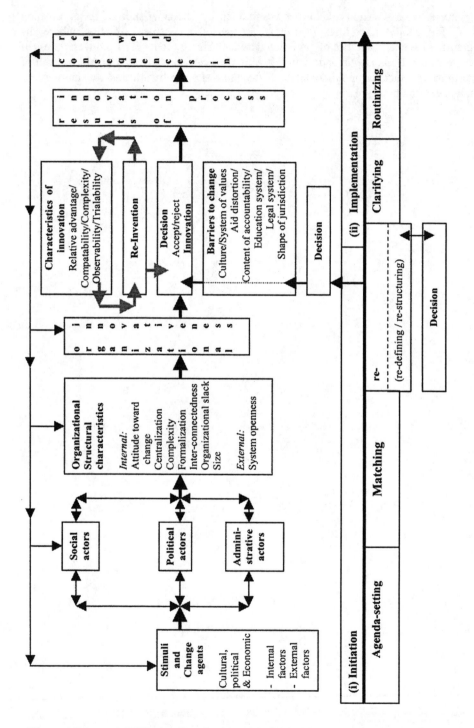

Figure 17.1.:   A Diffusion-Contingency Model for Government Accounting

17.3.1. THE MODEL SET-UP

The Model (lower section of figure 17.1.) provides a timeline sequence of five stages for the innovation process identified by Rogers (1995:391). He divides these sequences into two phases: the *initiation* phase, which contains two stages; and, the *implementation* phase, which contains the remaining three stages. The decision to implement the innovation marks the end of the initiation phase and heralds the commencement of the triple-stage implementation phase.

The Initiation Phase: Agenda-setting

Agenda-setting is an ongoing activity in all organizations. It is also the first stage of the innovation initiation phase of the diffusion process. Within this context, it comes into operation when organisational needs and problems are defined and solutions to them are sought. It combines both the identification and ranking of organisational requirements and the search, of both the external and internal environment, for potential innovations that might satisfy these needs and/or solve problems. Alternatively, the awareness of an innovation, rather than the need to solve a particular problem, may provide the catalyst. The awareness of an innovation, obtained through regular scrutiny of the environment, may prompt concerns about organisational performance and therefore trigger the start of the particular innovation process.

At the agenda-setting stage, the Model identifies the impact of internal and external stimuli and the impact of change agents (individuals who influence innovation-decisions in a direction deemed desirable by a change policy). In the case of many countries, particularly underdeveloped and transitional economies, international organizations can have a major impact, both directly and indirectly, on setting the agenda for innovation (Godfrey et al., 1996:1999). Agencies, such as the International Monetary Fund (IMF), the World Bank and other aid donors, can act directly as change agents (Husain, 1993). Structural Adjustment Policies promoted by the IMF act as a direct stimulus to social, economic and political change and innovation in many countries.

Also, in underdeveloped and transitional economies a more direct impact can be observed where international organizations require particular accounting innovations to be effected as a sine qua non of assistance being provided/funded. Similar effects can be observed also through the influence of competing, rather than complementary, aid/assistance programmes that include the transfer of expertise, technologies and/or systems. This can lead to severe problems of complexity where hybrid accounting systems can result from the impact of such aid distortion. Correspondingly, the creation of customized accounting systems that take more account of local circumstances and needs can be hindered (Godfrey et al., 1996:201). Indirectly, stimuli and change agent effects may be unrelated to aid or assistance programmes but conditioned by the culture, history (including colonial legacies see Godfrey et al., 1996, 1999) and openness of particular economies.

The Initiation Phase: Matching

The second stage in the initiation phase of the diffusion of innovations is *matching*, where an organisational problem is aligned carefully with an innovation; or alternatively, an innovation is perceived as a specific improvement to existing practice. Accordingly, this process involves the testing of the ability of the innovation to solve the organisational problem. For example, alternative international government accounting practices and systems may be considered as part of the agenda-setting stage of the initiation phase of the innovation process. However, only if a particular accounting innovation, which is planned to address the deficiencies of the existing practice or system, is perceived by the stakeholders of the organization to be a solution that matches the problems identified will the innovation process move into the implementation phase.

The two stages of agenda-setting and matching represent the initiation phase, at the end of which the decision will be taken either to proceed with implementation or to reject the innovation. Such innovation decisions can be of three types: optional, which are choices to adopt or reject an innovation made by individuals independently of other individuals' decisions; collective, which are decisions made by consensus; and, authority, which are decisions made by a relatively few individuals within a system who have power, status, or technical expertise (Rogers, 1995:29). Innovation decisions considered in this paper are clearly of the authority type.

The decision to adopt separates the two major phases of the whole innovation process. The second phase, implementation, involves three stages; re-invention (redefining/ re-structuring), clarifying, and routinizing.

The Implementation Phase: Re-invention

Rogers' Diffusion Theory identifies *Redefining/Restructuring (Re-Invention* or modification of the innovation, the organization, or both, to ensure a better fit) as the first stage of the implementation phase of the innovation process. We have some reservations with this proposition. Our view is that the implementation decision occurs at some point towards the end of the re-invention stage and not at the end of the matching phase. In fact, re-invention is an implicit part of the matching stage, where the innovation may be adjusted (redefined) and/or the organization altered (restructured) to allow full implementation of the innovation to take place. These processes help remove some of the uncertainty (technical, financial or social) that can present problems for the innovation process.

In other words, when the matching stage is near completion and the impact of the characteristics of the particular innovation and any barriers to change have been taken into account, some degree of re-invention may take place in order to reduce uncertainty and consequently facilitate acceptance rather than rejection of the innovation. This point is developed further below, where consideration is given to the impact of the characteristics of innovations on the decision process.

The Implementation Phase: Clarifying

Clarifying is the stage where, through wider use within the organization, much of the associated uncertainty surrounding the innovation is reduced and people begin to understand it more fully. The social interaction, both formal and informal, which takes place amongst stakeholders of the organization through the innovation being discussed and debated widely allows its meaning to be (socially) constructed over time.

The Implementation Phase: Routinizing
Routinizing is where the innovation loses its separate identity as it becomes incorporated into the regular activities of the organization. At this point, in the minds of the members of the organization the innovation changes its identity from 'new' to 'routine'. Accordingly, it is no longer considered to be an innovation and this marks the end of the innovation process.

17.3.2. ORGANIZATIONAL STRUCTURAL CHARACTERISTICS

At all stages in the innovation process internal and external organisational characteristics, as independent variables, impact on and determine the dependent variable, the level of innovativeness of the organization. If we define government as an organization (Rogers, 1995:5) then we can consider these organisational structural characteristics shown in figure 17.1.

Attitude towards change is somewhat self-explanatory in terms of both the leader(s) and the organization. Clearly, if attitude towards change is positive then organisational innovativeness will tend to be high. Interestingly, there may be barriers to change if the leader(s) and the organization display opposite attitudes. In other words, the leader(s) may be positive towards change but the organization, if negative, may stifle such innovative zeal, and vice versa. In underdeveloped and transition economies, political leaders may, for sound economic reasons, feel under pressure to agree to innovations suggested (or promoted) by international agencies such as the IMF and the World Bank. However, the successful implementation of such innovations may be more dependent upon the attitude to change of the government organization itself.

Normally, *centralization* (the degree to which power and control in a system are concentrated in the hands of relatively few individuals) is negatively associated with innovativeness. This occurs where organisational power is controlled by a small group of leaders, who are distanced from operational issues, and therefore are unlikely to generate many new ideas. However, in such organizations centralization may encourage the implementation of innovations, once the innovation-decision is made.

Complexity (the degree to which an organization's members possess a relatively high level of knowledge and expertise) is similar to the administrative structural variable of the contingency model. The organization members' range of occupational expertise and professionalism as expressed by formal training usually measure the level of complexity. High levels of complexity will have a positive effect on the innovativeness of the organization, as staff at all levels in the organization will tend to seek ways of overcoming problems and improving processes and procedures. Also, they will, as part of their ongoing professionalism, tend to scan the internal and external environment for potential innovations. In organizations exhibiting a low level of complexity the initiation, and more particularly the implementation, of innovation will be much more difficult. Indeed, the complexity of the innovation itself when combined with the complexity of the organization may generate the need to modify (re-invent) the innovation. If the potential innovation is highly complex, then it may have to be simplified before it can be introduced into an organization exhibiting a low level of complexity.

High *formalization* (the degree to which an organization emphasizes following rules and procedures in the role performance of its members) tends to have a negative impact on the consideration of innovations by members, but can have a positive effect on the implementation of innovations. A high degree of formalization appears compatible with a highly centralized organization and, not surprisingly, the effects are similar.

A high level of *interconnectedness* (the degree to which the units in a social system are linked by interpersonal networks) among the members of an organization will allow new ideas to circulate more freely. *Organisational slack* (the degree to which uncommitted resources are available to an organization) has a positive impact on organisational innovativeness in that it allows resources to be used to promote and develop innovations.

Consistently, the *size* of an organization has been found to be positively related to its innovativeness. However, Rogers points out that 'size is probably a surrogate measure of several dimensions that lead to innovation: Total resources, slack resources, technical expertise of employees, organisational structure, and so on' (1995:379).

System openness (the degree to which the members of a system are linked to other individuals who are external to the system) is identified by Rogers (ibid:377) as an external characteristic of the organization. A strong link would appear to exist between the level of system openness and the impact of external stimuli and change agents. Agenda setting and matching will be assisted through greater awareness of a wider range of innovative solutions that will be observed by an open, compared to a closed, organization.

17.3.3. CHARACTERISTICS OF INNOVATIONS

As we identified previously (Godfrey et al., 1999), the characteristics of innovations can have an important impact on the processes of initiation and implementation. These characteristics are relative advantage, compatibility, complexity, observability and trialability. Any assessment of *relative advantage* (the degree to which an innovation is perceived as better than the idea it supersedes) is influenced by economic factors; perceptions of social status; the effects of incentives; and, mandates for adoption. Obviously, economic factors drive many innovations, including accounting system change. In this context it may be that a country's social status will be an important trigger driving change, particularly at the *agenda-setting* and *matching* stages.

The current movement by many countries world-wide to change their government accounting systems to an accrual (commercial) accounting basis may, in some cases, be explained partly by the perceived (higher) social status of so doing. This desire for higher status may influence inappropriate change for some countries which have obvious difficulties in dealing with their existing accounting systems due to the, sometimes acute, shortage of technical skills and experience amongst the administrative cadre (weak administrative structural variables/low organisational complexity). The outcome of such innovation is likely to be negative unless considerable investment is made in the training and development of the administrative cadre. It could be argued that the IMF, the World Bank, the United Nations, and other international agencies, offer countries both incentives and, in some cases, mandates for change such as innovations in national accounting systems. Indeed, this argument could be extended to cover the impact of international and national accounting standard setting bodies, capital markets, economic communities such as the European Community, on commercial and public sector accounting systems, practices and procedures.

Compatibility (the degree to which an innovation is perceived as consistent with the existing values, past experiences, and needs of potential adopters) and *complexity* (the degree to which an innovation is perceived as relatively difficult to understand and use) have important roles to play at the *matching* and *re-invention* stages of the initiation and implementation processes respectively. As part of the matching process, potential innovations will be examined for their ability to solve the particular problem(s) identified at the *agenda-setting* stage. This assessment of the innovation's potential will be conditioned by perceptions of its ability to fit within the existing organisational values, experiences and needs set. These in turn will be reflections of the organisational structural variables in play at the time of the assessment.

If a positive decision is made to implement the innovation, compatibility and complexity will have further roles to play in the processes of *re-invention (redefining* and *restructuring)*. As identified above, most innovations will not provide a perfect fit for the implementing organization. In such situations, the innovation may be changed, and/or the organization itself restructured, to maximize the chances of a successful implementation. For example, a new accounting system may have to be customized to fit well within a new organization or cultural environment. Similarly, the organization itself may be adjusted to ensure the innovation is successfully implemented. For example, new technology may be introduced and/or a technical department may be established to provide training and trouble-shooting skills to facilitate the smooth introduction of the new accounting system.

Observability (the degree to which the results of an innovation are visible to others) and *trialability* (the degree to which an innovation may be experimented with on a limited basis) are likely to have a greater impact at the agenda setting and matching stages of the initiation sub-process. As was the case in both East Africa and North Africa (Godfrey et al., 1996, 1999) a close regional structural variable may allow both of these characteristics to be evidenced within neighbouring countries.

The cumulative impact of these characteristics of innovations can be either positive or negative, or it may result in re-invention of the innovation. This re-invention may involve an iterative loop where the innovation is adjusted and redefined in order to better fit the organization - or indeed the organization restructured to better implement the innovation (redefining and restructuring). This iterative process may allow the impact of some of the negative characteristics to change to a neutral, or positive, status. It may allow, also, some barriers to change to be overcome.

In summary, the Model operates in the following manner. Social, political and administrative actors interact as stakeholders of the government organization in seeking innovative solutions to perceived government accounting problems. Such interaction, which may be prompted in part by internal or external stimuli or change agents, is conditioned both by the internal and external organisational characteristics of the government, and by the characteristics of the innovation itself. The government's ability to innovate will be a function of its level of organisational innovativeness. In an open, decentralized and complex government organization the level of innovativeness will be high. However, the ultimate decision to initiate and implement an innovation will be affected by the impact of the characteristics of the innovation itself. If the relative advantage and compatibility characteristics of the innovation are positive, whilst its complexity is capable either of application or re-invention, then such innovation will be more likely to be successfully implemented, particularly if its application has been trialed and observed elsewhere.

17.4. Application of the Model to Government Accounting Innovations in Albania

Like many other countries, Albania is in a state of transition following the collapse of Communism. Having been subjected to more than forty years of authoritarian rule, it faces a formidable task. This task, arguably, is more formidable than that facing any other country in Europe: Albania was the most isolated of all the countries of Central and Eastern Europe; it is Europe's least developed country. Clearly, there are very many dimensions to the transition being attempted in Albania. In this section of the paper we apply the Model to innovations taking place in central and local government accounting in Albania. In particular, we will focus on the major government accounting reforms that are taking place which, at the central government level, will require ministries to produce accounts in line with a new (French influenced) accounting plan. In local government, similar reforms are taking place.

At the agenda-setting and matching stages of this innovation process in Albania, problems were identified regarding the appropriateness and applicability of the old accounting plan in delivering useful information for both public and private sectors within the nascent democratic economy. External stimuli were in operation, including the influence of international agencies acting in the role of change agents; examples might include the IMF's structural adjustment programme and World Bank funded programmes like, for example, civil service reform. Internally, political actors, partly in response to these external stimuli, sought new systems (including accounting systems) to facilitate the transition from a centrally planned economy to a market based system. Other external stimuli, identified as regional structural variables (Godfrey et al., 1996:199), that are likely to have influenced the mindsets of the internal political actors were the experiences of other former socialist states in similar transition scenarios. Thus, the matching process was in action with the search for innovations that might alleviate problems identified with the continuing use of the old accounting plan.

One common feature found in the former European socialist states is the central role played by the Ministry of Finance (MOF) in relation to all aspects of accounting systems, regulation, and control. Within the Albanian process of accounting innovation, the MOF performed the role of innovation champion and opinion leader. Rogers (1995:398) finds that the roles of innovation champions and opinion leaders can be critical throughout the whole process of innovation. Howell and Higgins (1990, quoted in Rogers, 1995) describe the former as charismatic individuals who throw their weight behind the innovation, thus overcoming the indifference or resistance that a new idea often provokes in an organization. The latter are described as individuals who lead in influencing others' opinions about innovations.

Whilst these definitions apply to individuals, it is clear that to understand more fully the innovation process in government (as an organization), it is necessary to interpret these functions as both organisational unit roles and individual roles. Correspondingly, the characteristics of opinion leaders (individuals) that are identified by Rogers (1995:293) (*external communication, accessibility, socio-economic status, and innovativeness*) must apply also to organisational units that perform similar roles. The primacy of the MOF within the government organization, especially in former socialist economies, provides equivalent characteristics such as organisational power (in place of socio-economic status for individuals), accessibility (particularly, access to all other organisational subunits of the government organization, and other organizations outwith government), external communication (particularly, through its macroeconomic management links with international agencies, and the world community), and, its own innovativeness (this may be a constraint in the case of former socialist economies as the Socialist Accounting Plan tended to dominate with, historically, little innovation taking place - clearly, this was the case in the isolated and autarkic Albania described below).

17.4.1.ORGANIZATIONAL CHARACTERISTICS OF THE ALBANIAN GOVERN-MENT

In the Model, the positive impact of such stimuli and change agents on political, administrative and social actors is conditioned and filtered by the level of organisational innovativeness of the government organization. This in turn is determined by the internal and external structural characteristics of the government organization. The main external characteristic is system openness, whilst the internal characteristics are: attitude towards change, centralization, complexity, formalization, inter-connectedness, organisational slack, and size.

System Openness
For much of its history, Albania has remained one of the worlds most isolated, closed and repressed countries. Images of Albania are grim and bleak and tend to be formed from what is known of the Communist regime of the post-war years. It is important to recognize, however, that Albania's isolation (and repression) predates this period. Indeed, it is no exaggeration to suggest that the Albanian people have been set apart from the rest of the world almost since the outset.

It is now generally accepted that by the seventh century BC certain tribes sharing a common Illyrian language and culture had settled in the territory now known as Albania (Vickers, 1995:1). The Illyrians were an ancient Balkan people and it would appear that all Illyrian tribes other than those in Albania disappeared during the Dark Ages. Thus, only in Albania did a separate identity and language remain intact. Nevertheless, the Albanian State only came into being at the end of 1912 – and it took until 1920 before it was recognized by the League of Nations. That is, the Albanians became the last Balkan nation to achieve their independence. Prior to that time, this region of the Balkan Peninsula had been subject to constant occupation by various forces; the most important of which was the Ottoman occupation that lasted for five hundred years from around the beginning of the fifteenth century.

Resistance to the Ottomans proved to be very costly for Albania. By the end of the fifteenth century (most of which had been spent fighting), the population was seriously reduced, the economy was all but destroyed, and the cities went into rapid decline. In short, what is now known as Albania became a decaying and isolated backwater of the Ottoman Empire (Vickers, 1995:10). Ottoman occupation had an equally profound effect. During the seventeenth and eighteenth centuries, almost two-thirds of the population converted to Islam (thereby providing them with the opportunity to rise to high office). By adopting the Islamic faith, an Albanian was automatically classified a Turk. This refusal to recognize the Albanians as a separate people proved to be a major obstacle to their cultural advancement - use of the Albanian language was not allowed in schools; a standard alphabet was not devised; books in Albanian were virtually non-existent. As a result, the rise of an Albanian national consciousness was delayed. A national movement did not start until the late 1870s, and it took a further forty years before Albania's frontiers were finally settled.

Even then, Albania's repression continued. Various occupations occurred during both the inter-war years and the Second World War before a Communist government seized control in 1944 and remained in power until 1990. During that time, the economy was reorganized along strict Stalinist lines. Albanian economic strategy represented a literal application of that set out in Stalin's last published work: Economic Problems of Socialism in the USSR. The formulations in the book were never implemented as policy in the USSR (Schnytzer, 1982:2). At different times, support was provided from Yugoslavia, the Soviet Union and China - the Communist government turning away from each in turn until by the end of the 1970s it implemented a policy of strict autarky, the result of which was to bring about economic ruin.

This brief history is necessary to explain the complete lack of openness of the Albanian system until very recently. It is only from 1990 that the economy has been gradually opened up to external influences and stimuli. That said, it is evident that Albanian society generally, including its political and administrative actors, has a strong desire to continue developing its nascent open, democratic system. Within the Model, therefore, the system openness variable is positive.

Attitude towards Change
Similarly to the degree of openness, the attitude towards change in Albania is positive - not the least because of the reality of former repression for the great majority of Albanians. However, there may be a tension in relation to attitude towards change in the government organization. It may be that the political leaders wish to implement change and correspondingly display a positive attitude towards innovations. However, the organization itself, because of the negative impact of other internal characteristics of the government organization, may inhibit the successful implementation of such innovations.

Centralization
Albania's government organization exhibits a high degree of centralization - perhaps unsurprisingly considering the impact of the forty-seven years of Communist dictatorship, which perhaps was more repressive and damaging in terms of institutional effectiveness and economic and social welfare than any other regime in Eastern Europe (Library of Congress, 1996).

Centralization was an essential feature of the old accounting plan. The former accounting plan was based upon the Russian model that was tweaked slightly by Albanian academics. Correspondingly, it was tied firmly to state central planning and was designed to maximize production with needs being satisfied using social criteria. It was resource constrained in that output was limited by the availability of resources. Prices and wages were set centrally and there were no associated inflation or exchange rate problems to contend with. The MOF and the Central (State) Bank controlled the uniform accounting system. This historically high level of centralization within the Albanian government organization continues to the present and, correspondingly, it may have a negative impact on the government's innovativeness.

Complexity
The implications of the former system were similar to those identified by Krzywda et al. (1995) in relation to Poland - that is accounting was perceived simply as a tool in exercising control. Within such a system, the role of the 'accountant' was that of a technician with corresponding low skill requirements and low esteem. As Bailey points out (1988:15), education and training processes were mechanistic, bureaucratic and conservative, providing limited skills and discouraging innovation. 'The command model for the management of the national economy does not encourage the development of the information function of accounting and leads to a decline in accounting' (ibid:16). Money management, accounts analysis and performance evaluation were conducted by the state bank. As a result, financial analysis and cost analysis were not developed as accounting tools. Power within such a system resided with the enterprises' chief economists, state bankers, state auditors and ministry officials. This low level of complexity within the government accounting cadre, equivalent to a weak administrative structural variable in the Contingency Model, is likely to have a negative correlation to the government's organisational innovativeness.

Formalization
Under the previous Communist regime, administrative actors were required to be extremely passive and a culture developed where considerable attention was devoted to avoiding both making mistakes and taking responsibility. Following orders and procedures was a non-negotiable requirement in such a system. Although social actors continue to demand increasing decentralization, political and social instability has delayed meaningful implementation. Accordingly, the government organization is still highly centralized and the level of formalization is high. High formalization, therefore, has a negative effect on the initiation of new ideas, however, it may assist in the implementation of innovations.

Inter-connectedness
Probably, because of the reality of existence within the former repressive regime, Albanian society - and its various organizations, including government - exhibits an extremely high level of informal inter-connectedness. The organisational inefficiency generated by the former repression and autarky in Albania meant that in order to get anything done it was essential to use personal contact networks. Such arrangements effectively bypassed the formal system and encouraged the social interaction of ordinary citizens in forming informal extended families and networks. This high level of inter-connectedness provides a positive counter effect on organisational innovativeness where, even if the formal organization struggles to effect change, the informal organization - if supportive - may assist the innovation process.

Organisational Slack
It is highly likely that there is considerable slack available within the government organization as organisational inefficiencies are still present. The resources represented by such organisational slack will be available to support aspects of both the initiation and implementation of innovations. Ceteris paribus, the existence of organisational slack will have a positive effect on governmental innovativeness. However, the other characteristics in Albanian government organization, such as high centralization and formalization, combined with low complexity, may have counter-balancing effects on this normally positive variable.

Table 17.1. summarizes the combined impact of these internal and external organisational characteristics - as independent variables - on the organisational innovativeness of the Albanian government organization - the dependent variable. The internal structural characteristic, size, has been ignored in this analysis as it is assumed to operate as a surrogate for other characteristics already described. If it is assumed that each independent variable has an equal impact on the organisational innovativeness of government, then the innovativeness of the government organization in Albania appears to be marginally positive.

Organizational Characteristic	Effect on Innovativeness
System openness	+
Attitude towards change	+
Centralization	-
Complexity	-
Formalization	-
Inter-connectedness	+
Organizational slack	+
overall effect	**4 positive/3 negative**
Conclusion: Government organizational innovativeness is marginally positive	

Table 17.1.: The Impact of Organizational Characteristics on the
               Innovativeness of the Government Organization in Albania

17.4.2. THE CHANGES IN ACCOUNTING RELATED TO THE BACKGROUND

Within this marginally positive innovative environment, the agenda was set for the introduction of a new national accounting plan to encompass both private and government sectors. In the early years of transition (the early 1990s), the MOF sought assistance in carrying out its role of innovation champion for this accounting change process. A leading academic was seconded to the Ministry to assist with the change process. Correspondingly, he took on the dual roles of opinion leader and innovation champion. In private discussions with the authors he very graphically described his predicament. He was faced with finding an innovative solution to the problems of the old accounting plan (the agenda setting and matching processes). He was never allowed to leave Albania to study abroad during the previous forty-seven years of Communist rule. Until recently, he was unable to study any accounting systems other than the socialist accounting plan.

He faced a very steep learning curve. However, he had learned to speak French and, not surprisingly, he soon developed an interest in the French Plan Comptable as a potential innovation to solve his problems. Such cultural random variables - acting as stimuli - have been observed elsewhere. In Romania, a similar accounting system transition conundrum existed and, partly because historically the elite of Romanian society always looked towards France as the center of culture and economics, a new French-based accounting plan was developed. This was in contrast to Russia, where the former Russian Plan was redefined and adjusted to meet new economic requirements (Richard, 1995:316-7).

Under the accounting law of 1993, the decision to introduce a new French-based national accounting plan was taken by the Albanian government. Under the same Act, some changes in the government organization (re-invention) took place. In 1993, a National Accounting Council (NAC) was established 'to effect the normalization of accounting in accordance with the dispositions of the present law as well as to ensure continuous methodological guidance' (Accounting Law, No. 7661, 1993: Chapter VI, translated). Under its terms of reference, the NAC reported to the Minister of Finance and was required to provide recommendations: for amendments to the legislation, for training of accounting specialists, for solutions to problems that might arise on implementation of the new accounting system.

A sister Act, the Law on Commercial Enterprises (1992), introduced the new national accounting plan for commercial enterprises and the 1993 Act signalled the intention of extending the new accounting system, subsequently, to government accounting. At the same time, further government organisational reconstruction took place with the setting up of an accounting department within the MOF. The academic seconded to the MOF as innovation champion was elected chairman of the NAC. He arranged for an officer of the accounting department (MOF), who specialized in public sector accounting, to undertake a one-year training programme in France. The officer returned with a considerable amount of materials, which were translated from French into Albanian. This extremely informal process constituted the beginnings of the development of the new government accounting plan in Albania.

Before a decision to accept or reject this new plan was taken, consideration was given (albeit indirectly) to the characteristics of this innovation. Table 17.2. summarizes the impact of these characteristics on this decision. Relative advantage was clearly positive. Part of the reason for adopting a French-based model may have lain in the need to reduce technical uncertainty in the sense that the French chart at least had some similarities to the old chart of accounts. There may have been, also, an element of risk management involved in terms of reducing both financial and social uncertainty. To develop a completely new national accounting system from a zero base would be too resource-expensive for the poorest country in Europe, and unacceptable in terms of both financial and social costs. Correspondingly, the adoption of a French accounting chart-based innovation, rather than an Anglo-Saxon model, provided a less risky solution to what, culturally and historically, is a heavily risk-averse society. Similarly, the new system provided compatibility (other than the complexity of the model when applied to the Albanian situation) for much the same reasons. Other positive characteristics were observability and trialability. Prior to this time, several other transition economies, for example Romania and Bulgaria, had adopted a French-based solution. Through the regional structural variable, this provided the opportunity for observation and, in a sense, trialability - at least at a distance.

Characteristic of Innovation	Effect on rate of adoption
Relative advantage	+
Compatibility	+
Complexity	-
Observability	+
Trialability	+
Overall effect	**4 positive/ 1 negative**
Conclusion: The rate of adoption of the innovation should be positive. Indeed, through the iterative processes of re-invention, redefinition, and restructuring, even the negative characteristic may be changed to positive - for example, through simplifying the innovation, implementation might be made easier within a low complexity organization.	

Table 17.2.: The Impact of Characteristics of Innovation on the Rate of
             Adoption of Government Accounting Innovations in Albania

However, the complexity of the French Plan was a problem, particularly when applied both to the very simple economy of Albania and to the potential problems of implementation by a weak and poorly trained accounting cadre. This negative variable generated the need for re-invention and redefinition. An iterative process came into play whereby the new accounting plan was subject to considerable simplification, thereby weakening the negative impact of the complexity characteristic and, perhaps, reducing the impact of some of the other barriers to change.

In summary, therefore, applying the Model has shown that government accounting innovation in Albania has progressed successfully through the initiation phase of agenda setting and matching. This process has been facilitated considerably by the operations of an innovation champion and opinion leader - the chairman of the NAC. At the point of decision to implement, some re-invention took place in the form of both redefinition - through simplifying the plan considerably - and restructuring, with the establishment of the NAC and the accounting department within the MOF. At present the new system is at the important clarifying stage of the implementation phase. It has not yet reached the routinizing stage, the end of the innovation process, where the new government accounting system is accepted fully as part of normal procedures within the government organization and, therefore, no longer represents an innovation.

17.5. Summary and Conclusions

The paper has attempted to develop a new hybrid diffusion-contingency model of government accounting innovations and to test it through analyzing its application to government accounting innovations in Albania. The Model brings together elements of contingency and diffusion theories to provide a better insight into the organisational, as well as socio-political and economic, factors affecting the innovation process.

The Model attempts to mirror, more accurately, the complex interplay of many variables on the innovation processes of initiation and implementation, which have been overlooked in previous studies. Independent variables, such as the internal and external characteristics of the government organization, affect the level of innovativeness of government, consequently impacting upon the positive stimuli emanating both from internal and external change agents and the actions of political, social and administrative actors. Further independent variables - the characteristics of the innovation itself, as well as other potential barriers to change - impact, through an iterative process of re-invention (redefinition and restructuring), on the decision to adopt or reject the innovation. Finally, the important processes of clarification and routinization involve an agreed social construction of the innovation which assists in the 'new' becoming the 'routine', and, therefore, accepted as no longer representing an innovation.

When the Model is applied to the introduction of the new French-based government accounting plan in Albania, it is observed that the level of innovativeness of the Albanian government organization is marginally positive. The proactive role of the innovation champion and opinion leader assisted the whole process of initiation through setting the agenda and matching, effectively, the new system to the perceived problems of the old. This, combined with the markedly positive characteristics of the new system itself - particularly after restructuring the government organization and redefining the innovation through simplifying the system to better fit the Albanian situation, allowed the implementation to progress. The present position is that the innovation process is at the clarifying stage of the implementation phase. This can be a critical stage, where the new government accounting system has little meaning within the government system. Through social interaction, administrative actors in particular, but also political and social actors as stakeholders of the government organization, gradually gain a common understanding of the new system. This social construction is important in allaying uncertainties and answering questions. Why has the old system been changed? How does the new one work? How will it affect me? Will I be able to cope with the change? The answers to such questions will be very important in the Albanian context where one barrier to change, the culture under the old regime, meant that one simply awaited orders. The great danger is that, if this culture still prevails within sections of the government organization, and if adequate training and staff development are not provided, the innovation may not be clarified and routinized as officers may be 'still awaiting orders'!

References

- Accounting Law No. 7661 (1993) Tirana, Albania: Ministry of Finance (translated).
- Bailey, D.T. (1988) *Accounting in Socialist Countries*, Routledge, London.
- Chan et al. (1996) Modeling Governmental Accounting Innovations: An Assessment and Future Research Directions, *Research in Government and Nonprofit Accounting*, Vol. 9, J.L. Chan (eds.), JAI Press, Greenwich, CT, 1-19.
- Godfrey et al. (1996) Governmental Accounting in Kenya, Tanzania, and Uganda, *Research in Government and Nonprofit Accounting*, Vol. 9, J.L. Chan (eds.), JAI Press, Greenwich, CT, 193-208.
- Godfrey et al. (1999) A Comparative Analysis of the Evolution of Local Government Accounting in Algeria and Morocco, *Research in Government and Nonprofit Accounting*, Vol. 10, P. A. Copley (eds.), JAI Press, Greenwich, CT, 201-234.
- Husain, I. (1993) A Comment on the IMF, the World Bank and Africa's Adjustment and External Debt Problems: Unofficial View, *World Development,* Vol. 21, No. 12, Pergamon, Oxford, 2055-2058.
- Jaruga, A., and Nowak, W.A. (1996) Toward a General Model of Public Sector Accounting Innovations, *Research in Government and Nonprofit Accounting*, Vol. 9, J.L. Chan (eds.), JAI Press, Greenwich, CT, 21-31.
- Krzywda et al. (1995). 'A Theory of European Accounting Development Applied to Accounting Change in Contemporary Poland'. *The European Accounting Review*, Vol. 4:4, A. Loft, A. Jorissen and P. Walton (eds.), Chapman and Hall, London, 625-657.
- Law on Commercial Enterprises No. 7638 (1992) Tirana, Albania: Ministry of Finance (translated).
- Library of Congress, Federal Research Division (1996) *Albania: A Country Study*, Web publication, http://lcweb2.loc.gov:8080/country-studies, Washington DC.
- Luder, K.G. (1992) A Contingency Model of Governmental Accounting Innovations in the Political-Administrative Environment, *Research in Government and Nonprofit Accounting*, Vol. 7, J.L. Chan (eds.), JAI Press, Greenwich, CT, 99-127.
- Luder, K.G. (1994) The Contingency Model Reconsidered: Experiences from Italy, Japan and Spain, *Perspectives on Performance Measurement and Public Sector Accounting*, E. Buschor and K. Schedler (eds.), Haupt, Berns, 1-15.
- Richard, J. (1995) The Evolution if the Romanian and Russian Accounting Charts after the Collapse of the Communist System, *The European Accounting Review*, Vol. 4:2, A. Loft, A. Jorissen and P. Walton (eds.), Chapman and Hall, London, 305-322.
- Rogers, E.M. (1995) *Diffusion of Innovations,* 4th ed., The Free Press, New York.
- Rogers, M. (1995) *Public Sector Accounting*, Stanley Thornes (Publishers) Ltd, Cheltenham.
- Schnytzer, A. (1982) *Stalinist Economic Strategy in Practice: The Case of Albania*, Oxford University Press, Oxford.
- Vickers, (1995) *The Albanians: A Modern History*, I.B. Taurus & Co Ltd, London.

THE EFFECTS OF REFORM ON CHINA'S PUBLIC BUDGETING AND ACCOUNTING SYSTEM

James L. Chan, Cong Shuhai and Zhao Jianyong

18.1. Introduction

Government accounting in the West does not have an exact counterpart in China. After the People's Republic of China (PRC) was established in 1949, 'government accounting', being associated with the previous regime, with its Western capitalist orientation, was replaced by socialist 'budget accounting'. The latter, with its explicit recognition of the vital role of the government budget in a planned economy, has been in use in China for almost fifty years. During its first three decades, the PRC had a highly centralized system, with the national government monopolizing virtually all aspects of the economy and the public sector. However, since 1978 market reform has gradually reduced the primary role of the state (including state owned enterprises) as the producer of goods and services. More recently, the central government has transferred some taxing authority and service responsibility to provincial and local governments.

These economic and institutional reform measures have affected virtually every aspect of the Chinese public sector economics and finance, including budget policy and accounting standards. This paper extends a series of papers that have examined the history of Chinese government accounting (Chan, 1995), new budget law (Chan, 1996), governance (Chan, 1997), and offbudget resources (Chan, 1998). Its primary purpose is to explore the relationship between economic and institutional reform and China's budget policy and accounting standards, while incorporating the most recent developments.

Section 18.2. will describe the reform measures, with an emphasis on their effects on government functions. Sections 18.3. and 18.4. will analyze how the changes in government functions have affected budget policies and accounting standards. The final section will argue that the future success of reform in China will depend on the development of the institutional infrastructure that delineates and enforces accountability.

18.2. Economic and Institutional Reform in China

Reform in China has radically altered the relationship between the government and the rest of the economy as well as the rules of the game (Schell and Shambaugh, 1998). A command economy that relied on allocations from the top has been gradually replaced by a competitive market economy mediated by exchanges. Direct state control of business enterprises is being replaced or at least supplemented by incentive contracts, resulting in a greater autonomy in decision making and management at the enterprise

A. Bac (ed.), International Comparative Issues in Government Accounting, 297-314.

level. While most public attention has focused on the emergence of a robust private sector in China, the restructuring of the public sector is no less remarkable. Financial burden and service responsibility have shifted from the central government to provincial and local governments, thus profoundly changing the dynamics of domestic economy and politics. In this section, we will focus on the changing functions of government in China.

18.2.1. FROM HIERARCHY TO AN 'ONION'

In an earlier paper (Chan, 1996), one of us has argued that the governance structure of China was changing from a hierarchy to one resembling an onion. Certainly the hierarchy still characterizes the formal structure. In a constitutional and political sense, the Chinese Communist Party (CCP) reigns supreme in policy making in China. The governmental structure itself is hierarchical. The Central Government ranks above provincial and local governments. At least constitutionally, the People's Congress oversees the executive branch and is increasingly assertive. The executive branch is organized as a hierarchy of administrative units. It is worth noting that an administrative unit can be very powerful by virtue of its authority to own or regulate state owned enterprises (SOEs) in a particular industry (e.g. transportation) or service institutions in a particular field (e.g. higher education). In the finance area, the State Planning Commission is extremely powerful in determining the basic direction of economic policies and approving major construction projects. In day to day operations, the Ministry of Finance oversees an extensive network of finance bureaus all over China. In the Chinese system, public finance agencies retain a remarkable degree of independence from the line agencies, which receive their appropriations from the finance bureau at the same level of government.

While the hierarchical arrangement still applies to the administrative units at the core of government, it no longer adequately describes the emerging realignment of social, economic and political institutions in China. This realignment may be best described as changing from a hierarchy to concentric circles like rings of an onion. The administrative units and the underlying Communist party policy-making structure will continue to function as a command center for governing China. However they are encircled by several organizational layers. The inner-most layer consists of public enterprises and institutions wholly owned by the state and directly controlled through administrative directives. The next outer layer consists of the quasi-public enterprises and institutions partially owned by the state. Under the new governance structure, profit or return on investment has begun to replace procedural control. Management is given a higher degree of discretion in running these entities and is free from frequent reporting requirements imposed on administrative units by accounting rules. Here we reach the outer parameter of what may be properly called the public sector. In the outer rim are private sector business and households whose economic conduct is regulated by law and contracts.

18.2.2. CHANGES IN GOVERNMENT FUNCTIONS

China is building a socialist market economy on the foundation of an orthodox socialist economy. Public ownership used to dominate the entire national economy, producing most of the goods and services. Social order was highly regimented. The social and economic functions of government are joined together. The economy as a whole may be characterized as 'government owned and government operated' (GOGO). State owned enterprises, being the extensions of government ministries, assumed the 'cradle to grave' caring of their employees, thus performing many social welfare functions of the state. It was hardly possible to differentiate the political, social welfare and economic functions of the state. In keeping with the dominant role of the state, the guiding principle of Chinese public finance for decades was 'unified expenditures and revenues'. This means the central government exercised a virtual monopoly over revenues and allocated budgetary resources to provincial and local governments (Wong, Heady and Woo, 1995).

That has changed under the unique system of socialist market economy with Chinese characteristics. China is attempting to retain the egalitarian features of socialism and introduce a competitive capitalist market economy (Naughton, 1998). It recognizes that all governments retain the ultimate responsibility for the people's general welfare. However, as a departure from the orthodox socialist system, the Chinese government has turned to market system for solving the nation's economic problems. The government retains the macro regulatory function, and refrains from direct control of micro economic activities at the enterprise level. The hope is that a market economy operating under state guidance and indirect control would satisfy the socialist ideals and take advantage of capitalist incentives (Cong, 1998).

China has pragmatically and gradually separated business from politics, and ownership from management. The CCP intervenes less frequently and forcefully in the operations of state owned business enterprises. While the state retains ownership of public property, it is increasingly willing to assume the role of investor, leaving business operations to professional managers. This system may be called 'government owned and contractor operated' or GOCO. The contractor is responsible for earning a negotiated rate of return on the state's investment and is allowed to retain the residual income. In order to be competitive, the cost conscious businessmen are disinclined to assume the social costs of life-time employment and an inefficient work force (Kernen, 1998; Tyler, 1998; Cheng, 1998). As a consequence, China's state welfare system has come under tremendous pressure from the almost 12 million unemployed in urban areas alone and 110 million people covered by the state pension system (Harding, April 14, 1999, p. 1).

In sum, the Chinese public sector is reinventing itself by shedding money losing state enterprises while keeping healthy and critical ones, by getting out of daily operations while strengthening regulatory regimes and macroeconomic fine tuning, and by devolving functions to lower-level government. By necessity, the public budgeting and accounting systems have to adapt to the new environment. The adaptations are described in the next two sections, beginning with the public budgeting system.

18.3. Budget System Reform

Reform has affected the Chinese public budget in four major ways: (1) the scope and the proportion of resources commanded by the public budget have been reduced; (2) multiple budgets have replaced the unitary budget; (3) offbudget funds have either been eliminated or placed under more rigorous control; and (4) state regulation of nonbudget funds has been tightened.

18.3.1. BUDGET SCOPE AND RESOURCES

Economic reform has greatly affected China's government finances. Government revenues increased more than six folds from 113.2 billion RMB in 1978 to 736.7 billion RMB in 1996 (approximately 8 RMB equal to US $1). As a percentage of GDP, however, it declined around 30% in the late 1970s to between 20-30% in the 1980-86 period. It further dropped below 20% since 1987 and steadily declined during the last ten years, reaching a low of 10-11% in the mid-1990s. This is a far cry from the situation in the pre-reform era. In 1960, nearly half of China's GDP was under government control (Cong, 1998, pp. 94-96).

Year	Revenues	Expenditures	Surplus (Deficit)	Debt
1970	66.3	64.9	1.35	
1971	74.5	73.2	1.26	
1972	76.6	76.6	0.07	
1973	80.9	80.9	0.09	
1974	78.3	79.0	(0.71)	
1975	81.6	82.1	(0.53)	
1976	77.7	80.6	(2.96)	
1977	87.4	84.3	3.09	
1978	113.2	112.2	1.02	
1979	114.6	128.2	(13.54)	3.5
1980	116.0	122.9	(6.89)	4.3
1981	117.6	113.8	3.78	7.3
1982	121.2	123.0	(1.77)	8.3
1983	136.7	140.9	(4.26)	7.8
1984	164.3	170.1	(5.82)	7.7
1985	200.5	200.4	0.06	9.0
1986	212.2	220.5	(8.29)	13.8
1987	219.9	226.2	(6.28)	16.9
1988	235.7	249.1	(13.39)	27.1
1989	266.5	282.4	(15.89)	28.3
1990	293.7	308.3	(14.65)	37.5
1991	314.9	338.7	(23.71)	46.1
1992	348.3	374.2	(25.88)	67.0
1993	434.9	464.2	(29.34)	73.9
1994	521.8	579.3	(57.45)	117.5
1995	624.2	682.4	(58.15)	155.0

Table 18.1.:   China's Government Revenues, Expenditures and Debt
               (Amounts in Billions of RMB)
Source: *China Statistical Yearbook*, 1996, Table 7-3 for Revenues and
               Expenditures, Table 7-20 for debt.

Escalating expenditures have outpaced revenues, resulting in greater deficits (table 18.1.). For the first time, the budget deficit of the central government reached 150 billion

RMB for fiscal year 1999, which is 57% more than the 96 billion RMB for last fiscal year (*Chinese American News*, March 12, 1999). In order to finance the deficits and stimulate economic growth, public debt increased from less than 10 billion RMB in 1985 to 155 billion RMB in 1995. Fortunately since China's GDP also increased during this period at annual rates between 20-35% a year, the debt to GDP ratio increased only from 1 percent to 2.7 percentage during those ten years.

The statistics cited above may be termed 'nominal' government revenues because they did not reflect such things as revenues off the budget (e.g. revenues collected and retained by local governments) as well as revenues regarded as nonbudget (e.g. local government special assessments). After adjusting for these items, which will be explained in the following sections, government revenues as a percentage of GDP increased from 22% to 34% in 1985 and from 11% to 22% in 1995 (Cong, 1998, p. 106).

Even so, the ambiguous and shifting boundaries of the public sector - both as a whole and in terms of its components - make it extremely difficult to interpret statistics about China's public sector. Does the public sector still consist of state-owned enterprises? How about the state-affiliated service institutions, such as hospitals and universities? Many of these institutions have created their own businesses. Many provincial and local governments set up financial institutions ('trust and investment companies') to borrow funds from domestic and foreign sources. When some of them collapsed, as in the case of Guandong International Trust and Investment with US$4.7 billion in liabilities and US$2.6 billion in assets (Landler, April 23, 1999, p. C2), the question 'Whose debt is it?' was not satisfactorily answered.

As the public sector's share of GDP - nominal or real - declined, concerns have been expressed about how well a fiscally feeble central government can effectively regular a robust economy to achieve economic and social goals (Wang, 1994). These have led in part to calls to scrutinize and regulate resources that flow outside of the official budget.

18.3.2. OFF-BUDGET REVENUES

Offbudget revenues are collected and retained for use by local governments, administrative units and until recently by state-owned enterprises and their supervisory agencies. The original intent was to give these organizations a modest degree of fiscal autonomy over certain revenue sources. For example, local governments were allowed to add a surcharge to some taxes and keep the receipts. Administrative agencies were allowed to collect fees for services. Finally state owned enterprises were allowed to retain a percentage of profit for employee welfare and equipment replacement. The amounts of offbudget revenues were quite modest during the era before reform: about 35 billion RMB or about one third of onbudget revenue in 1978 (Cong, 1998).

Under tight budget allocations, entrepreneurial government officials had every incentive to diversify their revenues by imposing a great variety for fees for public services (Chan, 1999). State owned enterprises were already charging for their products and services. Discretionary income for their managers came from earnings retained for legitimate purposes such as employee welfare funds as well as for their own prerequisites. As a consequence, offbudget revenues exploded ten fold to almost 400 billion RMB in 1992, when they almost equal to the amount of onbudget revenues. As a product of local autonomy and entrepreneurial spirit, offbudget revenues were susceptible to misuse, abuses and outright misappropriations. This led to demands to rein them in.

In examining the SOE offbudget funds, it has been noted that the SOEs themselves were in effect moved outside of the purview of the state budget. As independent economic entities, they contribute to government revenues by paying corporate income tax. Consequently, their retained earnings should not be equated with the unremitted revenues of governmental bodies. This reclassification reduced offbudget revenue by 242 billion RMB to less than 150 billion RMB in 1993 (Cong, 1998, p. 104).

New regulations have begun to emphasize that local government and administrative agencies are acting as agents of the state in collecting revenues. The money belongs to the state and may be spent only for public purposes. The intent of the new policy is clearly to take over what has become or at least perceived as the 'private' money of the collecting government unit. Judging from the continuous discussion of the issues, the control of these resources remains problematic.

18.3.3. NON-BUDGET RESOURCES

If budgeted revenues are the inner ring of the government revenue pie, offbudget revenues become the second ring. There still exists a third ring, the revenues outside of the government's financial system, or nonbudget revenues. These are also fees and assessments collected by administrative agencies and local governments. It has been estimated that they amounted to 23 billion RMB in 1985 and rose to 384 billion RMB or equivalent to about 62% of government revenues in 1995 (Cong, 1998, pp. 104-105). These figures are probably the lower bounds in view of likely underreporting.

Ironically, the burgeoning amounts of nonbudget revenues are a byproduct of devolution of government functions to local governments. As they assume more responsibilities and undertake more costly projects, they are tempted to resort to whatever means of financing available. It has been estimated that there were several thousand types of fees, competing with taxes and adding to the people's financial burden (Cong, 1998, p. 105). As there is even less transparency and accountability for these resources, nonbudget revenues are fertile breeding grounds for waste and corruption. Regulations have been enacted to bring nonbudget revenues into the fiscal system. Specifically, the imposition of fees requires the approval of the local People's Congress (Cong, 1998).

18.3.4. BUDGET SIZE RECONSIDERED

The existence of large amounts of offbudget and nonbudget revenues has rendered budget numbers less meaningful indicators of the size of the Chinese public sector. Analysts have adjusted onbudget revenue figures to arrive at a more accurate estimate of the total amount of government revenues (table 18.2).

Description	1985	1990	1993	1995
Nominal Amounts of Revenues	200.5	293.7	434.9	624.2
Subsidies for SOEs (1)	50.7	57.9	41.1	32.0
Offbudget Revenues (2)	27.7	63.6	143.2	240.4
Nonbudget Revenues	23.3	76.0	143.3	384.3
Actual Amounts of Revenues	302.2	491.2	762.5	1,280.9
Nominal Amounts of Revenues/GDP	22.4%	15.5%	12.6%	10.7%
Actual Amounts of Revenues/GDP	33.7%	26.5%	22.0%	22.0%

(1) Unlike the IMF-recommended practice of treating subsidies to state-owned enterprises as expenditure, the Chinese handled these as deductions from revenue.
(2) These originate from local governments and administrative units.

Table 18.2.:   Government Revenues of China (in billions of RMB, except %)
Source: Cong, 1998, Table 3-3, p. 104.
Original Source: *1996 Yearbook of Chinese Public Finance Statistics.*

The clarification of offbudget and nonbudget revenues has helped to delineate the scope and properly measure China's budgetary resources. Having dealt with the boundary issues, we next turn our attention to the question: Is the unitary budget concept still appropriate to the China that operates a mixed - socialist and market - economy?

18.3.5. MULTIPLE BUDGETS

Beginning in 1992, China's public budgeting system adopted the concept of multiple budgets to reflect the numerous and redefined roles of the state. The core of the state budget remains but it now separates regular expenditures and developmental expenditures. This has in effect created an operating budget and a capital budget. Another budget monitors the performance of business enterprises that use government-owned assets. A new social security budget has been created to take over the functions assumed by the social welfare funds scattered throughout the Chinese economy.

The transformation from a unitary budget to multiple budgets is an important step in the evolution of China's public budget. It seeks to balance consumption expenditures and development needs. It also enhances the transparency of financial distributions, revealing government fiscal activities and the causes of deficits, pushing the reform of the fiscal system, tax and investment systems, and the enterprise financial management system. Table 18.3. shows the operating and capital budgets for a recent year. The alert reader may notice that debt proceeds are improperly grouped under revenues in the capital budget.

Description	Amount
Current Revenues and Expenditures Item	
Total Current Revenue	601.9
Total Taxes	573.7
Subsidies for Lossmaking Nonproductive Enterprises	(13.5)
Adjustable Fund Revenue	3.5
Other Current Revenue	38.1
Total Current Expenditures	512.0
Non-productive Capital Construction Expenditures	25.3
Social Development and Welfare Expenditures	196.9
National Defense, Armed Police and Administration Expenses	158.3
Price Subsidies	36.5
Other Current Expenditures	95.0
Current Budget Balances	89.9
Constructive Revenue and Expenditures	
Revenue	
Current Budget Balances	89.9
Special Construction Revenue	41.6
Subsidies for Lossmaking Productive Enterprises	(19.3)
Sub-total Construction Revenue	112.2
Constructive Budget Balances	58.2
Total Revenue (Less Current Balance)	624.2
Debt Revenue	155.0
Domestic and Foreign Debt Revenue making up Deficit of Central Budget	66.3
Principal and Interest Payment on Domestic Debt Revenue	87.8
Borrowing from Abroad for Important Construction	0.4
Expenditures	
Production Capital Construction Expenditures	53.7
Technical Updates, Transformation and New Product Promotion Expenses	49.4
Expenditures Supporting Agricultural Production	22.1
City Maintenance Expenditures	28.6
Other Construction Expenditures	16.6
Total Construction Expenditures	170.4
Total Expenditures	682.4
Principal and Interest Payments on Domestic and Foreign Debt	87.8
Key Construction Projects Expenditures Using Foreign Debt	0.4

Table 18.3.:   China's 1995 Operating and Capital Budgets(Amounts in Billions of RMB)

Source: *China Statistical Yearbook*, 1996, Table 7-4

18.3.6 SUMMARY OF BUDGET CHANGES

Table 18.4. highlights the changes in China's public budgeting system that have resulted from the economic and institutional reforms. In general, the tight-knit unitary budget has become a set of budgets with specific objectives. The operating budget will focus on the core governmental functions of providing public goods. The capital budget will finance developmental projects. The state asset management budget in effect functions like a huge holding company, monitoring the contractors' return of investment on the nation's assets. Finally, the social security budget will become the safety net for the hundreds of millions of needy persons unloaded by business-minded enterprises unable or unwilling to assume the cost of caring for them.

	Pre-reform	Reform Measures
Scope of the Public Budget	All encompassing: vertical integration of all levels of governments; horizontal integration of executive units, service units and business enterprise units.	From integration to combination: a system of shared taxes for all levels of government; privatization, from GOGO to GOCO, market exchange replacing top-down allocation.
Content of the Budget	Unitary Budget: unit budgets are aggregated at each level of government; the budgets of all local governments in a province are aggregated for approval by the province; all provincial budgets are aggregated for approval by the national government; a general fiscal budget allocates all budgetary resources.	Multiple Budgets: governmental budgets for carrying out state functions; state assets management budgets to control the use of state assets by business enterprises (GOCO); social security budget to take over the welfare funds administered by units (including state owned enterprises).
Offbudget Funds	Defined as resources permitted to be retained for spending by local governments, fees collected executive units; special funds maintained by supervisory executive units; social welfare funds.	All fees collected are to be included in the budget. Local off-budget funds to be included in the budgets of local governments; investments in enterprises or return to the Treasury; social welfare funds brought into the social security budget.
Non-budgetary resources	All means of financing (including fees, borrowing) of local governments.	The levies of fees have to be approved through the legislative process; all financial resources subject to regulation and control.

Table 18.4.:   Changes in the Chinese Public Budget System

In light of these changes, what has become of the accounting system whose primary objective is to support budget execution? The next major section will attempt to answer this question.

18.4. Changes in Public Sector Accounting

18.4.1. INTRODUCTION

Chinese accounting standards have traditionally been grouped in three major categories: (1) accounting for budgetary resources administered by the Ministry of Finance and the finance bureaus at lower levels of government, (2) accounting for component units of government, and (3) accounting for business enterprises. This basic structure has not changed. However, component unit accounting has been subdivided into accounting for administrative units (such as the State Commission on Education) and accounting for service units (e.g. colleges and universities, research institutes). This change will be explained, as will some other substantive changes.

Before discussing the changes, it is important to acknowledge what has not changed. In the Chinese system of public finance, there exists a finance bureau in each government, with the Ministry of Finance at the top of the financial management superstructure. The Ministry of Finance and its local branches are responsible for budget preparation, distributing appropriations and the subsequent accounting and financial reporting. They are independent of the line departments and directly control the departments' fiscal affairs. This basic institutional structure has not changed. Neither has the strong budgetary control orientation of the accounting system maintained by the finance offices. After all, one of their primary missions is to execute the budget and report the results (Liu, 1997a and 1997b).

There is, however, a greater recognition that accounting can provide reliable information for macroeconomic regulation and for establishing fiscal policy. As the central depository of financial information, the budgetary accounting system is crucial for the implementation of financial policy. This was especially the case when local governments rely on the central government for their budgetary allocations. The decentralization discussed in the previous section has reduced the scope of control of the central government. However, the information system infrastructure is there to monitor the fiscal conduct of all governmental units (Liu, 1997b). A very important part of the infrastructure is the authority of the Ministry of Finance in setting accounting standards. We will now examine the extent to which these accounting standards have changed in response to budget changes and reform in general.

18.4.2. INCLUSIVE SCOPE OF ACCOUNTING

As discussed in sections 18.3.2. and 18.3.4., there were huge amounts of public sector resources lying outside of the official budget or even outside of the fiscal system. As long as accounting focused solely on budgetary resources, these would be resources - and liabilities - off the books of governments. The reform that drastically reduced the amounts of offbudget and nonbudget resources has brought them under accounting control. Specifically, all offbudget funds should be included in the budget and should be treated as revenues in the accounts, and expenditures financed by them should be similarly included in the total expenditures.

There remains, however, the much bigger problem of liabilities left out of the governments' balance sheet. To what extent is government responsible for the debt incurred by quasi-governmental organizations? Given the fuzzy nature of these entities, the line of accountability is often unclear. The further development of accounting standards on liabilities will have to await the resolution of legal and institutional issues.

18.4.3. SEPARATE ACCOUNTING STANDARDS FOR SERVICE ORGANIZATIONS

As the market economy expanded in China, services that were previously provided free of charge are increasingly sold for a price. For instance, public universities are now charging tuition; hospitals are requiring fees; patients have to pay for prescription drugs. These are only a few examples. These organizations - called service units, implying that they are component units of government - are doing so by necessity. Fees from customers are needed to make up for declining government budget allocations or subsidies. The pace is likely to accelerate to meet the government's goal of placing these organizations on a self-sustaining basis in three years.

As service organizations operate more like businesses, their links to the state budget is weakened. This is acknowledged by separating out service institutions - though still called service *units* - from the government's administrative units for purposes of setting accounting standards (Liu, 1997c and 1997d). The responsibility for setting their accounting standards has been shifted from the Bureau of Budget Management to the Accounting Bureau, which promulgates business enterprise accounting standards. New standards have abolished the classification of service organizations as being wholly subsidized, partially subsidized or self-sustained units. This classification is becoming less meaningful as financial self-sufficiency is the goal. (It is possible that government grants will replace direct appropriations, as the government realizes the need for public subsidies in order to achieve social equity.) Finally service organizations are required to use the accrual basis of accounting, just as Chinese business enterprises already are.

The decision to distinguish service units from administrative units has more than symbolic significance. It recognizes that these two types of organizations are different: service units can sell tangible services - private goods - to identifiable customers. In contrast, administrative units are charged with the formulation and implementation of public policies, which are public goods. In addition, the decision recognizes that in a market economy, a service unit has become an economic entity with its own rights and obligations - i.e. assets and liabilities - and has to earn adequate revenues to meet its expense to survive as a going concern. This requires a fundamental examination of their accounting model.

18.4.4 NEW ACCOUNTING MODEL

The primary objective of the accounting system of component units used to be the monitoring of budget execution. Its accounting model was represented by the accounting equation: sources of funds - uses of funds = fund balance. This model remains valid for administrative units. On the other hand, service organizations as autonomous accounting entities now require an accounting model represented by:

Assets - Liabilities   = Net Assets, and
Revenues - Expenses   = Profit

This model is endorsed by the service unit accounting standards that went into effect in early 1998. These standards also require the double-entry bookkeeping system and the adoption of the accrual basis of accounting. These recording and measurement methods are the foundation for preparing the balance sheet and statement of operations. Readers in the West would readily recognize these as the fundamental features of the corporate financial accounting model, which is based on the reciprocal nature of market transactions and service delivery as the basis of revenue recognition.

The recognition of assets, liabilities, net assets, revenues and expenses as five elements of the new service organization accounting model represents a paradigm shift in Chinese public sector accounting. Service organizations are being transformed from cost centers to revenue centers whose survival depends on the ability to serve and get paid by customers. In an unfettered market economy, the ability to pay is the predominant criterion for the allocation of goods and service. It is almost inevitable that this will lead to social inequality, which would require government intervention in serious cases. Even Western capitalist countries do not practice a pure market model when it comes to the production and distribution of merit goods such as education and health. It is difficult to imagine China embracing the market philosophy so totally that it will abandon socialist ideals completely. China will constantly be forced to resolve the contradictions inherent in a 'socialist market economy'.

18.4.5. SUMMARY

In addition to the above major changes, the new standards made other advances as well. First, they identified qualitative characteristics of financial information, such as relevancy, comparability, uniformity, timeliness, transparency, proportionality, materiality, objectivity. Second, they reaffirmed the cost principle for recording assets. Third, they prohibited transfers to special purpose funds. Finally, service organizations are urged to develop better cost accounting systems to facilitate management planning and control (Liu, 1997a).

Table 18.5. summarizes the major changes discussed in this section.

	Pre-Reform	Proposed
Unit Accounting	No differentiation between administrative (executive) units and service provider units	Clear differentiation between administrative (executive) units and service provider units
Classification of Activities of Service Institutions	All activities classified as fully subsidized, partially subsidized, and self-sustaining	No classification by extent of subsidy; entire service institutions expected to be self-sustaining in three years
Offbudget Funds	Administrative fees are regarded as offbudget	Administrative fees are included in budget and subject to budgetary control
Recording Method and Accounting Equation	Single entry bookkeeping method	Double entry bookkeeping
Elements of Financial Statements	Fund receipts, fund disbursements, fund balance	Assets, liabilities, net assets, revenues, expenses/expenditures
Basis of Accounting	Cash basis	Cash basis for executive units; service units may use cash or accrual basis of accounting

Table 18.5.:   Changes in Accounting Standards

18.5. Reform and Budgeting and Accounting

The economic and institutional reform in China during the last two decades has significantly altered the scope and function of the state. These have in turn had repercussions for public budgeting and accounting in China. We have found that public budgeting is more sensitive to environmental changes than accounting is. However, the effectiveness of budget reform depends in part on the availability of feedback information from the accounting system. Consequently accounting reform is at least as important as budget reform. While the budget remains an important fiscal policy instrument, there are also signs that the position of public sector accounting has been elevated. Market reform has created the need for reliable financial information for managing enterprises and institutions released from tight government control. Managerial accounting is ascending in importance as financial accounting has when firms try to raise capital from investors and creditors. As in the West, there is an emerging recognition of the importance of the balance sheets with information on assets and liabilities, away from the former exclusive emphasis on receipts and disbursements. As China engages in massive amounts of domestic and foreign borrowing for infrastructure development, the accrual basis becomes more imperative as it captures and presents information about long-term assets and liabilities.

18.5.1. PUBLIC POLICY ENVIRONMENT

The public budgeting and accounting developments in this chapter have taken place during a period when China was striking a delicate balance between the state, organizations and individuals. There is considerable concern over the ability of a weak state to ensure social and economic development. Within the public sector itself, the distribution between the central and local governments is a contentious issue. These

financial issues cannot be resolved in isolation as they are intertwined with China's economic and institutional development. Currently, Chinese budget and accounting policies are based on the following premises (Liu, 1997a, pp. 16-17):
- Public ownership will remain the main foundation of the China economy.
- Economic order shall be maintained.
- Public property should be protected.
- Private enterprises should be promoted within the framework of state regulation.

According to Gao Qiang (Liu, 1997b, pp. 2-3), former director of the Bureau of Budget Management, budgetary accounting changes should be consonant with other economic, finance and institutional changes in China. Specifically, public officials are encouraged to manage their units rather than just relying on state appropriations. The supply model is being supplanted by an entrepreneurial model. In the new model, the former system of tight central control is giving way to the practice of generating, accumulating and effectively using wealth. Furthermore, financial management regulations are being codified and elevated to the level of legal requirements. The current system of direct control by administrative edict will also be replaced by decentralized monitoring.

In keeping with the urgency of transitioning to a market economy, Chinese enterprise accounting reform has proceeded at a fast pace. The reform of public budgeting and accounting could not go faster than the institutional reform. Furthermore, budget reform has moved ahead of public sector accounting reform. But progress has been made. Service institutions are viewed as more businesslike, rather than like government agencies. After three years, the umbilical cord feeding service institutions from the state budget would be severed, leaving these institutions to float or sink on their own. Almost inevitably these former cost centers of government would gradually (or suddenly as the case may be) become revenue centers, creating a 'fee for service' culture and economy. They may be forced to borrow and find resources for capital maintenance and expansion. All of these changes would lead to the need for meaningful balance sheet, income statements and cash flows statements, which are the core of business financial reporting.

18.5.2. BUDGETING AND ACCOUNTING AS INSTITUTIONAL INFRASTRUCTURE

Accounting is a social and institutional practice (Hopwood and Miller, 1994). As such many seemingly technical issues discussed in this paper reflect China's evolving institutional structure. China is still in the midst of developing an effective tax system, defining the authority and functions of central, provincial and local governments, a legal system that protects private and public property rights. Only recently has China revised its constitution to recognize privately owned and managed economic entities as 'an important component of the socialist market economy' (*China Securities News*, March 17, 1999). These developments have - or should have - a direct impact on the resolution of accounting issues. Take the example of something as simple as the accounting equation: assets = liabilities + net assets. Before accounting measurement rules can be developed, property rights and financial obligations have to be recognized and enforced by the legal system.

By the same token, a strong accounting and auditing profession armed with rigorous standards and enforcement power is instrumental in cementing accountability relationships. The development of capital markets and lending on a commercial basis will enhance the leverage of investors and creditors. Investors and creditor will demand full financial disclosure. Transparency will be a key weapon for combating widespread corruption and other financial malfeasance. As analysts (Cheng, 1998; Oksenberg, Swaine and Lynch, 1998) have pointed out, effective public and private institutions will be essential for China's economic development. Budgeting and accounting are indispensable elements of the institutional infrastructure.

18.5.3. SUGGESTIONS FOR ACCOUNTING REFORM

Improving accounting policy and practice is a continuous process. China has made some initial progress; much more is needed to improve the performance of the Chinese institutions in the public and private sectors. We suggest that accounting policy makers pay greater to the following issues:

First, a closer coordination between budgeting and accounting reforms is required. For example, the requirement of a capital budget and social security budget is logically linked with the recognition of capital assets and long-term liability of government. The accurate determination of profits (or losses) of state-owned enterprise is essential for figuring out the amount of government subsidies and identify candidates for closing down. The resolution of these issues requires the cooperation of different agencies within the Ministry of Finance responsible for budgeting and accounting policies.

Second, budgeting and accounting for a variety of debts has become an urgent issue. By some estimates, public debt rose from 4.3 billion RMB in 1980 to 247.7 billion RMB in 1997. In recent years, budgeting and accounting standards have distinguished debt proceeds from revenues. Further research and standards are needed to go beyond bonded debt to recognize and measure many other liabilities, such as overdue salaries and wages, pension payable, social security benefits, insurance and loan guarantees. The bankruptcy and precarious financial condition of a number of huge investment and trust companies have exposed the government's vulnerability. These financial institutions, which borrow and invest billions are variously described as government owned, sponsored or related. Creditors have looked to their government backers only to face disclaimers.

The new requirement of the accrual basis will likely raise a host of implementation issues. Accrual is an illusive concept, and has been modified in varying degree for application in the public sector (Chan, 1998). Besides the technical issues of actuarial estimation, there will expectedly controversies surrounding the government's short-term and long-term liabilities as bureaucracies are reduced in size and state-owned enterprises unload their unproductive or unneeded employees. The accounting recognition of such liabilities would likely heighten the pressure to provide funding for the social safety net.

Third, cost accounting is badly needed in service institutions, as is management planning and control in general. As these organizations are compelled to be self-sufficient, they need to know the costs of services they provide to have a rational cost-based pricing policy to operate on a nonprofit basis. This will require the resolution of such problems as product costing, overhead allocation, and transfer pricing.

In summary, improved budgeting and accounting standards have been made possible by China's economic and institutional reform. The economic rationality they embody and the accountability they promote can translate China's economic growth into the greatest benefit for one quarter of mankind.

References

English Language Publications
- Chan, J.L. (1994) The Evolution of Government Accounting in China, In: V. Montesinos, J.M. Vela. Velancia (eds.), *International Research in Public Sector Accounting, Reporting, and Auditing*, Institut Valencia D'Investigacions Econo iques, Spain, 117-128.
- Chan, J.L. (1996) Budget Accounting in China: Continuity and Change, *Research in Governmental and Nonprofit Accounting*, 1-19.
- Chan, J.L. (1997) Two Paradigms for Managing China, *Advances in Comparative International Management*, 203-217.
- Chan, J.L. (1998) The Bases of Accounting for Budgeting and Financial Reporting, In: Roy T. Meyers (ed.), *Handbook of Government Budgeting*, Josey-Bass, San Francisco.
- Chan, J.L. (1999) A Sino-American Comparison of Budgeting and Accounting Coverage, In: E. Caperchione and R. Mussari (ed.), *Comparative Issues in Local Government Accounting*, Kluwer (forthcoming).
- Cheng, H-S. (1998) A Midcourse Assessment of China's Economic Reform, In O. Schell, D. Shambaugh, eds., *The China Reader: The Reform Era*, Random House, New York, 311-321.
- Harding, J. (April 14, 1999) China Faces Huge Welfare Burden, *Financial Times*, 1.
- Hopwood, A.G. and P. Miller 1994), *Accounting as Social and Institutional Practice*, Cambridge University Press, Cambridge, UK.
- Landler, M. (April 23, 1999) Down and Out at Failed Chinese Company: Gitic Bankruptcy Settlement Worse than Expected for Creditors, *New York Times*, C2.
- Naughton, B. (1998) The Pattern and Logic of China's Economic Reform, In: O. Schell, D. Shambaugh, eds., *The China Reader: The Reform Era*, Random House, New York, 300-311.
- Kernen, A. (1998) Out of Work in the State Sector, In: O. Schell, D. Shambaugh, eds., *The China Reader: The Reform Era*, Random House, New York, 348-356.
  Oksenberg, M.C. M.D. Swaine and D.C. Lynch, The Chinese Future, In: O. Schell, D. Shambaugh, eds., *The China Reader: The Reform Era*, Random House, New York, 505-530.
- Schell, O. And D. Shambaugh, eds. (1998) *The China Reader: The Reform Era*, Random House, New York.
- Tyler, P. (1998) Rural Poverty, In: O. Schell, D. Shambaugh, eds., *The China Reader: The Reform Era*, Random House, New York, 357-361.
- Wong, C.P.W., C. Heady and W.T. Woo (1995*) Fiscal Management and Economic Reform in the People's Republic of China*, Oxford University Press, Hong Kong.

Chinese Language Publications
- China Securities News (March 17, 1999) Revision of the Constitution of the People's Republic of China, *China Securities News*, 5.
- *China Statistical Yearbook* (1996).
- Chinese American Times (April 12, 1999) To Ensure 7% Economic Growth This Year, China's Fiscal Deficit Reaches a Unprecedented Huge 150 Billion, *Chinese American Times*, 1.

- Cong, SH, ed. (1998) *Chinese Macro Public Finance Policy*, Shanghai University of Finance and Economics Press, Shanghai, China.
- Liu, SB, ed. (1997a) *Fiscal General Budget Accounting*, China Finance and Economics Publishing House, Beijing, China.
- Liu, SB, ed. (1997b) *Strengthening Budget Managing by Regulating Budget Accounting*, China Finance and Economics Publishing House, Beijing, China.
- Liu, SB, ed. (1997c) *Administrative Unit Accounting*, China Finance and Economics Publishing House, Beijing, China.
- Liu, SB, ed. (1997d) *Service Unit Accounting*, China Finance and Economics Publishing House, Beijing, China.
- Wang, SG (1994) *Report on the State Capacity of China*, Oxford University Press, Hong Kong.

IMPLEMENTING THE MUNICIPAL ACCOUNTING REFORM IN FRANCE

Jean-Baptiste Gillet and Claude Heiles

19.1. Introduction

France has implemented since 1994 a reform of its municipal accounting legislation, towards a better accrual accounting system. The elaboration and implementation of this reform have shown the need for a medium-term solution between the traditional budgeting approach focused on the definition of an annual financial balance, and a full accrual accounting, consistent with the standards in use in the corporate sector.

19.2. Distinctive Local Government Rules create Strong Constraints for an Accounting Reform

French local authorities enjoy a wide autonomy, precisely guaranteed by the Constitution of 1958. The freedom of local government can be limited only by parliamentary statutes and not by Government regulations. Nevertheless, the financial management, budgeting and accounting of local authorities remain under distinctive rules, which were not substantially altered by the 1982 decentralization laws, and which became less and less adapted to new functions and liberties of local authorities.

19.2.1. SPECIFIC FINANCIAL MANAGEMENT RULES

Two distinctive rules characterize the French 'public accounting system'. These rules come from the administrative organization set up and matured from the middle of the 19th century.

Traditionally, financial accounting for France's public administration has been solely based on the annual budget. Bookkeeping aims at controlling and reporting on the execution of the budget. Budgeting and bookkeeping are focused on cash and control the use of money in accordance with budgetary appropriations. Annual accounts report sources and uses of money, and differences with the budget approved by the local assembly (the municipal council). Strict rules and procedures are meant to avoid errors and misuses.

A Common Budgetary and Accounting System
The French administrative system strictly separates the accounting responsibility from the administrative and political ones. Under this strict rule, local government accountants are civil servants employed by the ministry of finance. Public monies are placed under their exclusive control, for payment as well as collection, and they exercise a formal control over payment orders. Their accounts are judged by regional audits courts. In

A. Bac (ed.), International Comparative Issues in Government Accounting, 315-326.
© 2001 *Kluwer Academic Publishers. Printed in the Netherlands.*

addition to these basic accounting functions, they can act as advisors to the mayor, especially in smaller municipalities. It derives from this peculiar organization that two separate sets of accounts are held simultaneously by the local authority itself, and by the public accountant.

The first one is purely budgetary. It describes the budget forecasts and appropriations in terms of inflows and outflows. It derives from the democratic debate in the local assembly. The budget is focused on the definition of a short term financial balance i.e. the ability of the authority to match its annual expenditure - operating and capital - with its annual revenue. The budgetary accounting (administrative accounts) records the execution of operations. The description of events is not done in accrual terms, and the administrative accounts are held on a single-entry basis.

The second set of accounts is held by the public accountant with a double-entry system. It reflects the execution of the budget, and includes the cash description of operations ordered by the mayor. Budget and financial accounts are closely linked: every entry in financial accounting reflects a corresponding entry in budgetary accounting through 'payable' and 'receivable' accounts which determine the short term cash balance of the authority. Therefore, accounting rules automatically influence the budget itself.

Though derived from the general accounting principles, this second set of accounts was not held until the 1994 reform on an accrual basis. Moreover, in bigger municipalities, the budget was prepared on a functional basis (housing, education, ...) though accounting reflected the categories of the 'plan comptable général' (chart of accounts). These two distinct approaches made even more complex the accounting reform.

Cash Management under Strict Constraints
Unlike private companies, local authorities are bound to deposit their funds to the Treasury, without interest. This rule was perfectly understandable in times when local authorities were no more than local parts of the central State. It is now rather paradoxical after the decentralization carried out since the early 80's. However, this rule is part of a complex set of relations between the Treasury and local authorities:
- local taxes are collected by the Treasury on behalf on local governments, and the amounts are paid in advance by the central government which bears the cost of financing monthly advances as well as the risk of taxpayer's insolvency;
- the book-keeping service carried out by the treasury network of public accountants is nearly free for local authorities (though not for the national taxpayer).

This rule is often criticized and is subject to some exceptions. Bigger local authorities have been able to develop a 'zero-deposit' policy through sophisticated tools of cash management, often too complex for the smaller municipalities.

However, in depriving municipalities of the complete ability to manage their own cash position, this rule creates another important difference with private management, and consolidate a mostly budgetary approach.

19.2.2. THE PUBLIC FINANCING OF LOCAL BUDGETS

Local budgets are financed through three main sources of revenue: government transfers, local taxes, and fees charged on local services.

Local Taxes
Local taxes account for about a third of the total local budgets. Three principal categories of taxes are levied by local authorities:
- owners pay taxes on real estate, land and buildings;
- local citizens pay taxes on housing, whether owned or rented;
- companies pay taxes levied upon equipment and wages.[1]

Fiscal product is voted by local assemblies since 1980. This liberty has been widely used during the last 20 years in line with the decentralization laws voted in 1982: as a percentage of GNP, the fiscal revenue of local authorities as a whole accounted for 4.6% in 1980 and 7.0% in 1996 (including transfers from national budget).

As tax authorities, it is understandable that local governments should be careful about the fiscal implications of their decisions within their term of office, considering that the essence of budget is to match annual tax inflows against the same year outflows.

If we draw a comparison with local authorities in other European countries, it is interesting to note that French local authorities have a significantly high 'tax power'.

Sweden	60%
France	54%
Denmark	49%
Finland	46%
Belgium*	35%
Luxembourg	32%
Spain	<30%
Germany*	20%
Italy	<20%
Ireland	16%
United-Kingdom	14%
the Netherlands	8%
Portugal	7%
Austria*	5%
Greece	Low

* except federated states

Table 19.1.: Comparison with European Countries: Relative Tax Power
This table shows the percentage of fiscal revenue voted by the local assembly as a proportion of total revenue.
Source: Crédit Local de France

---

[1] The wage part of the 'taxe professionnelle' will disappear. It is being replaced by a government transfer.

From this table, we can see that French local authorities have a relatively wider fiscal autonomy than in other countries. Only Swedish local authorities have a larger fiscal responsibility. This point is important because it gives to local councillors a particular sensitiveness to financial problems when they may have fiscal consequences (even if the national budget compensates many tax exemptions for local taxpayers). In some cases, accounting can become a political problem, local councillors being sometimes more sensitive to short term fiscal consequences or level of service, rather than to medium/long term sustainability or inter-generation fiscal consequences.

Fees on Local Services
Local authorities carry out quasi-commercial services: water supply, sewerage... The legal principle, sometimes politically challenged, is that these activities, usually called '*industrial and commercial*' must be financially balanced by themselves, and not been financed through general taxation.

This is why the first accounting reform which took place in the municipal sector in the early 90's was the reform of the 'industrial and commercial services'. The accounting reform has fully implemented the principles of the 'plan comptable général' in use for corporate and commercial entities. In this sector, the accounting reform presented little specific difficulties: for instance, identification and valuation of assets used in these services could be carried out on common grounds.

The accounting reform carried out in these industrial and commercial services set up the basic principles of accrual and cost accounting in the municipal sector. Local authorities managers and public accountants got acquainted with these principles and techniques, thus opening the way to the more general reform of municipal accounting later in the 90's.

19.2.3. FINANCIAL PRINCIPLES DERIVED FROM TRADITIONAL BUDGET RULES

The mostly fiscal nature of local revenue makes it perfectly legitimate to maintain the traditional budgetary system where annual forecasts and appropriations are voted by the local assembly, and the bookkeeping aims at controlling and describing as precisely as possible the use of public money.

French local authorities are subject to the traditional budget principles, which have not been altered by the accounting reform. Two principles must be shortly outlined.

The Budget is an Annual Forecast
Budget forecasting aims at determining the appropriate level of taxation and cash inflows, necessary to match the annual expenditure. This traditional approach is mostly 'cash-based' rather than accrual and can sometimes lead to short-sighted decisions.

However, many local managers and politicians have developed new management techniques more oriented towards pluri-annual decision making and in 1992 bigger municipalities have been entitled to vote pluri-annual spending authorizations for capital expenditure.

The Annual Budget must be balanced

The strongest budgetary principle imposed upon local authorities is the legal requirement of balancing the budget. Unlike the central government, this is a strict limit against financial risks in local government. This rule is maintained under strict control by the budgetary control of the préfet and regional courts of audit.

This rule has several important aspects:

- the equilibrium is determined separately for the operating section and the capital section of the budget. The operating section must be balanced by current revenue, and any imbalance has to be financed either by raising taxes or by cutting in non mandatory expenses;
- the capital section (capital expenditure including capital repayment of loans) is financed by capital revenue, the surplus of the current section, and fresh loans; the balance rule means that the capital repayment of loans must be financed by capital revenue and operating surplus, and not by new loans;
- the equilibrium must be reached on a yearly basis. In case of a deficit (ex-ante or ex-post if it is of a substantial amount), the budgeting responsibility is transferred to the 'préfet' (central government representative), advised by the regional court of audit.

19.3. The Municipal Accounting Reform: Introducing a Better Accrual Approach

About ten years after the decentralization reform of 1982, the reform of the municipal accounting system took place in 1994, and was implemented between 1995 and 1997. In the late 80's, some municipalities met financial difficulties. These problems outlined that the financial and accounting system of local government, left unreformed by the 1982 legislation, had serious flaws. Therefore, this reform was a part of a wider move which principal aims were:

- to give better financial information on local government to elected members, citizens, taxpayers and lenders;
- to improve management tools and techniques;
- to strengthen financial control over local budgets.

The basis of the reform was the implementation of the principles of the 'plan comptable général' adopted in 1982, upon which public sector accounting system must be based. This involved the application of an accounting classification based on the structures of the general accounting system: five classes for the balance sheet, two classes for the statement of revenue and expenditure, and the application of general accounting principles: prudence, consistency, fairness, ...

Another axis of the reform was to provide a functional presentation: the functional system created in the 1960's was rather complex. The reform created a functional code consistent with the European 'functional classification of the administrations', which provides 10 main functions and about 50 sub-functions. All municipalities over 3 500 inhabitants must use this functional code. Municipalities over 10 000 inhabitants can even use this functional presentation to vote their budgets.

19.3.1.AN EVOLUTION TOWARDS ACCRUAL ACCOUNTING

Whereas the traditional budget system gives the annual view of cash inflows and outflows, the reform aimed at introducing accrual accounting principles, based upon the standards set up in the 'plan comptable général'.

The Introduction of Basic Accrual Principles

The introduction of the basic accrual accounting principles needed to be done in accordance with some of the principles of the public accounting system: one of the cornerstones of the budget system is the commitment accounting. When an authority creates a financial obligation (e.g. through a contract), the commitment must be recorded by the budget authority for its full amount.

This idea of commitment differs from the notion of accrued charge used in accounting and described by the 'plan comptable général' in accordance with international rules. For instance in the case of an order for a good purchase:
-   the commitment is recorded when the order is placed;
-   the charge is accrued when the good is delivered.

In the French budget system, the commitment accounting is a single entry system which describes the amount of authorized spending, the amount of existing commitments already recorded, and the amount available for future spending. It is kept by the authority (i.e. not by the public accountant), it is not reconciled with the financial accounting and it is not publicly disclosed. As such, it is rather an internal management tool than an accounting system. In the budget accounting, the expense is recorded on issuance of a payment order by the authority spending officer. The record of the payment order is done both in the budget system and in the financial accounts by the public accountant. Both accounts are reconciled at the end of the year.

The accounting reform has introduced a new cut-off mechanism for municipalities over 3.500 inhabitants: the authority must identify within its commitment accounting which charges are actually accrued in order to record them in the financial accounting as 'payable', even if the payment order has not been issued at the end of the year.

Reflecting the Assets employed for Public Purposes

Except for 'heritage' or community assets, the mission of municipalities doesn't imply the possession of assets of an essentially different nature from most private entities. Therefore, most concepts used in the 'plan comptable général' for the description of assets could be used in the case of municipalities, on the basis of historical costs.

The biggest practical difficulty was, and still is, the drawing up of assets inventories: capital expenditure recorded in the financial accounts were seldom reconciled with physical inventories. Currently, except for municipalities which used to keep permanent registers of their assets, this work is still being done and the deadline initially 31/12/1997 has been postponed twice until 31/12/1999. However, if the interest of assets valuation is sometimes challenged as a basis for full cost accounting in the public sector, the need for accurate inventories is now widely admitted, as a basic principle of 'domestic economy'.

Another difficulty encountered in the reform was the need to describe precisely the situation of assets belonging to an authority and utilized on contractual or legal grounds for the delivery of services by another body, such as another authority or an inter-municipal body, or a non-profit organization... This leads to complex situations which must be accounted for as accurately as possible, whether the ownership of the asset is transferred from an entity to another or not.

19.3.2. THE NEED FOR A MEDIUM TERM SOLUTION

The municipal accounting reform introduced the basic principles of accrual accounting in the French municipal sector. However, it was necessary to find some medium-term solutions: accounting principles have sometimes to be adapted to real facts:
- most French municipalities are very small, about 32000 municipalities out of 36500 have less than 2000 inhabitants; this has led to ease the burden of a complex accounting system for the smallest authorities, though maintaining a 'full' system for bigger ones;
- due to the obligatory link between budget and financial accounting, and to the high sensitivity to fiscal consequences of accounting, some 'safety nets' were designed in order to limit the most abrupt consequences of the new rules on the budget balance.

Two points must be underlined as characterizing the adaptation of financial accounting to budgetary constraints: the use of provisioning as a 'warning' system rather than real provisioning, the limitation of the effects of the amortization mechanism.

Provisions as a Warning Mechanism
The new system creates two types of provisions:
- Provisions for risks and charges: in essence, these provisions don't differ much from the standard rule;
- 'mandatory provisions': these provisions were created to limit financial risks which occurred in some local authorities in the late 80's. Three items are subject to a mandatory provision:
    - credit guarantees granted by the local authority to other entities;
    - judgment debts when the first instance judgment has been given against the authority, and regardless of a pending appeal;
    - deferred loan repayments ('balloon'), with specific calculation rules.

Due to the obligatory link between budgetary and financial accounting, and due to the mandatory equilibrium of the budget, the creation of provisions has an impact on the budget: a provision is charged as a current expense in the budget and must be financed, either through tax raises (or other current revenue) or through cuts in other (cash) expenses. At this point, it is easily understood that accounting becomes a political problem for local governments who must explain why future or even uncertain expenses must be financed by today's taxation. This is particularly true for the third item of mandatory provisions: it is actually difficult to explain why the capital repayment of a loan in the future has to be charged today as a current expense and financed immediately by a tax increase.

This is why it has been admitted that the amount of provision could be accounted for as capital revenue in the capital section of the budget, thus allowing additional capital expenditure. In other terms, provisions are dealt with as capital and reserves in budgetary accounting. Therefore, when the risk will occur, the provision will no longer be available as a budgetary resource, and it will be necessary to raise new resources to face the actual expense. In that sense, provisions function as a simple 'warning mechanism'. However, many local managers are of course perfectly aware of the fundamental soundness of a 'real' provisioning mechanism, and it is hoped that in future reforms for other levels of local government, provisions will be dealt with in a more academic way.

Though this system could be described as unsatisfactory, we can draw a comparison with the State budget:
- when the provisioning mechanism has been used by the State, it has been technically used as a real provision mechanism: in 1989 the Government created the 'plan d'épargne populaire (PEP)', i.e. saving plans designed for the middle class, with a financial incentive as a government premium paid normally after 8 years of continuous savings. The amount of premium due by the budget accrued year after year but would not be paid before the 8th year of the system. Therefore, it was decided to provision the amount of premium accrued calculated after the banks' information. This amount increased the annual deficit of the State's budget without actual payment. Eventually when the premiums were paid in 1997, the provisions accumulated were used to finance the actual expense, therefore with no impact on this year's budget balance;
- however, in the State budget, the provisioning mechanism is nearly not in use: it would be hard to find other examples of provisioning in the State budget. In that respect, one could find that the municipal accounting reform has gone further than the State accounting system.

Limiting the Fiscal and Budgetary Effects of Assets Depreciation
Another significant example of limitation of budgetary and fiscal effects of accrual accounting is the case of assets amortization. As for the provisions, the annual amount of amortization is charged in the financial accounting to the profit and loss account, and must be balanced in the budget either by taxation or by cuts in other expenses in order to maintain the budget equilibrium.

In a perfectly legitimate way this amount of amortization is accounted for in the budget as a current expenditure and as a capital revenue.

However, it was necessary to limit the consequences of amortization on local budgets. Two main limitations were introduced by the reform:
- The field of mandatory amortization is limited to some categories of assets i.e. renewable assets (vehicles, equipment, furniture, machinery,...) and fixed assets (buildings) when used for commercial purposes or producing revenue. Consequently, 'heritage' assets, buildings used for administrative purposes or schools, and public works on roads and highways are not subject to amortization. In the same respect, smaller municipalities (under 3.500 inhabitants) are not obliged to amortize assets of whatever nature. Within this restricted field, only new assets are covered by

mandatory amortization, though local authorities can decide to amortize older assets. Similarly, they have the faculty to amortize outside this mandatory field.

In some cases, the absence of amortization reflects the absence of depreciation, or the implicit recognition that the asset will not have to be replaced (heritage assets). In the case of roads and highways, it can be admitted that they will maintain their value provided that heavy repair and maintenance is adequately carried out and that it is not necessary to depreciate them in the balance sheet. However, administrative buildings and schools hardly fall into one of these categories, even given adequate maintenance.

- The second limit aims at preventing fiscal consequences of the introduction of mandatory amortization. If the amount of amortization leads to an increase of over 2% of the fiscal revenue of the local authority, the amount in excess can be deferred off-balance. This mechanism works as a 'safety net', but until 1997 has been used by only three municipalities. However, its mere existence illustrates the ambiguity of accrual accounting in the public sector.

19.4. Towards a new Frontier

19.4.1. THE NEED FOR A TRUE FINANCIAL REPORTING

Municipal accounting, similar to other levels of Government, is organized to provide a legal and political control, either of local assemblies or of government control and audit bodies. However, beyond the publication of accounts developed under a logic of conformity, there is still a lot to do on the way of 'accountability' as it is understood in many countries, as 'the cornerstone of all financial reporting in government'. [2]

The French legislation has introduced a minimum level of financial reporting in 1992 (Jean Claude Scheid, 1994).[3] Local authorities must disclose as an annexe to the budget a number of documents or information:
- synthetic data (ratios) on the financial situation of the municipality;
- aggregation of the principal and secondary budgets;
- list of subsidies to non-profit organizations;
- table of guaranteed loans;
- synthetic data on inter-municipal organizations in which the municipality participates;
- balance sheet of commercial and non-profit organizations in which the municipality has a stake or incurs a risk.

However, it is doubtful that this information forms a proper financial reporting for three principal reasons at least:
1. Technically, the data disclosed is not consistently collected: periods of reference are not necessarily the same for the different entities, the content of the information is not homogeneous, significant information is missing, the definition of organizations

---

[2]   GASB 1987, 'concepts statement' N°1
[3]   Law of the 6th Feb. 1992, known as 'loi sur l'administration territoriale de la République'

in which the municipality is at stake or incurs a risk is doubtful, the ratios can be misleading or misinterpreted...

2. The data collected is not professionally controlled: whereas accounts of local authorities are held by professional accountants (civil servants, controlled by the regional courts of audit), the presentation of this information is done under the sole responsibility of the mayor, with no control other than political. Therefore, the quality of information cannot be professionally guaranteed, even if in most cases, the collection of the information is done with great technical ability and seriousness.

3. The information gathered in accordance with the law is not actually presented in the view of helping citizens or elected people to conceive a sound and proper judgement over the authority's achievements, performance or costs. It is rather some raw material, which need further elaboration to be practically useful for most people. For instance, a basic information such as the total manpower costs of the local authority is not directly available through the aggregation of principal and secondary budgets.

Some local authorities have voluntarily decided to disclose financial information in a more professional manner, and have developed a true financial communication policy. This is mostly the case of big municipalities or authorities, which provide and publish high quality documents. These documents are often directed to financial markets were the bigger authorities can raise funds. However, the lack of common standards and professional control give no real guarantee over the technical quality and soundness of these reports.[4]

Compare this situation to the purpose assigned to financial reporting e.g. by GASB (1987): 'Financial reporting should provide information to assist users in assessing the service efforts, costs, and accomplishments of the governmental entity [...]. This information helps users assess the economy, efficiency and effectiveness of government and may help form a basis for voting and funding decisions', one can assume that there are still some steps ahead.

19.4.2. THE NEED FOR CONSOLIDATION OF LOCAL ACCOUNTS

Another shortcoming of financial reporting in the local government is the question of consolidation.

This matter is particularly true in the French public sector for two reasons:

1. An increasing part of local authorities activities is undertaken by dependent bodies rather than the authority itself. This situation is not unique in France but has significantly developed either through secondary budgets, public bodies (with autonomous budgets and separate accounts) or semi-public corporations [5] ...;

2. due to the considerable number of municipalities of mostly small size, inter-municipal co-operation has widely developed in France: on top of about 36.000 communes, more than 20.000 inter-municipal bodies have been created for various

---

[4] This opinion doesn't apply to the reports issued by the few authorities who have been formally rated.

[5] Sociétés d'économie mixte, (SEM) which combine public and private funds for the delivery of certain types of services, for instance housing.

purposes and the number is rapidly growing. Sine 1992 new forms of inter-municipal bodies can be created, with an autonomous tax power: nearly 18.000 municipalities are now federated in 1577 of these groups which cover more than 50% of the French people. They are managed by an assembly designated by the local councils of the participating municipalities among their elected members. Their budgeting and accounting system is based upon the same model as the municipalities themselves. These inter-municipal bodies create a very complex pattern: one municipality can participate in several bodies for different purposes.

In this context, the consolidation of local accounts poses many complex problems (Vicente Pina and Lourdes Torres, 1998). The definition of the reporting entity is very complex. No method derived from the private sector, such as participation in the capital and the degree of financial control exercised, is directly available,. Other methods have to be defined in order to assess either the political or administrative control or a more financial concept based upon financial dependency or financial risk in the event of a bankruptcy. The method of consolidation must equally be paid adequate attention.

Given the fast development of this form of organization of local services, this matter questions the transparency and accountability of the local government as a whole, and is the real new frontier in local government financial reporting in France.

19.5. Conclusion

Though the need for a modern accounting system in the public sector is now widely acknowledged, there were, and perhaps still is, some scepticism about the implications and consequences of a 'private sector' accounting system in the French municipalities: some doubts about the fact that private accounting would improve accountability and transparency to the local citizen and taxpayer, doubts about the need of a cost/performance measurement system for most public services, and some doubts about the need for an additional burden imposed on small local authorities and the real 'value for money' of this new form of bureaucracy designed by some civil servants.

The municipal accounting reform carried out in France is by no means a universal model. However one can feel that it has reached a reasonable compromise between the somewhat idealized purity of the private accounting model, and the more traditional budget model which is designed to answer the basic taxpayer's question who wants to know 'where his tax money goes'.

This conclusion can be extended to other levels of government: after the municipal sector, workgroups on the reforms of the 'département' and 'région' accounting systems have been launched, and are still deliberating. Some pilot sites would hopefully implement the reform in 2001.

The further step will be the question of the State budget and accounting system itself. The Ministry of Finance has launched since 1996-1997 several workgroups on 'patrimonial accounting': no doubt that the municipal experience will serve as a guide and a partial reference for a reform yet to come.

References

- Jean-Claude Scheid, Revue Française des Finances Publiques, N° 49, 1994 '*Le reporting communal: pratiques Américanes et loi ATR*'.
- Vicente Pina and Lourdes Torres, proceedings of the EIASM-conference '*Accounting for the new public management*', San Servolo 1998, '*Decentralization of services and consolidation of annual accounts of local governments*'.

CHAPTER 20

LOCAL GOVERNMENT ACCOUNTING IN NORWAY:
CENTRAL NORMS CREATE CONFUSING INFORMATION
AT THE LOCAL LEVEL

Helge Mauland and Frode Mellemvik

20.1. Introduction

Norwegian local government consists of 435 municipalities and 19 counties. There are approximately 4.4 mill. inhabitants in Norway and 90 % of them are living in 10 % of the local governments. The Norwegian Act of Local Government (ALG) enacted in 1993 has detailed regulations concerning the preparation of local governments' budgets and accounts. In accordance with the ALG the Ministry of Local Government and Regional Development (MLGRD) has issued comprehensive central regulations for budgeting and accounting procedures. Most probably Norwegian local governments are facing extensive changes in budgeting and accounting rules. Several years ago a pilot project for more precise recording of local government data to the government was implemented. The pilot project was terminated in 1997 and has been evaluated as a success in 1998. Full-scale implementation with minor amendments is expected in 1999 and 2000 in all of Norway's 435 local governments. The implementation of a new local government reporting system necessitates another set of central regulations replacing the 1993-regulations. The intention is to put the regulations in force from the beginning of the year 2000. By Norwegian standards this is a very ambitious time schedule.

The new reporting system involves essential alterations in the local government reporting system to the central government concerning activities and functions. The main report of to-day (MLGRD, 1993) including an operating statement, a capital report and a balance-sheet, will not be changed after the implementation of the new reporting system. This means no changes in the fundamental financial accounting principles. Kommunal Rapport (1998) has summed up the changes in this way:
- the main purpose is to facilitate the surveillance of local governments' service production and use of resources;
- local governments (municipalities and counties) will have to report production of services in accordance with a more detailed classification;
- for all services volume produced, demand and use of resources have to be reported;
- ease comparisons between local governments.

It is noteworthy that focus is on resource allocation, which means that the term of costs (in contrast to expenditures) probably will be far more central in future than in the existing system.

A. Bac (ed.), International Comparative Issues in Government Accounting, 327-339.

The Act of Accounting (AA) which came into force 01.01.99 comprises most organizations including public services (electricity, water supply, transport etc.), local governmental and governmental organizations not comprised by the ALG and other legislation which except them. Financial accounting of the central government is also excepted.

Our main concern is whether the local government accounting system should be harmonized with either the rules of the Act of Accounting or the accounting system of the central government. The central government budgets and accounts are prepared according to the principle of cash-basis accounting. This seems to be in accordance with international governmental accounting practise. In the last years however there has taken place a change towards practising accrual-basis accounting principles in the governmental sector. Pioneers in this context are New Zealand and Australia (Guthrie 1993, 1997), but also the Swedish governmental accounting system has now been adapted to the principles of accrual-basis accounting (Falkman, 1998).[1] The question which is focussed on in this paper is what kind of information the Norwegian local government accounting system produces, including a discussion of problems and possible changes.

20.2. A brief Review of the Norwegian Local Government Budgeting and Accounting System

The local government accounting system of today is a hybrid. Local government accounting statements are partly prepared on an accrual-basis, partly on a cash-basis. In addition repayments on long-term loans as well as some types of applications of equity are recorded in the operating statements. The matching principle is adapted for some revenues and expenditures, but not for others. It is a common belief among accountants in general that local government accounting reports are prepared on a cash-basis principle, but this is not the truth. Changes in liquid assets are not shown explicitly in financial reports, they have to be worked out separately.

The income statement shows in principle all changes in owner's equity due to operations. This is true also for the Norwegian local governmental accounting report, but in addition it includes a lot of transactions unknown in income statements of enterprises. In a Norwegian local government accounting report we could also find for instance repayments on long-term loans, new loans, loans to others, fixed capital acquisitions, acquisitions of long-term shares, sales of long-term shares. The report will also include many so-called internal financial transactions. These internal transactions are so numerous that in many reports they overshadow the external transactions reported.

The Norwegian local government accounting report includes four statements:
- the operating statement;
- the capital statement;
- the fund flows statement;
- the balance-sheet.
A rough outline of the operating and the capital statements is presented in table 20.1.

---

[1]   For a detailed analysis and discussion, see Olson et al. (1998).

Operating Statement (OS)	Capital Statement (CS)
+ Operating revenues	+ Gross acquisitions and investments
- *Operating expenditures*	+ New long-term loans
= Gross operating surplus	+ *Fund allocations*
- Net interests	= *Funding requirements*
- *Repayments on long-term loans*	*Funding*
= Net operating surplus/deficit	New long-term loans
Application of net operating s/d	+ Central government contributions
Funding of expenditures in CS	+ Transfers from OS
	+ Other contributions
+ *Net fund allocations*	+ *Use of reserves (equity)*
= *Surplus of the year (residual)*	= *Sum of funding = funding requirement*

Table 20.1.:   Fundamental Structure of Local Governments' Operating and Capital Statements

This system is not adopted by the central government. In the accounting (and budgeting) system of central government the OS and the CS are integrated into one statement. Until 1993 local governments had a version of same system, but then it was changed[2]. Local governments are preparing their budgets and accounts in a unique way. No other Norwegian organizations have adopted similar principles and regulations. It is not far beyond reason to assert that the system is 'home-made' in the ministry traditionally staffed by people who have not much formal accounting competence. Many of them have a juridical education making them good in developing norms and rules. In our research so far we have not found an international parallel to the Norwegian local government accounting system.

We will in this paper not explain in details every item in the statements. It is noteworthy, however, that three different 'operating surpluses/deficits' occur in the operating statement. Media normally focus on the bottom line, surplus of the year, which is a residual. In our opinion this item gives no information that could be interpreted in a consistent way. A local government officer can manipulate this figure for instance via net funds allocations. The gross operating surplus is in many ways parallel to the operating profit of an enterprise, but local governments are not profit-oriented organizations. The second term, the net operating surplus, is influenced by repayments on long-term loans, an alien item in the income statements of an enterprise.

The capital statement (CS) includes acquisition of fixed assets, shares and long-term loans. These items are recorded as expenditures, but simultaneously they are recorded in the balance sheet. Thus, fixed assets are recorded as expenditures the year of acquisition and at the same time depreciated in the OS. We find these kinds of peculiarities also in the accounts of the central government, but to a less extent.

Transfers from OS to the CS are important funding sources, which emphasizes the close connection between the OS and the CS. Until 1993 the OS and the CS were integrated in one statement, but then they were separated into two statements. The CS cannot formally

---

[2]   See Mellemvik and Monsen (1996).

be closed with a deficit. A deficit must in worst case be compensated by using the so-called liquidity reserve, which is an equity account. In many Norwegian local governments the liquidity reserve is negative. In such a case the accounts are closed with a deficit though this is not allowed. In the budgetary process the CS cannot be closed by drawing on the liquidity reserve, this is exclusively an accounting phenomenon.

The balance sheet (BS) is very much a copy of such a statement for an enterprise, and as shown below the structure and the items are the same as found in the private sector. The outline of the structure is presented in table 20.2.

Current assets	Short term liabilities
	Long term liabilities
Fixed assets	Equity

Table 20.2.:   Main Structure of Balance Sheet of
                Local Governments

From 1999 the order of presentation is reversed for Norwegian enterprises starting with the fixed elements and ending up with current. This more or less cosmetic change was made as a part of a reform aimed at adjusting Norwegian enterprise accounting to the standards of the EU.

Equity is defined as total assets minus total liabilities. The composition of the equity in Norwegian local governments is very peculiar. In table 20.3. we present a brief overview of the different items included in the local government equity concept.

- Restricted operating funds
- Unrestricted capital funds
- Restricted capital funds
- Unrestricted operating funds
- Accumulated accounting deficits this year and earlier
- Accumulated surpluses not yet allocated
- Liquidity reserve operating statement
- Liquidity reserve capital statement
- General equity account

Table 20.3.: Local Government Equity

Norwegian local governments have nine different kinds of equity accounts to keep up with. The regulations concerning the equity accounts are difficult to understand and give local government officers a huge battery of possibilities to play on when closing the accounts. In the regulations issued by the MLGRD much attention and importance are given to each item on the equity list. From an accountant's point of view the economic realities and the solidity of an organization are unchanged when a figure is transported from one account to another on the list above. Some of the concepts may even be misleading. The concept of liquidity reserve causes much confusion. It is a common belief that liquidity reserve indicates bank deposits or cash. To explain that the account of the liquidity reserve may be used even if the organization is insolvent represents a considerable pedagogical challenge.

It will be far beyond the scope of this paper to fully explain the equity account. For a more detailed description and discussion of the equity account, see Mauland and Mellemvik (1998). To understand the use of this account it is however, essential to understand the functioning of the local government accounting system[3]. Briefly expressed, this account can be classified as an account of adjustment, and how it is used is illustrated below. Above we explained the acquisition of fixed assets. When e.g. a building is acquired, the amount is recorded both in a CS-account as an expenditure and in a BS-account as a fixed asset (both debit records). The credit records are a bank account and the general equity account. For most accounting students these technicalities are doubtless difficult to understand.

20.3. Capital Acquisitions, Depreciation and Operating Surplus/Deficit

The problems of capital acquisitions, depreciation and operating will be illustrated by an example from a local government named Capdep. In the beginning of year X0 Capdep acquired equipment for 2000. The equipment is funded by means of unrestricted capital fund. The data of local government of Capdep is presented in table 20.4.

Balance Sheet local Government of CAPDEP 01.01.X0	
Bank deposits	2,000
Unrestricted capital fund	2,000
In the beginning of year X0 capital equipment to be depreciated linearly in 5 years is acquired for 2000	
The capital equipment is funded by means of unrestricted capital fund Operating income and expenditures are 20,000 and 19,600 respectively for each year. Depreciation is not included in the amount of 19,600.	
A surplus is to be allocated to the liquidity capital reserve account by the first ordinary budgetary treatment, which means two years later	

Table 20.4.: Local Government of Capdep, Illustrative Data

Before presenting the annual reports in accordance with ALG and the local government accounting regulations, the solution according to general accounting principles in the Norwegian AA will briefly be demonstrated in table 20.5.

---

[3]   See Sunde (1998) for further details

Financial reporting according to the AA					
Income Statement	Year X0	Year X1	Year X2	Year X3	Year X4
Operating profit before depreciation	400	400	400	400	400
Depreciation	-400	-400	-400	-400	-400
Operating profit	*0*	*0*	*0*	*0*	*0*
Balance Sheet 31.12	Year X0	Year X1	Year X2	Year X3	Year X4
Fixed asset/equipment	1,600	1,200	800	400	0
Bank deposits	400	800	1,200	1,600	2,000
Total assets	*2,000*	*2,000*	*2,000*	*2,000*	*2,000*
Owners equity	2,000	2,000	2,000	2,000	2,000
Retained earnings	0	0	0	0	0
Total liabilities and equity	*2,000*	*2,000*	*2,000*	*2,000*	*2,000*

Table 20.5.: Local Government of Capdep

The example is trivial, but it illustrates some of the problems using Norwegian local government accounting reports.

Annually operating profit after the deduction of depreciation allowances, is 0^4. At the end of year 4 the equipment is completely depreciated, and at the same time bank deposits are sufficient to replace the original equipment, provided no inflation or specific change in prices. The use of the actual equipment measured in monetary terms, is taken into consideration through depreciation. The effect of depreciation is that sufficient cash is retained to ensure replacement. In the balance sheet total assets are 2000 each year, but the composition of assets changes from equipment to bank deposits/cash annually.

The story is not quite so simple when the reports are prepared in accordance with the Norwegian local government accounting regulations (LGAR). The reports are presented in table 20.6. In this example there are no financial items. Consequently gross operating surplus and net operating surplus are identical. The bottom line of the operating statement is 400 annually compared to 0 when reported according to general accepted accounting principles. Depreciation is recorded both as a revenue item and an expenditure item. The LGAR does not allow depreciation to influence neither net operating surplus nor the bottom line. This may be characterized as an odd way of accounting. It is due to the fact that capital acquisitions in reality are recorded as expenditures. Depreciation could have been left out entirely. However, according to the accounting regulations it is important to show the use of capital equipment in the accounting reports. Another reason for including depreciation is that most public services are priced according to full costing principles and depreciation is part of full cost. These calculations are also often part of the basis for governmental contributions and transfers from the central government to local governments. Thus, it is important to include depreciation in the local government accounting system.

---

[4] For the case of simplicity all problems concerning taxation are left out.

In the announced new LGAR it seems to be much emphasis on the real use of resources involved in the production of goods and services. The central government view (public servants of central government always have the final word when new LGAR are issued) is that accounting reports will not give a true view of resources used if depreciation is omitted. In the new LGAR depreciation will influence gross operating surplus, but not net operating surplus and the bottom line. This means that the technically complicated accounting regime will continue. The recording is complicated, and we are afraid understanding of local government accounting reports will still be confined to few persons, and especially to the initiators of the accounting regulations.

Operating statement	Year X0	Year X1	Year X2	Year X3	Year X4
Gross operating surplus before depreciation	400	400	400	400	400
Depreciation in operating statement	-400	-400	-400	-400	-400
Depreciation in operating statement	400	400	400	400	400
Use of accumulated non-allocated fund	0	0	400	400	400
Transfer to CS	0	0	-400	-400	-400
Non allocated net margin	**400**	**400**	**400**	**400**	**400**
	Year X0	Year X1	Year X2	Year X3	Year X4
Capital statement					
Capital acquisitions	-2,000	0	0	0	0
Liquidity reserve allocation	0	0	-400	-400	-400
Need to be funded	**-2,000**	**0**	**-400**	**-400**	**-400**
Transfer from OS	0	0	400	400	400
Use of restricted capital funds	2,000	0	0	0	0
Total funding	**2,000**	**0**	**400**	**400**	**400**
Balance sheet report 31.12	År X0	År X1	År X2	År X3	År X4
Cash/bank deposits	400	800	1,200	1,600	2,000
Fixed capital equipment	1,600	1,200	800	400	0
Total assets	**2,000**	**2,000**	**2,000**	**2,000**	**2,000**
Unrestricted capital fund	0	0	0	0	0
Liquidity reserve capital	0	0	400	800	1,200
Accumulated net operating surplus	400	800	800	800	800
General equity account	1,600	1,200	800	400	0
Total liabilities and equity	**2,000**	**2,000**	**2,000**	**2,000**	**2,000**

Table 20.6.: Reports in Accordance with Local Government Accounting Regulations

The annual surpluses coincide with the annual changes in bank deposits. Apparently surplus of the year is identical with change in bank deposits, but this is due to the fact that no items are accrued except for depreciation. There are no short-term receivables and no current liabilities in our example, but this is an unrealistic assumption in the real Norwegian local government accounting word. These items are left out in an attempt not to draw attention away from what we consider the central point in this context. A surplus at the bottom line of the OS is in fact identical with the change in working capital. The annual budget has to balance, i.e. neither surplus nor deficit are allowed. A surplus is in many ways an unintended change in working capital. This is one of the main reasons why the Norwegian local government accounting system often is characterized as a financially oriented accounting system.

In the CS the capital acquisition is recorded as expenditure. At the same time the acquisition is recorded in the balance sheet. To accountants this seems to be a contradiction. To give a better understanding of how this functions, we show in table 20.7. how this technically is recorded.

	Debit	Credit
Plant and equipment (balance sheet account)	2,000	
Bank deposits (balance sheet account)		2,000
Capital acquisition/investment (CS-account)	2,000	
General equity account (balance sheet account)		2,000

Table 20.7.:   Recording of Equipment in Local Governments

In accounting we are familiar with the first debit-credit entry. In the Norwegian local government context we have in addition a debit-record in the CS met by a credit-record in the general equity account. Thus the system may be characterized as a double-double entry recording system. The general equity account is in many ways an account of equity adjustment. The debit-record of 2000 in the CS influences surplus (and thus equity) in a negative way. This is compensated by crediting the general equity account by an identical amount.

20.4.   Unrestricted Use of Accumulated Surpluses

The ALG describes in a detailed way how surplus and deficit in the OS has to be allocated. According to the rules a surplus can be allocated to any purpose, but it contains no instructions about time. The local government council has to decide upon how surplus is to be allocated. Until now it has been usual to allocate the surplus in the first ordinary budget. Let us return to the example. The surplus (bottom line) is figured and becomes known during springtime X1. The first ordinary budgetary debate takes place in the local government council in autumn 19X1 when the council decides upon the operating budget for 19X2. This budget has to be decided upon within 31.12.X1. It is illegal according to ALG to start operations in 19X2 without an approved budget. In our example allocation to liquidity capital reserve account is preferred, but there are no obstacles in making allocations to capital fund. In the end of 19X2 the accumulated surplus is 800, but it will not grow any further.

Accumulated surplus is credited to an operating revenue account in the OS. The law demands that a surplus in the OS has to be allocated in the OS. If the council wishes to use the surplus to build up a capital fund for future investments, a transfer from OS to CS has to be made. It is indeed a complicated system to understand and overview.

20.5.   Local Government Accounting Reports gives Misleading Information

Applying this example, what kind of information do we have from Norwegian local government accounting reports? In our opinion the value of information is very questionable. Readers of these reports are given partly misleading or even wrong descriptions of the financial position and economic strength of the local government. At the same time the statements must be characterized as cumbersome and not easily available, even for skilled accountants. In our example an amount was allocated to the liquidity capital reserve account. Allocations of this kind are however made on a voluntary basis. The surplus may be allocated to current operations without being in conflict with the ALG.

The previous ALG did not permit this kind of allocations. A supreme principle in the previous ALG was the preservation and maintenance of fortune. In the 1993 ALG there is far less emphasis on capital preservation. In the latter part of the 1980's and in the beginning of the 1990's some local governments, especially in the north, got into serious financial trouble. The consequence was a new section in the 1993 ALG, stating that the local council had a particular responsibility to monitor the liquidity of the local government. The local council has according to the ALG an obligation to ensure sufficient funding of current operations. If general accounting principles had been applied, the question in matter would not have arose, due to depreciation allowances.

20.6. The Acquisition of Shares and Decline in Share Values

In this chapter we are going to take a closer look at the acquisition of shares, the decline in share values and how these phenomena are recorded in local government accounting reports. To grasp our main message in an easier way we once more apply an example, which is presented in tables 20.8., 20.9. and 20.10.

An organization, which applies local government accounting rules, starts up activities 02.01.X1. The opening balance sheet is as follows:
Bank deposits 0   Equity 0
During the first year of operations revenue and expenditure data are:
Operating revenue   10,000
Operating expenditure   9,000
In the end of year X1 the organization acquires shares in a publicly owned corporation for 1000 in an attempt to save employees' jobs. The acquisition is funded by a transfer for OS to CS. The revenue and expenditure data are identically for year X2. In the end of X2 the publicly owned corporation ends its activities due to financial trouble. The shares are to be considered worthless and are fully written down in the accounts.

Table 20.8.:   The Acquisition of Shares and Decline in Share Values

The financial statements according to the Norwegian AA are presented in table 20.9. Again the illustrative material is quite trivial. It is obvious that profit is 1000 in year X1 and 0 in year X2.

Statement of income	Year X1	Year X2
Operating revenue	10,000	10,000
Operating expense	-9,000	-9,000
Realized loss on shares		-1,000
Profit	1 000	0
Balance sheet	**31.12.X1**	**31.12.X2**
Shares	1,000	0
Bank deposits	0	1,000
Total assets	1,000	1,000
Equity	1,000	1,000
Total equity and liabilities	1,000	1,000

Table 20.9.:   Financial Statements according to Norwegian AA

Let us now turn to the government solution in year 1 (table 20.10.).

Operating Statement	**Year X1**
Operating revenue	10,000
Operating expenditure	-9,000
Net operating surplus	1,000
Transfer to CS	-1,000
Non allocated surplus	**0**
Capital Statement	**Year X1**
Acquisition of shares	*-1,000*
Transfer from operating statement	*1,000*
Balance Sheet Report	**31.12.X1**
Shares	*1,000*
Equity	*1,000*

Table 20.10.:   Local Government Solution in Year 1

As we explained above all capital acquisitions have to be recorded in the CS. This is equivalent with recording the acquisition as expenditure and recording the acquisition as an asset in the balance sheet simultaneously. The reader immediately discovers that profit according to the AA and net operating margin according to the LGAR varies in opposite direction. The AA income statement shows a profit margin of 1000 while the LGAR operating statement shows 0. It is up to the reader to decide upon what he or she considers give the most correct reporting.

The reporting of year 2 in accordance with the LGAR are shown in table 20.11

Operating Statement	Year X2
Operating revenue	10,000
Operating expenditure	-9,000
Net operating surplus	**1,000**
Transfer to CS	0
Non allocated surplus	1,000
Balance Sheet Report	**Year X2**
Shares	0
Total Assets	**1,000**
Non-allocated surplus year X2	1,000
Equity	0
Total Liabilities and Equity	**1,000**

Table 20.11.: The Reporting of Year 2 in accordance with the LGAR

It is remarkable that loss on shares is not reported at all. On the contrary, in year X2 an operating surplus of 1000 is reported. Total assets, liabilities and equity are identical in both years.

This example illustrates that applying the LGAR it is difficult to be sure what is a surplus and what is a deficit. The most serious problem is that the reporting according to the LGAR is not connected to or tied up against any generally accepted accounting principles. Consequently, it is difficult to interpret the information in an any reasonable way.

20.7. Summary

In the last years there has been much focus on operating surplus/deficit, performance, performance indicators, effectiveness and efficiency in public sector accounting (see e.g. Olson et al., 1998). Until now this has been most evidently recessed in central government regulations and reports. Norwegian governmental institutions, for instance universities and state colleges, are now instructed to make internal accounting reports exhibiting current revenues and expenses caused by different activities. The central government accounting system is still based upon the cash principle. The implication is that systems converting accrual accounting data to cash accounting data have had to be available.

For local governments, and not least the MLGRD issuing the accounting regulations, it must be essential to establish a better framework for accounting reports. In practice two main directions exist. On the one hand the MLGRD can issue regulations based on the accounting principles based on the AA. Choosing this alternative special arrangements have to be made reflecting the fact that local government institutions are non-profit organizations. On the other hand the MLGRD can cultivate cash-based accounting systems and specify the main accounting report of local governments to be a cash flow statement. In this context the MLGRD is in the lucky position to draw on important experience obtained through experimentation and research in this field (see Mellemvik and Olson, 1996).

Norwegian local governments have since 1991 the opportunity to make accounting reports adjusted to own requirements. An express condition however is the conversion of data produced in alternative accountings systems to the template of the LGAR. Conversion systems are often costly to run and cumbersome to maintain. Very few local governments have taken the opportunity of alternative accounting systems so far. Accounting competence and capacity are restricted in most Norwegian local governments, and many local government officers have hands full keeping up with the existing complex regulations. To run two different kinds of accounting systems is a problem in itself.

The LGAR has been changed several times during the years. The application of accounting ideas and principles derived from private sector accounting was until few years ago not on the agenda. In the last years on LGAR amendment occasions it is quite often referred to the private sector arguing that accounting reports of local governments must be as reliable as those prepared by enterprises. Until now this reliability has not been attained. The main weaknesses of the LGAR of today can be summed up as follows:
-   the complicated book-keeping system;
-   equity and liability transactions are mixed up in a way that causes confusion;
-   net operating surplus and surplus of the year are influenced by repayments on long term loans and recording and reporting of capital acquisitions as expenditures;
-   the accounting system does not focus on neither the use of resources (expenses) nor cash-outflows.

References

- Aavik, P (1998) Kommuneregnskapet er uforståelig for fagfolk, *Kommunal Rapport, nr. 24.*
- Falkman, P. (1998) *Statlig redovisning enligt bokföringsmässiga grunder: en redovisningsteoretisk analys*, CEFOS, Göteborg.
- Guthrie, J. (ed.) 1993: *The Australian Public Sector: Pathways to Change in the 1990s*, IIR Conferences, Sydney.
- Guthrie, J. (1998) Application of Accrual Accounting in the Australian Public Sector, Rhetoric or Reality?, *Financial Accountability & Management*, No. 1, Vol. 14, 1-19.
- Kommunal og regionaldepartementet (1997) *KOSTRA - Rapportering av data om kommunal økonomi og tjenesteproduksjon*, Oslo.
- Kommunal og regionaldepartementet (1997) KOSTRA, Forskrifter for forsøk med alternativ rapportering av økonomi og tjenestedata, Oslo.
- Kommunal- og arbeidsdepartementet (1993) *Nye forskrifter for kommunale og fylkeskommunale budsjetter og regnskap*, Akademika, Oslo.
- Kommunal rapport (1998) nr. 13.
- Mauland, H. og Mellemvik, F. (1998) Regnskap, budsjettering, økonomistyring i offentlig sektor, Cappelen Akademisk Forlag, Oslo.
- Mellemvik, F. og Monsen, N. (1996) Fire norske regnskapsverdener - en studie av statens innvirkning ved fastsettelsen av regnskapsstandarder, *Beta*, No. 1, 17-38.
- Mellemvik, F. og Olson, O. (red) (1996) *Regnskap i forandring: utvikling, spredning og bruk av kommuneregnskap*, Cappelen Akademisk Forlag, Oslo.
- Olson, O., Guthrie, J. Og Humphrey, C. (eds.) (1998) *Global Warning. Debating International Developments in New Public Financial Management*, Cappelen Akademisk Forlag, Oslo.
- Sunde,Ø. (1998) Kommuneregnskapet etter god regnskapsskikk, *Kommunerevisoren, NKRF Tidsskrift*, nr. 4, 4–11.

CHAPTER 21

BUDGETING AND ACCOUNTING PRACTICES FOR SUBSOVEREIGN DEBT ISSUERS

Krzystof Cichocki, Jeanine Kleimo and James Ley

21.1. Current System and Debt Issuance Situation in Poland

21.1.1. INTRODUCTION

Economies emerging from central planning, such as Poland, still suffer from a statist orientation in their local governments. The fundamental characteristics of financial reporting involve municipal responsibility to communicate and to be accountable to central ministries or other authorities which often continue to provide large measures of the budgetary resources available to municipal governments. Financial reporting focuses on expenditure management, or ensuring that budgeted resources - over 60 percent of them obtained from the central government - are expended for eligible purposes in keeping with the budget, and on minimizing deficits. There are few gains to be obtained from generating operating surpluses, as these - in the case of Poland - cannot be held in reserve for future expenditures or assigned to particular projects for which they were not budgeted. Instead, a budgetary surplus is carried over to the next year to finance what may otherwise be a deficit, or for whatever purpose the municipal board and council decide.

Debt management is one of the most important elements of public finance. It includes all processes related to issuance of debt, its service and monitoring, as well as identification and control of various types of risk associated with borrowing or issuing debt. Loan proceeds, credits and municipal bonds in Poland are the means of financing budget deficit, while debt service, including principal and interest, extends over many years and is a real burden for local government budgets in the future.

The development of Poland's subsovereign debt markets has been truly remarkable. Several studies have chronicled the growth of Poland's subsovereign debt markets over the four years, 1994 -1997. These studies reveal that the market, while still quite small relative to the entire Polish public and private debt market system, grew swiftly over the four-year study period. However, information flows in the present system fail to contribute to an environment in which decision - makers have access to the information and analysis they need for effective and open operations. Ideally, information should flow from municipalities to the state or central government, from the central government to municipalities, from one municipality to another, and from municipal employees to the public and to the municipal council. At present, there is only effective communication from local governments to the center in accordance with guidance and regulations issued by ministries and other state authorities, and some communication between municipal employees and the municipal Council.

A. Bac (ed.), International Comparative Issues in Government Accounting, 341-357.
© 2001 *Kluwer Academic Publishers. Printed in the Netherlands.*

21.1.2. GMINA BUDGET STRUCTURE

The basic revenue of a Polish *gmina* or municipality is guaranteed by the Law on Local Government. Standard-setting laws passed by the Parliament define revenue types and methods of calculation. The sources of funds that flow into municipal budgets are defined at various levels of detail by the Constitution of the Republic of Poland, the Law on Public Finance (substituting for Budget Law since January 1999); the Law on the Revenue of Local Government, and the Local Self-Government Act. Expenditures, borne by units of local government, are defined by the Local Self-Government Act and the Law Amending the Scope of Responsibilities of Certain Cities, according to the specificity and the scope of their responsibilities. Although the Law on Public Finance introduces many new provisions regarding debt issuance and management, it draws on provisions of the old Budget Law, and repeats many of its drawbacks. These will be discussed further in the following sections.

Allowable total revenues of local government (gminas) as defined by Polish law consist of:
-   local revenues (locally collected property taxes, vehicle tax and other taxes, and user fees and charges);
-   gmina shares of the personal and corporate income taxes;
-   general subvention, including the educational subvention and the compensation subvention for poor gminas;
-   earmarked grants from the central government, including grants for delegated tasks and for financing investments projects.

With the exception of earmarked grants, most of these revenues are easy to forecast for financing investments projects for which allocation procedures are not transparent. Some cities are allocated additional shares of personal income tax. Municipal revenues also include budgetary revenues of budgetary units accounting to municipalities and a budget surplus of budgetary enterprises, which are considered off-budget organizations.

There is also substantial differentiation in the robustness of municipal revenues across cities of different sizes; the situation in rural gminas is substantially worse than average. This is due, in part, to lower own-revenues from the property tax and other local taxes. In addition, Poland's farmers have yet to be included in the personal income tax system. Until this year, however, rural gminas received some of the shared personal income taxes generated in urban jurisdictions because tax shares were calculated on a per-capita basis for the entire voivodship (a political subdivision which includes multiple gminas). The new Law and Local Government Revenues eliminates the voivodship basis for calculating shared taxes and thus will give each local government shares of only those taxes generated within its jurisdiction.

Gmina expenditures, as defined by Polish law, consist of all recurring personnel and operating expenditures, interest payments on short- and long-term debt, gmina guarantees of municipal enterprise (e.g. public utility) loans, and capital investment expenditures made from current revenues or the proceeds of borrowed funds. Recurring operating expenditures do not vary dramatically from year to year, unless major changes in the types or levels of services offered have occurred. Budgetary classification of expenditures is similar to the functional classifications of the International Monetary Fund. The relative proportions of operating expenditures are assigned to health care, education, municipal services, and other activities, although differences do exist.

The Law on Public Finance, previously known as the Budget Law, defines local government budgets as annual budgets and does not recommend setting up multi-year investment plans. The Law defines a budget surplus or deficit as the difference between the total revenue and the total expenditure of a gmina, and thus accepts the possibility of gminas incurring budget shortfalls (deficits). It also specifies sources gminas may use to cover the deficit.

The budget surplus or deficit is not a good measure of the financial condition of the gmina in consecutive years. It would be misleading to base an assessment of a gmina's financial condition on the difference of revenue and expenditure defined by law. This is due to several factors. First, analysis of only the revenue and expenditure statements of the gmina can lead to false conclusions, if not supported by a more in-depth analysis of the revenue and expenditure structure. Second and more importantly, the definition of gmina revenues does not include loan proceeds, bond issuance proceeds, surplus from previous years, and proceeds from privatization or sale of gmina property. These are used instead to offset the budget deficit. Third, the definition of gmina expenditures does not include amounts allocated for the repayment of loan principal. Fourth, cash based accounting is predominantly observed in the local government budget as a part of the Polish public finance system. Actual payments made in a given budget year are considered as the revenue and expenditure, irrespective of the period to which they refer and when they became due. Therefore, an analysis of the financial condition of a gmina cannot be based upon budget data for a single year. It is necessary to analyze budgets of several consecutive years. Some grants, for example, shares in income taxes transferred to local government by the central authorities, are allocated based on accrual accounting principles. An assessment of any further debt carrying capacity (e.g., to finance a capital project) is possible only with the knowledge of the structure of gmina finance, including the ratio of the revenue to the external sources of funding.

In order to obtain an actual and undistorted picture of the financial status and financial management in the gmina, one should base the analysis on the revenues and expenditures, as defined in the Public Finance Law, on additional resources, defined in the budget as non-revenues (*przychody*), and non-expenditures (*rozchody*), and on the actual cash flows between the gmina and other entities. In addition, accumulated deficits prompt a closer look at the actual impact of the future debt service, especially within the context of the risk related to a change in interest rates.

21.1.3. OPERATIONAL AND CAPITAL EXPENDITURES AND THE NEED FOR SEGREGATION

Up until early 1999, the Budget Law governed local self-government in Poland and did not stipulate the need for or benefit from separate operating and capital budgets, contributing to the overemphasis on current operations at the expense of longer term development. The new Law on Public Finance, despite efforts by local government representatives, does not introduce separation of operating and capital budgets.

However, it does require preparation of an investment expenditure plan for two years following the budget year.

Despite this improvement, there is still a tendency to emphasize annual operating requirements and subsequent demands for municipal resources. When there is a desperate need for a particular capital project, the annual budget is 'robbed' of its resources to pay for large, one-time investments. Even in cases without this extreme competition between operating and capital resources, there is unlikely to be rational planning based on the execution of strategic decisions or on a long-term perspective of the needs of the city or town.

The new law provides only a partial solution. With few exceptions, gminas do not have a capital budget. Municipalities do not compare the costs and benefits of undertaking desired capital investment activities in a manner related to the cost of financing options, including internal financing. Neither do they compare options for internal financing or external financing of the same project. Further, in most municipalities there is not a system in place for establishing criteria and priorities for capital outlays, as these must compete with operating expenses for scarce budgetary resources. Finally, the failure to segregate capital and operating budgets tends to result in a failure to account for (and report on) the impact of debt on the budget in a useful manner from the standpoint of internal financial management.

Decision making would be enhanced by such segregation, especially those related to rehabilitation versus new construction of municipal facilities, including housing and technical infrastructure. Capital budgeting techniques would make it possible to assess the costs and benefits of alternative capital development scenarios and to compare them with budget resources. Without a separate capital budget, there tends to be an overemphasis on rehabilitation and maintenance instead of construction and replacement, as the annual or apparent budgetary implications are reduced. In an environment in which there is neither separation of capital and operating budgets nor accounting for depreciation, distortions in resource allocation often result, leading to less than efficient use of scarce budgetary funds. If depreciation were entered into the accounts, there would be a record and report of the value of fixed assets which may be used by managers to determine their replacement schedules. Lacking such crucial information, managers who attempt to minimize annual or operating budget impact will often seek to allocate funds to maintain the current stock of fixed assets rather than to assess, in an objective manner, whether replacement makes better long-term financial sense.

Setting up a separate capital budget requires the commitment of resources for this collective purpose. This means, in practice, informed judgment regarding the amount of funds required to meet operating demands, leaving the remainder for capital projects. Alternatively, commitments of resources to capital projects can be made first, leaving residual resources for operations. Ideally, a strategic plan would set out capital investment requirements for the gmina for the intermediate or long term and resource commitments to the capital side of the budget could be made accordingly.

Effective budget management requires not only separate capital and operating budgets, but also the application of realistic projection techniques and the ability to commit to multi-year appropriations. One way to introduce multi-year appropriations is to create reserve accounts for maintenance of major facilities.

The identification and implementation of long-term capital improvement plans necessitates the allocation of resources towards the achievement of a clear investment agenda. This, of course, demands that a separate capital budget be devised to allocate and monitor the distribution of resources towards this purpose. In other words, the lack of segregation between the operating and capital budgets impairs the ability to undertake capital improvement planning by failing to make a clear resource allocation to the capital side of the budget. Planners concerned with economic development, infrastructure adequacy and expansion, and other public works would find their work made easier by an overall division of operating and investment resources.

Once resources are segregated, it becomes possible to undertake additional steps towards rational and efficient resource allocation and utilization. Capital improvement planning is just one component of this increased transparency and efficiency. Within capital improvement planning efforts, local government managers can choose to establish priorities for the use of available investment resources. It is more difficult to attempt such prioritization without an agreed-upon level of investment in the budget; furthermore, the results of doing so will be less evident.

With operating and capital resources segregated, the formulation and application of basic priority criteria is not a difficult process - if there is the political will to do so. In many cases, political and other subjective, non-efficiency-oriented criteria guide the allocation of capital resources, and the will to change is the first step towards recognizing the merits of objective criteria and priorities. These criteria and priorities are best evolved at the municipal level in line with either formal strategic plans or simply with intermediate to long term goals in mind. The simple goals of improving certain infrastructure, improving service access, or reducing service costs are sufficient for competent municipal staff to use to generate such criteria.

21.2. Debt Management and Reporting; Limits on Debt and Deficits

21.2.1. DEMAND FOR INFRASTRUCTURE FINANCE

Issues in documenting capacity to issue debt must be linked with the demands of private sector investors to finance profitable investments. Investors and underwriters who undertake due diligence also seek to have this effort facilitated by the issuer. Accounting and financial management structures which are not transparent and which do not reveal clearly the streams of revenue and expenditures anticipated are difficult if not impossible for investors to accept. Furthermore, billing and collection systems for municipal services supported by debt must be businesslike and demonstrate an effective collection effort to justify the investment.

Traditionally, borrowing has been undertaken solely for the purpose of financing budgetary deficits. Under the Budget Law, loans could not be explicitly obtained for the purpose of financing long term capital investments such as public works projects, not even for essential infrastructure. Instead, capital projects were financed and built slowly, utilizing whatever resources could be spared from each year's annual budget with some concessionary financing, for example from environmental funds. As revenues from service charges have typically been nominal and rather distant from rates needed for cost recovery, there was no perceived need to alter this system or to utilize receipts from service charges to cover the debt service on loans.

21.2.2. NEEDS FOR IMPROVEMENT OF MUNICIPAL SERVICE QUALITY

Rates or charges for municipal services, including water, sewerage, electricity, street cleaning, solid waste collection and disposal, and district heating (for homes as well as public buildings) were established during the central-planning era. It was expected that the state would subsidize these services as part of guaranteeing that everyone had access to publicly-generated benefits. During the past ten years, while goods produced in the private sector have, of course, come to be priced at market levels, goods and services produced in the public sector have not reflected market forces. There is considerable public resistance to higher rates due to a combination of factors, including a strong residual belief that public-sector services belong to the people and should cost little. The lack of transparency in service cost and price determination exacerbates public opinion that service charges do not need to be increased and, conversely, that increases will not result in improved or expanded service.

In planning, budgeting, and operating terms, rate-setting and rate collection are divorced from critical management accounting issues such as cost recovery and efficiency. In many cases, municipal services are only expected to cover operating costs and not to contribute to the purchase of capital items such as infrastructure. In many cases, revenues are insufficient to provide for adequate maintenance of service networks and generation capacity and quality. Most fixed assets were allocated to utility divisions or companies themselves, which may or may not receive operating subsidies from the municipality. Many municipalities have deteriorating infrastructure and service quality which suffers from the lack of reinvestment. It is, however, difficult to attract investment to operations which are not at all profitable. Further, the constraints on a utility's ability to raise rates to levels necessary for repayment of debt service that would, in turn, attract capital investment, create an environment in which debt issuance backed by revenue flows to municipal utilities alone is difficult.

Once reasonable estimates of annual maintenance costs can be determined, this can be reflected in charges for municipal services, with short-term surpluses committed to a reserve account to be available to cover maintenance expenses. This would reduce the impact on the annual operating budget of municipalities which seek to implement and manage service charges that reflect the true level of cost recovery.

21.2.3. LONG TERM DEBT AND ITS SERVICE

Long-term debt is that issued for a period longer than one year and generally for purposes of financing the construction or rehabilitation of large and expensive capital infrastructure. The basic legal statutory framework in existence appears to provide a sufficient basis for the issuance of valid and enforceable long-term debt obligations. Existing banking laws and regulations, such as the bond Law of 1995, donor interventions in the financial sector and the strong interest of some gminas, all led to an estimated 611 internationally or domestically denominated market rate bank loans, with an estimated value of 979,984,000 Polish zloty (PLN) and the issuance of locally denominated 44 bond issues with a total par value of PLN 481,900,000 in the three year period from 1995 to 1997. The number and par value of commercial bank loans and bond issues closed in the last four years testifies to the fact that the banking and securities laws and enforcement mechanisms have permitted growth of the subsovereign debt market. Total concessionary lending for the same three-year period has been estimated at PLN 801,700,000 (approximately US $230 million).

Nonetheless, other indicators suggest that it is time for a significant refinement of this crucial part of the subsovereign debt market framework. These indicators suggest that only one public offering has been executed to date and that no retail market has developed.

Typical Limitations
Under the provisions of the Polish public finance law and requirements of the European Union, all Polish governments singly and combined cannot have total debt outstanding greater than 60% of their total annual revenues. Any proportion over 50% results in additional restrictions on new debt issuance until previous debt is retired to a level below 50%. These limits were prescribed to meet macro-economic standards set by the Maastricht Treaty for members of the European Union. However, no EU member has written such provisions into its domestic law. It is not entirely clear how individual countries will be able to calculate public debts when accounting and budgeting standards still differ widely within the EU itself.

Debt service is defined as principal and interest payments on debt outstanding, municipal bonds redemption and interest on bonds, as well as guarantees and sureties of municipal enterprise debt. According to Poland's Law on Public Finance, long-term debt service as a percentage of total revenues of a gmina cannot exceed 15%. When the value of total debt outstanding exceeds 55% of revenues, then debt service by law cannot exceed 12%. It should be noted that debt service is a fixed obligation that commits a municipality's resources for many years into the future. While there are economically sound reasons for issuing debt, its usage must be carefully monitored over time to ensure that a gmina does not assume more debt that it can afford to repay. The above 'stock' and 'flow' limitations are restrictive, but they are quite typical types of limits central governments use to regulate subsovereign debt.

Linking Subsovereign and Central Government Debt Limitations
Less typical is a set of debt limits that link the borrowing of subsovereign governments to the borrowing of the central government if the total consolidated public debt (national and subnational combined) exceeds 50% of Gross Domestic Product (GDP). When the consolidated public debt exceeds 59% but less than 55% of the GDP, then the ability of local governments to borrow is limited to the same deficit to revenue ratio as is enacted in the national budget for the central government. Moreover, once the 55% threshold is crossed, but is below 60%, local government borrowing is limited (by an algorithm) to

share of between 1% to 99.9% of the central government's deficit to revenue ratio. When the total consolidated public debt exceeds 60% of GDP, all borrowing both in the central government and subsovereign governments must stop. It should be noted that the debt of Polish central government is currently estimated to be close to the 50% threshold and could be above it if the Polish zloty loses value against the western currencies.

Specific Limitations

The new provisions (delineated in article 50) of the Public Finance Law require that:
1. the debt must be serviced at least once a year;
2. the discount can not exceed 5% of the nominal face value of debt (bond);
3. interest capitalization is not allowed.

As discussed in a subsection of 21.2.3., the Public Finance Law defines debt service as principal and interest payments on debt outstanding. If we observe provision 1 above, the gminas could not issue zero-coupon bonds for a period longer than one year, because, if they did, no debt service payment would occur in selected years.

Provision 2 restricts local government in their negotiations with potential lenders, although the objective of its implementation is doubtful. It will not limit substantially long term accumulation of debt repayments. It is also difficult to understand the role of the third provision. Computing interest at least once a year does not mean that interest capitalization contributes to accumulating long term payments.

Article 51 of the new Law contains a provision that the face value of a loan, denominated in Polish zloty, be determined on the day of signing a loan contract. This provision practically precludes local governments from taking credits nominated in foreign currency.

New Administrative Division

New levels of local governments were introduced in Poland in 1999. A group of gminas is called a *powiat*, and a group of *powiats* is called a *voivodship*. *Powiats* and *voivodships* will have the right to borrow and this right could prove dangerous when combined with their low revenue generating capacity, limited expenditure flexibility, and the possibility of significant unfunded or underfunded mandates. Indeed, comparative experience suggests that irresponsible sub-sovereign borrowing is most prevalent among entities that are highly dependent on the central government for their revenues, relatively constrained in the expenditure choices, and short of funds overall. Thus, it is essential that Polish gminas approach borrowing with extreme caution. Polish powiats and voivodships may not pursue the issuance of debt simply because their financial and institutional circumstances are different.

Current Bond Issuance

Between 1996 through 1998, fifty Polish gminas issued municipal bonds for the total sum of PLN 525 million. Only one such bond was a public issue, while all others were executed as private placements. In 1997, the value of bond issues was 2.5 times greater than the value registered in 1996, with the number of issues nearly doubling. It is expected that the 1999 Law on Bonds will be amended to allow for both the issuance of revenue bonds and for the creation of bond pools.

21.2.4. SHORT-TERM DEBT SERVICE

Short-term debt is defined as debt with a maturity of one year or less and which requires repayment within the budget year. It is generally issued to maintain adequate cash flows. Gminas should strive to forecast and manage their needs for cash such that they avoid altogether the need to issue short-term debt. Effective cash management programs can meet gmina cash flow needs internally by a variety of measures such as maximizing interest earnings on gmina bank deposits and short-term investments, and by scheduling tax collection due dates more evenly throughout the year. Gminas should strive to avoid the issuance of short-term debt. The overall average of the gmina own revenues, which gminas collects themselves, was approximately 40% for the period 1992-1996; therefore, only this share of revenues was available for debt service.

If the increase in spending in greater than can be accounted for by inflation or the addition of new services, it may also indicate declining productivity; i.e., the government is spending more money to support the same level of services.

21.3. Other Deficiencies in the Current System

Internal information, which serves as the basis for effective and efficient decision making is poor. Municipalities use a cash basis accounting system by law, thus impairing their capacity to assess their financial position in keeping with standards of information and decision making applied in the private sector. Efficient and effective cash management systems are lacking, and few treasurers trained in the days of central planning have the requisite skills to devise methods of cash management which could maximize their liquidity and provide opportunities for a rate of return.

Beyond cash and revenue management, there is no real debt or liability management at the municipal level. In fact, local governments lack even the mechanisms to determine safe and sustainable levels of debt. Their capacity to undertake long-term planning for infrastructure development is limited both by design (i.e. the law) and by experience

21.4. Needs for Poland

21.4.1. RECENT EFFORTS

Recent efforts to introduce internationally acceptable budgeting and accounting practices would enable local governments to attract needed investment through the emerging debt market must address the needs of potential investors for reliable financial information. There are at least two possible approaches. The current Public Finance Law does not require that municipalities and their divisions prepare financial statements or multi-year investment plans (i.e. capital improvement plans.) Central government support for local government initiatives to attract investment could be realized most effectively by changing the legal requirements requiring municipalities to provide accurate and transparent financial information and reports to decision makers, the public, and investors and by requiring local governments to generate capital improvement plans. Such plans should define how municipalities expect to secure the resources necessary for the improvements proposed.

In the absence of such an initiative, some municipalities have been able to attract private investment through the bond market in order to finance long-term investments. These gminas have produced the kind of information needed by private sector investors; however, guidance is still needed to develop formats, financial statements and reports. At a minimum, municipal officials must be able to formulate financial reports and statements, financial performance indicators, and be familiar with techniques of financial forecasting and project analysis. This would allow them to understand whether private financing, on defined terms, might benefit them as well as to assure investors that conditions related to their potential investment will be met.

21.4.2. ACCOUNTING AND FINANCIAL REPORTING

The Need of Accounting Regulation

Among the changes which must be reflected in the information generated by gminas is the presentation of financial statements which use an accrual rather than cash basis of accounting. Long-term investments dependent on revenue flows to local governments must, of course, reflect comprehensive or accrued values. As mentioned above, the segregation of capital and operating expenditures is critical. The management of financial assets in a manner designed to protect investors and to ensure the availability of surplus funds to meet financial obligations requires the adoption of reserve accounts to restrict the use of such surpluses and their exploitation for non-project purposes. Again, the most effective step to insure such performance is the creation of accounting regulations which permit the creation of such accounts. In the absence of such regulation, municipalities themselves must establish such measures to demonstrate their capacity to provide necessary assurances to investors.

Despite this lack of government policy and practice to enhance municipal capacity to communicate effectively with the private sector regarding financial opportunities, mechanisms have been found, nevertheless, which can assist in closing the gap. One such measure which offers potential is the creation of an International Accounting Standards Conversion Model as part of an effort to improve accounting practices among municipal enterprises, particularly water and wastewater entities, which are owned and operated by gminas. This conversion model is based on case studies of careful investigation at the municipal level which reveal many areas of divergence between current practice and international standards, and which outline the information which must be converted for the generation of IAS-conforming financial statements. The model itself is an Excel-based computer spreadsheet which permits local financial managers to 'translate' the information they record in accordance with the government's budgetary classification and reporting system and convert it into statements which potential private sector investors can read. This can be achieved through clear steps which are easy to follow by anyone with access to the requisite information. While regular generation and use of standardized financial statements and reports would familiarize local officials with revealing information, it would also provide a second best solution that enables officials to communicate more effectively with the private sector.

As there are no financial statements by division, there are no consolidated financial statements at the municipal level which would provide an overview of local government financial status and capacity to investors. There is a need for financial statements at all levels which delineate outstanding debt and that make it possible for potential investors to ascertain the capacity to service additional debt. Similarly, as financial reports have the sole purpose of reporting on annual budgetary activity to the central government, there is no information which reports long-term projections, including debt.

As noted elsewhere, there must be a shift from financial management practices which focus solely on expenditure management to those which are comprehensive enough to include liability management. The introduction of financial statements that conform with international standards, the routine application of performance measures or standards to these statements for internal as well as external assessment, and the adoption of standard audits would contribute substantially to closing the gap between local government investment needs and potential private sources for long-term investment. While considerable legislative change and human resource development will be required to bring about such reforms in a truly effective and comprehensive manner, limited initiatives such as the application of the IAS conversion model may enhance communication in the short term. The introduction of credit analysis and ratings and the adoption of long term debt reporting within the current context would, at least, permit private investors to obtain the assurances needed to mobilize resources for local government capital projects in Poland.

Bases of Accounting
The basis of accounting determines when revenue and expenditures are recorded. Use of accrual and modified accrual bases of accounting enhances the usefulness of financial statements for creditors and investors. Financial statements prepared using these bases of accounting provide better information about a gmina's future ability to repay debt or generate positive returns on investors' funds.

Any local government entity that wishes to operate on a commercial basis, thus having more attraction to private investors, is advised to adopt the full accrual accounting basis. For all other gmina units and subordinate units, the use of the modified accrual basis of accounting is proposed, with revenues reported if they are both measurable and available to pay liabilities of the current period. For example, a gmina would record a revenue when it sends a property tax bill to a taxpayer, if the bill is payable by the taxpayer within the current period.

Under the modified accrual basis, expenditures are recorded when the gmina incurs a liability that it expects to liquidate within the current period. The expenditure is typically recognized when the invoice and goods are received from a vendor. Long-term liabilities (such as principal on long-term debt) are not recorded as expenditures. Expenses that do not require cash outlays (such as depreciation) are not recorded as expenditures. Finally, 'losses' (e.g. early retirement of a fixed asset) are not recorded as expenditures.

Consistent Accounting Practices
Subordinate units must adopt consistent accounting and reporting conventions so that their respective financial information can be shown within the same set of financial statements. Consistency is needed on practices relating to valuation of investments and fixed assets, depreciation, revenue and expenditure accruals, distinctions between short and long-term assets and liabilities, and definitions of fixed assets, to name just a few.

As discussed elsewhere in this paper, the need for consistency does not mean accounting practices must be uniform among all units and subordinate units. Consistency requires that accounting standards be primarily established and modified by the accounting profession rather than by State regulation.

Consolidated Financial Statements
A gmina's financial statements should be both comprehensive and consolidated, that is, they should present information for all its budgetary units and subordinate units (the commercial code and joint stock companies) in a set of single financial statements. Users of comprehensive and consolidated financial statements are able to obtain a better picture of the fiscal condition of the gmina as a whole.

There are at least five requirements that must be met for financial statements to be comprehensive and consolidated. All units and subordinate units of the gmina:
- should use a common classification system;
- are either included or excluded from the financial statements in accordance with clear criteria for defining the gmina as a financial reporting entity;
- must use consistent accounting practices;
- must prepare at least some common financial statements, and
- must report transactions that occur within the gmina entity in such a way that would prevent double counting of revenue and expenditures.

21.4.3. CLASSIFICATION SYSTEM

Consolidated financial statements show results of operation, balance sheet information, and cash flows for multiple gmina units and subordinate units within a single set of financial statement. Use of the same classification system by all gmina units makes this possible. It would be useful if the standard classification system conformed to international financial reporting standards since this would enable comparisons of Polish public sector financial activity with that of other nations.
There are three levels of budgetary classification currently used by gminas: title (*dzial*), chapter (*rozdial*), and paragraph. We suggest to introduce changes at each of these levels. At the paragraph level, the classification system utilizes the United Nations Classification of Functions of Government (UNCOFOG) methodology. It should be noted that the existing classification system closely resembles the UNCOFOG classification methodology. At the paragraph level, the model adopts the International Monetary Fund's methodology for classification of revenue and expenditures and for transactions between levels of government.

While changes at the rozdial classification level are not required for purposes of conformance with international reporting standards, the model recommends that extensive reforms be made at this level. There are several problems with the existing rozdial classification. Several important competencies that were devolved to gminas in 1990 are not reflected in the rozdial classification level. The objective of classification at the reformed classification level are twofold:
1. for the operating budget, rozdial classification is based upon a gmina's unique organizational structure, and

2. for the capital budget, rozdial classification reflects the individual investment projects undertaken by the gmina.

21.4.4. USE OF RESERVE ACCOUNTS

Reserve accounts are managed as restricted equity or fund balance accounts, and the financial resources they represent are available until spent and belong to the gmina or to the entity to which resources are assigned. In cases in which local governments seek to attract credit, investment, or other forms of private-sector cooperation, their ability to demonstrate the value and use of reserve accounts may be helpful in demonstrating that the gmina in questions is financially viable and has an attractive investment opportunity. Ideally, a reserve account is established for each facility or group of like fixtures (such as the maintenance of water lines, pumps, and other elements of the water distribution system.).

21.4.5. FIXED ASSET REPORTING

There are two principal reasons for creating a system of fixed asset reporting beyond the obvious one of conformance with Generally Accepted Accounting Procedures. These are:
1. using fixed assets as collateral for loans and investments, and
2. improving internal efficiency of resource use. These will be discussed in turn.

Fixed Assets as Collateral
In order to utilize fixed assets as collateral, their value must be established and a basis for valuation must be determined (e.g. by historical cost). First, there must also be a definition of fixed assets that takes into account the practical needs for this information. For example, items likely to be utilized fully within the year of purchase should be excluded. A definition should be prepared by financial managers and approved by local officials following an explanation of the rationale underlying the definition. Lacking any other starting point, municipal financial managers may wish to begin with the definition of fixed assets as being those items with a useful life exceeding one year and whose purchase price (or current replacement cost) exceeds 500 PLN.

Fixed assets must be viewed as productive assets, that is, those which actively or potentially generate a return and which generate or help to produce some benefit to the local government through more efficient functioning of some aspect of gmina responsibility. Obviously, fixed assets include such major capital investments as water treatment works and district heating plants; however, fixed asset definitions should encompass office equipment and furnishings, vehicles, and other items needed to make non-revenue generating local government activities more efficient.

Defining fixed asset value is critical to ensuring the commitment of adequate resources for their maintenance and related preservation of value. In many local government cases, fixed assets and their current value are not maintained in a manner which would ensure their long-term preservation. Instead, asset purchases are simply recorded as one-time expenditures, similar to any outlay of funds. This results in a failure to link asset purchases with a corresponding schedule of maintenance and improvement. The key decision is reduced to how much should be spent from the current budget. Typically, maintenance costs are less than replacement costs, so this process likely results in an overemphasis on reducing current expenditures and, thus, on allocating resources for maintenance rather than replacement. No cost/benefit analysis is typically performed; therefore, maintenance outlays may be budgeted beyond the point which maximizes the utility of current expenditures versus capital expenditures (in the form of replacement costs). Further, due to the emphasis on minimizing expenditures, maintenance outlays may not even be adequate to keep fixed assets in optimal working order, with the result that potential benefits may be reduced relative to a financial management system that is able to focus on maximizing assets and their contribution to the delivery of government services. Without the life cycle view of fixed assets that permits the optimization of their value, it is difficult to make the best resource allocation decisions.

The management of fixed assets as productive assets which generate streams of benefits (if not revenues), along with financial statements and reports which link assets to cash flows, provides a basis for borrowing or issuing debt to finance improvements and expansions to the gmina's capital base. For this reason, the value of assets can become an important component of the collateral which a local government may have to offer in order to attract investment or credit. Regardless of whether assets are presented as collateral or not, the fact that fixed assets are managed in a businesslike fashion is critical to the perception of municipal officials as competent managers of additional capital assets. Whether new equipment, buildings, or other facilities acquired through loans or debt issues are to be repaid entirely from project-generated revenues or not, the capacity of managers to demonstrate that these assets will be developed and managed effectively and efficiently does much to assure lenders and investors of the viability of the financing proposal which they are to consider.

Improving Internal Efficiency of Resource Use
Record keeping and monitoring/maintaining the condition of fixed assets is the first step towards determining trends as to whether asset use is improving or declining in productive value. Standard accounting systems focus on the recording of the transaction in which assets are acquired and typically do not maintain information on the efficiency of the asset's use. Financial managers would be well advised to develop fixed asset maintenance records which note maintenance and other reinvestment actions. This should be combined and compared with information about asset performance, especially the monitoring of the asset's contribution to service or agency output or efficiency. Such indicators as cubic meters of water generated, kilometers of road paving completed, or units of district heating delivered may be compared with both direct (service-related) and indirect costs for purposes of both tracking trends in performance efficiency and understanding and controlling costs of units of service. In fact, the concept of unit cost for services is helpful for monitoring efficiency. Computations may be made based on a starting point such as the date at which an asset is first put into service, relating total costs to the units of service delivered. The cost per unit can then be monitored effectively as well as compared with those of other cities, other service providers, or other service delivery alternatives available for consideration. Interagency comparisons can be particularly useful both for purposes of internal management and for possible communication about asset values to potential buyers or sources of private sector capital. To achieve this, municipal associations, organizations of financial officers, or municipal

service and utility chambers may be encouraged to develop and promulgate performance indicators which address fixed asset utilization as well as other topics.

The matching of asset purchase and maintenance costs with service charges is, of course, one objective for defining and monitoring unit of service costs. Revenue forecasts may also be made on a unit cost basis; ascertaining the unit cost of production is essential to the determination of cost-recovery rates or charges. Rate increases and new investments are easier to justify with this base of information as well as to project with some measure of accuracy.

Asset valuation and estimate of useful life are essential background for establishing and accounting for depreciation, an important source of funds (as sources and uses of funds concept is introduced). Cost accounting is possible to introduce once there is fixed asset valuation and reporting, leading to more efficient and transparent service pricing. Of course, it is important to develop 'industry standards' or tax agreements related to the determination of useful life and related depreciation computations.

Assigning operating and maintenance resources by facility or facility type creates incentives for efficient facility management and resource use and illustrates areas of improving and declining efficiency, thus enhancing transparency along with decision making and enabling decision makers to compare the effectiveness of their efforts with those of their counterparts in other municipalities. The result is both more efficient service delivery at the local level and the creation of industry standards among all municipalities to use as benchmarks for effective operations.

21.5. Summary and Conclusions

Poland has not shifted away entirely from a municipal financial management system designed to address the needs of central government officials rather than local managers. There is a tremendous backlog of demand for infrastructure finance and for resources for other long-term capital investment in Polish gminas. To meet this demand requires that local officials understand how to communicate their financial position and their project or service capacity to provide solid returns to investors in terms which potential lenders and investors can understand. This requires the adoption and implementation of new accounting and budgeting procedures.

The legal environment in which gminas operate has undergone substantial changes in recent years; and these changes are not yet complete. In this somewhat uncertain environment, it is possible for gmina officials to meet the informational needs of private sources of capital while conforming with the requirements of the central government in its continued role as provider of the largest share of operating funds for local government. The challenge for gmina officials seeking access to long-term resources from Poland's expanding capital markets is to satisfy the provider of operating funds (the central government) as well as those of new financial resources (the private sector). This must include assurances to both that recent and proposed changes in the law will not substantively affect in any negative way the contractual relationships which gminas may initiate with private sources of finance.

The crux of the problem continues to be central government emphasis on annual operations and the expenditure side or budget, which is in conflict with private investor demands for capital investment planning, for cost recovery rates, and for sound long-term management planning that includes the maintenance of fixed assets. Central government policies, notably its treatment of multi-year financial commitments and of the depreciation of fixed assets, are at odds with solid, long-term fixed asset maintenance and operation.

While there is no clear path for gmina officials to follow, they may be encouraged both by the volume and number of recent local government bond issues and by the apparent recognition of the central government, as reflected in recent legislation, that changes must be made. The determined gmina may find a way to issue debt in the current market. Its officials are encouraged to adopt features of International Accounting Standards which are not in conflict with the Public Finance Law and to strengthen their financial management and information systems in ways which will attract outside investment. The adoption of multi-year investment planning, the preparation of capital improvement plans, and the use of improved budgeting and forecasting techniques may be sufficient to induce additional investment at the gmina level. Gmina officials and policy makers are encouraged to examine the ways in which central government demands for information and expenditure management can be harmonized with the requirements of private sector lenders and investors. There need not be conflict between the huge demand for resources and for infrastructure's contribution to economic growth among gminas and the provision of adequate rates of return required by the expanding private sector.

References

- Bitner, M. (1996) *Municipal Bonds in Poland: General Overview of the Bond Market*, Municipal Bond Center at MDA, Warsaw.
- Bitner, M. (1997) *Municipal Bonds in Poland-Market Characteristics*, Municipal Bond Center at MDA, Warsaw.
- Bitner, M., Cichocki, K. (1998) *Risk Indicators for Assessment of Local Government Debt Repurchasing by Commercial Banks*, Internal Report, BIG Bank, Warsaw (in Polish).
- CERA (1998) *Municipal Bond Markets as of October 15*, Warsaw.
- CERA (1998) *Pending Issues of the Municipal Bond Market*, Warsaw.
- Cichocki, K., Leithe, J. (1999) *Gmina Financial Aid Indicators*, Report of the Local Government Partnership Program, USAID, Warsaw
- Cochran, T., DeAngelis, M., Levitas, A. (1999) *Continuing Development of Poland's Subsovereign Debt Markets: Impediments and Opportunities*, A Briefing for USAID Regional Housing and Urban Development Office, Warsaw
- Levitas, A. (1997) *The Development of the Polish Municipal Capital Market 1994-1996*, Research Triangle Institute, Warsaw.
- Regional Office In Koszalin (1998) *Commercial Credits Drawn by the Communes and Communal Companies in the years 1995-1997*, Koszalin; a report for the Council of Regional Clearing Houses.